From Lumumba to Gbagbo

From Lumumba to Gbagbo

*Africa in the Eddy
of the Euro-American Quest
for Exceptionalism*

K. Martial Frindéthié

McFarland & Company, Inc., Publishers
Jefferson, North Carolina

LIBRARY OF CONGRESS CATALOGUING-IN-PUBLICATION DATA

Names: Frindéthié, Martial K. (Martial Kokroa), 1961–
Title: From Lumumba to Gbagbo : Africa in the eddy of the Euro-
    American quest for exceptionalism / K. Martial Frindéthié.
Description: Jefferson, N.C. : McFarland & Company, Inc., Publish-
    ers, 2016. | Includes bibliographical references and index.
Identifiers: LCCN 2015048282 | ISBN 9780786494040 (softcover :
    acid free paper) ∞
Subjects: LCSH: Radicalism—Africa—History—21st century. |
    Nationalism—Africa—History—21st century. | Africa—
    Foreign relations—Western countries. | Western countries—
    Foreign relations—Africa. | Africa—Social conditions—1960– |
    Africa—Economic conditions—1960– | Postcolonialism—
    Africa. | Exceptionalism—Western countries.
Classification: LCC DT30.5 .F75 2016 | DDC 960.3/2—dc23
LC record available at http://lccn.loc.gov/2015048282

BRITISH LIBRARY CATALOGUING DATA ARE AVAILABLE

ISBN (print) 978-0-7864-9404-0
ISBN (ebook) 978-1-4766-2318-4

Front cover photograph of protestors in Africa © 2016 Peeter
Viisimaa/iStock

Printed in the United States of America

McFarland & Company, Inc., Publishers
  Box 611, Jefferson, North Carolina 28640
  www.mcfarlandpub.com

Table of Contents

Preface   1

Introduction   3

1. Why Are We So Blest? The Euro-American Anxiety
   with Exceptionalism   11

2. Africa Caught in the Eddy of the Euro-American Quest
   for Exceptionalism   27

3. The Euro-American War on Algeria: Could a Mother So
   Yearn for Freedom but Keep Her Children in Bondage?   47

4. The Sarkozy-Obama Epic African Adventure   67

5. Hunting Laurent Gbagbo   85

6. Côte d'Ivoire: The International Community Hiding
   No More   127

7. Côte d'Ivoire: The International Community's Panglossism   168

8. We Shall Remember as Far Back as Lumumba   197

9. The Congo's Bumpy Road to Independence   213

10. There Shall Be Wars of Liberation   233

Conclusion   247
Chapter Notes   251
Bibliography   263
Index   271

Preface

The process of researching for this book and writing it has been emotionally draining for me as a person of African origin. At every bend, around every corner, the Euro-American injustice towards Africa and the African people jumped at me, taunted me, wielded a license of impunity in front of me. Nevertheless, I made it my duty to persevere in digging through the multitude of variegated scattered evidence, in sorting it, and in synthesizing it in one place, in order to inform those who want to know the truth about the nature of the Euro-American relations with Africa. The verdict of this book is confounding: After six hundred years of duplicitous relations with Africa, the West's outlook on the continent has not changed much. The Euro-American powers continue to throw their military weight around, brutalizing and coercing the African people into accepting propped-up autocracies that are relevant only insofar as they cater to all of the Euro-American exigencies first, leaving Africa depleted. Even worse, the hubris-drunk Euro-American powers directly commit human and economic genocides on African soils, convinced that no criminal court can ever hold them accountable for their crimes on the African populations.

With the election of a man of African heritage as president of the United States, many Africans had hoped that the Euro-American outlook on their continent would gain in a little more sensitivity. They were disappointed. In general, President Barack Hussein Obama's election brought nothing positive to Africa. In fact, many would argue that Obama sanctified the destruction of the continent more than any other American president in modern times could have. From Libya to Côte d'Ivoire, passing through Egypt, Obama underwrote the transformation of once-stable nations into permanent war zones whence orphans and widows take to the uncertain seas, in unfit inflatables, in search of better lives elsewhere.

Should we obliterate from the narratives we reserve for future generations the Euro-American jingoism that has caused so much distress to Africans? Some, like Joe Scarborough and Charles Krauthammer, say we should forget and move on, for much of it is "ancient history" long ago atoned for. Yet we cannot advance without historical memory, as if in a world that has no beginning and goes nowhere. So, to satisfy the harbingers of historical amnesia who urge that we not go back 800 years while keeping what humans have as their most precious gift—memory—I turned my gaze back only to try to understand, through some representative cases in *recent* history, how much has really changed in the rapports between the West and Africa. And from Lumumba to Gbagbo, hardly anything has changed. In fact, things look too strikingly similar to not worry about the Euro-American pattern of destruction and assassination. The capture and deportation to The Hague of President Laurent Gbagbo by the Euro-American imperialist power, like the assassinations of Muammar Gaddafi and Patrice Emery Lumumba, were meant to curtail the development of Africa, and it ought to be inscribed in history as such.

Today, with the worldwide deployment of academics, activists, and heads of states in support of Gbagbo, with the African Union's protest against the European Union's instrumentalization of the International Criminal Court (ICC) as a tool for picking marionette leaders in Africa, with the growing discredit that the lack of sufficient proof against Gbagbo has brought on the ICC, and overall with the far-reaching mobilizations and discussions that are taking place upon the arrest of Gbagbo, President Gbagbo's story deserves to be known. Most important, Gbagbo's story, along with Gaddafi's and Lumumba's and other instances of Africa's arrested development, deserves to be told against the background of the anxiety for exceptionalism that too often leads the Euro-American powers to act as mere buccaneers. *Lumumba to Gbagbo*, which started as a paper I read at the invitation of the Pan-Africanist Movement in Washington, D.C., is a book that the general public desiring to be informed on African politics–as well as scholars of African studies, African history, and international politics–will find highly resourceful. Besides reading historical events from new perspectives, the book goes through the rigorous work of finding, analyzing, and synthesizing for the reader the wealth of scattered information on the very recent political crises in Tunisia, Libya, and Côte d'Ivoire, among other places, and in relation to contemporary political debates in France and in the United States.

Introduction

The problem examined in this book is that—in its rapports with the Third World, and particularly with Africa, over the last two centuries—the Euro-American power has neither demonstrated ingenuity nor made significant headway. Instead, driven by a concern to actuate mythical exceptionalism, the Euro-American power continues to faithfully rehearse the brutish and warlike habitus typical of the first North-South encounters, recklessly throwing its military weight in the midst, particularly in Africa. The book pledges to demonstrate this thesis by examining the West's rapports with Africa from Patrice Lumumba to Laurent Gbagbo and those in-between. But can a book with such an objective effectually fulfill its responsibility to its readers without examining the necessary historiographical and sociological drives which, before Lumumba and after Gbagbo, have inscribed the West's "relationship" with Africa in the register of mere buccaneering? Thus, although Côte d'Ivoire and the Congo remain central themes in the book, *Lumumba to Gbagbo* functions as a metaphor for analyzing the Euro-American abusive relationship with Africa from the years leading up to the 1885 Berlin Conference to the present day.

In the first chapter, "Why Are We So Blest? The Euro-American Anxiety with Exceptionalism," the book establishes that the principle that has taken over Euro-American "diplomacy" is the affirmation of exceptionalism. This principle, though dressed in gaudy declarations and ostentatious political pageantries, is in its naked form nothing more than flag-waving hubris and jingoism. Today, no candidate for the American presidency can realistically hope to be elected without waving the saber of war in some foreign country, and no respectable journalist (by American standards, of course) can hand his microphone to a politician without pressing his interviewee on where the latter plans to wage his own war. Every American president and presidential hopeful must have a war of his (or her) own in a foreign country, and the gorier the war the better. As evidenced by the 2016 presidential hopefuls' predilection for positioning themselves as the most warlike candidate, the ability to take the American army to foreign places, crush some flesh and bones, make widows and orphans, scar the landscape, and destroy foreign countries' entire infrastructures in the name of exceptionalism has become a natural and expected prerequisite for being president in the United States.

This burden of American exceptionalism, misleadingly drawn from Alexis de Tocqueville's, in fact, contrapuntal characterization of America as unexceptional, has been a heavy conundrum for American presidents to bear: Peace and prosperity are attainable only through constant wars. And so, from Woodrow Wilson's 1916 campaign slogan, "He Kept Us Out of War," that got the 28th American president reelected, the modern-day catchphrases have turned fanatically bellicose to the point that President Barack Hussein Obama's Nobel recognition for his "likelihood" to cultivate peace rather than war resounded as if it were a betrayal at home. Democrats and Republicans alike beat on the American president for flirting equally with Muslim and Socialist/Communist agendas. And so, in order to ascertain that he is a son of America, raised within an American ideology to safeguard the continuance of America's exceptionalism, Obama reclaimed America's foundational myth of superiority wrested in America's martial tradition and sought wars of his own. In a bizarre self-hating gesture, Obama's doctrine of "Don't Do Stupid Shit!" in general, turned to "Don't Do Stupid Shit to Powerful Nations, but to Africa, You May!" Consequently, Obama made Africa his primary target. Under Obama's pugnacious watch, Egypt, "the cradle of civilization," has been reduced to ruins and its geological and cultural riches expatriated to the West; Libya, the departure point for Africa's total economic independence, has been reduced to a lawless zone where armed militias fight for control of territories and oil resources; and Côte d'Ivoire, once an example of success in sub-Saharan Africa, has been transformed into a rogue state of human rights abuses, ethnic and religious cleansing, anti-intellectualism, and poverty.

Nevertheless, the chapter argues that Obama's strategic vision driving foreign policy is in fact no strategy at all, and that, all along, he was being co-opted and led by former French president Nicolas Sarkozy. Having perceived Obama's weakness at home, and the American president's unsuccessful effort to convince a skeptical American public that he, too, believed in American exceptionalism, Sarkozy—just as would proceed a hermit crab—had decided to give contents to the American president's empty shell, in order to satisfy his own Napoleonic designs.

Truly, Sarkozy, like the French presidents who preceded him, had big shoes to fill. Since Napoleon Bonaparte's glorious years, France has been beset by a number of military defeats—the most monumental of which were the two losses to Germany in 1871 and in 1940, the loss in Indochina in 1954, and the loss of Algeria in 1962—that have diluted France's professed "exception française." As if the pressure on Sarkozy to recapture the lost Napoleonic paradise were not a heavy enough burden, the world economic crisis of the late 2000s had placed

France's economic strategy and credibility under the strict gaze of Standard and Poor's and threatened to push France over the financial edge. It thus became imperative that, in order not to be once again irrelevant, as was the case in the last century, France, which had historically prospered by attaching itself to Third World nations as a leech attaches itself to a foreign body, made a tacit deal with Obama to ensure that its hegemonic siphons were solidly fastened to and tapping into the economies of the developing nations, especially the former French colonies of Africa.

Chapter 2, "Africa Caught in the Eddy of the Euro-American Quest for Exceptionalism," historicizes the Euro-American obsession with exceptionalism as ultimately staged in the two European wars, during which Africa's human and economic resources were heavily strained towards restoring the dignity of the Euro-American powers, while at the same time Africa was being figured as mere accessory. The chapter registers Africa's extraordinary contribution to the victories of the Triple-Entente in the first war (1914–1918) and to the triumph of the Allies in the second war (1939–1945). The chapter especially focuses on the role played by the African infantry corps (the *tirailleurs sénégalais*) on the battlefields of Europe as well as on the roles played by the African populations in Africa in keeping Europe standing by feeding Europe's soldiers, supplying Europe's local markets, delivering raw materials to Europe's war factories, and keeping Europe's financial machine running by investing in European war bonds. In spite of Africa's extraordinary contributions, the continent and its people could not escape ridicule by Europe, as witnessed in the 1931 Exposition coloniale internationale.

Nevertheless, European racism and intolerance towards Africans during the First World War, in the interim between the wars, and after the Second World War had a boomerang effect. It occasioned a strong black consciousness whose demands for recognition progressively evolved from mere claims of total assimilation into the political, economic and social fabric of France to determination for full autonomy. In the context of four humiliating historical events—France's 1940 speedy surrender to and occupation by Germany, the 1945 final liberation of France by the Allied forces, the May 7, 1945, signature of the Armistice in Reims during which the Americans and the Russians marginalized France as the weakest link in the Allied forces, and France's 1954 military defeat in Indochina—French Africa's demand for independence was especially perceived by the colonizing country as a provocation, an impertinence reminding France of its unexceptional stature in the world, an affront that could not go unpunished unless France was once and for all admitting its lack of exceptionalism. So, *la patrie* (the motherland) that so yearned for freedom in 1945 went to war against her daughter who committed the ultimate sin of demanding her own independence.

Chapter 3, "The Euro-American War on Algeria: Could a Mother So Yearn for Freedom but Keep Her Children in Bondage?" gives an account of the Euro-American war on Algeria, a consequence of the North African country's demand for self-determination. On V-Day, May 8, 1945, the very day that millions of French revelers in metropolitan France and abroad were busy celebrating their liberation from German occupation, in Algeria, the country that had sent more 150,000 of its children to Europe in order to help free France from German oppression, French colonial authorities and troops exhibited blatant hypocrisy. In the Algerian towns of Setif, Guelma, Kherrata, Darguina, and Aokas, French troops and armed European militias went on a killing spree: 45,000 Algerians massacred. By raising the question of their independence on the day France was celebrating its regained exceptionalism, the native Algerians had committed heresy. The May 8 massacres, the callousness of which was to quell any Algerian inclination for independence, actually came as a few more somber chapters of France's cruelty in Algeria, which, added to the Algerian people's collective oral memory, further strengthened their resolve for full independence.

The chapter recalls the narratives of subjugation and defilement which, since the June 14, 1830, French invasion of Algeria, older generations of Muslim Algerians had been passing on to their progenies up to that fatal day of May 8, 1945. It is a collective memory filled with stories of military brutality, genocidal attempts, islamophobia, coerced apostasy, racism, and land expropriation—so many mistreatments that the May 8, 1945, demand for Algerian independence sought to end. And if the cruelty of the French troops and militias in Sétif, Guelma and Kherrata was intended to stifle the Algerian will to freedom, it had the contrary effect, as it further radicalized the native Algerians who riposted with the creation of the Front de Libération Nationale (FLN), whose armed branch, the Armée de Libération Nationale (ALN), opposed the French ferocious offensive military operations in the countryside as well as in the European urban centers, inflicting the invaders innumerable military and civilian casualties.

In Algeria, France was deeply entrenched in a war yet dared not give it that name. Between 1954 and 1962, France had deployed its country's heaviest artillery, had sought the counsel of its most ruthless military commanders, especially those that had served in Indochina, and sent more than 2 million young Frenchmen across the Mediterranean Sea to fight the FLN Mujahidins. Algeria, the French authorities estimated, was not just a French colony. It was a French department inhabited by French settlers. It was out of the question that Algeria be surrendered, for losing Algeria would be like losing the Alsace and Lorraine all over again. France's defeat in and flight from Algeria dealt its claim of exceptionalism a heavy blow and compounded the difficulties to overcome in the effort of recapturing the mythical Napoleonic paradise. After France's defeat in Algeria,

France's resolve was to be on the winning side of every issue no matter the acrobatics that such resolution would require.

Chapter 4, "The Sarkozy-Obama Epic African Adventure," shows how performing complicated gymnastics in order to be on the "right" side of every issue posed no problem for Sarkozy. The movement of protest in the Arab world that had been opportunistically tagged "Arab Spring" had started in Tunisia. At its inception, the French president was against it and had even offered to send a French police force to his good friend, Tunisian president Zine El Abidine Ben Ali, to quell the demonstration. After the defeat in Algeria, it was out of the question that Tunisia, too, should fall into the hands of ultra-nationalists that would jeopardize France's financial interests in the Maghreb and further complicate the quest for exceptionalism. So, in a feat of agitation, Sarkozy made a decision that proved thoughtless. However, as the tides started to change and Ben Ali was undoubtedly about to fall, Sarkozy quickly took up the cause of the Tunisian revolutionaries and inaugurated himself the champion of "freedom and democracy" in the Arab world. Though dusted with the zest of a particular nervousness, Sarkozy's duplicity in Tunisia was not occasional but lay at the very core of a cynical French foreign policy; and as the French president dragged a popularity-deficient President Obama in his international quest for exceptionalism, Sarkozy's off-the-cuff, irrational, and reckless political decisions endorsed by Obama would remain indelible stains on Obama's legacy in Africa.

Sarkozy and Obama's first big joint venture started in Libya with the passing on March 17, 2011, of United Nations [UN] Security Council Resolution 1973–2011 and ended with the capture and assassination of Libyan Guide Muammar Gaddafi by an infiltrated French secret service operative on October 20, 2011. Sarkozy had clear motives for wanting Gaddafi dead. The Libyan Guide had started a vast program of economic and financial enfranchisement of Africa, which, if successful, could relegate an already down-spiraling France to the backroom. Furthermore, Gaddafi's promises to help France's economy get back on its feet had not materialized; and as Sarkozy's relationships with Gaddafi broke down, a $50 million financial scandal was brewing that could cut short Sarkozy's political career.

A regime change could efface all traces of the imminent scandal, reshuffle the cards, and give France privileged access to Libya's so coveted huge oil and cash reserves. Sarkozy had the will but lacked the resources to take on Gaddafi alone. He needed the support of the United Nations Security Council and NATO's military apparatus; in other words, he needed Obama. Eager to show his warlike fortitude, which was being questioned at home, Obama underwrote Sarkozy's requests, and to war Sarkozy and Obama went under the pretext of "saving poor African lives" from Gaddafi's dictatorship. The war on Gaddafi did prove lucrative. By the time it was over, the European Union (EU) and the U.S.

had, respectively, pocketed 45 billion euros and $32 billion of Libyan money, thanks to information given them by Mohammed Layas, head of the Libyan Investment Authority (LIA). Furthermore, in Libya, Sarkozy was able to test his unproven, thus unmarketable, Rafales and finally get France some belated purchase orders from India, Qatar, and Egypt. After the death of Gaddafi, all happened as if the mission in Libya was accomplished. The Euro-American philanthropic saviors of the Libyan people packed their bags and left a torn-down country to become the theater of armed militiamen vying for control of the once stable Libya. The thousands of Libyan refugees taking to the sea, risking their lives on unsafe boats in the hope of reaching the coasts of Europe, is evidence that in Libya the Euro-American objective was not to save Libyans from themselves. It was to destroy an African country that had become ambitious to the point of threatening to displace the center that the Euro-American power has made its private province.

As Chapter 5, "Hunting Laurent Gbagbo," will also show, fear of being economically decentered motivated the Euro-American war against the West African country of Côte d'Ivoire, although there, too, Obama was being led and misled by Sarkozy, rather than leading. The economic turning point that Côte d'Ivoire—the world's major cocoa beans producer and the world's third largest coffee beans producer—had initiated since the early 2000s under the gambit of President Gbagbo's politics of Refondation was threatening to undermine France's economic monopoly in the country. In addition, since the early 2000s, a failed coup attempt against Gbagbo's government had morphed into a protracted rebellion that had occupied the northern part of the country and was openly supported by the French government.

From the day he took office, Sarkozy had maneuvered to find a resolution to the Ivorian crisis that would satisfy France's monopolistic position in the country. His predecessor, President Jacques Chirac, had started the work but could not finish it before the end of his mandate. Evidently, the best solution was to get rid of President Gbagbo and replace him with Alassane Dramane Ouattara, the former International Monetary Fund (IMF) executive in whose name the Northern Rebellion had been undertaken. As the chapter shows, Gbagbo was only the third target of France's attempt at regime change as early as 1999; one successful coup against President Bédié and several failed coups against General Gueï were undertaken with the purpose of installing Ouattara. In any case, from 2002 to 2010, after several failed attempts to strip Gbagbo of his executive power by the French government and the UN Security Council posing as arbitrators, it became evident that direct military intervention was no longer possible and that only through a manipulated election would Gbagbo be pushed out.

However, as discussed in Chapter 6, "Côte d'Ivoire: The International Community Hiding No More," the electoral manipulations of 2010 were so unashamedly obvious that it shocked most of the independent observers present in Côte d'Ivoire, except, of course, the Western power led by France, the United Nations, and the United States. French Ambassador Jean-Marc Simon and American Ambassador Philip Carter III directly intervened to change the vote results and proclaim Ouattara the winner of the election. President Gbagbo demanded a vote recount as the only condition for him to ascertain the true results of the election. For UN Secretary-General Ban Ki-Moon, President Sarkozy, and President Obama, a vote recount was against all democratic rules and would "set a bad precedent." Gbagbo—they were inflexible—had to cede power to Ouattara. On March 20, 2011, with the strong support of Obama's UN Ambassador Susan Rice, the UN Security Council passed Resolution 1975 (2011) authorizing Sarkozy to openly arm the Ivorian rebels and to use French and UN helicopters to bombard Abidjan, kill thousands of Ivorian civilians, and finally arrest President Gbagbo. In 2012, after months of detention in Côte d'Ivoire, in order to silence Gbagbo's supporters and ensure Ouattara a peaceful presidential tenure, Gbagbo was deported to the International Criminal Court at The Hague to be judged for crimes against humanity. President Gbagbo, as well as the millions of Ivorians whose lives have been disrupted by the violent intrusion of the Euro-American power in Ivorian politics, have been simply sacrificed on the altar of the Euro-American quest for exceptionalism.

As discussed in Chapter 7, "Côte d'Ivoire: The International Community's Panglossism," in Côte d'Ivoire things happened as if one had awoken from a deep slumber to find that vote recount—a method that had proven efficacious in resolving electoral dispute in the United States in 2000, in the Bush versus Gore case, as well as in several other countries—had been written off as undemocratic. This, however, was not the only absurdity being played out in Côte d'Ivoire. In its venture to assert its innate superiority over Africa, the Euro-American power has, as was the case during the two European wars, been able to rely on some local informants, some modern African tirailleurs, in the figures of some of the most corrupt African heads of state, such as Blaise Compaoré of Burkina Faso, Abdoulaye Wade of Senegal, and Goodluck Jonathan of Nigeria. Furthermore, the puppet government installed in Côte d'Ivoire under the guise of promoting democracy became, in a matter of a few weeks, a promoter of ethnic and religious cleansing. In Côte d'Ivoire, three entities—France, the United States, and the United Nations—had managed to replace a democratically elected president with a dictator. This, however, was predictable, given the undemocratic pattern that had characterized Ouattara's political strategy since 1993.

The fate of President Laurent Gbagbo is like that of Patrice Emery Lumumba, which the book discusses in chapters 8, "We Shall Remember as Far Back as Lumumba," and 9, "The Congo's Bumpy Road to Independence." Chapter 8 revisits the Congo of the Belgian kings, from Leopold II to Baudouin I, and the pattern of abuses and exploitation that has characterized the administration of the Congo from 1885 to 1909. Chapter 9 argues that, like Gbagbo's outlook on Côte d'Ivoire, the first Congolese prime minister had for his country a vision of a unified, independent nation in full control of the natural resources of which it had custody. Such a vision was antithetical to the Euro-American will to domination expressed through the smoky appellation of exceptionalism. Like Gbagbo, Lumumba could be brash and impetuous, which had made him some enemies from within the West was only too delighted to capitalize on. In 1961, just six months after he was elected, Lumumba was assassinated and the Congo relapsed under the abusive tutelage of the Euro-American power.

Chapter 10, "There Shall Be Wars of Liberation," cautions the Euro-American world that its politics of wreaking havoc in Africa are not sustainable. It will continue to radicalize the masses until such day when the Africans are adequately armed and ready to oppose their oppressors in a full-blown war of liberation on a scale greater than has been witnessed in Algeria. The past wars have proven that the Euro-American powers are not invincible. They are simply better armed. Yet, reason must teach us that no one will forever have arms supremacy, as the brains that forge the weapons that give the Euro-American power its temporary military supremacy are available in Africa as well. Consequently—unless the imperialist West is disposed to line up millions of its youths against millions of African youths determined to be free from coercion—sincere diplomacy, rather than brute force, shall be the order of the day in international dispute resolution.

CHAPTER 1

Why Are We So Blest?
The Euro-American Anxiety
with Exceptionalism

*I contend that we are the finest race in the world and that the more of the world
we inhabit the better it is for the human race.*
        —CECIL RHODES, "Confession of Faith," 1877

*There are big countries and small countries.... We are all different, but when
we ask for the Lord's blessings, we must not forget that God created us equal.*
        —VLADIMIR PUTIN, President of the Russian Federation

In France, when it comes to teaching the chapter on the decolonization of
the former French colonies of Africa, high school teachers are officially instructed
to emphasize two forms of decolonization: on the one hand, an accidentally violent decolonization that took place in North Africa, and of which the Algerian
decolonization is illustrative, and, on the other hand, a typically peaceful decolonization that presumably took place in sub–Saharan Africa.[1] In hiding the fact
that equally in North Africa, or the Maghreb, and in sub–Saharan Africa France's
repressive military machine has killed hundreds of thousands of Africans, French
authorities intend to impress on French students' minds the myth that French-
professed "*exception française*" was attained with grace and refinement.

Likewise, in America, the genocide and material dispossession of the Native
Americans is not part of the public school curriculum. Public school students
are not taught the capture of blacks, their shackling, raping and selling, all done
in the same manner mere livestock are commercialized. Disclosing the explicit
links between liquidation, land grab, slavery, and America's economic magnificence seems to run counter to the idea of American patriotism and American
grandeur supposedly achieved through honest, hard work and perseverance
against an indomitable and hostile nature.

Yet, historical truth can be stubborn, truth that has survived by leaving in
its passage a trail of evidence that sooner or later uncover the hidden ethnocentric

atrocities that have made up the foundation of the Euro-American myth of exceptionalism. In the United States, for example, a growing number of people are discovering that American exceptionalism came at a vile cost. Lately, scores of American corporations, among them Wachovia Bank, Bank of America, JP Morgan, *USA Today*, and Tiffany and Co., to cite only a few, have admitted to have profited from the despicable business of slavery.

The Euro-American propaganda meant to imprint in young minds that nonwhite lives—especially black—have no value, and that massacres against blacks—military and civilian alike—commissioned by Euro-American governments can be easily suppressed from history books seems doomed to fail.[2] Though from the perspective of the so-called civilized nations, sympathizing with nonwhite victims may run counter to the idea of "patriotism," it won't, however, eliminate the fact that the Euro-American society is a violent society, one whose wars—those waged against peoples in faraway places as well as those that saw brothers cannibalize each other—such as the first European war (1914–1918) and the second European war (1939–1945), are attributable to one, and only one, foundational myth: The belief that one is of the chosen people, and that, consequently, all the resources of the world, be they in one's backyard or in that of the neighbors, should be requisitioned to satisfy one's voracious appetite first. Only then, should there be anything left, can that leftover be used to address the rest of the world's hunger.

This is the reality that the Euro-American world has misinterpreted as a measure of grandeur and that it names exceptionalism. In the name of exceptionalism, many nonwhite peoples have been terrorized and even exterminated.[3] It is highly unlikely that within the next generation any Western political leader will be extradited to an African court to answer for any crimes committed against the people of Africa in the name of exceptionalism. Yet this is not for lack of past and present crimes against humanity commissioned by Western leaders against Africans, in Africa.[4] Western societies seem to have sanctioned the belief that "strong leaders" are particularly those state men and women who have a few foreign wars under their belts, and the gorier the wars, the higher the esteem that is bestowed upon the leaders who wage them. There is a Western revaluation of values, whereby those who offer iron and blood to the world are the most adulated. In October 2012, the European Union awarded itself the Nobel Peace Prize, for "holding [its] union together" economically and politically. The ugly reality that no self-congratulatory celebration can gloss over is that the European Union's supposed harmony came at the cost of wreaking political and economic havoc elsewhere, especially in Africa, and with the help of America.

The overall condition of the Third World is closely linked to the Euro-American actuation of its myth of exceptionalism. As de Tocqueville mocked American plebeian nature and praised French uniqueness, he could not imagine that Napoleon Bonaparte had marked the end of France's exceptional era, and that America, which he had burlesqued in his *Democracy in America*, would one day own the word "exceptionalism," with whatever misfortune it could bring to people both abroad and at home.[5] If the *disease* of exceptionalism—this tendency to throw one's military weight around, bully the weakest, and steal their resources—had for long been the prerogative of western Europe, in modern times it has been appropriated by America to the point of becoming an expected prerequisite for the American presidency. As notes William Pfaff, "The American government now has become institutionally a war government, which finds its rationale in waging war against small and troublesome countries and peoples, in the generalized pursuit of running the world for the world's own good. In this effort, one war is pretty much like another, and every president, to be reelected, needs one."[6]

Of all the U.S. modern leaders, President Jimmy Carter is probably the one who has shunned war the most. Apart from his April 24, 1980, failed attempt to rescue 52 American hostages held in Iran, President Carter never formally engaged America in the kind of ghastly wars that have come to define American presidencies. And the price that President Carter has paid, and is still paying today, for his reluctance to wade in the gory and the gruesome is well known. Carter was not reelected, and he is looked upon by most Americans, Democrats and Republicans alike, as a weak president. America no longer has the unwarlike wisdom of yesteryear, as remarks Steve Chapman: "The campaign slogan of 'He Kept Us Out of War' that got Woodrow Wilson elected ninety-six years ago would not have much success today. Today, the presidential trend is to get into war."[7]

For a moment, President Barack Obama had contemplated walking in the steps of Wilson or Carter and doing away with the American tradition of warlike foreign policy. It did not last long. Obama turned out to be one of the most fervent upholders of American pomposity, and in the same stride the modern American president whose warlike arrogance has been the most destructive to the African continent. Under Obama's presidency and thanks to Obama's reckless foreign policy affected by a determination to appear pugnacious, the proud African country of Egypt, the cradle of human civilization, is in shambles; Libya, the linchpin of Africa's resurgence, is a lawless hub of uninhibited inter-militia wars; Côte d'Ivoire, the "African Elephant," has birthed a dictator; and Kenya, the country of the great Jomo Kenyatta, would have fallen into civil confrontation had the Kenyans not been wise enough to reject Obama's ill-advised interference in their presidential elections. And yet, from the outset, it all seemed as if President Obama would be more of a sensible American leader, one really deserving of the Nobel Peace Prize that he was awarded on the mere potentials of his campaign speeches.[8]

Obama: I Believe in America's Exceptionalism

On September 11, 2001, Al-Qaida launched several deadly terrorist attacks inside the United States. On October 16, 2002, a joint resolution of the United States Congress signed by President George W. Bush guaranteed Bush the right to order a punitive war against Iraqi president Saddam Hussein's Baathist government, which Bush accused of harboring terrorist groups in the Middle East and stockpiling chemical weapons of mass destruction. On October 2, 2002, in a speech he delivered in Chicago at an anti-war rally, then–Senator Obama strongly condemned President Bush's imminent war in Iraq, calling it "a dumb war. A rash war. A war based not on reason but on passion, not on principle but on politics."[9] Actually, Obama was not shying away from the United States' confrontational ideal. His argument was just that the terrorist organization Al-Qaida, not Iraqi president Saddam Hussein, should be the target of Bush's military actions. Be that as it may, Obama's stance on the Iraq war won him the label of an appeaser by neoconservatives. In his May 15, 2008, address to the Israeli parliament President George Bush blasted candidate Obama for being a mollifier, a contender soft on terrorism and not fully committed to Israel's security:

> Some seem to believe that we should negotiate with the terrorists and radicals, as if some ingenious argument will persuade them they have been wrong all along. We have heard this foolish delusion before. As Nazi tanks crossed into Poland in 1939, an American senator declared, "Lord, if I could only have talked to Hitler, all this might have been avoided." We have an obligation to call this what it is—the false comfort of appeasement, which has been repeatedly discredited by history.[10]

Besides being called an appeaser and unpatriotic, Obama also faced accusations of espousing Socialism. On October 12, 2008, during a campaign stop in Ohio, a plumber by the name of Samuel Joseph Wurzelbacher—concerned that if the Illinois Senator had his way, Obama's prospective tax plan would prevent him from acquiring the business he had been working for—approached candidate Obama with this question: "I'm getting ready to buy a company that makes 250 to 280 thousand dollars a year. Your new tax plan is going to tax me more, isn't it?" In his attempt to reassure his interlocutor that his proposed economic policy would not affect him negatively, Obama replied, "When you spread the wealth around, it's good for everybody." Seizing on the exchange a few days later, Republican presidential hopeful Arizona Senator John McCain accused Obama of Socialism: "Joe, in his plainspoken way, said [Obama's tax plan] sounded a lot like Socialism. And a lot of Americans are thinking along those same lines. In the best case, 'spreading the wealth around' is a familiar idea from the American left. And that kind of class warfare sure doesn't sound like a 'new kind of politics.'" McCain traced Obama's politics beyond the "American left" to

French Socialism when he added, "At least in Europe, the socialist leaders who so admire my opponent are upfront about their objectives. We should demand equal candor from Senator Obama."[11]

Thus, Obama was some sort of Western European socialist mole who, under the guise of devising for Americans a better social program, was in fact seeking to Europeanize America by diluting its exceptionalism with the virus of social democracy. According to President Bush and the Republican Party, not only would Obama undermine America-Israel relations in order to appease the Muslim world, but his economic plan inspired by European Socialism would also undermine America's economic stability. Despite these criticisms, in November 2008, Obama was elected president of the United States. But his election did not rid him of the label of Socialist tagged on him by neoconservatives nostalgic of the Bush doctrine.

Of Obama's alleged socialist inclination, *Forbes* contributor Paul Gregory has argued that, though it would be absurd to think of Obama as a socialist in the sense that Lenin, Mao or Castro would be, Obama falls "within the mainstream of contemporary socialism as represented, for example, by Germany's Social Democrats, French Socialists, or Spain's socialist-workers party." Obama's political vision satisfies the principles of the Party of European Socialists, such as put forth in November 2011.[12] Merrill Matthew concurs that Obama's economic policies mirror French president François Hollande's. Both Hollande and Obama, he argues, intend to make the rich pay for economic growth by raising taxes on them; they both intend to raise the dividends tax; they hassle financial and oil industries, promote renewable energies projects with taxpayers' money, and increase public subsidies to small businesses.[13] Likewise, characterizing Obama's healthcare program (mockingly baptized Obamacare by Obama's critics) as just a minute component of a larger "vision for forced sharing of American assets," O'Reilly described Obama's vision as one in which "the state should provide all citizens a certain lifestyle, at the expense of other citizens…. If healthcare is a constitutional right, then everything associated with good health … would fall into the civil rights category." The state would have to pay for such needs as housing, food, clothes and transportation for those who cannot afford them, which would not be feasible "without the state seizing the assets of everyone else." Thus, Obama's social politics are inspired by socialist-communist ideology, O'Reilly concluded.[14] So President Obama was still haunted by the faults imputed to candidate Obama.

During his presidential campaign, Obama had promised to address the Muslim world from a major Muslim capital. He did fulfill his promise to Muslims on June 24, 2009, in Cairo. But before flying to Cairo, Obama attended the April 3–4, 2009, NATO 60th anniversary celebration in Strasbourg, France. There, as a press conference concluded, Obama skillfully navigated a question by *Financial*

Times journalist Edward Luce, who asked him whether he believed, like his predecessors, in America's myth of exceptionalism:

> I believe in American exceptionalism, just as I suspect that the Brits believe in British exceptionalism and the Greeks believe in Greek exceptionalism. I'm enormously proud of my country and its role and history in the world…. Now, the fact that I am very proud of my country and I think that we've got a whole lot to offer the world does not lessen my interest in recognizing the value and wonderful qualities of other countries, or recognizing that we're not always going to be right, or that other people may have good ideas, or that in order for us to work collectively, all parties have to compromise and that includes us.[15]

Conservatives in American took notice of Obama's hesitation to delve effusively in the legend of American uniqueness, and would not let him so easily off the hook, especially as Obama continued to give them rhetorical rationalizations for their accusations. As Alaska Governor Sarah Palin would later write in her *America by Heart*, "Many people don't believe we have special message for the world or a special mission to preserve our greatness for the betterment of not just ourselves but all of humanity. President Obama … doesn't believe in American exceptionalism at all. He seems to think it is just a kind of irrational prejudice in favor of our way of life."[16]

At Cairo University, in the speech he promised and whose title, "A New Beginning," implied a departure from the way successive American governments, and especially the Bush administration, had engaged the Muslim world, Obama elaborated on his Strasbourg reply. Appealing to Muslims, Obama stated that he had "come [to Cairo] to seek a new beginning between the United States and Muslims around the world; one based upon mutual interest and mutual respect; and one based upon the truth that America and Islam are not exclusive, and need not be in competition." Obama called for an end to the cycle of suspicion and discord between Muslim nations and America, assured that American troops would be pulled out of Iraq and Afghanistan in order to make room for stronger economic partnerships, and promised to uphold what he saw as his "responsibility as President of the United States to fight against negative stereotypes of Islam wherever they appear." Obama appealed for peace between Palestinians and Israelis, whom he described as "two peoples with legitimate aspirations" who must live up to their obligations in order to reach out to a lasting peace.

Obama's speech was balanced and in stark contrast to the usual disproportionately pro–Israel stance of his predecessors. The discourse was cautiously applauded by most Muslim and Israeli leaders. At home, however, conservatives were raging. The Obama of the Cairo Speech—in which he stated, "Just as Muslims do not fit a crude stereotype, America is not the crude stereotype of a self-interested empire, [that] given our interdependence, any world order that elevates one nation or group of people over another will inevitably fail"—was far from the herald of American exceptionalism that Conservatives would have liked their president to be. So, the criticism of pro–Muslim and anti–Israel sentiments leveled against Obama intensified and came to compound on those of him as an appeaser and a socialist, especially as the Nobel Institute awarded Obama the Nobel Peace Prize for his celebration of multiculturalism and universal brotherhood.

Obama's reluctance to clearly embrace what some liberals might qualify as American chauvinism, his unwillingness to influence foreign policy with America's military might, and his timidity in unequivocally endorsing American Christian precepts, such as the sanctity of life whose inception Conservatives locate at the moment of conception and whose inviolability, they claim, should be partly preserved with the defunding of abortion, for instance, have lent him harsh denunciations by Conservatives. Ultraconservative radio show host Rush Limbaugh accused Obama of being ashamed to acknowledge the values of free markets, opportunity for everybody, capitalism, competition, liberty, and the rule of law that made America stand out.[17] House Minority Leader John Boehner was aghast that Obama should establish some moral equivalence between Palestinians and Israelis. Time and again during his second presidential campaign Republican presidential hopeful Governor Mitt Romney attacked Obama for using foreign soil for an apology tour about America's foreign policy. On March 31, 2012, in his remarks at the Wisconsin Faith and Freedom Coalition Forum, ahead of the state's April 3 Republican primary, Romney had this to say about his belief in American exceptionalism and what he suspected was President Obama's embarrassment to recognize and embrace America's uniqueness: "There is no other nation on earth like America…. I always knew inside [that] I had a special gift no one else had. I was an American. No question in my heart that it was special to be an American…. Our President doesn't have the same feeling about American exceptionalism."[18] On October 7, 2011, in his foreign policy speech delivered at The Citadel, Romney attacked Obama again for his hesitancy to unambiguously espouse America's exceptionality and for his contemptible answer to America's exceptionalism: "God did not create this country to be a nation of followers…. I believe we are an exceptional country with a unique destiny and role in the world…. In Barack Obama's profoundly mistaken view, there is nothing unique about the United States."[19]

On September 11, 2012, terrorists in Libya attacked the American embassy in Benghazi and killed U.S. Ambassador Christopher Stevens and two CIA contractors, Tyrone Woods and Glen Doherty. Obama's supposed aloofness to America's ideals and apologetic posture on America's foreign policy and his perceived weakness by America's enemies were indicted as the causes of the attack. Had he shown courage and determination in American foreign policy, had he unambiguously embraced American exceptionalism, no one would have dared such a bold move on an American embassy, his critics lamented. Of course, such a premise was totally dismissive of previous terrorist attacks on American infrastructures under more aggressive American presidents. Nevertheless, Obama found himself on the defensive. By all indications, he must have felt compelled to embrace and proselytize the gospel of American exceptionalism in order to avoid accruing Republican charges of his dispassion for the ideal of American magnificence, in order to appear more committed to working for the continued preeminence of the United States.

On May 2, 2011, Obama had successfully ordered American Special Forces in Afghanistan to track and eliminate America's number one enemy. During his electoral campaign, he had promised to take the war directly to Osama bin Laden, who had commissioned the September 11, 2011, attacks on America. He kept his promise and had bin Laden killed. Nonetheless, Obama was not getting any credit for remarkability. In fact, Bush's Secretary of Defense Donald Rumsfeld posted on Facebook that recognition for bin Laden's death was also due to his former boss: "All of this was made possible by the relentless, sustained pressure on al-Qaida that the Bush administration initiated after 9/11 and that the Obama administration has wisely chosen to continue." While congratulating Obama for showing no stress as the operation to kill bin Laden was underway, Alvin Felzenberg also insisted that credit for the killing of the terrorist chief should be shared between Obama and Bush, the latter for speaking "confidently and courageously to the world about the values that made the United States a great and just nation. This weekend, the military carried out that promise [of killing bin Laden] in his name."[20] Even in his ultimate show of fierceness Obama was not getting credit for exceptionality. He was still perceived as a fragile, insipid, and above all unexceptional president that was, in the best case, only capable of finishing a work his predecessor had set up for him. Obama needed to convince the American public that he was a president in the full sense of the term—that he met America's warlike expectations. Obama needed a war of his own, started by him and won by him. This is a proposition which should make some small country somewhere in the world quake in fear, as is the case any time an American or European president feels the need to show his people that he is a determined custodian of their exceptionalism.

In Syria, right in the aftermath of the war on Gaddafi's government, a dream occasion for Obama to rid himself of the soft, socialist label that had stuck on him since his opposition to the Iraq war presented itself. Bashar al-Assad was allegedly "killing his own people," a most inadmissible offense for the West, which in its killing extravaganzas had supposedly not stooped so low as to kill its "own people." Killing other peoples was justified. So, on the night of September 10, 2013, in a televised speech to the nation, Obama set about to sell his prospective war in Syria as an imperative dictated by America's exceptionalism: "[W]hen, with modest effort and risk, we can stop children from being gassed to death, and thereby make our own children safer over the long run, I believe we should

act…. That's what makes America different. That's what makes us exceptional."
Obama was resolute to go to war against Syrian president Bashar Al-Assad for
"using chemical weapons against his people." He seemed to care less that on May
6, 2013 (the very week U.S. Secretary of State John Kerry was headed to Moscow
to convince President Putin to shift his alliance from Assad to the U.S.), in an
interview with Swiss-Italian television, Ms. Carla Del Ponte—a former Swiss
attorney-general and prosecutor with the International Criminal Tribunal (ICT)
for the former Yugoslavia and since 2011 investigator of the United Nations Independent International Commission of Inquiry on Syria—declared that, although
she could not rule out the use of chemical weapons by Assad's troops, she was
"a little bit stupefied by the first indications [she] got … they were about the use
of nerve gas by [Assad's] opposition."[21] It mattered little that in the name of
exceptionalism America was gearing up to punish Assad for a crime that the
opposition to Assad's government *may* have committed. In the wrong as in the
right, America was exceptional, and its truth was The Truth.

So, on September 24, 2013, at the United Nations 68th General Annual
Assembly, President Obama reiterated his gospel of American exceptionalism:
"Some may disagree, but I believe America is exceptional, in part because we
have shown a willingness, to the sacrifice of blood and treasure to stand up, not
only for our own interests, but for the interests of all." In the audience, Obama's
speech triggered some hilarity. Russian U.N. Ambassador Vitaly Churkin and
Russian Foreign Minister Sergey Lavrov could not contain themselves. They
chortled and giggled as Obama dove into his sententious speech about America's
exceptionalism and high moral judgment. But Churkin and Lavrov were not the
only ones chuckling. In a September 2013 *New York Times* op-ed, Russian president Vladimir Putin took issue with Obama's Syria speech:

> It is alarming that military intervention in internal conflicts in foreign countries has
> become commonplace for the United States. Is it in America's long-term interest?
> I doubt it. Millions around the world increasingly see America not as a model of
> democracy but as relying solely on brute force, cobbling coalitions together under
> the slogan "you're either with us or against us" … I carefully studied [President
> Obama's] address to the nation on Tuesday. And I would rather disagree with a case
> he made on American exceptionalism, stating that the United States' policy is "what
> makes America different. It's what makes us exceptional." It is extremely dangerous
> to encourage people to see themselves as exceptional, whatever the motivation.
> There are big countries and small countries, rich and poor, those with long demo-
> cratic traditions and those still finding their way to democracy. Their policies differ,
> too. We are all different, but when we ask for the Lord's blessings, we must not
> forget that God created us equal.[22]

The reactions to Putin's open letter to President Obama were immediate
in the U.S. Democrats and Republicans alike circled the wagons around Obama

and launched all sorts of name-calling against Putin. In the squabbles, Senator John McCain of Arizona distinguished himself. Thinking that he was writing a rejoinder to Putin's letter in *Pravda*, a major Russian paper that actually went defunct in the 1980s, McCain took to the Web to chastise Putin in an obscure online publication, pravda.ru, calling Putin a tyrant and oppressor of the Russian people and a corrupt leader. McCain's mistake caused Russians to scoff at him, arguing that he was really stuck in the past. Nevertheless, McCain's defense of Obama's rhetoric of American exceptionalism was good enough proof that, as patriotism went, Obama no longer had anything to prove to conservatives. Or had he?

Had Obama proven beyond any reasonable doubt that he fully embraced the foundational myth of American superiority? Had he proven it to himself? Apparently not, for the American president must have felt the need to be a little more assertive in his support of America's hubris against the conviction of "reciprocity" that won him the Nobel recognition when, in his May 28, 2014, commencement address to the class of 2014 at the U.S. Military Academy at West Point, he carefully treaded water between the currents of those who accused him of selling out America's ideal of uniqueness and those who accused him of insensitivity. On that occasion, Obama tried to explain American exceptionalism as one that compels Americans to uphold, more than anyone else would, international expectations of decency: "I believe in American exceptionalism with every fiber of my being. But what makes us exceptional is not our ability to flout international norms and the rule of law; it's our willingness to affirm them through our actions." So then, in order to quash the criticism of socialism, weakness, and lack of patriotism leveled against him, Obama had adopted a different tone, one that was perceptible already in mid–2010. If, as Matthew Rothschild wrote, Obama "genuflected on the altar of American arrogance" at West Point, we hardly saw both knees touch the floor.[23]

The Obama Doctrine: "Don't Do Stupid Shit!" to Powerful Nations

At West Point, Obama did his kneeling to American hubris, all right! But he did it with only one knee on the ground. From mid–2010 onward, Obama had, if not fully embraced America's foundational myth of exceptionalism, at least oscillated between that belief and his supposed faith in reciprocity, with a more pronounced leaning toward the former. This was nothing new. Oscillation, ambiguity, confusion, and hesitation have always characterized Obama's approach to foreign policy. Most American presidents have had some strategic vision driving their foreign policy. Clinton believed that in an interconnected world, nothing was absolutely isolated, and therefore, events apparently geographically far from America could indeed have deep implications for the lives of Americans. As terrorism and wars breeding instability were on all fronts, America's role was, Clintonians would argue, to police the world in order to *prevent* the festering of foreign conflicts from reaching the coasts of America.

President Bush's doctrine was preemption. He believed in hitting America's enemies first, even before they had the opportunity to act; and when it came to America's security, cumbersome negotiating, such as that habitual at the United Nations or even in Congress, Bush believed, could be circumvented. Bush would strike first and ask other world leaders to either fall in line or to dissent and assume the consequences of their choices, such as not having any claim in the loot sharing. Thus, to punish France for not supporting the United Sates in the Iraq war, the Bush administration would not let the country of Jacques Chirac have any "fat contracts" in the reconstruction of Iraq.[24] At one point, the French authorities, who had wanted to ascertain their independence from America's growing paternalism since 1945, had even feared America's punishment against France to be war, as Secretary of State Collin Powell had confusingly suggested on the *Charlie Rose Show.*[25] It took French authorities months of schmoozing and self-humiliating diplomacy to regain America's trust. Rightly or not, Bush's strikes on Afghanistan and Iraq were predicated on his firm belief that these countries constituted threats to the U.S. Even those who question his true motives in Iraq would remember that Bush said once of Saddam, "After all, this man wanted to kill my Dad," which verified the preemption doctrine: Strike your enemies before they have a chance to strike your kin.

So, there seems to be some strategic vision driving foreign policy with Obama's immediate predecessors. On the other hand, one has yet to figure out what Obama's doctrine is. Obama's principles guiding foreign policy appear nebulous, like one of those metaphysical conjectures that are meant to efface their own traces as soon as they are posited. Anything and its contrary are possible at the same time. One can lead by being led at the same time. One can be sure and uncertain at the same time. One can speak now or later at the same time, for time can be and cannot be of the essence at the same time. This is a complicated political dance, the steps of which are not easy to understand. Nile Gardiner, who believes he has figured out Obama's doctrine, writes that "the Obama doctrine is really an empty shell, one predicated on American weakness rather than strength ... the decline of the American superpower, with no clear U.S. leadership ... a willingness to kowtow to strategic adversaries, the scaling down of America's defenses, and the downgrading of key partnerships, including the Special Relationship."[26]

If one is to believe former Secretary of State Hillary Clinton, who, after serving in the Obama administration from 2009 to 2013, left early enough to distance herself from her former boss and pursue her own bid for the 2016 presidential election, the Obama doctrine is as unassuming as "Don't Do Stupid Shit!" Criticizing Obama for lacking gumption in Syria, Hillary Clinton defended herself as being one insider who, against Obama's extreme caution, was pushing for more military action in Syria. In other words, against Obama's doctrinal fear of "doing stupid shit," she was the brave one, the exceptional one, as true as exceptionalism rhymed with military bravado. Hubris and show of military chutzpah constituting the organizing principles of American exceptionalism, Hillary was positioning herself as one who, unlike her former boss, was prepared to lead America: "The failure to help build up a credible fighting force of the people who were the originators of the protests against Assad—there were Islamists, there were secularists, there was everything in the middle—the failure to do that left a big vacuum, which the jihadists have now filled…. Great nations need organizing principles, and 'Don't do stupid stuff' is not an organizing principle."[27] This was the innermost repudiation of his foreign policy and accusation of nonexceptionalism Obama had received.

From within as well as from outside his administration, from the point of view of neoliberals, as well as from that of neoconservatives, Obama's perceived overly cautious and conciliatory foreign policy approach was betraying the foundational myth of American exceptionalism. To affirm his power at home against the neocon nihilism and nostalgia, Obama had to show firmness. So, resolute to give the world his fair share of iron and blood, as we will later see, Obama was going to lend his support to the most egregious and groundless wars. He was going to blindly follow, in its conquest of the world, a 21st Napoleonic spirit in the form of French president Nicolas Sarkozy and contribute, more than any other U.S. president of the last two centuries, to the destruction of the African continent.

The labels of anti-patriot and socialist tagged on Obama were not fading. The American president needed to offer, not just his critics but also his international peers, bold acts of nationalistic grandeur. In the least case, Obama needed to redeem himself by showing that his predecessors were not rash, dumb and stupid for going to war, but rather that war was the quintessential way for American presidents to actuate Americans' innate disposition to do only good deeds and carry out their heavenly responsibilities of pulling others from the Dark Ages. The idea of going to war to ascertain one's superiority is as ancient as the world and as appealing to humans' most brutish and most bestial instincts as one can find. Since time immemorial, people who thought of themselves as superior beings have sought to save others despite themselves; and war has been the method of choice that "exceptional beings" have used to save "inferior beings" from themselves. American Conservatives' relentless accusations of Obama as betraying the great American ideal and Obama's celebrated weakness at home, either factual or rhetorical, rendered the American president highly susceptible to foreign co-option, precisely to French co-optation. This made him the sidekick of French president Nicolas Sarkozy, who also had a paradise lost of exceptionalism to recapture.

"I'm going to ask Obama to walk ... and he'll do it"

Indeed, every French leader since Napoleon Bonaparte's faded "magnificence" has had to carry the heavy burden of reconstructing and sustaining France's unstable myth of "*exception française.*" Sarkozy's presidency, like the ones that preceded it, inherited lingering painful images of France's humiliation that needed to be jettisoned—images of France as the most cowardly nation in Europe, as the weakest link of European grandeur. The most monumental examples are France's two losses to Germany (1871 and 1940), de Gaulle's subaltern position during the 1945 signing of the armistice in Reims, the defeat in Dien Bien Phu (1953–1954), and the 1962 defeat by the Front de Libération Nationale (FLN) in Algeria. These failed military campaigns have had enduring traumatic consequences on the French collective consciousness and have remained a stain on France's claim of exceptionalism—as true as exceptionalism rhymes with successful military campaigns, territorial occupation and resources requisition. From the day he took office, Sarkozy had aspirations not merely of reinventing a Napoleonic era of glory for France, but also, above all, an ambition of embodying Napoleon himself. And of Napoleon I, the 23rd French president seemed to have only retained the warlike disposition, the expensive as well as expansive military campaigns, and the lucrative pillaging. For Sarkozy, it was a mistake for his predecessor (Jacques Chirac) to have kept France out of the last Euro-American bellicose intervention in Iraq, a golden chance to erase France's gloomy past and restore its lost glory.

Since his 2007 election, Sarkozy was set to redeem France and install it on the *highest* pedestal. American president Barack Hussein Obama was going to play a major role in Sarkozy's master plan, for what greater success could a leader have than to lead the leader of the United States, and the *tallest* in generations, too. There is abundantly documented evidence that in Sarkozy's relationship with world leaders, and especially with President Obama, size did matter and that the French president tended to bring everything down to a personal level. Indeed, when in September 2009, five-foot-five Sarkozy visited Faurecia, a technology plant in Caen, his aides made sure that only smaller-height workers were selected to greet him. It was out of the question that Sarkozy and those who were watching him around the world on TV be made aware of a "defect" he had been trying his hardest to conceal: his diminutive height.

[Sarkozy] stood before the cameras flanked by white-coated workers and suited executives, very few of whom were taller than him. A journalist reportedly asked one of them later: "Is it true you were all picked to appear alongside the president because of your height—because you shouldn't be taller than the president?" The worker answered: "Exactly that." And French TV news showed 20 relatively small Faurecia workers from a total workforce of 1,400 being bussed to the press conference from other parts of the site.... Sarkozy's aides were keen to ensure no repeat of the D-day debacle in June [2009] when, just along the Normandy coast in Colleville-sur-Mer, Sarkozy had stood next to 6ft 1in Barack Obama and 5ft 11in Gordon Brown during the 65th anniversary commemoration ceremony. French virility had been symbolically castrated by an Anglo-American height conspiracy.[28]

For Sarkozy, to beat Obama, the tallest president of the most exceptional country, amounted to beating his own symptoms and resurrecting Napoleon and thus France's glorious years. Sarkozy had dreams of making Obama walk to his pace, and he did not hide it. So, as Obama was being discredited in the United States, Sarkozy was going to use Obama's home front handicap to his advantage. Sarkozy (was it a symptom of his Napoleonic complex?) had never held a high opinion of Obama; but yet again, Sarkozy had never held a high opinion of anyone else but himself. "In the world according to Sarko," as writes Nile Gardiner, "President Obama is weak, inexperienced and badly briefed.... [Obama] has a subtle mind, [is] very intelligent and very charismatic," but he lacks the experience that makes a great leader. Having never held any high government office responsibility before being elected to the White House, "[he] is not always operating at a level of decision-making and efficiency." When Sarkozy succeeded in getting Obama to come to an official visit in France for the D-Day landing anniversary, he proudly declared to his associates, "I am going to ask [Obama] to walk on the Channel, and he'll do it."[29] Sarkozy had decided to lead on the world stage and make Obama follow. Whatever conservatives thought of Obama in America, he was still the leader of America, and to get him to take orders would be for Sarkozy a great exceptionalism boost. In reality, Sarkozy and Obama needed each other: Sarkozy needed Obama to further his Napoleonic image and Obama needed Sarkozy's agitation to exorcise his own alleged weakness. Eye to eye, Obama and Sarkozy seemed to be saying to each other, "Tell me what you don't have; I've got it!" So, it was just a matter of time before Sarkozy and Obama would embark together on an exploration into exceptionalism.

The France that Sarkozy had inherited was like that of his predecessors, a bundle of defeats and *ressentiments* that needed redressing. De Tocqueville's French exceptionalism, so celebrated in 1835, would be lost 36 years later and not recovered for almost half a century. In 1871, France's arrogance was flung back in its face, when, in some excess of self-importance and seeking to reclaim the privileged position in Europe it had lost under Napoleon Bonaparte, France, this time under Napoleon III, declared war on the German Empire, only to be overpowered, severely beaten, severed from her territories of Alsace and Lorraine, and tendered a war reparation bill of 5 billion francs (the equivalent of $1 billion) to be paid within three years. While one would think that such humiliation would tame France's hegemonic drive, on the contrary, upon German invitation to join other European powers in the looting of Africa, some politicians in France were thinking of recapturing the Hexagon's lost exceptionalism by building a larger colonial empire through wars of conquest.

Between November 15, 1884, and February 26, 1885, German Chancellor Otto Von Bismarck convened a meeting of European leaders in Berlin for the purpose of collectively coming up with guidelines that would regulate European nations' stranglehold on African territories. The European powers' rush to stake claims in Africa was very disorganized and conflicts were frequent amongst them. Rules needed to be established for a "civilized" looting of the Black Continent. The French, who had just come out of two losing wars, one against Germany (1870–1871) and one against China (1883–1885) and who were also engaged in frequent skirmishes against militants seeking independence in occupied Algeria, had very little enthusiasm for more conquest wars and needed some strong convincing.

So, five months after the Berlin Conference, a debate between proponents and dissenters of France's colonial expansion erupted on the floor of the French *Assemblée Nationale*. Jules Ferry (who had been twice prime minister of France, once from September 1880 to November 1881 and another time from February 1883 to April 1885) represented the first group. He made his arguments in favor of colonial expansionism on France's need to reaffirm its exceptionalism lost to Germany after 1871. France, Ferry explained, would be well inspired to seek a colonial empire for several reasons. Economically, with the competition of Germany and the United States, two increasingly protectionist countries of intense industrial and agricultural outputs, it was imperative that France should find new markets outside of Europe and America for its export commodities. From a humanitarian standpoint, Ferry added, France, as a member of the "higher race," had a heavenly right and responsibility to civilize the "inferior races" and to pull them from the Dark Ages. From a political and patriotic perspective, France needed to ensure its place in the world by performing acts of exceptionality. For France to abstain from pursuing a colonial empire when all the other European countries were seeking colonial expansion, he insisted, would amount to surrendering for an indefinite time to the other European nations its privileged position in Europe. To reestablish its honored place on the international exchequer, France would need to start exporting to faraway places its language, its customs, its flag, and its genius.[30]

In his rejoinder to Ferry, Georges Clemenceau (leader of the Radical Party) took issue with Ferry's dichotomy between "superior races" and "inferior races." Clemenceau recalled that in the days leading up to the Franco-Prussian war, German social engineers had also argued that Germans constituted a race superior to the French race and therefore were more likely to win a war against the inferior French. So Clemenceau asked Ferry whether the Germans' 1871 victory verified the thesis of German exceptionalism. Clemenceau then advised his fellow countrymen not to repeat this German axiom against African nations by trying to disguise violence under the cunning designation of civilization. He explained that the justification of divine right, or duty to civilize and lead others, was nothing but a right to brutality that scientifically advanced societies would claim in order to take possession of less advanced nations and torture their citizens and exploit them for the benefit of so-called superior races. Clemenceau added that to make civilization a justification for colonization was to add hypocrisy to violence. His appeal was not heard, and by the late 1800s and early 1900s several pro-colonialist pressure groups—such as the Comité de l'Afrique française, the Comité de l'Égypte, the Comité de l'Asie française, and the Comité de Madagascar, all unified under the banner of the Parti colonial—convinced the French government to resuscitate France's exceptionality in the world by colonizing further.

In 1885, then, Germany was the magnificent nation, and Germans were the superlative race, the beautiful people. Battered France was thus the inferior nation seeking to recapture a vanished glory through the building of a larger colonial empire. After its 1871 victory over France, Bismarck knew, in spite of Germany's extended hand to France, that—in spite of the fact that Germany had invited France to take its rightful seat among the "nations of plunderers" of the African continent, and in spite of the fact that though being in a better military disposition to snatch for itself a greater number of colonies Germany had let France get away with the lion's share of African territories—France was obsessed with one idea: to assuage the humiliation dealt it by Germany, take its revenge against Germany, reverse the tides, and sit, once again, on the pedestal of beauty and glory.

Germany was aware that sooner or later it would have to go to war against France. In anticipation of that war, Germany had signed the Triple-Alliance, a defense agreement with Austria-Hungary and Italy, on May 25, 1882. In preparation for its war to reconquer its exceptionalism, France also signed a defense agreement with Russia and Great Britain, the Triple-Entente (Triple Friendship), on August 18, 1892. When, in July 1914, Austria-Hungary declared war on Serbia for the assassination in Sarajevo, by a young Serbian, of Austrian Archduke François-Ferdinand and his wife, Sophie de Hoenberg, these alliances would indubitably drag the whole of Europe into the misnomer that came to be called World War I.

CHAPTER 2

Africa Caught in the Eddy of the Euro-American Quest for Exceptionalism

The first and second European wars, which started because of the Euro-American quest for exceptionalism had profoundly affected the lives of millions of Africans. France, especially, had used the people of its African colonies in the most proficient way in its quest to restore France's lost standing in the world. Long before its 1871 bitter loss to the Germans, and by way of takeovers, deportation and assassination of freedom fighters, double-dealing, and unmatched techniques of divide and conquer, France had annexed a number of countries and was ruthlessly administering their indigenous populations. By the early 1950s, if exceptionalism, as defined by the heralds of colonial expansion, meant brutal occupation of foreign territories, then France was without any doubt exceptional, as it had colonies on every continent of the globe, with variegated administrative set-ups, such as slave colonies, settlement colonies, protectorates, and the like. Even though the local populations in the colonies did not have the same rights as the citizens of France, France's colonial acquisitions were governed as extensions of France, and the colonial populations were expected to take part in the economic well-being of the mainland as well as in its defense.

Africa in the First European War

The French colonies were instrumental in defending France against its foes. Hence, the first European war saw the drafting of important contingents of colonial populations in the French army who not only had to endure French racism but also discrimination from the European enemies of France. More than 135,000 conscripts from the French colonies were sent to Europe to fight on behalf of France in a war about which they understood very little and in a social and climatic environment with which they were not familiar at all. Over 35,000 of the

African draftees, called Senegalese *tirailleurs* (sharpshooters), lost their lives fighting for France. In spite of their designation, the Senegalese tirailleurs did not all come from Senegal, though Senegalese constituted the first contingents of this colonial infantry corps. They came from all the French colonies. Despite the difficult and unfamiliar conditions encountered in Europe, the soldiers from the colonies fought with distinction and discipline even when outnumbered, as was often the case:

> Then, the disaster and carnage ... the tirailleurs rushed, rolled, encircled, are submerged by the irresistible wave of attackers. They sell their lives dearly with terrible blows. However, what can this handful of heroes do against the great number? One by one, they succumb. At noon, there are only a few men left, who, having managed to escape to the limit of grassland through the tranches filled with water, will join the 4th company and renew superhuman acts of bravery.[1]

They also contributed to important victories on the battlefields of Europe. Of them, a Belgian paper once wrote, "The black tirailleur, by his heroism, his courage, his strength, and his tenacity, showed the universe that he is not an inferior. He was, of all, the most feared by the German."[2] Were the African tirailleurs feared by the German soldiers for their heroism, courage and strength? Were they feared for the "beastly" appearance, half-man half-beast charging human German soldiers? Or did the German soldiers consider it beneath their standing to fight against an inferior race? The African fighters on the European battlefield were not tolerated by their white counterparts, especially by the Germans, as evidenced by a letter written by German volunteer Hans Friedrich Blunck. The soldier's letter, which a German propaganda paper published in 1915, was meant to be part of the arsenal of racial war fought alongside the war in the trenches. In his letter, Blunck accused nonwhite, and particularly black soldiers, of sullying with their dark, bestial blood a marvelous, civilized, white war fought on white soil.

> In this night, the marvelous fighting has become disgusting to me. The foe deployed Senegalese Negroes and Indian auxiliaries against our glorious volunteers, and it was as if, through the stream of blood that covered the battlefield, the trembling beastly smell of the dark-colored people emerged. As if together, with the inferior blood of these strangers, something would pour into the soil plaguing the country, as if the earth knew that it would never again be able to become green after the African feet had touched it.... The German had seen the black flood, the dark mud devouring him and his men. He had not been able to fight man against man, as had been the dream of his life; the enemy had sent half-animal peoples of Africa, whom he had not expected; the enemy had mobilized Asia and betrayed thousand years of old Europe.[3]

Though in a less racially charged tone than that used in his comrade's letter, in his December 1914 message to his parents another German soldier, Kurt Schlenner, was delighted that, unlike the very colorful, racially diverse enemy troops that lacked cohesion, German troops were solid by their natural racial unity. They could boast a perfect spirit of comradery, while, on the other side, the task of building a strong unit would be arduous, for "one cannot respect a Negro as a comrade after all."[4]

After the Armistice of 1918, still a considerable number of tirailleurs remained in France, some of whom the French government deployed to Rhineland in order to give them a full sense of France's superiority over Germany, a French supremacy which, once they were repatriated and as African emissaries of French magnificence, they were expected to carry over to their respective countries and convey to their peoples. Furthermore, by stationing black troops in occupied German territories, France was hoping to express to the world that its pledge to republican principles was heartfelt and that France marked no difference between its white and black soldiers. The reality was quite different.

In the early months of the war, the French media's representations of the African soldiers in Europe differed little from those offered by German propaganda papers. Some French cartoons portrayed African soldiers as savages and barbarians wearing necklaces made of German soldiers' ears as trophies.[5] Incidentally, the use of necklaces of ears as war trophies was a method that Marshal Thomas Bugeaud's French troops had developed in 1842 during France's violent conquest of Algeria; and it is interesting that this barbaric method initiated by the French against Africans in Algeria should be attributed to the African troops fighting for France's liberation in Europe. Also, the tirailleurs were not given permission and, unlike their French counterparts, could not visit their families in Africa. Furthermore, the African troops fighting in Europe were given a very summary training and were not allowed to rise above the position of captain. Even at the highest admitted grade, African soldiers were under the supervision of French officers, sometimes of lower status.[6] The French authorities went to great lengths to prevent their African soldiers from mingling with the French general population.[7] As recalled Kandé Salifou Kamara, a conscript from Guinea, "Even when we were marching through a [French] town, [white] officers would be on your right and your left saying: 'one two, one two' ... and if you turned to look at the people cheering, they would slap you so hard you would actually see the fire of hell."[8] As reports Richard Fogarty, at the highest level of French administration the idea of taunting Germans with the presence of "Black Shame" importing "their savage methods of warfare into the heart of civilized Europe" was not always appreciated. While some French lawmakers, in charging the Germans with hypocrisy for having inaugurated the most abject methods of warfare in occupied Belgium and France, called for blacks to be deployed in the Rhineland, Marshal Pétain of France as well as the British and American administrations did not approve of the idea.[9]

Actually, neither France nor America nor Great Britain had resolved their own anxieties about race yet. The British reproached the French with using black soldiers against white enemies; the French resented having blacks around their women, and the Americans were afraid that the "freedom" afforded to black French soldiers could be deleterious among black American soldiers at home. As evidenced in the encrypted message of an anonymous sender to the French Director of the Colonial Troops, the presence of the tirailleurs was a precarious issue in France: "We cannot remove them. Public opinion, the national interest, some influential men, including the Tiger [Clemenceau], won't allow it. But on the other hand, you will not be able to leave them in France … [as] (socialists) … Americans in particular, hoteliers and therefore the southern departments agree on that. The theme is found: praetorians, as you saw in the meeting of 29 December."[10]

It was thus decided that the black soldiers should return to Africa; but for how long? For as has been so clearly stated by the mysterious correspondence there was also the question of national interest. And in 1918, national interest required that France's workforce, especially the men killed on the battlefields, be replaced immediately. "The cause was heard; the 'Senegalese' [tirailleurs] would not remain in France—although some [among the French authorities] wished they would. However, there was no question to demobilize them immediately to their country of origin; on the contrary, they would be employed as replacements to French in the metropole."[11]

The debate on the presence of blacks in a white war was meant only for the primary protagonists of that war to try to pull the claim of defender of "greater civilization" toward their respective arguments. Of all the protagonists of the first European war, Germany and Great Britain had perhaps the most coherent attitude regarding their racist anxieties. They thought that blacks were an inferior race that did not deserve to spill precious white blood; and they kept blacks away from the battlefields of Europe. As for all the others, including the United States, they hated nonwhites when it suited them but were quite open to use them to fight their war. Italy's attempt to deploy 2,700 soldiers from Libya failed when half of the troops died from pneumonia upon their arrival in Italy and the other half was subsequently returned to Africa. The Belgian government considered but never actuated their plans to send Congolese soldiers to Europe, and the Portuguese, like the Belgians, hesitated until the end of the war to send soldiers to Europe.[12] The French, with their 800,000 men from the colonies, had set both a precedent and a record. As they helped the forces of the Triple Entente secure the occupied territories of the Rhineland in Germany, some of the tirailleurs dated or married German women and had biracial children. These interracial encounters, though clear indications that not all Europeans were racists, were not approved of by all Germans, and the malaise of the "Black Shame" would linger until 1939. In France's twisted, unacknowledged racism it was still the blacks that France used in 1914 to reinstate its lost prestige. It was, once again, the blacks that would come to the rescue of France in 1939, when France lost its freedom under German occupation. The fact that the German notion of "Black Shame" and the French notion of "black force" were both tinged with racism says much about the general concert of minds in the whole of Europe regarding blacks before, as well as after, the first European war.

Europe's and Africa's Outlooks Toward Each Other in the Interwar Period

Truly, blacks' prowess on the battlefields of Europe won them an ambiguous representation in the European imagination after the first European war. In the interwar period, blacks were no longer regarded simply as primitives or savages. Blacks' portrayal by the European media, especially the French media, started to undergo a metamorphosis, mainly because of a conscious effort by French officials, as early as 1915, to authenticate France's victory in the first war. In response to Germans' accusations that France had introduced black barbarism in a white, civilized war, the French started to work towards softening the image of the African tirailleur in order to present France's victory over Germany as having been won fairly, by the white rules of the game of war. Thus journalist Alphonse Séché, for instance, wrote in the French weekly *L'Opinion* that "for the black man, the white man's orders, the chief's orders are summarized in one phrase that he repeats over and over again '*y a service*'.... He won't discuss; he does not try to understand. He would kill his father, mother, wife, child to obey the orders he has received.... In all the Blacks' acts, we find this mixture of child-like nature and heroism."[13] From this new perspective then, the tirailleur was no longer a lawless blood-thirsty warrior who would go on uncontrollable killing sprees; he was, rather, a disciplined soldier whose respect for white authority—as most of the officers from whom the African troops took their orders were white—was almost mechanical. As they were being praised for their courage, blacks were also, and paradoxically, being portrayed as epitomizing brute force and natural stamina, and these exoticized images were exploited by industrial entities to commercialize any product that was dark or expected to have potent merits, such as coffee, tea, cocoa, or even motor oil.[14] The various exploitations of the black's image in commercials in the aftermath of the first war were only symptomatic of a larger, more systematized, exploitation to come during the interwar.

Between the first and the second European wars, France had come to realize the true potentials of its colonies. As Albert Sarraut, Minister of the Colonies,

stated in his *La Mise en valeur des colonies françaises*, the true economic and political values of the French colonies were revealed to the French public during the
first war. In the 1914–1918 war, Africans, Asians, West Indians, Malagasies and
Indochinese fought for France or filled French factories to curb the country's
labor deficit or both. Though it is difficult to give exact statistics on what the
colonies contributed to the war effort in terms of men, goods, and money from
the beginning of the war to the end of the war, conservative statistics available
between 1916 and the end of 1918 indicated that the colonies' contributions were
sizeable. At least 800,000 men from the French colonies were sent to France to
help in the war effort, of whom 600,000 were combatants and 200,000 laborers.
In French North Africa, 172,000 men from Algeria, 60,000 combatants from
Tunisia and 37,150 volunteers from Tunisia were recruited and deployed to
France. Of these 270,000 combatants from the French Maghreb, 28,200 were
killed and 7,700 were unaccounted for. French East Africa sent 17,910 to France;
French West Africa contributed 163,602 combatants; and Madagascar contributed 10,000 men to work in heavy artillery. By 1918, between 1,500 and 2,000
men were still in formation to be deployed to France. To make up for the labor
deficit in France, a concomitant recruitment of laborers was taking place with
the recruitment of soldiers. Between 1915 and 1919 a total of 220,600 laborers
were recruited from the French colonies, of whom 75,564 were from Algeria,
18,538 from Tunisia, 35,010 from Morocco, 48,918 from Indochina, and 5,535
from Madagascar. Furthermore, 1 billion francs of war bonds were sold in the
colonies to raise money for the war, and 1,600,000 tons of diverse materials were
provided by the colonies to France, of which 714,296 tons of goods (grains, sugar,
alcohol, vegetable, tobacco, rubber, oil, cotton, wood, meat, leather, hide, nuts,
etc.) were contributed by sub–Saharan Africa and Madagascar alone.[15]

Undeniably, as wrote Sarraut, "The colonies were no longer just those distant countries that fed the dreams and fantasies of writers! They were countries
overflowing with an intense life, rich in men and in raw materials, which have
demonstrated their vitality in the hour of greatest danger. For these achievements,
the 'colonial enterprise' proved that it is 'profitable.'"[16] In fact, the people of the
metropole, having understood that the colonies could, and did, contribute enor-
mously to France's military and economic vitality during the war, had a significant
number of speculators looking to make money in colonial ventures grow the
business volume in the colonies. By the end of fiscal year 1930, for instance, the
six main colonial banks (the banks of Martinique, Guadeloupe, Reunion, Guyana,
West Africa, and Indochina) had a general business volume of 6 billion francs,
of which one-sixth was from French West Africa.[17] The contributions of France's
colonies to the war effort had somehow vindicated Jules Ferry and the champions
of colonial expansion.

Nevertheless, as deplored by Sarraut, things could have been done in a more functional and less precipitous way. The contributing resources of the colonies, which truly did help France win the first war and reaffirm its exceptionalism in Europe, seemed to have been collected haphazardly. For instance, the recruitment of the colonial forces was disorganized and undertaken in unfit hygienic conditions. The recruits were not selected sensibly with respect to their fitness and intellectual capacities, and they were submitted to long and tiring marches from their villages to their training camps, which led to many losses of men that could have been put to better use in France. Because, explained Sarraut, "beautiful, strong, and educated men," as needed by France, "could not be created in just a few months," and colonial administrations would better serve France if in the future they would put more effort in, above all, "perfecting the racial and individual characteristics" of the colonial subjects.[18] In the interwar, French social engineers, through the voice of Sarraut, henceforth intended to systematize the colonies' productivity rather than leave it to mere chance. "Indeed, more enlightened now on its colonial empire and on the value of elements of renaissance, reconstitution, and national vitality that it can draw from it, France, now organizing its future on more powerful bases, will demand that its colonies and protectorates provide men for its army, money to alleviate its budgetary expenses, materials and products for its industry, its commerce, its sustenance, and its trade."[19] Sarraut was right. France was going to need its colonies more than before, as the global economic crisis of 1929 was approaching.

Though the early to mid–1920s were a period of relative prosperity in France marked by postwar reconstruction initiatives, by the late 1920s and early 1930s the global economic crisis which had started in 1929 hit the heart of France. The devaluation of the British pound in September 1931 followed by more devaluations in Europe caused French products to be out of reach for its economic partners and therefore undesirable. Industrial and agricultural production in France fell 17 percent, and as a consequence, unemployment rose progressively, from less than 20,000 people affected in 1929 to 250,000 in 1932 and 500,000 in 1934. The French wanted bread, rent subsidies, and financial help.[20] In the 1930s, the future was uncertain, and the general mood in France was more about preserving any little money one had than taking financial risks in the colonies.

Consequently, apart from the few risk-takers who had undertaken economic ventures in the colonies at the end of the first war, the general French public needed to be persuaded that their colonies were not money pits, that personal economic investments in the colonies were likely to be lucrative, and that their country's greater colonial involvement would not imperil their daily lives any further. In the perspective of sensitizing the French public to Sarraut's vision of structured colonial exploitation, and in order to get the full consent of the French public for a more substantial colonial venture, Sarraut's enthusiasm was put on display.

An international colonial fair was staged from May 6 to November 15, 1931, in Paris to celebrate *La plus grande France* (the Greater France, that is, France and its colonial empire). On that occasion, not only was the general French public invited to witness the wonders of France's colonial empire—some simulations of colonial scenes set up more for the purpose of appealing to French people's need for the bizarre and the exotic than for depicting the lived realities of locals in the colonies—but so, too, were academics, pre- and in-service teachers as well as schoolchildren and students, to whom the Ministry of the Colonies offered free excursions to the site. The goal was to educate educators and their young learners about the benefits that France drew from its colonies and instill in them a sense of pride in the colonial enterprise, to be carried over to future generations. And educated the guests were, indeed, as posted materials at various locations of the colonial exposition gave the public information about the many advantageous aspects of France's colonial venture. Thus, visitors at the Exposition coloniale internationale of 1931 could read, for instance:

> The total number of imports from Overseas-France amounted to 20 billion francs; the part of European-France in this total is 11 billion francs. The total number of exports from Overseas-France amounted to 15 billion francs, the part of European-France in this total being 7 billion francs. The total trade of Overseas-France is 35 billion francs. Did you know these numbers? Meditate on them and, keeping in mind that Overseas-France buys 11 billion francs of merchandise to European-France against 9 billion purchased abroad, imagine how more severely the current economic crisis would be felt by European-France if it did not have this wonderful market overseas, if these 11 billion export sales were to be cut off from the national revenue.[21]

So then, in the words of French officials themselves, and contrary to the purported philanthropic objectives trumpeted hitherto by the European powers that were present at the 1885 Berlin Conference, France's colonial expansion was more a profitable venture for France than for the natives of the colonies. The first war proved it beyond any doubt expressed by such reticent politicians as Clémenceau. In fact, he was so impressed by the contribution of the black troops to the defense of France during the war in 1818 that Clémenceau himself backed General Ferdinand Foch's proposal to raise an elite colonial force for the following year to be led from behind by French troops. It was hoped that, thanks to their "natural warlike abilities," the black soldiers, with the technical support of their French counterparts, would perform at their best against the Germans. Actually, French war engineers were so convinced that warlike abilities were innate to particular tribes that they recommended recruiting in specific tribal proportions. "Thus, in the fall of 1919, the War Minister demanded that the quotas be compounded as much as possible in the following proportions: 35 percent Mandingos (Bambara, Malinke, and Senufo), 30 percent from Upper Volta (Mossis, Bobos, Habbé), from Pula, Sereres, Ouolofs (20 percent), etc."[22]

Henceforth, with an outlook laden with prejudice, France was headed to making the colonies that had given so much during the first war an even more profitable enterprise for France after the war, especially given the economic uncertainty of the 1930s. The problem with systematizing the profitability of the colonies after the first war was that it also implied systematizing the abuses imposed on the colonies during the first war, and thus exacerbating the discontent of the natives of the colonies; for, in order to satisfy the demands of France during the first European war, the French administration's intervention in the social, political and economic lives of the locals in the colonies was more invasive than before.

The contributions to the war effort imposed by France on its colonies had devastating effects on the colonial populations. Among other burdens endured, such as the significant reduction of Africa's labor force and the disruption of its societal and familial structures, in the urgency to feed the French first and the Africans last Africa's agricultural resources were depleted when entire subsistence economies were diverted to extensively producing export crops to satisfy the needs of the metropole. Côte d'Ivoire for instance was made to specialize in the production of coffee and cocoa in its western and central regions, rubber, palm nuts, and coconuts in its southern region, and cotton and grains in its northern region. In Côte d'Ivoire, the transportation—to the southern port of Abidjan through the northern savannah and then the thick forest of the South—of the 4,200 tons of grain imposed as contribution by the colonial administration necessitated 2,500,000 days of portage distributed over 25,000 individual porters.[23] Likewise, the French Sudan (today's Mali), a region of weak population density and very scarce transportation and one that had never exported grains before the first war, was asked to raise its grain production by 60,000 tons. As a consequence, the region had the major part of its population requisitioned for the production, packaging, and transportation by land and river of grains. Sarraut's *mise en valeur* was asking for more effort from the colonies in supplying France with such raw materials as were needed by its factories. French colonies, he insisted, must help their motherland resolve its uninterrupted trade deficit and enfranchise its economy from the servitude imposed upon it by its economic partners (Germany, Great Britain, and the United States). Regarding products such as fatty matters, cotton, wood, wool, gum, rubber, leather, and minerals that were needed by France, "the metropolitan soil does not produce them, they can be found in inexhaustible quantities in our colonies," he declared.[24]

France's eagerness to press the colonies for more resources as a solution to its own economic difficulties would progressively strain its relations with the colonies and would lead from sporadic rebellions to more vociferous calls for independence. In the interwar period, the colonial representations of Africans did not change much. France continued to see Africa as a partner only insofar as Africa was exploitable and expendable and Africans as overgrown children who needed intellectual guidance from the motherland—*la patrie*. The image of the African as a big child was a colonial stereotype that had found its way, through the first war, into the interwar. Before, the black soldier was believed to be an impetuous and aggressive fighter, but a savage fighter all the same, lacking the intelligence required in a white war.[25] In the interwar, black people in general were figured as people with "unique physical prowess, limited intelligence, and special talent for music and dance,"[26] and their lands were figured as bountiful, savage territories waiting to be tamed for the benefit of Europe. What France failed to recognize was that, though its image of Africa had practically not changed, Africans' images of themselves and their representations of France and the French people had profoundly been affected by the war. The interwar era was for Africans a time of political *prise de conscience.*

One of the objections that German officials raised in 1915 against France's use of nonwhite soldiers was, as Koller's words encapsulate so well, that "if African and Asian soldiers saw white nations fighting each other and were allowed to participate in those fights and experience the white soldiers' vulnerability, they would lose their respect for the white race once and for ever."[27] Notwithstanding the obvious racism in the Germans' objection, the Germans were on point in their prediction. Truly, the African soldier—posted in the Rhineland to humiliate the vanquished racist German and return home as an ambassador and proselytizer of French exceptionalism—had actually returned to his people in Africa with a demystified image of Europe and of the Europeans, France and the French in particular. On the battlefield, in the villages and in the big cities, the black soldier had seen the whites collapse under pressure and fear. Whites, the black soldiers realized, were neither invincible nor infallible. In fact, they were neither more intelligent nor less intelligent than blacks on the battlefield. Whites were much like blacks, ordinary humans with normal apprehensions and hopes, and their privileges in Africa, which were supposedly based on a myth of superiority, were actually undeserved. The postwar era witnessed the emergence of "new Africans" who were ready to question the values of the European society that they had served.[28] The tirailleur who came back from the war was of this new breed. Thus, in words that clearly situated where the spirit of evil and savagery really lay, Bakari Diallo, the first Senegalese tirailleur to put his war experience on paper, had this to say:

> We are facing the German troops, in Marne. It is 4 a.m. … the guns, canons, and other war instruments that kill their masters have quieted down for a while. The Squads are refueling with some coffee and nutritious food. Everything was prepared at night and you have to eat to have the strength to die. A German who ended up in the wrong lines was caught, with his coffee in hand, by a Senegalese sentry. When he was surrounded by the tirailleurs, his entire body was shaking. Poor guy! Did

you not anticipate this moment as you had already counted your gold and glory? The Blacks that you regarded as savages have captured you at war, but instead of putting an end to your life, they have made you a prisoner. Tomorrow, after the war, let your fear not stop you from proclaiming in your country the sentiments of justice that will rehabilitate their names among the human races, equally savage.[29]

War and the Birth of a De-Territorialized African Intellectual Elite

The intellectual front as well the war had given rise to a new black consciousness, though filled with contradictions, which would start challenging white hegemony. Elected in 1914 to the French Assemblée nationale to represent Senegal under the gambit of France's politics of Assimilation, Senegalese Blaise Diagne had used the burdens of the war to insist that the tirailleurs be treated like other French soldiers—that there be no race-based objection to their deployment to the Rhineland, as they, too, were essential to France's victory and, thus, deserving of recognition. Diagne's demands that black soldiers be treated equally, that they be provided with the necessary material conditions to survive the harsh German winter, for instance, signaled the advent of a new African leadership that was not intimidated from claiming its rights.[30]

In the aftermath of armistice, as French authorities, faced with the depletion of France's workforce, were looking for more recruitments in Africa to relieve the French soldiers and replenish the factories with Frenchmen, Diagne had proposed to Clémenceau that military conscriptions be made mandatory in Africa. This idea was actually that of Lieutenant-Colonel Mangin, an officer of the French colonial army, who, as early as 1910, had argued in his *La Force noire* that France should make its African colonies a reservoir of native soldiers to be used to fight France's wars in order to help save the lives of young Frenchmen. However, Mangin's proposed conscription program came with a judicial stipulation that neither Mangin himself nor nationalist lawmakers were ready to accept. A legislative proposal that was meant to meet France's recruiting goal by incentivizing conscription had linked military service with French citizenship. Like several French lawmakers who were not eager to see blacks become French citizens through conscription, Mangin argued that France should not feel obliged to reward its subjects for their service to their "generous" motherland. In fact, as early as 1895, when the debate about the linkage of military service to French citizenship started, colonial journalist Ulysse Leriche stated that France had no obligation to offer its colonial subjects French citizenship. What France needed, Leriche insisted, was "soldiers, not electors." Therefore, he proposed, France should carry on with its longtime policy of "using" people in the colonies without feeling compelled to offer them anything in return.[31] The general sense was that, instead of France feeling guilty for exploiting its colonial subjects, it was rather France's colonial subjects that should be grateful to France for bestowing on them civilization, justice, health, and prosperity. This idea, on May 1930, on the site where the French invading forces landed in Algeria a century before, would be encapsulated in the unveiling by French president Gaston Doumergue of a 9-meter-high statue celebrating the centenary of the invasion of Algeria: "The monument's centerpiece," as described, "was comprised of two female allegorical figures: on the one side, France, maternal and generous, and on the other Algeria looking upward for protection and guidance."[32] Other critics were against the idea of conscription *tout court*, be it accompanied with citizenship or not. For them, it was a dangerous idea to arm black soldiers. They could one day turn their guns against the French in African rebellions.[33] When, in October 1919, Diagne's proposal to recruit more black soldiers was ratified and put into practice, "on the one hand, Mangin could estimate to have reached his goal of creating a large black force, and, on the other hand, Diagne could be satisfied to have inaugurated the cornerstone of Africans' access to French citizenship, which, for the African 'elites' of the time, constituted the ultimate goal of the assimilation program."[34]

Diagne was the epitome of the French African intellectual elite of the postwar era, an elite of de-territorialized Africans wandering at the crossroads of Africa and Europe. Born in 1872 on the Senegalese Island of Gorée, Diagne, a Catholic by faith through adoption by a Christian family, studied in France and worked as a civil servant in several colonial administrations (French Congo, Reunion, Madagascar, and Benin) before being elected as the representative of Senegal's *Quatre Communes* (Saint-Louis, Dakar, Gorée, Rufisque). In 1916, Diagne, the first black at the French *Assemblée*, convinced the French Parliament to pass the "*Loi Blaise Diagne*," giving full citizenship to the colonial subjects of the *Quatre Communes*, who, though granted the rights of French citizens since the Revolution of 1848, were still faced with enormous obstacles in claiming their privileges as French citizens. Diagne's eagerness to seek French citizenship for the African elites betrayed, on the one hand, a certain malaise with his native culture, which he could no longer claim entirely, and, on the other hand, a forced entry into a French society that was not spontaneous in greeting him in its midst.

Other black intellectuals would follow in Diagne's path and request for their people equal social rights. Senegalese poet, philosopher, and political figure Léopold Sédar Senghor was also of this new breed of African intellectuals resolute to ask of France that it fulfill its promise of assimilation while heeding the call of a fleeting African societal order. The postwar African intellectual elites' fascination with France and things French made it difficult for them to utter the word "independence" where and when it was needed, even when this embryonic intellectual realization found support and impetus in such progressive entities as the French Communist Party and the Surrealist Group.

Indeed, in 1931, a group of forty surrealists, among them Aragon, André Breton, René Char and Paul Eluard, had protested the *Exposition nationale*— meant to showcase Mother-France with its savage colonial children—as exploitive, degrading and imperialistic. They denounced the show through pamphlets that read "*N'allez pas à l'Exposition Coloniale!*" (Do Not Go to the Colonial Exposition!). In lieu of the colonial exposition, the French Communist Party and the surrealists organized a counter exposition, the "Anti-Imperialist Exposition," which, though not heavily attended, did not go unnoticed. Although the Surrealist Group and the French Communist Party became some of the strongest advocates the African intellectuals of the 1930s had in Europe, these supporters of the African cause were, nonetheless, not infallible. Despite all their good intentions, the lenses through which they approached African realities were first and foremost culturally, socially and politically European.[35] Their fight with(in) Europe was one of class warfare. Africa's fight and the fight of the people in the colonies against the colonizing countries could be nothing short of self-determination. The French Communist Party and the Surrealist Group could not clearly articulate the black's fundamental question of independence; they could even constitute a dead weight on the ankles of the African nationalists. In fact, after some years of flirting with the Communist Party the black intellectuals of the French colonies finally chose to go their separate ways. Martinican Aimé Césaire's resignation letter to Maurice Thorez is often cited for this divorce.[36]

As a proof, when in 1940 France was once again besieged by Germany the French Communist Party was one of the strongest proponents for the recruitment of blacks to fight in France for an independence that was denied them at home, for, as Raphaël Granvaud notes so well, "In France ... the only concern, shared by military authorities and political movements of all kinds (even the Communist Party), is the restoration of the Empire, and through it the 'greatness' of France, in order to wash the humiliation of years of occupation."[37] And yet, it was clear that if won, France's victory would only reinforce the power of the French oppressor and further delay the independence of the oppressed black, as years before the start of the second European war Africans' fervor for independence was being ruthlessly crushed by colonial authorities in several places in Africa. "Faced with the pre-insurrectional climate developing by the early forties in most colonies, all the French military effort, once the war ended, and even before, would be devoted to quelling rebellions in blood. Colonial officers even recommended that rebellions be created with provocations in order to better crush them preventively and make examples."[38] If in the French imagination, even in the French liberal imagination, blacks were overgrown children that had no use of independence they were nonetheless fierce, aggressive, and warlike children who had proven their worth during the first European war and could be used again. It was paradoxical that black intellectuals like Diagne and Senghor should see recruitment of blacks in a white war as a path to autonomy while what Africa needed was independence and not double-standard citizenship. In the colonies, France had not always fulfilled its promises to the war veteran considered as French. Often, his pensions came late or were simply forgotten; his physical and mental wounds were not tended to; and the job that he was promised upon his return was nowhere to be found. It is paradoxical that instead of asking for full independence the African intellectual elites should want to remain in a French political arrangement that was that discriminatory against blacks.

1939–1945: "The future of Europe ... in our hands"

On October 11, 1914, a downhearted and grave U.S. Ambassador to London Walter H. Page summarized the beginning of the first European war to his friend Colonel Edward M. House in a letter to America:

> Germany (that is, Prussia and its system) cut out like a cancer; England owning still more of the world; Belgium—all the men dead; France bankrupt; Russia admitted to the society of nations; the British Empire entering on a new lease of life; no great navy but one; no great army but the Russian; nearly all governments in Europe bankrupt; Germany gone from the sea—in ten years, it will be difficult to recall clearly the Europe of the last ten years. And the future of Europe more than ever in our hands.[39]

Thus, as far back as the beginning of the first European war, America was convinced that Europe was economically and physically bankrupt, and that the future of Europe belonged to America. One cannot measure the gravity of such a conviction, considering that only a few months before, Europe was persuaded that the future of *the world* was in *its* hands. And indeed, the future of Europe, from 1914 onwards, was shaped across the Atlantic, in America, a situation that became even more unmistakable by the end of the second European war in 1945.

The American gradual fervor for exceptionalism in modern times stems from a claim of entitlement in the aftermath of the second European war. It is as if, having rescued Europe, and particularly France, from German occupation, America henceforth regarded itself as the rightful inheritor of exceptionalism, in lieu of Europe, the battered and humiliated continent. This verity Europe, particularly France, has never digested and, in a distorted double libidinal gesture of condensation and transfer, France has set about to make Africa pay for the humiliation it suffered on the world stage.

On June 22, 1940, French General Charles Huntziger signed the recognition of France's capitulation to Germany in the forest of Compiègne. For a more dramatic effect, Hitler had insisted that the official text of France's defeat be signed in the same train car that had hosted the signature of the 1918 armistice that shamed Germany. So, there, in the same wagon, through General Wilhelm Keitel—for Hitler had judged it below his standing to sit through the whole ceremony and had left early to contemplate his conquered territory—Germany handed the French authorities the terms of the occupation. All the northern part of France, including all its coastal areas, down to the city of Bordeaux on the western coast (a total of three-fifths of the French territory) were declared Occupied Zone. The *Zone occupée*, with its capital in Paris, was under direct German military and executive control. The southern part of France was the *Zone libre* or *France libre* (Free Zone), a misnomer, indeed, for the "Free France," with its capital in Vichy, was actually administered on behalf of Germany by Marshal Henri Philippe Pétain, the very "national hero" of the mythical battle of Verdun of the first European war, who had by then become head of the French government. The two zones were separated by a 50-kilometer demilitarized buffer zone, called *zone de démarcation*. Furthermore, the territories of Alsace and Lorraine were back into German territory. The French armed forces were disbanded, except the police and the gendarmerie committed to the enforcement of order, and France was ordered to pay a daily reparation bill of 400 million francs to Germany in addition to picking up the tab for the German occupation. Hitherto disgraced and overtaken by France, Germany was now at the top of Europe; and France was, henceforth, a de facto German protectorate from 1940 to 1944.

Nonetheless, refusing France's precipitous capitulation to Germany, General de Gaulle fled to London to rally the troops for resistance. On June 22, 1940, in a radio address aired on BBC, de Gaulle appealed to the French, asking them to have faith in their worldwide human and material resources and urging them to carry on the fight.

> Yes, we have suffered a great defeat. A bad military system, mistakes committed in the conduct of operations, the spirit of abandonment of the government during these battles caused us to lose the battle of France. But we have a vast empire, an intact fleet, a lot of gold. We have allies whose resources are immense and dominate the seas.... I invite all the French who want to remain free to listen to me and follow me.[40]

The human and material resources of the colonies were certainly on the mind of General de Gaulle as he made his appeal for resistance; and indeed, from the start of the war, the colony had been paying a hefty price for the liberation of France. The division within France along the lines of pro–Vichy (or pro–German) and pro–Paris (or pro–Allies) had profound consequences in the French colonies. Africa, too, was partitioned along pro–German and pro–Allies lines. And if only France introduced foreign fighters on a European battleground during the first European war, the second European war would see all the imperial nations within the Allied forces recruit heavily from among the populations of their colonies. Thus, while the French colonies of West Africa were committed to the Vichy regime, the colonies of France in Equatorial Africa, along with English West Africa, Liberia, English East Africa, the South African Union, Cameroon, and the Belgian Congo were co-opted by the Allies. As for Great Britain, it had 334,000 soldiers from South Africa, 100,000 men from Egypt, 77,767 men from Southern Africa (Lesotho, Botswana, Swaziland, Zambia, and Zimbabwe), 289,530 soldiers from East Africa (Kenya, Tanzania, Uganda, Malawi), 243,550 soldiers from English West Africa (Nigeria, Gambia, Sierra Leone, Ghana), 6,500 men from Mauritius and Seychelles, and 30,000 Ethiopian patriots fighting on its sides. France, both Vichy and free, had 190,000 men from Algeria, Senegal, Mali, Burkina Faso, Benin, Chad, Guinea, Côte d'Ivoire, Niger, and Republic of Congo in its ranks. Italy recruited 60,000 troops from Eritrea, and Belgium drafted 24,000 men from the Congo.[41] The second European war was not fought just in Europe; it was also transported to the African continent, as African armies correspondingly fought respective enemy positions on the African continent. For instance, the African troops of French Equatorial Africa and Cameroon were commissioned to harass and conduct sabotage operations against the Italian positions in Eritrea and against Erwin Rommel's formidable Afrika Korps in Libya. In fact, America's Operation Torch was facilitated by the participation of thousands of African troops needed to secure North Africa and also French West Africa to the cause of the Allies.

The African colonies' monetary contributions to the second European war effort were also considerable. For instance, the British West African colonies contributed about 931,127 pounds to the Allies, of which 44 percent were from Nigeria, 38 percent from the Gold Coast, 16 percent from Sierra Leone, and 1.2 percent from Gambia. French Africa's heavy taxations and war bonds generated a total of 1.5 billion francs to the war effort. In the Belgian Congo, hundreds of thousands of people were requisitioned to harvest rubber to supply Firestone with raw materials that could no longer be acquired from Asia or to mine copper and uranium for war industries.[42]

In the second European war, as was the case in the first European war, when France, confronted with a powerful German military power, faced the risk of total colonization and complete loss of its independence, African troops and civilian populations in the French colonies were solicited, and they responded to the cry of the "motherland." However, by 1945 Africa had undergone growing awareness about the nature of its relationship with France and was going to put the truthfulness of Mother France's love for her dark-skinned children as well as her propounded commitment to liberty, equality and fraternity to the test. After all, could a mother yearn for freedom and prevent her children from attaining their own freedom? Could self-determination be appropriate for the people of France but inappropriate for the peoples of the French colonies? The second European war precipitated the question of independence for the colonized peoples. A fervor for independence that had started in Indochina was spreading to Africa like wildfire, first to the Maghreb, and then to sub–Saharan Africa, with such urgency that on April 20, 1947, in Dakar, French president Vincent Auriol vowed to use force to prevent France's colonies from obtaining independence— this Indochinese concept that, in reality, would not be of much use to the majority of those who are asking for it.

> France, [Auriol] said, "will overcome any inertia, all your misgivings, and all selfish-
> ness and will break all the dissociation attempts. France rejects force, but when
> imposed violence, it also knows how to be firm. From all the weight of its power, it
> defends its children, whatever their race, religion, color, and protects their property,
> their customs, their traditions, their lives because it is its duty expressly stated in
> the Constitution to ensure the safety of all and to preserve the common good." The
> fact is that in Indochina and elsewhere some minorities are seeking to eliminate
> France and to seize power in the name of independence that would not come true
> for all the populations.[43]

Independence was good for the French but useless for the peoples of the colonies is, in essence, what Auriol was saying; and two years earlier, indeed, France's duplicity hit one of its highest notes.

It was May 8, 1945. The streets of Paris were bustling with revelers drunk with joy and singing patriotic songs. It was V-Day. General Charles de Gaulle had just announced on the radio to the French people the victory of the Allied forces, the unconditional surrender of Germany, and the liberation from German occupation of the French people. The French flag could be hoisted again without fear of German retribution. In his June 22, 1941, appeal to French soldiers to keep fighting, de Gaulle had urged them to trust the "immense resources" of France's allies, and especially the "gigantic possibilities of the American industry" to deliver victory to France. De Gaulle was well-advised. France's allies had lived up to the General-resistant's expectations and dealt a decisive blow to Germany.

France was free, of course, but there remained on the whole country, on its people and on its institutions a lingering malaise, a stain, a sense of humiliation and dishonor that even the final ratification of the victory document in Reims seemed to have amplified rather than effaced. Apart from the honor that was afforded de Gaulle the day after the armistice signature to announce the victory to his people, on May 7, 1945, everything else indicated that, first and foremost, the triumph over Germany actually belonged more to France's allies than to France. And to make it clear enough to the French authorities, Lieutenant General Walter Smith, Chief of Staff to General Eisenhower, Supreme Commander of the Allied Forces, and Soviet General Ivan Susloparov signed the German

Instrument of Surrender on behalf of the winners. As if in a moment of after-thought, the Allies then asked French General François Sevez, Chief of Staff of General de Gaulle, to countersign the document as a mere witness. This was a very explicit way for America and Russia to signal to France that, though free now, France remained, nonetheless, a less than exceptional, less than ordinary nation.

The French army, which had been up to then advertised as the most formidable army in Europe, had fallen to Germany in record time. On June 17, 1940, six weeks after the war had started, Marshal Pétain had ordered his troops to stop fighting, and the French government fled to the city of Vichy, whence it would administer occupied France on behalf of Nazi Germany. France's allies, especially America and Russia, had intended to remind the French authorities that the victory was not of France's doing; and indeed, France would not have been liberated if two determining military presences had not changed the course of the war: the Soviet Red Army and the United States Army, the first by having made tremendous human sacrifices and having shown extraordinary resilience and formidable fighting spirit, the second for having broken its isolationist policy and entered the war with one of the most terrifying killing machines the human inventive mind had ever created.

On December 17, 1941, the United States naval base at Pearl Harbor, Hawaii, was attacked by the Imperial Japanese Navy. From that day onwards, the American isolationist and neutral doctrine was totally abandoned. In fact, even before the attack on Pearl Harbor, America's sales and escort of arms to Great Britain and America's "shoot-on-sight" policy following the attack of USS *Greer* had already started to wean the United States of its neutrality in the second European war. After Pearl Harbor, America entered the war militarily, first with its offensive against German troops in Tunisia, in November 1942. On the Eastern Front, after surviving a two-and-a-half-year German siege in Leningrad (today's Petersburg), from September 1941 to January 1944 that cost the lives of 1,000,000 Russians, the Red Army started a counterattack heavy in casualties (27 million Russian dead) that would lead Russian soldiers to the gates of Auschwitz on January 1945 and to the heart of Berlin on April 24, 1945.[44] The new owners of world exceptionalism were henceforth the United States of America and the Soviet Union, two allies whose junction on River Elbe, on April 27, 1945, officially sealed the Allied forces' victory on all fronts.[45]

Rewriting a Humiliating Victory

France was free but humiliated. Of France's participation in the second European war, history will mostly remember its cowardly surrender in six weeks, its occupation by Germany, and its deliverance by the Russian and Anglo-American forces. In the ensuing years, a French movie industry would make it one of its national objectives to mythologize the role of *La Résistance* in liberating France and to not only erase the image of cowardice associated with the French army during the second war but also attenuate the American and Russian ownership of the victory that has been lingering in the collective memory since 1945. If America's great influence on the second European war has been very difficult to expunge, the Cold War helped the Euro-American coalition cover the great sacrifices the Russians made in the second European war. While the war against Nazi Germany claimed roughly 300,000 soldiers and civilians in Great Britain against an astounding 27,000,000 people in Russia, still "95 percent of young people in the UK believe Germany was an ally of their country in that war, whereas the Soviet Union was the enemy."[46] Of the Red Army's contribution to the second European war, many have endeavored to emphasized tales of violence and rape. And when confronted with evidence of Russian triumphs and obliged to say a word on the Red Army's military might, some would choose to attribute Russia's victory to its felt boot, which, contrary to the German boots, were allegedly better suited for the harsh conditions of winter.[47] Other influential historical voices, as critics like Peter Cheremushkin deplore, have simply chosen, out of mere jingoism, to ignore Russia's contribution to the second European war.

> In Tom Brokaw's book *The Greatest Generation*, there is a brilliant collection of individual stories of individual men and women, American citizen heroes and heroines who came of age during the Great Depression and the Second World War. However, the role played by America's Soviet allies is largely ignored. Brokaw's book, which was recently translated into Russian, has only one mention of Russia—describing the greatest generation standing "fast against the totalitarianism of their former allies, the Russians," in their post-war lives. "I was much more concerned about the prospects of the Cold War than the lessons of the war of my early years," Tom Brokaw has said. It would be good if such a recognized celebrity could look a little deeper in his evaluation of the greatest generation.[48]

Looking deeper is the least of the worries of a Euro-American coalition seemingly anxious to maintain its exclusive standing on the pedestal of exceptionalism. Indeed, America's industrial power, though it entered late in the war, and Russia's extraordinary human resolve on the Eastern Front did put a decisive end to the second European war. However, like the first war, the second European war had demanded enormous human and material sacrifices from the French colonies. Be that as it may, in the post-second European war, America was the new "owner" of exceptionalism. The world's center had been displaced, and France's myth of grandeur was forever shattered.

For France, an event even worse than losing its exceptionalism had taken place in its colonies that would have grave consequences for its future: The second war had enfranchised the Africans from supposed childhood to adulthood and had restored the French from the myth of super-humanity to the reality of mere humanity.[49] At the end of the second European war, French authorities had suspected that new challenges would arise for them in the colonies. The fact that, as Ali Mazrui noted, "at the end of that war the World omnipotence was no longer in Western Europe, but was divided between Washington and Moscow," had also infused unforeseen boldness in Africans.[50]

> But what makes the French imperial enterprise unique over all others is that it is shrouded, from the Third Republic until its last day, with a major moral justification: that of the civilizing mission of France. Because the colonizing nation was not ordinary. It was one that intended to enlighten the world by exporting the Enlightenment. It was one of human rights. On behalf of the same principles of liberty it embodied, it appealed to the right of a people to be civilized and transform another people.[51]

That shroud of moral justification was shredded by 1945. The people of the colonies came to understand that what actually made the French imperial enterprise unique was its inherent duplicity, and that—as history had proven twice in less than 30 years—France was neither the quintessential nation nor a nation endowed with any divine mission as its social engineers had trumpeted. For the second time in less than 30 years, the peoples of the colonies had seen France's myth of exceptionalism crumble.

CHAPTER 3

The Euro-American War on Algeria: Could a Mother So Yearn for Freedom but Keep Her Children in Bondage?

On May 7, 1945, it was not an exceptional France but a less than ordinary France, a weak France, a cowardly France that was celebrating its liberation. It was not an exceptional nation but a crouched nation, with its hunkered people and its broken institutions infiltrated by dealers in abdication and corruption, that still was trying to hold on to some semblance of dignity. Nevertheless, on that day of France's liberation, would it not have been logical—if only for the sake of the principles of liberty, equality, and fraternity, to which France professedly held dear, or at least for the sake of the principle of the right to self-determination guaranteed to every people in the Atlantic Charter of April 14, 1941—that France's guns of repression be quieted for a moment to allow the peoples of the colonies some contemplation of their own independence? Was not May 8, 1945, to be a day of thanksgiving, a day of unpretentiousness and of the celebration of freedom?

So, in Sétif, the Algerians, too, were gearing up for their own independence. How could they have known that they would have to wait 17 more years to experience it, that their freedom would require more blood and sacrifices? How could they have known that this France, to which they had given 150,000 of their own children to fight German occupation, would not hesitate, on the very day of its liberation, to turn the guns of oppression against them, its liberators? Yet the spilled blood of the massacred Algerians that had paved the way to France's occupation of this North African country had not entirely dried. The ancients remembered it as if it had happened a few days before and still told it to their grandchildren so they would know how they went to bed with empty bellies while the French roamed insolently overfed in their country, how they were pushed to the rocky, sterile desert to make room for the newcomers on the arable coastal lands.

The Invasion of Algeria

The invasion of Algeria started in 1827, when Dey Kodja Hussein of Algeria, plagued by his own economic difficulties, summoned French Ambassador Pierre Deval and urged him to transmit to the French authorities his insistence that France repay a long-due loan that his country had made to France during the 1899 Napoleonic wars. The Dey's demands were greeted with the French Ambassador's insolence. During a heated argument, the exasperated Dey swatted Deval with his flywhisk, calling him a "wicked, faithless, idol-worshipping rascal."[1] The Marseille business community, which had been eying Algeria for years, used that as an excuse to beat the drum for the invasion of Algeria in the press. And King Charles X, who was willing to use an invasion in Algeria to divert attention from his unpopularity at home, borrowed invasion plans that were designed in 1808 by Napoleon (who also had thought of invading Algeria to supposedly protect French ships from Algerian pirates) to invade Algeria in order to wash away France's humiliation, end piracy, and save the Algerian people from evil by bringing them into the realm of Christianity.[2] On June 14, 1830, France landed 37,000 troops in Algeria. On July 5, the Dey was deposed. Heeding Charles X's promise to save the Algerians from the evil of Islam by converting them to Christianity, the French troops took over mosques and transformed them into cathedrals.

First projected by the French war engineers to be a quick and easy success, the Algerian invasion not only faced a fierce resistance but the invading army, confronted with a treacherous and unfamiliar terrain, dysentery, and malaria, also suffered many losses. Though in the 1830s the majority of the 3,000,000 Algerians were Sunni Muslims, the toughest resistance to the French invasion took place between 1830 and 1847 under the leadership of a 25-year-old charismatic Sufi Muslim, Sultan Abd el-Kader. The glue of the Algerian resistance was Islamic faith. As notes Evans, "[The Algerians] inhabited the 'world of Islam' and it was their sacred duty to defend where they lived from what, in popular Arabic, was known as al Roumi: the Christian invader."[3] Under the young Abd el-Kader, the French troops suffered enormous setbacks and in 1836 had to call in to the rescue a brutish veteran of the 1808–1814 Spanish war, Marshal Bugeaud. Using his legendary ruthless strategy of scorched earth and a combination of cold-blooded techniques, Bugeaud defeated Abd el-Kader on December 23, 1847, and the Sultan was deported to France to be imprisoned. As remarks Youssef Girard, in their conquest of Algeria, the French military did not go in for subtleties. The "pacification" of the country was achieved at the cost of the systematization of "raids" by General Lamoricière and the establishment of a policy of "scorched earth" by Marshal Bugeaud. From 1830 to 1871, France began a genocidal policy of war crimes and crimes against humanity. In 1880, the depopulation of Algeria was so alarming that in a study entitled *La démographie figurée de l'Algérie,* Dr. René Ricoux, head of the demographic and medical statistics of the General Government of Algeria, predicted the annihilation of the Algerians. According to him, the Berbers and Arabs, "inferior races" and especially "degenerate races" were bound to "disappear in a regular and timely manner."[4]

Nevertheless, the Sultan's arrest did not immediately end the war. Faced with a number of unfair practices perpetrated by the French occupiers, such as arbitrary land grabs and racial discrimination, the Algerian resistance carried on in sporadic pockets until the 1880s and beyond the Berlin Conference. The land grab that has been the consequence of the Algerian invasion had generously rewarded the newcomers while dispossessing the native Algerians. The biggest landowners in Algeria were nostalgic aristocrats who acquired substantially large acreages with dreams of reproducing a prerevolution regime in Algeria. Other landowners were soldier settlers the French authorities rewarded with land at the end of their military service and religious congregations, such as the Cistercian monks, who were offered more than 1,020 hectares of farmland. In fact, well over 450,000 hectares of tribal land were seized from their owners, who were summarily executed or deported, and these lands were redistributed to the newcomers.[5] When the French invaded Algeria, about 22,000 Algerian Jews were living in the mainly Muslim country as second-class citizens. They had to pay taxes to practice their faith. These Jewish populations saw the French invasion as a way to enfranchise themselves from Muslim hegemony. So, they supported the invasion and on October 24, 1870, asked for and were bestowed French citizenship, thanks to the Cremieux Decree, a ruling bearing the name of its Jewish-French initiator, Joseph Cremieux. As French citizens, these Jews were henceforth politically and socially above the Muslims, who not only could not vote when Algeria was declared a French territory by the French government in 1881 but were also governed under a different code, *le Code de l'Indigénat,* a very discriminatory and abusive "native code." In fact, the Algerians' position of subalterns on their native land was compounded when, in 1889, a French identity was sealed among all the settlers with the conferral of French citizenship to the other half of the settlers (430,000 people) who had immigrated to Algeria from countries such as Spain and Italy. Once and for all, the Algerians where on one side, facing the French along a dividing line of segregation.

In 1871, the French defeat by Germany in the Franco-Prussian War infused more energy in the Algerian resistance, which sought to capitalize on France's weakness. The Algerian rebellion, which in 1871 gained new impulsion and made successful gains by inflicting heavy casualties on the French and occupying key positions, fizzled quickly and occasioned more repressions by the French army and more abuses by the colonial authorities. This, however, did not stifle the Algerians' resolve to reclaim their country. The more repression the occupying army exerted over the people of Algeria, the more hatred was generated and the more resistance was engendered. A war is not won with brutish means only, but also with diplomacy and backroom subtleties. This was lacking in the French repressive campaign. In fact, in 1894 one of Bugeaud's successors as governor-general of Algeria, Jules Cambon, had warned French authorities that the inhuman techniques used in Algeria, especially during the Bugeaud era, could reduce the Algerian countryside to "a human dust" on which France would have "no influence" and in which "unknown movements" would be birthed.[6] Cambon's remark was insightful. The invasion of Algeria and the dispossession of the Algerian people became part of a collective oral memory that kept the ideal of independence alive for years to come:

> Muslims were told to remember the brutality of Bugeaud. They were told to remember the humiliation of Islam, such as the conversion of the Ketchawa mosque, one of the largest and most beautiful in Algiers, into a cathedral on 18 December 1832. They were told, too, to remember the dispossession of their land. The original sin of invasion could never be forgiven. All their subsequent ills—racism, religious humiliation, material dispossession—were seen to flow from this event and on this basis a large part of the population could never accept French rule under any circumstances.[7]

Despite recent revisionist efforts by French authorities, France's past genocidal campaigns in Algeria are well documented, not only in the collective memory of Algerians, but also in a trail of correspondence left by the official perpetrators of the gruesome policy at a time when their sense of impunity had reached an unimaginable degree of inhumanity. Thus wrote Lieutenant-Colonel Montagnac, "All the good soldiers that I have commanded know not to bring me an Arab alive.... [K]ill all the men fifteen and above, put all the women and children on boats, send them to the Marquesas Islands or elsewhere; In short, destroy everything that does not crawl at our feet like a dog. Here, my friend, is how you fight the Arabs."[8] This was a "pacification" method that Governor General of Algeria Bugeaud, in charge of the expeditionary mission, rationalized when he wrote that "there is no other way to succeed in submitting this extraordinary people."[9]

On V-Day, of All Days

On May 8, 1945, V-Day, on that day, of all days, could imperialist France not be wise enough to hold itself from relapsing into its barbaric proclivity? The Algerians, who had sacrificed their sons and daughters for the liberation of France, had certainly thought France's genocidal instincts were dead and buried, that France would remember their martyrs and honor them. So, on that day of the fall of Nazi Germany and of the liberation of France from German colonization, the people of Sétif, Guelma, Kherrata, Constantine, and other places in Algeria had gathered for a peaceful march to demand that they, too, be recognized as deserving the inalienable right of all men for self-determination. Brandishing American, British, Soviet, French, and, of course, Algerian flags, the Sétif crowd headed towards the monument of the unknown soldier to lay a wreath in memory of all the fallen soldiers of the second European war. There was a fervor for independence in the air at the end of the war, especially on that day, so the Algerian crowd were also carrying signs with slogans such as "Down with colonialism," or "Long live the Atlantic Charter," or "for the liberation of the people, long live free and independent Algeria," or "long live Messali."[10]

Messali Hadj, a Sufi Muslim, son of a shoemaker, was a conscript of the first European war. He was an unreserved anti-imperialist, anti-colonialist, strongly against assimilation, and a fervent nationalist. Messali's L'Etoile Nord-Africaine, founded in July 1926, was the first political party to unambiguously ask for Algerian independence.[11] The Algerian crowds on that day of celebration were escorted by members of the young Muslim Scouts, an organization that sprung from another nationalist Muslim leader, Sheikh Abd al-Hamid Ben Badis. Contrary to Messali, Ben Badis was of a noble beginning. His father was a tax collector for the French administration who backed France in Algeria and was even decorated by Napoleon III. Though French-educated, Ben Badis pretended not to speak French and would express himself only in Arabic. Committed to the revival of a language that the French administration had declared a foreign language, Ben Badis worked for the establishment of a Muslim press in the 1920s and 1930s, founded the Association of Algerian Ulema in May 1931, which around 1935 opened a number of Arabophone schools, cultural associations, sports clubs, and theaters, of which the young Muslim Scouts were part and whose principal goal was to counter the one-sided and discriminatory education offered by the French and to celebrate the pride of Algerian essentiality. The Association of Algerian Ulema's motto was "Islam is my religion, Arabic is my language, Algeria is my country ... and independence is a natural right for every people of the earth."[12] Such a program made no room for negotiation with the French settlers. It was a revolutionary program that was disseminated through radical songs. Considering that Ben Badis was—and still is—regarded as the most respected Algerian nationalist—because, as scholars agree, it was the religious doctrine of the Association of Algerian Ulema that had primarily kept the nationalist ideal alive and going—it would not be fanciful to assume that the songs of Ben Badis's Association of Algerian Ulema were part of the procession.[13] On May 8, 1945, the Muslim crowds must also have been chanting one of the freedom songs of the Association of Algerian Ulema: *From our mountains rise up the cries of free men. They demand independence, the independence of our country.*[14]

This time, the demands were no longer claims for assimilation. It was a nation, *their* nation, the Algerians were demanding. The wait for assimilation had lasted too long. At one time, liberal General Governor Maurice Violette had hoped that assimilation would come to be a reality in Algeria, that his European compatriots would understand that it was both in their interest and in the interest of the Algerian people that they all should merge into a common nation: "Muslim students," he dreamt, "while remaining Muslim, should become so French in their education that no Frenchman, however deeply racist and religiously prejudiced he might be … will any longer dare to deny them French fraternity."[15] And when, in an ultimate effort to push the passing of a law that would assimilate just 25,000 Algerians—exactly the number of Algerian soldiers who died for France during the first European war—out of the 6 million Algerian people, the Oran Senator retorted with words reminiscent of Mangin's and Séché's, that "the *indigènes* had fulfilled their duty *vis-à-vis* ourselves and deserve to be recompensed. But to do this, is it necessary to resort to imprudent measures?"[16] The heartbroken Governor had warned of a storm to come: "When the Muslims protest, you are indignant; when they approve, you are suspicious; when they keep quiet, you are fearful. *Messieurs*, these men have no political nation. They do not even demand their religious nation. All they ask is to be admitted into yours. If you refuse this, beware lest they do not soon create one for themselves."[17] Prophetic, indeed, were Violette's words.

The political mutation of Ferhat Abbas, one of the leading revolutionary figures in Algeria, is a prime illustration of how an exhausted call for assimilation could, in the end, be superseded by a radical demand for total independence. Abbas was a successful pharmacist in Sétif, and "everything about Abbas was orientated towards the West, specifically France, and a bourgeois France at that," notes Horne. More at ease in speaking French than in expressing himself in Arabic, married to a French woman after divorcing his Algerian wife, "a man of pacific temperament," straddling two cultures, French and Algerian, Abbas was a perfect example of the sort of assimilated Algerian that Violette had dreamt of, but one who, nevertheless, had by French racism and unyieldingness been entirely tipped over to his Muslim side. Abbas's move from being a champion of assimilation to a herald of Algerian autonomy would have been unthinkable given his declaration of a few months earlier, which had won him the sobriquet of instrument of the colonial establishment. In 1936, Abbas had this to say:

> Had I discovered the Algerian nation, I would be a nationalist and I would not blush as if I had committed a crime…. However, I will not die for an Algerian nation, because it does not exist. I have not found it. I have examined History, I questioned the living and the dead, visited cemeteries; nobody spoke to me about it. I turned to the Koran and I sought for one solitary verse forbidding a Muslim from integrating himself with a non–Muslim. I did not find that either. One cannot build on the wind.[18]

And so, the destructive storm so dreaded by Violette had come to the birthplace of Ferhat Abbas; and, with the converging winds of the end of the second European war and the demystification of France, the storm had come threatening to blow the Algerian pillars of inequalities. For the French authorities, the Sétif march was felt to be a provocation, a conscious effort by the colony to rub in the insult of having capitulated in 1940, to remind France of its recent past of subaltern under German occupation and of mere fixture in the 1945 signature of the Instrument of German Surrender; the apprehension was palpable.

> So in Sétif, birthplace of Ferhat Abbas, the Muslim rally began to form very early, around 7 or 8 a.m. on the side of the Algerian town…. Specifically, the Algerian event was to go from the Muslim quarter to the European quarter, at the War Memorial, where a wreath would be laid…. In any case, the head of Muslim Scouts was summoned by the sub-prefect Butterlin early in the rally. Is the event "patriotic" or "political"? That was Butterlin's question. And as the manager replied that he could not see the difference, the sub-prefect insisted that there should not be any banners with slogans—that would be "political"—and, of course, no Algerian flag. On this condition, they could march … [and] the procession moved on. Behind the scouts, there must have been between 7,000 and 8,000 demonstrators, including a large group of students. Along the way, banners appeared and, at some point, the Algerian flag—amidst the Allies' flags.[19]

The sight of the Algerian flag was more than the police chief could bear. He pulled his gun and shot the flag bearer point blank. Bouzid Saal, a twenty-two-year-old Algerian housepainter, was the first Algerian killed in Sétif on that day of France's liberation. He would be the first of a long list to come on that day and the following days when, fearful of possible retributions, the French authorities distributed weapons to French civilian militias to help the police patrol the French quarter. The next day, 35 Algerians were killed for violating a curfew. In Guelma, too, on May 8, at 5:00 p.m. it was the same scene. Guelma was already a violent place for the Muslim populations. There, a zealous subprefect, André Achiary, was ruling almost independently from the central administration. He had established an "emergency court" and a "committee of public safety" in the town, staffed with armed European militiamen. As early as April, Achiary had sensed the tension and distributed weapons to his militia.[20] Now he knew that the event was coming to his town, and he had his men positioned on each street corner with machine guns. So he was prepared when, during the Guelma march organized by Algerians to celebrate the end of the war and the fall of the Nazi regime, the Algerian flag was waved in the middle of the Allies' flags. At the sight of the white and green Algerian banner and of some signs calling for Algerian independence, Achiary went into a trance, pulled his gun and shot Bouzma, the young Algerian flag bearer. Four other Algerians were killed by the police on that day in Guelma.

The same day, V-Day, May 8, 1945, the town of Kherrata was packed with vendors, traders, and customers. It was market day, and the news of what happened in Sétif and Guelma had spread. Anger, disbelief and agitation were tangible in the crowd of Algerians. The colonial administration would not take any chance; the French officials distributed weapons to the Europeans in the city before declaring a curfew. The next day, 10,000 Muslims, convinced that they were being set up like their brothers and sisters of Sétif and Guelma, had converged on the town center to prepare for their defense with everything they could find. They would not be mere sitting ducks. The crowd broke into government offices and stole a few weapons. They set some houses on fire. They killed the colonial administrator and the judge. The Muslims fell in the trap of 500 heavily armed militiamen strategically posted with explicit orders to shoot to kill. As they were retreating to the mountains, the Algerians killed 10 soldiers and wounded 4 others. That day, all day and all night, from helicopters and the Duguay-Trouin cruiser, Kherrata and its neighboring villages were shelled by the French army. Thousands of Algerians were killed. The French rationale for these massacres? War on terrorism! And this "war on terrorism" would last the whole month of May with orders to shoot any gathering of native Algerians. As Algerian writer Kateb Yacine testified,

> It was in 1945 that my humanitarianism was confronted for the first time with the most atrocious realities. I was twenty. I've never forgotten the shock I felt before the ruthless slaughter of thousands of Muslims. It cemented my nationalism.... [T]he demonstration of May 8 was peaceful. We were taken by surprise. The leaders were not prepared for what happened. It ended with tens of thousands of victims. In Guelma, my mother lost her memory.... We saw bodies everywhere, in every street. The repression was senseless; it was a great slaughter ... [and] whole douars were decimated, villages were burned, dechras and families were burned alive.... The soldiers grabbed the infants by their feet, twirled them around and threw them against the stone walls where their flesh splattered on the rocks.... [T]he French army had planned the extermination of thousands of Algerians. For that, the French soldiers had gathered all the populations bordering the coast east of Bejaia in Bordj Mira to Darguina, Souk El-Tenine, and Aokas. All the people in these areas were forced to regroup on the beaches of Melbou. The occupier wanted the physical liquidation of all these people. Armed soldiers went door-to-door through the city of Sétif and some surrounding areas, and forced men, women and children out, onto trucks ... the truck of death. Thousands of Algerians were unloaded from the truck at the bottom of the gorge of Kherrata. The horror was not over for those poor "bougnouls" as the French colonists loved to call them. "Banana" Helicopters flew over the site of the massacre to finish the wounded. A real human butchery site that would later be invested by scavengers.[21]

The repression was not just French. It was Euro-American. The American and the British provided logistical support to France in the massacres of May

1945.[22] The cruelty of the May 1945 repression seemed to have reassured the French, seemed to have comforted them in their conviction that Algeria was once and for all pacified and that no major event could really upset their hegemonic power in the occupied country.[23] Algeria, they thought, was henceforth like a dead volcano that would now and then emit some impulsive fumaroles without ever relapsing into its old wild ways. And yet, if there was at least one lesson that the French should have drawn from their own recent history, it would have been that no violence however great, that no intimidation however powerful was enough to tamp down a trodden-on people's yearning for freedom. The French should have known that they could not maintain the Algerian populations in the slums of political, social and economic poverty forever. In fact, British Consul to Algeria John Cavell was more perceptive than the French authorities. On June 12, 1945, in a letter to the British Foreign Office, Cavell judiciously warned of the embers smoldering under the ashes:

> It is probably safe to assume that the Algerian nationalist movement has been checked but it would be unwise to assume that it has been killed. The ruthless destruction of villages and the indiscriminate slaughter of women and children will never be forgotten. The movement will of necessity go underground for the time being and will come to the surface in another form.[24]

And in another form, indeed, the Algerian nationalist movement emerged nine years later.

Nine years after the massacres of May 8, 1945, all the sociological ingredients—racism, the juxtaposition of two utterly different societies (one white and opulent, the other Muslim and deprived), general political discontent, rising unemployment of growing youth confronted with lack of prospects and other ills—were in place for an Algerian offensive against France's hegemonic grip on Algeria. The Algerian resistance, which was random and disorganized at first, had developed into what would be its most structured and formidable organization, the *Front de Libération Nationale* (FLN), which, between 1954 and 1962 would strain France in a war for independence that would have France send more than 2 million of its young men born between 1932 and 1943 across the Mediterranean Sea to fight in the hope of maintaining France's stranglehold on Algeria.[25] The FLN came into full view through deadly offensive actions under the young leadership of Karim Belkacem, Mohamed Boudiaf, Hocine Ahmed, Ahmed Ben Bella, a group of revolutionaries who were convinced that, given France's intransigence, given its continuous dismissal of the Algerians' demands for political and social changes, and given the French authorities' determination to respond to any dissent with repressive military methods, only an armed insurgency had a chance of bringing about an Algerian democratic state founded on the principles of Islam.

Of course, six years earlier, on October 18, 1948, the French authorities had initiated a program of social reforms supposedly meant to improve the conditions of all the Algerians (Muslim Algerians and Algerians of European ancestry) in the rural sector. However, that program contributed little, if anything, to changing the native Muslims' socioeconomic conditions. On the contrary, it drove an increasingly dissatisfied Muslim population into the embrace of an FLN that for the average Muslim could usher in liberation from French occupation and better social, economic and political prospects. Among the promises made by the French authorities in 1948 was the purchase of some lands from rich European landowners to be returned to native Algerians dispossessed during the French invasion of 1830, the outfitting of farmers without land of their own or of farmers striving on arid, unproductive lots with adequate cultivable land. Other assurances were to make farmers' credit union loans easily accessible to all farmers, to train all farmers to modern agricultural methods, or to give famers, collectively, access to tractors and other farming machines. A significant budget of over 1 billion francs was allotted to the program.[26] In 1954, the program of rural sector revitalization had not delivered its promoted results, at least as far as the Muslim farmers were concerned. The farmers who effectively benefited from the revitalization program were mostly the Europeans farmers or those of European descent. The conditions of the native Algerian farmers (the Muslims) had deteriorated.

In fact, in 1954, at the time of the FLN's first significant offensive, the Muslim community constituted 89 percent of the total population of Algeria and 98 percent of the farming population of the country. The country's citizens were significantly rural people, with a high percentage of youth, the highest in the world at the time (52 percent of the Muslim population were less than 20 years old). About 2,573,500 Muslims were farmers; but among them, only 488,948 owned their land. They held less than 10 percent of the cultivable land of Algeria, of which only 4 percent could be considered "productive land." Most of the Muslims worked on a single family lot or as paid workers on other people's lots. On the other hand, only 14 percent of the European population were in the farming business. Yet, 87 percent of the cultivable lands of the country were the properties of just 6,385 farmers of European descent. The lands owned by the European farmers or farmers of European descent were generally vast, rich, and homogenous, and in revenue, those vast European farms yielded 96.5 percent more than the Muslims' lands would generate.[27] Inequality in land distribution based on racial difference, whereby lands with soils likely to produce expensive crops were attributed to the Europeans and dry lands were left to the Muslims, increased the pauperization of the Muslim masses.

Most of the lands with rich soils suited to rich cultures (600,000 hectares) are in the hands of European operators. Three quarters of the irrigated lands belong to them; a hectare of irrigated land produces 10 times more than a hectare of dry land ... [and] the gross yield per hectare presents essential differences depending on the crop grown: it increases from 13,000 francs for cereals and dry vegetables (crops primarily grown by Muslims) to 77,000 francs for industrial crops, 95,000 francs for fruit, 140,000 francs for vines (more practiced by Europeans).[28]

These discrepancies were mainly attributable to an arsenal of opportunity distribution that paid lip service to equality but remained plagued by racial prejudice. For instance, in 1954, a total of 75 percent of the local credit unions' clients were native Algerians. European farmers received 80 percent of the loan distributions that the banks made, against only 4 percent for the Muslims. This was to be expected, as the October 1948 announcement of the rural development program cautioned that Muslim farmers should not expect the same treatment as their European counterparts.

> This is not to say though that we can consider integrating all Muslim agricultural activities in the building of the normal credit and cooperation at this time. For, let's face it: if the cells that make up the program (cooperatives and mutual agricultural credit banks) are accessible to all, and if one already has twice as many Fellahs as European farmers, the great mass of Muslim farmers cannot access it yet. They cannot present the personal or real guarantees usually needed.[29]

In other words, one only lends to the rich, and preferably to the Europeans. The land reform had benefited only the rich European landowners; and the credit reform was undertaken only to loan money primarily to the already very well-off European farmers. At its inception, and even before the 1948 rural development program, the Algerian banking system had the dice loaded against the Muslim populations. "The Algerian banking system handed an inbuilt head start to those settler speculators who understood the system of borrowing and credit, an advantage reinforced by the fact that usury was forbidden by Islamic law. This access to finance capital was the final pillar in a system that dispossessed Muslims on a grand scale."[30] This segregate development pattern was reflected in the makeup of the Algerian society.

Of the vast stretch of land that made up the country (2,205,000 square kilometers), only a minute portion (68,000 square kilometers) was made available to the Muslims for permanent agricultural exploitation. Thus, on average, 210 farmers were struggling to make a living on 1 square kilometer of generally arid land for which they had little if any subsidies in seeds, tools or fertilizers. The land reform failed the Muslims, and so, too, did the agricultural subsidies and loans that were promoted to supply them with seeds and fertilizers. In 1954, about 47 percent of the Muslims in the agricultural sector were unemployed or underemployed. No aspect of the lives of the Muslim populations was spared by the social inequality that the system of colonization instituted. In 1954 Algeria fit the typical picture of the colonial society. In the colony, whereas unemployment and poverty were the daily grinds of the native populations, these burdens were practically unknown to the nationals of the colonizing nation. Relatively speaking, in the colony there were no poor or unemployed whites. As Benot noted, the colonies have always ensured an outlet for many kinds of workers from the metropole—transit workers, railway workers, postal workers and teachers—who would be twiddling their thumbs in boredom in their own countries or would constitute potential pockets of demonstrations and of social antagonism. In the colonies, many of these *petits Blancs* could afford to have a home, which would be unthinkable for them in their countries. This is not to say, however, that the settler community was a homogenous one. Even within that community, distinctions existed among the "authentic French," who came originally from France, especially the territories of Alsace and Lorraine (the good patriots who were given vast stretches of land and who made up the bulk of the *"grands colons"* wielding economic and political influence), the French from the Midi, who, though French, came to Algeria to seek better conditions and ended up being the *"petits Blancs"* with the small jobs, and lastly the naturalized French from Southern Europe (Italians, Maltese, Spanish, etc.), who did not have the "right origin" or the "right language."[31] Nevertheless, in Algeria, as in most colonies, "the citizen of the colonizing nation, rich or poor, [was] always privileged, willing or unwilling."[32] At the bottom of the Algerian classification was the dispossessed Muslim. In Algeria the affluence of the urban centers that concentrated most of the white settlers gave the Muslim Algerian of the rural areas a false sense of possible opportunity outside of the beaten farms.

Hence, there began a massive rural exodus toward the Algerian urban centers, whose populations jumped 5.2 times between 1900 and 1954. Poverty was rampant in the rural areas. Still 81 percent of the Muslims resided in the rural zones, as the urban centers presented no better prospects either. If in the rural zone vast stretches of land made the differences between the Europeans' and the Muslims' standards of living slightly inconspicuous in the urban centers, Muslim poverty and European wealth were living in close proximity and were eye-catching. Fanon, in his *Wretched of the Earth,* gave vivid descriptions of these two spaces, which epitomize the exclusive reciprocity characterizing the colonial society.

> The settlers' town is a strongly built town, all made of stone and steel. It is a brightly lit town; the streets are covered with asphalt, and the garbage cans swallow all the leavings, unseen, and unknown and hardly thought about. The settler's feet are never visible, except perhaps in the sea; but there you're never close enough to see them. His feet are protected by strong shoes although the streets of his town are clean and even, with no holes or stones. The settler's town is a well-fed town, an easygoing town; its belly is always full of good things. The settlers' town is a town

of white people, of foreigners. The town belonging to the colonized people, or at least the native town, the Negro village, the medina, the reservation, is a place of ill fame, peopled by men of evil repute. They are born there, it matters little where or how; they die there, it matters not where, nor how. It is a world without spaciousness; men live there on top of each other, and their huts are built one on top of the other. The native town is a hungry town, starved of bread, of meat, of shoes, of coal, of light. The native town is a crouching village, a town on its knees, a town wallowing in the mire. It is a town of niggers and dirty Arabs.[33]

These were the contradictions that the Algerian urban centers presented on the eve of the Algerian offensive against the colonizers' interests. While only 6.3 percent of the European populations were illiterate, within the Muslim populations 94 percent of men and 98 percent of women could neither read nor write. The mortality rate within the Muslim populations was significantly higher (190 per 1000) than the rate in the European populations (9 per 1000). In fact, in the crowded urban centers, only one-seventh of Muslims had a job. The urban center accentuated the social divide between Europeans and Arabs. The urban centers as well as the rural areas of Algeria became resentment neighborhoods and fertile recruiting grounds for the Algerian revolutionaries opposed to French occupation. For how could the Algerians not be resentful, how could they not want to take the place of the occupier that made them toil in their own country for a life of misery? Was it not fair that "the look that the native [turned] on the settler's town [should be] a look of lust, a look of envy; [that expressed] his dreams of possession—all manner of possession[?]"[34]

In a shocking way the urban centers revealed to the Algerian the stark contradiction between his wretched life and the comfortable life of the French colonist. The urban center allegorized for the Algerians the injustice of their circumstances and the urgency to take action and to write an antithesis to a course of history that was in the process of making them the fall-guys. Yet it was from the rural zones particularly that the Algerian revolution would take off. As notes Lequy, "The war in Algeria took place mainly in the poorest rural areas, those where the colonization of the plains slowly repressed or simply contained the populations whose growth rate is among the highest." It was in the rural areas that the first subversive operations of the Armée de Libération Nationale (ALN), the armed branch of the FLN started. The FLN was able to easily recruit within the disaffected peasantry for its seditious operations against colonial installations. Given the blatant inequalities in the distribution of opportunities to which they were subjected, the recruits of FLN were not difficult to persuade in carrying out the destabilizing program of the organization.

During the night of October 31–November 1, 1954, the Front de Libération Nationale launched its first actions: 70 coordinated commando attacks on several colonial, military and police targets in various parts of the country (police stations, army barracks, a radio station, a gas station, several agricultural installations, and some industrial plants). The insurgents set fire to scores of houses, barns, crops and fields that belonged to Europeans settlers. They assassinated agents who were in the fields implementing the discriminate program of the Agriculture Ministry, and even Muslims that were suspected of collaborating with the European settlers were killed. The attacks claimed about nine lives. Pamphlets left on the scenes of the attacks indicated clearly who the perpetrators were and what motivated them:

> To the Algerian People
> To the Militants of the National Cause
>
> To those of you who are called upon to judge us ... we shall enlighten you on the underlying reasons that led us to act, by explaining our program, the meaning of our action, and the legitimacy of our views whose purpose remains NATIONAL INDEPENDENCE in the North African context. Our desire is also to avoid the confusion that imperialism and its crooked administrative and political agents may want to create in your minds.... The name of our reform movement is FRONT DE LIBERATION NATIONALE, thus refusing all possible compromises and offering the possibility to all Algerian patriots of all social strata, from all parties and movements purely Algerian to join in the liberation struggle without any other consideration.
>
> GOAL: NATIONAL INDEPENDENCE through:
> The restoration of the Algerian State, sovereign, democratic and social within the framework of the Islamic principles
> The respect of all fundamental liberties without distinction of race or religion
>
> INTERNAL OBJECTIVES: POLITICAL CLEANSING through:
> The recovery of the true path of the National Revolutionary Movement and the destruction of all vestiges of corruption and reformism, sources of our current regression
> The gathering and organization of all the healthy energies of the Algerian people for the elimination of the colonial system.
>
> EXTERNAL OBJECTIVES:
> The internationalization of the Algerian problem
> The actualization of the North African unity in its natural Arab-Islamic framework.
> Within the framework of the United Nations Charter, the affirmation our active sympathy towards all nations willing to support our liberating action
>
> MEANS OF STRUGGLE: In accordance with the revolutionary principles and taking into account internal and external situations, the continuation of the fight by all means in order to achieve our goal....[35]

In Algeria, past the first moments of shock, began the rounding up of any Muslim suspected of having once expressed some disagreement regarding French rule; and more strenuous measures were taken to inhibit insurgence, which implied that "the evil must be pursued where it is to be found and the ringleaders routed out where they are ... [and] no weakness [shall] be tolerated."[36] In France, though the general public and the media showed little interest in the event, for the government it was a big embarrassment and not reacting would constitute proof of weakness. For Paris, Algeria was France; it was out of the question to sever France from one of its integral parts. That was the general consensus in France—and insofar as France was the protector, that was the general consensus among the European settlers in Algeria. Bellowed Prime Minister Pierre Mendès-France at the Assemblée Nationale, on November 12: "One does not compromise when it comes to defending the internal peace of the nation, the unity and the integrity of the Republic. The Algerian departments are part of the French republic. They have been French for a long time, and they are irrevocably French.... Between them and Metropolitan France, there can be no conceivable secession.... *Ici, c'est la France.*"[37] French Socialist Interior Minister François Mitterrand would add to this political intransigence military inflexibility: "The only possible negotiation is war.... Algeria is France. And who, among you, *Mesdames* and *Messieurs*, would hesitate to employ all methods to preserve France?"[38] The wink of the eye was understood: *use all methods available to preserve France.* And all methods, indeed, legal as well as illegal, the French army did use in order to keep Algeria in the bosom of France. And the gorier the methods used by France, the more inflexible was the Algerian nationalists' determination to fight back and to fight on for their independence. The attacks carried out by the mujahidins of the Armée de Libération Nationale intensified over time rather than subsided. November 1954 witnessed 178 attacks; December saw 210 insurgencies. After a recess in March 1955, the attacks intensified up to 501 in June. In the villages, young men enlisted in the ALN; women supported the revolution by providing food, water, and clothing to the fighters.[39] In the urban centers, Algerian women even took part in combat operations, placing bombs and fighting on the side of the ALN.

Confronted with the growing guerrilla activities, the French authorities' solutions were usually improvised, reactive, and irrational. In 1954, between the FLN's insurgents' arsonist actions on the Algerian forests on the one hand, and on the other hand the French army's attempt to dislodge the revolutionaries by "smoking them out," about 75 percent of the Algerian forests were burned down.[40] In March and April 1956, a number of decrees taken by the French government increased military support and interventions to Algeria and divided Algeria into three manageable zones: operation ("to crush the rebels"), pacification (to protect the European and Muslim populations), and forbidden (interdicted to the Muslims, indiscriminately regarded as sympathetic to the FLN, the interdicted zones were to be evacuated and their populations gathered elsewhere in internment camps). By 1959, Algeria had 1,000 internment centers, each containing around 200 families.[41] The French authorities' strategy of land grab and cantonment of the Muslim populations exacerbated the poverty of the native Algerians. Entire fields were left uncultivated, the unattended cattle died, famine set in. In December 1959, a letter published in *La Revue de l'Action Populaire* told of the destructive effects of the internment strategy on the Muslim populations:

> Prior to November 1954, this tribe was stretched on the thousands of acres that belonged to it. It was the time of material property ownership: the herds were healthy and their sales guaranteed a comfortable life. The poorest had the freedom and security to gather alfalfa where it grew best. Summer 1958: internment and end of nomadism. Nothing for the animals, nothing for the people (3000 persons). No work, impossible to move around.[42]

The colonial administration was losing the native populations, even those among them that were reluctant to join in the insurgency of the FLN (at the beginning, not all the Algerian peasants were willing participants in the revolution, and many of them had to be aggressively converted by the FLN) were now willing to be part of the growing insurgency. Parked by the occupiers in the slums of poverty, where their only choices were to die passively of hunger or to fight with the hope of attaining freedom, dignity, and a decent life, the native populations of Algeria, in their great majority, chose to fight to rid their country of the invaders. In 1954, neither de Gaulle's 45,000 massacred Algerians of Sétif, Guelma, Kherrata, Darguina, and Aokas (this is the official Algerian number) nor the arbitrary massive incarcerations of Algerian political leaders or the daily harassments of the Algerian populations could stifle the Algerian people's determination for independence. From then onwards, a march for independence was underway, which, from sporadic acts of sabotage and harassment of the occupying forces, would develop into full-fledged confrontations between Algerian independentists and the French army. By 1954 the Algerian urban centers, where most of the European populations and vital economic interests were concentrated, were already infiltrated by FLN sympathizers and would constitute hotspots for the counterinsurgency brigade to worry about.

To counter the Algerian insurgency, the cruelest methods by the most ruthless of France's war engineers were put to work. French generals who had overseen the vicious counterinsurgency war in Indochina had become the authorities on war strategies at the French Ministry of Defense. Their courses were taught at war schools in France; their conferences were applauded at expert gatherings; their papers were published in major journals. And, above all, they were advising on how to conduct the Algerian counterinsurgency. In fact, Algeria became a laboratory where their theories were put into practice. Algeria became also the site of redemption where officers who had failed in Indochina would wash away the shame of defeat.[43] From that standpoint, it was out of the question that the *war* in Algeria be lost. A defeat in Algeria would signify the total loss of France's already bruised exceptionalism.

Though never officially admitted by the French authorities, by 1954 it was undeniable that France was fighting a full-grown war in Algeria. The French army was present in Algeria. It intervened in Algeria as a belligerent force at war in a context that was not officially designated as war context, while "the principle function of an army is to wage war." From the standpoint of the French officials, the military operations in Algeria were being undertaken in the strict context of the implementation of civil law and order; admitting it was war would mean on the one hand that France was at war with itself—a civil war, since Algeria was declared a French department since 1848—and on the other hand that the opposing faction had legitimate claims of independence.[44] The ambiguity was not just about the designation of the operation; it also applied to the vague rules of the ambiguous operation. In July 1, 1955, the French Ministry of National Defense and the Interior Ministry made official a set of instructions which emphasized that "every rebel carrying a weapon or believed to be carrying a weapon is ... to be shot immediately."[45]

It is easy to understand how such orders could leave ample room for abuses. Would a creative interpretation not make *any* Algerian a "rebel," as most Algerians were resentful of French rule and likely to rebel against some aspect of it? Also, in a social context where the police system was so repressive and the justice system so expeditionary that it was in the interest of any native Algerian to avoid both the police and the colonial justice system, would not any Algerian trying to run away from the police be regarded as a suspect and therefore a candidate for summary execution? Furthermore, the classification of France's war in Algeria under the rubric of "police operations" and outside the jurisdiction of formal war allowed for a number of cruel methods that would not officially violate any war laws because they remained unreported to the overseeing authorities of war crimes. And the war in Algeria was marked with a cocktail of violent acts of torture such as, beating, hanging upside-down, electrocuting, waterboarding, and raping. The technological advances had made it easy for the French army to take portable *gégènes* (slang for generators) on the field, along with guns, clubs, and masculine libidinal savagery, and thus make electrocution a mobile form of torture alongside beating and raping; the latter was a creative way to psychologically weaken an otherwise formidable Algerian enemy. As an Algerian recalled, "Once the soldiers have removed [the men] from their homes and have penned them up outside the village in order to ransack the houses, [the men] know that the sexual organs of their daughters and their wives will be ransacked as well."[46] The goal of raping, as Branche argued so discernibly, was to attack the foundational pillar of the Algerian society based on the virility of the man as the protector of the society, and the purity of the woman as the cultural pride.

Indeed, the much hierarchized traditional Algerian family, which was based on the principle of "*El Ayla*," or extended family, was headed by the family patriarch, or *Wali*, the supreme guardian. The authority of the Wali was absolute. He assigned family space, roles and responsibilities and regulated any conflict within the familial setting, and his decisions had the force of law. But more than anything else, it was in the Algerian woman's behavior in society, in her purity and in her exemplary reputation that the pride of the Algerian family resided, of which the father was the guarantor. It thus fell to the unmarried young woman and to the wife to remain chaste and faithful, respectively, so as not to sully the family honor. To ensure that the chastity of the women preserved the "*horma*" (or sense of honor and respectability), the Algerian tradition instituted a space delineation system, a separation of the familial life into two spaces: women's space and men's space. While men's space was generally the public arena, women's space was the space of interiority. The traditional Algerian woman was to remain theoretically invisible to the outside world. In public, she had to protect herself against the gazes of men, preferably by covering herself; at home, apart from her close relatives, who could be around her, she had to avoid men, too. Her spaces were generally the bedroom, the kitchen and the terrace. An Algerian word that characterizes this female interiority is "*Hajba*," a word that suggests confinement, cover, and veiling. Traditionally, Hajba was a month-long period of time during which the new Algerian fiancée was locked in a dark chamber where she would be abundantly fed and embellished for her wedding day. During that period, the bride would be instructed by her old aunts as to her future duties and responsibilities towards her husband and her in-laws. Thus, as some would say, in this traditional "patriarchal society based on male privilege, and where according to the cultural habitus the father [was] the worshipped foundational referent of the social norm, in this society where the woman [was] a capital, kept safe from suspicion and offense, so that her behavior [would] not affect the honor (the horma) of the family and the nation by extension," the rape of a woman was a dishonor to the community.[47]

The French war engineers knew that by allowing their soldiers to rape the Algerian women, they attacked the foundational pillar of the Algerian society and the most powerful arsenal of the Algerian revolutionaries: their cultural strength. So, as a form of torture that was recurrently used by the French army in its war against the Algerian freedom fighters, rape belonged to these unconventional weapons in the French arsenal that French authorities officially denied using while secretly allowing soldiers to carry on in order to, as Branche would put it, "advance state interests."[48] The war in Algeria was simply that: a colonial war, one that took military violence to a whole new level and with rules different from those applicable in wars against Europeans nations. The violence of that war was not directed just against an enemy force (the FLN), it was also directed against the civilian populations. It was "not justified by the law of the strongest, but by that of civilization"; it was the violence of civilization against primitivism.[49] The paradox of the French repression is that the ghastlier it was, the faster it made the FLN sympathetic to the Muslims in the countryside and the more it helped the ALN in recruiting. Even a great part of the elected Muslim leaders openly joined the nationalist cause. It was not just the Algerians that found the French war methods abhorrent. Within the French forces, too, disapproval of torture, especially of Massu's cruel techniques, was expressed at the highest echelons.

> On March 28, 1957, General Paris de la Bollardière asked to be relieved of his duties. He could not allow the use of torture, which he had experienced and fought against during the German Occupation. The Chaplain of the Fourth Paratroopers' Division responded declaring: "one cannot fight against revolutionary war except with methods of clandestine actions." General Paris de la Bollardière was sentenced to sixty days in prison on April 15, 1957.[50]

Another French officer, Secretary-General of the Algiers police, accused Massu of having disposed of 3,024 Muslims in unconventional ways. Massu submitted his resignation in 1957.[51] These dissensions within the French war apparatus, which came to public view just a few months after General Massu—appointed on January 7, 1957, to oversee the pacification of Algeria, having infiltrated the FLN and killed or arrested its local members—had declared the end of the dismantlement of the nationalist organization, signaled increasing uneasiness about the way France conducted itself in Algeria. The war in Algeria had drawn much unwanted international attention towards France. Internationally criticized, France was increasingly pressured by its allies and by the United Nations to seek a "democratic solution" to the Algerian question, a situation that had now become complicated with the bounty that lay underneath as well as on the surface and above the Algerian desert.

In fact, in 1956, French Régie Autonome des Pétroles (RAP) had discovered oil in the Algerian Sahara, and for the first time France would have control of oil resources that were "outside the Middle East and beyond the reach of ... the unreliable 'Anglo-Saxons.'"[52] If France knew that the independence of its African colonies was inevitable, Algeria, on the other hand, was never envisioned to be outside its sphere of influence, as it was part of France by all the French authorities' accounts. In fact, with Algeria as the anchor point, a plan to continue a parallel exploitation of French Africa beyond independence was drafted. France had hoped to strengthen its power in Africa from the country of Algeria. Besides its energy sources, the Sahara was also a prized testing ground for atomic experimentations. Algeria was too juicy a bite for France to just cough up.

It is thus understandable that France used all means at its disposal to maintain the status quo in Algeria until the very last moment. After a century of French domination, Algeria gave French Africa the measure of what it takes to be free. In 1962, Algeria snatched its independence from France at the cost of purgative violence and sent the occupiers scurrying for boats home. French history books refuse the proposition that France was defeated in Algeria. In Algeria, French schoolchildren are taught France "left" on its own volition. The falsification is grotesque. Be that as it may, Algeria was France's last significant defeat in a series of losses that had plagued the country since the Napoleonic wars. And since Algeria, the Hexagon seemed to have vowed to be on the "winning side" of history no matter what acrobatic prowess it would require. Sarkozy's changing positions in Tunisia was illustrative of this Hexagonal resolve.

CHAPTER 4

The Sarkozy-Obama
Epic African Adventure

Tunisia: A Prelude

Sarkozy and Obama had a rendezvous with history. They both needed to perform political acts of grandeur, the former to recapture a lost Napoleonic paradise and the latter to belong, to acquire approval of the American electors after years of marginalization as being seen as unfit for the American presidency characterized by hubris and jingoism. They both needed to perform acts of exceptionality. Tunisia was a warm-up session, a prelude to Sarkozy and Obama's epic African adventure. An event had started in Tunisia that was quickly termed the "Arab Spring," to which leaders of the so-called free world needed to quickly anchor themselves, an event that they even needed to achieve their aims. For, indeed, at the beginning, Sarkozy was not onboard with the so-called Arab Spring. Nevertheless, by some remarkable acrobatics, the French president succeeded in inaugurating himself as the champion of "democracy" in the Arab world, and, *dans la foulée*, dragged the exceptionalism-lacking-American-president-in-need-of-recognition into some of the world's biggest international frauds.

On December 17, 2010, after trying unsuccessfully to recover his confiscated fruit cart from the Tunisian police, Tarek Bouzizi, a young Tunisian fruits vendor, set himself on fire and died two weeks later. Tarek's hopelessness and anger, symptomatic of the condition of so many Tunisian youths living in poverty and under the repressive system of President Zine El Abidine Ben Ali, spontaneously ignited a protest that grew larger the more brutally the Tunisian authorities tried to quash it. Seeing his good friend Ben Ali in difficulty, Sarkozy offered to send him a force to crush the protest. The president of the "country of human rights" had found no other solution to the Tunisian crisis than to offer more repression to the Tunisian people. At the French Assemblée Nationale, the members of the French Socialist and Communist parties displayed feigned vexation at Sarkozy's "lack of good judgment." They knew, however, that it was the rule of the game to openly protest the policy of the opposing party, which in reality they would rehearse as soon as they would be in position to govern.

French politicians are groomed to wallow in war, violence and corruption. In recent memory, no French president has left office without some sort of international scandal. It is one measure of French exceptionalism. In 1979, President Giscard d'Estaing had gone to war against Central African Emperor Jean-Bedel Bokassa to hide a personal diamond deal gone public. François Mitterrand had his moment of affirmation of French exceptionalism in Rwanda. Mitterrand sent the Hutu army 500 French paratroopers and 150 military advisers. In 1992, Mitterrand directly helped the Hutus slaughter the Tutsis in Rwanda. And it was a French military authority that confessed it: "It is true that in February 1992 we were very hard. We used the occasion to test some experimental weapons, some light mountain tanks and some combat helicopters equipped with a dozen rockets on each side."[1] After Mitterrand, Jacques Chirac had two moments of exceptionalism; the first in 1997 when, in his effort to help oil giant Elf (now Total) recapture some lost dividends from the fiscally hostile Congolese government of Lissouba, he decided to return Dictator Sassou Nguesso to power, sending the latter scores of military advisers along with 25 tons of military materials to help him massacre Lissouba's supporters and finally take over power. Chirac's second moment of exceptionality came when in 2004 he ordered French soldiers in Abidjan, Côte d'Ivoire, to shoot and kill unarmed Ivorians protesting French political interference in their country.[2] Sarkozy had hardly started. He would be exceptional, too, like all his predecessors. He had been carrying on Chirac's war in Côte d'Ivoire, but thus far Chirac's Ivorian heritage had not brought him moments of grandeur. Sarkozy needed to diversify; he needed to distribute his eggs into several baskets.

For the time being, Sarkozy's open support to Ben Ali looked a lot like a big gaffe. By all indications, Ben Ali was about to fall, and Sarkozy needed to perform some winning acrobatics to save face and reposition the "country of human rights" on the right side of history. So, when on January 14, 2011, Ben Ali finally fled Tunisia, Sarkozy, who three weeks earlier had offered to help him repress the Tunisian revolution, had this to say: "France's policy is based on two unbroken principles: Non-interference in the internal affairs of a sovereign state and the support of democracy and freedom…. For several weeks now the Tunisian people have been expressing their aspiration for democracy. France, which has enduring ties of friendship with Tunisia, is determined to be by its side." Sarkozy's Tunisia policy was a failure. But if it was carried on, the "Arab Spring" could still help restore France's exceptionalism. The most important thing was to learn one's lesson and to be henceforth positioned on "the right side"—to know when to drop one's friends and make new ones.

In France, the center-right government of Sarkozy, aided by a "philosopher of war," Bernard Henry Levy, was fanning the flames of confrontation in the Arab world. Sarkozy had philosophical support to go to war, even against a president that months earlier he had called his "brother."[3] Duplicity, which is one of the organizing principles of French exceptionalism, was actuated by Sarkozy when, in order to save himself from a brewing scandal, the French president launched into a war against Gaddafi, a war Obama, too eager to shed the label of "weak president," perhaps not-so-naively supported and heavily participated in.[4] After Tunisia, a rendezvous with the "Arab Spring" was in the making for all "democracy lovers" in the world, which Obama would rather not miss. Sarko, who was now an expert in detecting the direction of the wind, was going to help Obama perform acts of exceptionalism.

To Kill Gaddafi and with Him Africa's Elan Vital

On October 19, 2011, Gaddafi was captured alive by a frenzied Allah-shouting mob of Libyan "revolutionaries" a few minutes after NATO fighter jets had shelled his 50-car convoy and cut short his escape from his hometown of Sirte. Found hidden in a sewage culvert, Gaddafi was dragged out, then shot and killed execution-style by the throng. One of his executioners, a bearded man in full combat apparel, admitted that Gaddafi was captured alive and killed moments later. Right on the scene of the murder, he animatedly said to a TV reporter, "We caught him and we shot him…. [O]ne guy shot him." That mysterious "one guy" who shot Gaddafi, a report by French weekly Le Canard Enchaîné and several investigations would later reveal, was an infiltrating French secret service assassin who had taken advantage of the tumult created by Gaddafi's capture to approach the Libyan leader close enough to shoot him on orders of NATO, and Nicolas Sarkozy particularly. According to Le Canard Enchaîné, neither Obama nor Sarkozy wanted Gaddafi to emerge alive from the bombings of Libya. Gaddafi knew too much, and given a chance to speak he could reveal some very damaging facts about his relations with some Western leaders. The weekly's version refutes NATO's account that "Gaddafi was trying to escape Sirte in a convoy, when French and American drones fired on his convoy, leaving him wounded. NTC [Libyan National Transitional Council] forces later captured and killed Gaddafi." Le Canard Enchaîné reported, instead, that on October 19, 2011,

> a few hours before Gaddafi's convoy was shelled in Sirte, a colonel at the Pentagon had called a leader of the French Military Intelligence, which was tasked with chasing after the Libyan leader, and had told him that "Gaddafi has fallen into the trap, the U.S. drones have located him in a district of Sirte and it became impossible for him to escape the grip of his chasers." The U.S. chief told the French leader, "Leaving Gaddafi alive will turn him into a nuclear bomb."[5]

This story was substantiated in 2012 by Mahmoud Jibril, interim prime minister of Libya after the fall of Gaddafi. Jibril told Egyptian TV that "it was a foreign agent who mixed with the revolutionary brigades to kill Gaddafi." Rami El Obeidi, the former head of foreign relations for the Libyan transitional council, admitted that he was aware that Gaddafi was being stalked through his satellite communications system as he spoke with President Bashar Al-Assad of Syria. The NATO assassin knew where Gaddafi was at all times and chose the right moment to eliminate him.[6] The United Nations' call for an investigation to elucidate the circumstances of the Libyan leader's death was merely a melodramatic contortion, especially when it is demonstrated that the UN has never been able to lead any investigation to fair conclusion, especially when everything indicates that the UN, this outpost of the Euro-American imperial power, was in on the kill. Why was Gaddafi such a threat to the Euro-American imperial power, and what is the origin of Sarkozy's vendetta against Gaddafi?

In 1988, Gaddafi was accused of sponsoring the bombing of Pan Am Flight 103 over Lockerbie, Scotland, which caused the deaths of 270 passengers and crew members. As a punishment, the Libyan Guide was shunned by the Euro-American coalition. However, on May 15, 2007, U.S. Secretary of State Condoleezza Rice announced the removal of Colonel Gaddafi from the U.S. terror list and the resumption of regular diplomatic relations with Libya for, said she, "the excellent cooperation Libya has provided to the United States and other members of the international community in response to common global threats faced by the civilized world since September 11, 2001."[7] Even before the U.S.'s decision, European leaders were busy courting Gaddafi, who, according to a British diplomat in Libya, had "way more cash than he knew what to do with." On March 25, 2004, Tony Blair had tea under a tent in the Libyan Desert with Gaddafi. There, as he was negotiating a $1.2 billion gas exploitation contract for BP as well as important sales of British missiles and air defense systems, Blair expressed a deep-felt relief in the Euro-American leadership: "It's good to be here at last after so many months."[8] Soon after Rice's announcement, relieved Euro-American leaders were in Libya wooing Gaddafi. The Libyan Guide's huge cash reserve had no black powder scent on it, and Europe was in dire need of economic resurgence. Between 2008 and 2010, Tony Blair visited Libya four times, doing business with Gaddafi's son Saif el-Islam Gaddafi and with Mohammed Layas, head of the Libyan Investment Authority (LIA) on behalf of JP Morgan.[9] Gaddafi had supposedly made amends in the form of surrendering two suspected Libyans to be tried at The Hague for their role in the bombing of Pan Am 103, surrendering his Weapons of Mass Destruction Program, severing ties with terrorist organizations, accepting responsibility for the Pan Am 103 bombing, and paying $2.7 billion in compensation to the victims of the bombing. Having been welcomed back into the "Concert of Nations," Gaddafi undertook to tour world capitals.

In December 2007, Gaddafi was greeted in Paris by Sarkozy with the highest honors. Nothing was refused him. He was even allowed to set up tent at the Elysée. On that occasion, high-level exclusive discussions were had between France and Libya for a deal that would guarantee France the supply of military equipment to Libya. In July 2010 an important French delegation in Tripoli had been negotiating the signature of several lucrative military armament contracts with Libyan authorities for two weeks. Gaddafi was poised to purchase from Dassault Aviation, Thales, MBDA, and CMN 14 Rafale fighter jets, important communication materials, some radars, and a modern naval fleet. This was potentially a 4.5 billion-euro market, a huge oxygen tank for the struggling French economy hit by the global economic crisis.

Built in the mid–1980s, the French Rafale, a fighter jet with dubious performance, had never been sold outside of France before Gaddafi's prospective purchase. If Gaddafi's acquisitions materialized, it could be a confidence booster for the Rafale, and other markets could open up for France's military aviation industry, especially as Brazil and India were waiting to see how Libya would rate its new acquisitions. The deal with Gaddafi went bust and, in a domino effect, Brazil acquired Gripen jets from Swedish Saab instead, and India gave itself more time to shop around.[10] Sarkozy, who had hoped to be the French president who would finally sell a Rafale, was disheartened and humiliated, especially after so much drumbeat around a possible first sale of the Rafale in more than 23 years and the ensuing scorn and ridicule he harvested at home. Gaddafi was going to pay for making a fool of Sarkozy's Napoleonic ego. In a twinkling of an eye, the good client of a few weeks earlier turned out to be a dictator. On March 13, 2011, at the Elysée, Sarkozy greeted the first Libyan opposition government in exile and pledged his country's support to Gaddafi's opposition.

A month earlier, social protests by Libyans demanding better living conditions and a more democratic system had put Colonel Gaddafi at odds with the opposition in Libya. The protesters had become armed militias attacking Libyan army outposts, and Gaddafi ordered his police to respond with disproportionate force. This was opportune: by violently cracking down on the protests, Gaddafi had handed the West a priceless occasion to rehash its worn-out phrase "killing his own people,"—as opposed to killing *other* peoples, as is customary for Western powers—an invaluable pretext to do away with him. On February 26, 2011, a French-sponsored resolution (Resolution 1970–2011) was voted by the United Nations Security Council to refer Gaddafi to the International Criminal Court, to impose an arms embargo on Libya, to inflict a travel ban on Gaddafi, his relatives and his associates, and to freeze Libya's economic assets on member states' territories, purportedly to be used at a later time for the Libyan people or to be used by member states for "justified extraordinary expenses." Resolution 1970–2011 also set up a committee to monitor the sanctions imposed on the Libyan government. The sanctions did little to inhibit Gaddafi's crackdown on the protests, and France, through its Foreign Minister Alain Juppé, introduced another resolution (Resolution 1973–2011) on March 17, 2011, which was successfully voted on by the UN Security Council, to establish a no-fly-zone over Libyan territory. Following Sarkozy's previous call for Gaddafi to resign, with Resolution 1973–2011, the Security Council officially affirmed the illegitimacy of Gaddafi's government.[11]

Upon the adoption of Resolution 1973–2011, Juppé sententiously spoke of the right of the Libyan people to "breathe the fresh air of democracy" and of the international community's responsibility to "help the people of [Libya] build a new future." Mark Lyall Grant, the United Kingdom's Permanent Representative to the United Nations, urged NATO and the Arab League on behalf of the United Kingdom to act fast in order to free the Libyan people from a government that has "lost legitimacy." For Peter Witting of Germany, it was important to send Gaddafi and his associates the message that "their time [was] over and that they must relinquish power immediately." For U.S Ambassador to the United Nations Susan Rice, the saintly Security Council had "responded to the Libyan people's cry for help."[12] On March 16, 2011, when *Euronews* asked Gaddafi's eldest son about his response to France's, and especially Sarkozy's, ardor to intervene in Libya, Saif-al-Islam Gaddafi accused Sarkozy of hypocrisy and asked that the French president return $50 million of Libyan money allegedly given him by his father to finance his 2007 presidential campaign. Saif threatened to publish proof of the not-so-legal transaction:

> First of all, Sarkozy must return the money he received from Libya to finance his electoral campaign. We did finance his campaign, and we do have proofs of that. We are ready to reveal everything. The first thing we want this clown to do is to return this money to the Libyan people. We gave him this money because we expected him to work in favor of the Libyan people, but he has deceived us. Return our money. We have all the details, the bank accounts, the documents, the transfer operations. We will reveal everything soon.[13]

First denied by Sarkozy and dismissed by the French as a desperate move by the son of a cornered dictator, Saif's allegations were confirmed on October 25, 2011, by former Libyan prime minister Baghdadi Ali al-Mamoudi in a Tunisian court. Subsequent investigations by French judges revealed a few disturbing elements but no smoking gun; and key Libyan witnesses who had much to lose by confirming Saif's story took the safe road and refuted it. The story of Gaddafi's money being poured into Sarkozy's campaign gained traction again when, in a documentary aired in 2013 and in 2014 by France Télévisions, Gaddafi's former interpreter, Moftah Missouri, confirmed that the Libyan leader told him personally that Sarkozy had received from him $20 million, a revelation that in April 2013 prompted a French judge to order that Sarkozy's personal phone, along with those of two of his former ministers, Brice Hortefeux and Claude Gueant, be tapped. The surveillance of Sarkozy's phone conversations did reveal at least that he was concerned enough to try to obstruct the investigations against him. On the very days of the two incriminating broadcasts, he phoned Patrick Calvar, the director of the Internal Intelligence Office, to inquire whether Calvar was still loyal to him and whether he intended to subpoena Gaddafi's interpreter. Gaddafi used to tape all his communications and archive them. Coincidentally, all records of Gaddafi's conversations have disappeared with the NATO bombing of Tripoli. A French investigation team still hopes to recover them as they seem to be at this point the only material evidence likely to explain the former French president's relations with the fallen Libyan Leader.[14]

In any case, after March 16, 2011, Sarkozy's enthusiasm to go to war against Gaddafi became obsessional. It all took on a personal coloration. It was no longer "for humanitarian purpose" that Sarkozy was going to war; it was more for the purpose of saving his political career. If proven—and Sarkozy's attempts at obstructing justice indicated that he was not as clean as he had claimed to be— Saif's allegations could sink his public and personal lives. A French president before him had fallen upon evidence of corruption, and Sarkozy would not be another disgraced French president. Upon Saif's threat to release the evidence that his father had financed Sarkozy's political campaign in a quid pro quo arrangement, Sarkozy's agitations turned epileptic. The French president wasted no time lobbying for his peers' support at the UN in favor of an airstrike against Gaddafi. So hardly had UN Resolution 1973–2011 been voted on than the French air force was out pounding Gaddafi's positions, apparently to prevent the Libyan leader from massacring his own people. Since we know that France has really never cared about African lives, since France has always abided by de Gaulle's dearest maxim that "France has no friends but only interests," Sarkozy's alacrity to "save African lives" by attacking Gaddafi, under whose feet just a few months ago he unfurled the red carpet, rang suspect.[15]

Could it be that through his precipitous airstrike, Sarkozy was, among other hidden motives, trying to cover up some embarrassing evidence, just like his predecessor, Valerie Giscard d'Estaing, in Central Africa? The Euro-American power's purported intention to save lives and insure the pursuit of democracy in Libya was a fallacy. The West's true impulses for wanting the Libyan leader out of the picture resided elsewhere. The motivations were personal, economic, and geopolitical. Gaddafi was working for the betterment of the African continent, and as such, against the continuation of the Euro-American dominance in Africa. As Russian Foreign Minister Sergei Lavrov noted, "At the center of the U.S. philosophy is only one thing: 'We are number one and everybody else has to respect that....' The United States wants all the same to dominate the world and cannot merely be a first among equals."[16] As we shall see, in Africa Gaddafi was the only head of state who not only could undermine this American hegemonic proclivity but also had the political will and the social and economic program as well as the financial means to shift the world center of influence from north to south.

Africa is one of the most resourceful continents in terms of geological and agricultural riches. However, the elites of Africa are also the most impressionable. Elsewhere, we have treated the African elites' seduction with an idea of globalization whose principal theorem is to make the black continent the perpetual camel of the world and the transporter—as opposed to transformer—of Africa's riches to the "First World."[17] Gaddafi had understood that in order to emerge as a political and economic power to be contended with, Africa would have to disalienate itself, mentally and materially. The elites of postcolonial Africa—most of whom are direct products or progeny of the yields of the colonial school and of the colonial church of mental estrangement that taught them to hate themselves and love everything Occidental—will need to come out of their stupor and break the spell of maintenance and perpetuation of the ideology of Western dominance. Gaddafi's proud posture, his proposed rearticulation of Africa's social lives around African values, was meant to outfit the African elites with a sense of worth and reverse their mental dependence on the West. Materially, Gaddafi was placing African nations in the necessary conditions for them to reject Western countries' poisoned gifts of aid and loans. Gaddafi's active Pan-Africanism was outfitting several sub–Saharan African countries with economic infrastructures that could free them from their abusive relationships with the West, especially France. Nearly all the sub–Saharan African countries benefited from Gaddafi's generous Community of Sahel-Saharan States Investment Bank lodged in Tripoli. In every African country, Gaddafi's financial footprints were noticeable at every level of development, from tourism to heavy industry.

Of course, while leading African nations to develop their own investment systems and emancipate themselves from their manipulative "friendship" with the Euro-American world, Gaddafi had his own dream of becoming the Fundamental Leader in Africa. On August 28, 2008, in Benghazi, Gaddafi was inaugurated "King of kings" at a ceremony that he orchestrated, and which gathered more than 200 African traditional kings and chiefs as well as some African mayors—another accolade for Gaddafi, who just a year earlier had been a pariah on the world stage! This was all it took for French newspapers to turn apoplectic and belittle all those who took part in the crowning ceremony. Gaddafi, *L'Express* wrote, "was accompanied by seven African 'kings' in traditional costume covered in shiny metal."[18] Notice the disdainful quotations around "kings." Notice the contemptible mention of not gold but "shining metal." In other words, These African kings were not kings in the real sense of the word. They were not kings like the king of Spain, the queen of Denmark, or the queen of England. And these pseudo-kings, who wanted to pass for "real" kings, were bedecked in "shining metal." In other words, Africa, the continent of gold and diamonds, a continent that for the last 600 years has been pillaged by the Euro-American swashbucklers, could afford only "shining metals" for its not-so-real kings. Perhaps *L'Express* is right, in that Africa's precious metals are to be found in the coffers of the Euro-American banks. Still, what baseness! What a discharge of uncontrolled abhorrence!

It was not just the Euro-American imperialist power that was afraid of Gaddafi's geopolitical positioning. In Africa, too, a certain African elite infected with the poison of self-hatred saw Gaddafi as a threat to its power, a power that it has held thanks to its allegiance to rapacious Occident's neocolonial program. Many of Gaddafi's African peers, though they did glean from his bountiful reserve of petro-dollars, secretly loathed him. It is even remarkable that it was the African heads of state whose countries benefited the most from Gaddafi's not-so-disinterested kindness—lets us admit it—that failed to come to his defense when he needed them most. It is remarkable that they even supported the West's assault on Libya. And yet, they had more to gain with Gaddafi's presence than with his absence. Gaddafi at least was investing in Africa, which could not be said of most of his African peers nor of the Euro-American powers that usually give with one hand and take back tenfold with the other. The African leaders who had benefited from Gaddafi's generous donations to later turn on him were simply still under the spell of the slave mentality that caused the house Negro to prefer the comfortable bondage in the master's house to the uncertain future in liberty. The mentally enslaved African leaders enjoyed little dictatorial powers the Euro-American coalition afforded them under bondage and secretly loathed Gaddafi, whom they perceived as a threat to their privileges. The West, in its assassination of Gaddafi, was going to make use of this brotherly suspicion.

The imperial powers of Europe and America cannot stomach the idea of a unified and competitive Africa. The Euro-American powers cannot envision with serenity an Africa that emerges to become a serious alternative to them on world stage. China had placed them on unstable grounds. India was threatening to shove them to the margin of indispensability. Should Africa rise undisturbed, they could become totally irrelevant. Of all the African leaders capable of putting Greedy West out of business in Africa, Gaddafi's was the most formidable. Gaddafi believed that African states should make it their mid-term objective to leave the Bretton Woods institutions, these insatiable organizations that have thriven by cultivating misery in Africa. Gaddafi was on his way to enfranchising Africa from the international usurers that the World Bank and the International Monetary Fund are in reality.

In *"Les vraies raisons de la guerre en Libye,"* Jean-Paul Pougala enumerates some of the grievances that the West had against Gaddafi, which are some of the real motives of the Euro-American war against the Libyan president. The West had never forgiven Gaddafi for freeing Africa from its stifling information tutelage by offering the continent its first Regional African Satellite Communication Organization (RASCOM) in 2006. Before RASCOM, as notes so perceptibly Pougala, calling from and to Africa was the costlier communication in the world. For this service, Europe would bill Africa $500 million per year. If Africa wanted its own satellite in order to circumvent this hefty annual tab from Europe, the continent would have to come up with $400 million. Gaddafi disbursed three-fourths of the money needed so that Africa would not have to borrow it from the gluttonous lenders of international finance, the rest coming from the African Development Bank and the West African Development Bank. Another one of Gaddafi's ventures was to contribute to the creation of three African banks— precisely, a $42 billion African Monetary Fund to correct the rapacious activities of the IMF in Africa—that would be headquartered in Yaoundé, Cameroon, an African Central Bank headquartered in Abuja, Nigeria, and an African Invest-ments Bank headquartered in Sirte, Libya.[19] These were Gaddafi's biggest projects for Africa. His militant economic Pan-Africanism was a threat to the West's hege-monic intentions in Africa. The development of these financial institutions, as Celestin Bedzigui pointed out, would have accelerated African countries' enfran-chisement from the World Bank and the International Monetary Fund, both instruments of the Euro-American maintenance of Africa in debt and in a per-petual state of backwardness, and would have brought the end of the CFA franc, the currency that 14 former French colonies are forced to use. Furthermore, Gaddafi's economic influence on the world stage was growing at a rate that could not be to the liking of the Euro-American imperial power: "The combination of water and oil has given Libya a sound economic platform. Ideally placed as the 'Gateway to Africa,' Libya [was] in good position to play an increasingly influ-ential role in the global economy."[20]

In fact, in the 1950s, oil exploration in the Libyan southern desert had unex-pectedly uncovered a huge basin of fresh water about 40,000 years old. If exploited, the aquifer could supply Libyans with fresh water for the next 200 years. Furthermore, its exploitation could be considerably less expensive than desalinating seawater or importing overpriced water from Europe as was then the case. With the technical know-how of South Korea, Turkey, Germany, Japan, the Philippines, and the United Kingdom, in 1984 Gaddafi injected $25 billion of Libyan oil money into what his fellow countrymen proudly coined "the eighth wonder of the world," a system of underground pipelines to bring much-needed fossil water from the desert to the Libyan people. Gaddafi's Pharaonic "Great Man-Made River Project, [GMMRP]" as Libyans noted, was a turning point: "The water changed lives. For the first time in our history there was water in the tap for washing, shaving, showering ... [and] the quality of life is better now, and it's impacting the whole country."[21] And indeed it was. Thanks to the GMMRP, 130,000 hectares of land were irrigated to make new farms; lands were distributed to small farmers to grow produce and supply the local markets, and large farms were established to produce export crops, such as wheat, oats, and barley. For Europe, the GMMRP not only meant that Libya would no longer rely on its costly water market, but it also meant that Libya was henceforth targeting the European markets and becoming a formidable economic force to reckon with. This was more than the Euro-American imperial power could stomach. Gaddafi, the arrogant leader from Africa who dared to dictate his economic rules to the Euro-American power, had to be stopped.

Besides killing any hope of Africa's economic independence by eliminating Gaddafi, the West, like a throng of predatory Vikings, had its eyes on the huge riches to loot in the ensuing chaos of a war against Gaddafi. Libya was a huge reservoir of oil and gas, for which Europe also has a voracious appetite. Furthermore, the estimated $150 billion Libyan foreign investment portfolio, which was managed by the Libyan Investment Authority (LIA), had the cash-stricken West green with envy:

> Just before the military raid on Libya, the Euro-American ruling circles looted these funds in the greatest act of piracy. They were helped by Mohamed Layas, the representative of the Libyan Investment Authority, who, in a January 20 diplomatic correspondence published by WikiLeaks, informed the U.S. Ambassador in Tripoli that LIA had deposited $32 billion in U.S. banks. Five weeks later, on 28 February, the U.S. Treasury reportedly "froze" these assets. This money—which, according to U.S. officials, constituted the "the largest sum of money ever blocked in the United States"— Washington declared, would be safeguarded "in trust for the future of Libya." In reality, the money was used to revitalize the debt-stricken sinking U.S. economy. A few days later, the European Union, too, "froze" 45 billion euros of Libyan funds, apparently for the same purpose.[22]

For Sarkozy, besides looting Gaddafi's country, would it not be even better to resuscitate France's economy by selling a few of the country's unwanted Rafale fighter jets? For, after all, one of the main reasons why the Rafale has remained unsold was that, contrary to the Mirages fighter jets that became popular after Israel tested them during the six-day war, the Rafale's trumpeted technological prowess had never been verified on the battlefield. So Libya was also to be the testing ground for the clientless French jets. Thoughtless French troops had spilled the beans about Sarkozy's macabre plans in Libya. Indeed, whoever had seen the news on French TF1 on March 25, 2011, and had decided to go back to the same site the following day to review the coverage of the war in Libya would notice one thing: The news video reportage on French airplane carrier *Charles de Gaulle* has been shortened. The embarrassing portion of the reporting, where a careless French soldier stated as a matter fact that the airstrike on Gaddafi's army offered great opportunities to test new military equipment and to train new pilots, was edited out of the tape. The order to amend the news footage came certainly from the Elysée, as it is a fact that the French media is one of the most policed media in the world despite statements to the contrary. It was hoped the French military sorties against Gaddafi would make France's target weapon buyers, India and Brazil, take notice of the Rafale's firing power. Testing new weapons in Africa in order to recruit new buyers has long been part of France's marketing campaign. Mitterrand had done it in Rwanda. Creating havoc in Africa as a means to augment the French economy is a fashionable strategy among France's social engineers.

In its exceptional barbarism, the Euro-American imperial power has in fact destroyed the countries it purportedly came to save. As James Petras and Robin Eastman-Abaya note, just as in Iraq where the West's intervention has resulted in "well over a million civilian deaths, four million refugees and the systematic destruction of a complex society and its infrastructure, including its water supplies and sewage treatment, irrigation, electricity grid, factories, not to mention research centers, schools, historical archives, museums and Iraq's extensive social welfare system," in Libya in the early days of the raid the bombing had caused the total destruction of civilian infrastructures, of airports and roads and seaports, of communication centers, and caused the flight of scores of multinational corporations and the mass migration of hundreds of thousands of people from Asia, the Middle East, and sub–Saharan Africa.[23] The most lasting damage done to Libya by the Euro-American power has been the foreclosure of the country's prospects for democracy and development. The Euro-American power has killed the future of Libya; the Euro-American power has ensured that Libya should never again be a threat to its own hegemony in Africa; the Euro-American power has made sure that Libya should never get back onto the rails of democracy, by transforming into a thousand tiny chaotic spaces, each controlled by a warlord and his army of thugs, a country that despite some political imperfections invested oil money into one of the largest civil engineering ventures in the world in order to bring to its people, from miles underneath the scorching desert sand and through a 4000-kilometer network of pipelines, *potable water, a most fundamental human right.*

> In July 2011, [the Euro-American power] not only bombed the Great Man-Made River water supply pipeline near Brega, but also destroyed the factory that produces the pipes to repair it, claiming in justification that it was used as "a military storage facility" and that "rockets were launched from there." Six of the facility's security guards were killed in the NATO attack, and the water supply for the 70 percent of the population who depend on the piped supply for personal use and for irrigation has been compromised with this damage to Libya's vital infrastructure.[24]

The Euro-American power's attack on Libya was a grave breach of the Libyans' human rights, if only for the destruction of Gaddafi's water project. But there was more than that. Schools, hospitals, personal properties acquired by thousands of Libyans over many years, jobs vital to families' subsistence, and the serenity of the Libyans were destroyed.

Gaddafi's execution after his capture and the fact that his body was put on display in a circus-like carnival in Misurata for old and very young to taunt were indications of the true genealogical spirit of the Libyan newfound "democracy" under the saintly aegis of Europe and America. The signatories of the Libyan "democracy" had just revealed the measure of their "independence." It was couched in human rights abuse and lawlessness. Intellectual honesty demands that we ask ourselves whether a democracy that has *lynching* at its very core is a sustainable democracy. Is it not rather the fact that the moral urgency of such a democracy is already thwarted by its very performativity? After wishing for and ordering the assassination of Gaddafi, the Euro-American operatives came out exhibiting their sense of exceptional ethics. Yes, they do kill. But theirs are clean killings, sanitized killings, and not the indecorous and undignified butchery offered the world by "these Arabs," one could read in their declarations of outrage. For Andrew Mitchell, the International Development Secretary, "[the circumstance of Gaddafi's murder] was clearly a very confusing moment and I would have preferred that he had faced justice either in a Libyan court or in the International Criminal Court in The Hague, but it is difficult for us in Britain to put ourselves into the position of the soldiers and those who were involved in the capture of Gaddafi and I think the best accounts were those that have come from the Libyans themselves."[25]

Phillip Hammond, the British Defense Secretary, said, "It's certainly not the way we [civilized people] do things, it's not the way we would have liked it to have happened…. The fledgling Libyan government will understand that its reputation in the international community is a little bit stained by what happened." In reply one is tempted to ask this question: What of the reputation of the Euro-American power that has commissioned the total destruction of Libya, the murdering of thousands of innocent Libyans, and the assassination of Gaddafi, all under the false pretense of saving Libyan lives and building a democratic society in Libya?

Today, Libya is burning; Iraq is burning; Egypt is burning; Syria is burning. The imperialist West is scurrying away from the crime scenes. The United States, Great Britain, and France have packed their belongings, closed their embassies, and fled from the furnace they have helped ignite. The Occidental proclivity to rush into a foreign country, take it to the brink of collapse and backwardness, and then, when things become unbearable, run away and blame the autochthonous populations for not being up to the principles of "democracy and civilization" will always amaze decency. All the social engineers in the West who had theorized the erection of superlative societies with the fall of Saddam, Gaddafi, Mubarak, and Bashar are spinning a new story, erasing and rewriting pages of the "History Book" they have become expert at falsifying. Will the imperialist West once, just once, concede that being endowed with a high degree of gluttony and destructive drive does not necessarily give one the primacy of human intelligence? Will the imperialist West admit its responsibility in this long, distressing Arab tragedy at play before our eyes, which in the West's precipitous self-congratulatory gesture it had baptized "the Arab Spring" and which has turned out to be a very long winter?

A Most Profitable Partnership

Obama was right to be elated and proud when he declared that "all of this was done without putting a single U.S. troop on the ground." Of course, the operation had cost America at least $2 billion according to Vice President Joe Biden; but this was small change compared to what was spent in other wars. Furthermore, America had gained at least $32 billion of Libyan money. This was a profitable war for the Euro-American coalition. Indeed, on this April 3, 2011, exactly seventeen days after France has battled at the United Nations to have UN Resolution 1973–2011 authorizing war on Gaddafi adopted, a letter signed by the Libyan National Transitional Council and intended for the Emir of Qatar, a copy of which was obtained by the French paper *Libération*, indicated that French oil exploration companies, of which Total is the leader, had played an important role in effecting the Euro-American war in Libya. The Libyan CNT had guaranteed France an additional 542,000 barrels of oil per day in Libya for its support in toppling Gaddafi, on top of the 1,550,000 barrels it was exploiting before the beginning of the West's offensive on the Libyan people. As the leadership of the CNT promised, "regarding the agreement on oil signed with France in exchange for recognition of our Council," the letter stated, "as the legitimate representative of Libya, we have delegated the brother Mahmoud [Shammam, Minister in charge of media at the CNT] to sign this agreement assigning 35 percent of total crude oil to the French in exchange for full and ongoing support to our Council."[26] The chaos that ensued after the Euro-American shelling of Libya and the assassination of Gaddafi, the fact that Libya is now a lawless state divided into four unruly zones (Benghazi, Sirte, Tripoli, and Pheasant) does not inconvenience Total the least. Despite the chaos—and some critics would suggest that it is precisely thanks to the chaos—Total continues to thrive in Libya undisturbed.[27] In fact, Ivorian economist Tiémélé noted,

In spite of the official clamors and agitations cynically advocating defense of democratic values and respect for human rights worldwide, the presence and activities of TOTAL and other major Western oil companies in Libya eventually convince us of the hypocrisy of the Western leaders, for whom, in fact, only their petty interests matter.... Here lies the answer to all these wars conveniently promoted over the recent decade in countries with the largest oil reserves (Iraq, Libya, Syria, threats against Iran, and Sudan then South Sudan, Ivory Coast, Mali, Central African Republic, Chechnya and Asian countries of the former USSR, the threat of war against Russia itself, instability in Nigeria with the sect Boko Haram, etc.).[28]

If Total's unorthodox commercial methods in Libya look so familiar to those who have been following the history of France's presence in Africa, it is only because Total's former name was Elf-Aquitaine, a company that General de Gaulle had established in the late 1950s, along with the CFA franc (created in 1945), for the sole purpose of pillaging the African continent. In imagining the future Franco-African relation in 1958, General de Gaulle had an apprehensive eye towards the deleterious effects of France's looming defeats in Indochina and Algeria, such as the imminence of Sub-Saharan Africa's independences and France's consequent loss of influence on the continent. So de Gaulle resigned himself to independence for France's African colonies only in theory, while keeping them reliant on France in practice. If, as de Gaulle was convinced would be the case, France was to grow the way it had always grown, that is, by attaching itself to Africa in the same manner a parasite attaches itself to a host body, then a system was to be put in place that would find a few corrupt African elites who would participate in the feast at the detriment of the great majority of Africans. So de Gaulle instructed Jacques Foccart, his chief adviser for African affairs, his "man in the shadow," to build the system that would fulfill this objective. Thus Foccart proposed the creation of Elf-Aquitaine.

Scandal-ridden oil exploration company Elf-Aquitaine was the multinational that would be the financial force behind France's neocolonial ambition in Africa. Led by a ruthless manager, French secret services director in London during World War II, former Defense Minister, and ex-director of French atomic program, Pierre Guillaumat, Elf-Aquitaine was a take-no-prisoners-minded offshore company that skillfully mixed business operations with military and intelligence tactics. Guillaumat was the Head Chaperone of the corrupt African leaders that Foccart picked to secure France's parasitic existence by siphoning Africa's resources into France's economy. The goal of this criminal organization was dual. First, it was to reward compliant African elites with financial and military assistance as well as freedom to loot their countries and silence dissent with impunity. Second, defiant nationalists and their most loyal supporters were to be simply eliminated.[29] African dictators propped up by Elf were, among others, Mobutu of Zaire, Bongo of Gabon, Bokassa of the Central African Republic,

Gnassingbé of Togo, Nguesso of Congo-Brazza and so on, the kinds of dictators who were considered "good nationalists" in the West, precisely for displaying an utter lack of nationalist fiber and for their collusion with the predatory Western states. Political assassination and massacres directly committed or ordered by Elf were, among others, the massacres of the Bamiléké people of Cameroon between 1958 and 1964, the assassination of Togolese pro-independence president Sylvanus Olympio in 1963, the contracting of mercenary Bob Denard for the assassinations of two Comorian presidents (Ali Soilih in May 1978 and Ahmed Abdallah in November 1989, not to mention the toppling of a number of others), and the execution of nationalist president Thomas Sankara of Burkina Faso in 1987.

An investigation undertaken by Judge Eva Joly on a matter that was not directly related to Elf led her to stumble upon the elaborate criminal network woven around the oil exploration giant. When Judge Joly completed the report of her investigation, it was a 100,000-page summary of evidence that uncovered several billion French francs of misappropriation and which led to the indictment of about 37 people.[30] The international disgrace of Elf and its subsequent stock market backlash led the multinational's executives to seek a salvaging solution through integration and name change. In 1999, French oil company Total-Fina acquired Elf for 46 billion euros. In 2003, Elf changed its name to Total. Elf's newfound name did not, however, put an end to the multinational's bullying methods and criminal activities. On the contrary, evidence shows that Total has been on all fronts of the buccaneer-inspired wars that France has been waging on Africa. Rather than causing France to reduce its brutish, predatory campaign on the African continent, the criticisms leveled against Elf/Total's criminal activities have, on the contrary, inspired France to adopt a policy of concealment by diversification, whereby a plethora of other French conglomerates now supplement Total in raping Africa for the economic furtherance of France.

Besides Total, the first French investor in Africa, which draws about 31 percent of its production from the continent, accounting for a profit of 8 billion euros in 2011, for instance, other major French multinationals operating in Africa are Areva, Bouygues, and Bolloré. In Niger, where the bulk of Areva's uranium extraction venture is concentrated, the French multinational insists that it should be held to its 1968 contract with Niger, by which it has paid a mere 5.5 percent royalty rate to Niger over the last 50 years. In the Canadian province of Saskatchewan and in the country of Kazakhstan, where Areva also operates, the French multinational pays, respectively, royalty rates ranging between 15 percent to 20 percent and 13 percent to 18 percent. In Niger, Africa, Areva insists that the rate of 12 percent Niger demands is excessive. The explanation given by Areva is that it has been losing money on its investment in Niger. Consequently, Areva would not comply with Niger's new fiscal obligation instituted in 2006.[31]

However, whoever is familiar with Areva's propensity for "cooking the books" will understand that this is another case of insincerity by the French multinational. Indeed, on June 3, 2014, the French financial brigade searched the home of former Areva CEO Anne Lauvergeon, suspected of "presenting or publishing inaccurate or false accounts, disseminating false or misleading information and engaging in forgery." In this case, it was France itself, the main stakeholder, which was complaining of having been deceived by Areva executives, and which therefore had lodged a complaint against one of its proudest multinationals.[32] If Areva could be deceitful to France itself, one can only imagine what the company has in store for the defenseless country of Niger. Indeed, in Niger, too, as elsewhere, Areva's executives were lying: Areva was not losing money in Niger. It was making a lot of it. In 2013, Areva made a 9-billion-euro profit on its Niger operations. Niger's whole budget in 2013 was only one-fifth of Areva's profit that same year.[33]

Though French oil exploration and mineral extraction companies in Africa are by far the most devious of the French multinationals operating on the continent, they are, nevertheless, not the only dishonest ones. In their vast expansion of sugarcane and palm tree plantations, French agricultural multinationals have distinguished themselves for their arbitrary land grab without local population consents. All these multinationals have more or less made themselves guilty of worker abuse, local populations' health endangerment, and in some cases civil war funding. According to the *Conseil français des investisseurs en Afrique* (CIAN), which includes the French companies on the African continent, about 1,000 companies operate in Africa, with 80,000 employees and a turnover of 40 billion euros, that is, 75 percent of the French activity in Africa.[34]

As for this other machine of subjugation, the CFA franc currency—created on December 26, 1945, as a currency to be used within the French African countries—has been the most powerful instrument of France's financial hegemony in Africa. In explaining the logic for the creation of this currency linked to the French franc and guaranteed by the French treasury, French Finance Minister René Pleven justified it as an altruistic decision by Mother France to protect France's colonies from the devaluation of the French franc that resulted from France's ratification of the Bretton Woods consensus. As Gary K. Busch showed well, only the contrary is true. The CFA franc has allowed France to tighten its grip on Africa by making CFA member states as financially dependent on France as a minor child would be on its parents.[35]

Today two different CFA francs in two monetary zones are used by 14 African countries. One is in circulation in the West African Economic and Monetary Union (WAEMU) zone (Benin, Burkina Faso, Guinea-Bissau, Ivory Coast, Mali, Niger, Senegal and Togo), and another CFA is in circulation in the Central African Economic and Monetary Community (CEMAC) zone (Cameroon, Central African Republic, Chad, Republic of Congo, Equatorial Guinea, and Gabon).

The CFA franc is regulated by a monetary policy set by the French Treasury that makes it impossible for the member countries of the CFA zone to have control of their own finances. The French Treasury is not obliged to refer to the central authorities of the Central Bank of West African States (BCEAO) and the Bank of Central African States (BEAC) for its operation of the CFA. However, the Central Bank of each CFA member state must save at least 65 percent of its foreign exchange reserves in an "operations account," which is retained at the French treasury, and another 20 percent to cover its financial liabilities. In other words, at least 85 percent of the foreign reserves of the CFA member states are held in "operation accounts" at the French treasury. In addition, the CFA Central Bank sees that no country is extended a credit more than 20 percent of its public revenue of the previous year, and any overdraft operation by any member state must be first approved by the French treasury, "which has invested the foreign reserves of the African countries in its own name on the Paris Bourse" to generate interests for the French treasury rather than for the African countries that are the legitimate owners of these funds. As Busch notes, "The two CFA banks are African in name, but have no monetary policies of their own. The countries themselves do not know, nor are they told, how much of the pool of foreign reserves held by the French Treasury belongs to them as a group or individually." In fact, everything happens as if the member states of the CFA zones were immature children who need guidance from France as to how to manage their money. Even worse, in French Africa the French treasury and the French multinationals, supported by the French governmental institutions and the French army, have always functioned as a criminal organization on a conquered territory, racketeering and plundering with extraordinary good conscience. Wherever these French devices of exploitation are challenged, the French government comes to the rescue, with a sequence of aggressive punitive actions that can range from simple intimidation to full-blown wars. The very first day he took office, on October 26, 2000, former Ivorian president Laurent Gbagbo had committed the ultimate sin of threatening France's hegemony in Côte d'Ivoire. For that, he was hunted, captured, and has been sitting in a jail cell at The Hague since November 29, 2011, thanks to a cooperative endeavor by Sarkozy, Obama, and UN Secretary-General Ban Ki-Moon.

CHAPTER 5

Hunting Laurent Gbagbo

"He is a Socialist"

Gildas Le Lidec, who served in Côte d'Ivoire between 2002 and 2005 as French Ambassador, reported that French president Jacques Chirac once confided in him that the reason he resented President Laurent Gbagbo of Côte d'Ivoire was because Gbagbo was a Socialist. For Chirac, Gbagbo being a Socialist justified a plot for his removal. As a Socialist, Gbagbo was perceived to be a danger to French private ownership of strategic Ivorian companies, as he could be inclined to nationalize former state-owned enterprises that his predecessors had ceded to French multinationals.

In fact, when President Gbagbo was elected in 2000 a number of French multinationals had been awarded contracts by the previous governments of Côte d'Ivoire in conditions that were not necessarily transparent. Furthermore, those French multinationals had manifested little fervor in fulfilling some of their pledged obligations. For instance, the Abidjan-Niger railway system, which former prime minister Dramane Ouattara had conceded to his friend Bolloré in the early 1990s, was supposed to be renovated and its services improved by the new buyer. Instead, by 2000 Bolloré had not yet fulfilled his responsibilities. Likewise, Côte d'Ivoire's power company (EECI) and water company (SODECI), two very strategic sectors of the Ivorian economy granted to the Ouattaras' friends Bouygues at the price of one symbolic franc, had not been modernized as agreed upon. They were still in outdated conditions in 2000, and power and water interruptions were common occurrences in Abidjan and its suburbs as well as in the hinterland. Not only had the French companies breached the terms of their contracts with Côte d'Ivoire, but they were also fleecing the Ivorian economy by overcharging the government and the populations for their services. Thus, for instance, the contract of a third bridge to be built in Abidjan was ceded to the French concrete king Bouygues, although Chinese COVEC had expressed willingness to build it for one-third of what the French had asked for.

An anecdote that would take us ahead of the story of the dishonesty of the French multinationals operating in Côte d'Ivoire is that the construction of the

Third Bridge was delayed for several years, until the fall of President Gbagbo, the circumstances of which we shall discuss soon. After Ouattara was installed as president of Côte d'Ivoire in 2011, Bouygues was finally awarded the contract for the bridge and completed the edifice, initially planned to be a free bridge, as the first toll bridge in Côte d'Ivoire and just in time to be inaugurated on December 16, 2014, as a "Christmas present" to the Ivorian people. The inauguration of the Pont Henri Konan Bédié (HKB), thus named in honor of former Ivorian president who had rallied to Ouattara in 2010, was euphoric, carnivalesque and Ubuesque.

The bridge was described as "the symbol of the Ivorian Great Jump Forward." Sometimes it was applauded as an illustration of French superlative know-how, and at other times it was admired as the expression of Ouattara's futuristic vision for his country. The government freely bussed populations of the hinterland to Abidjan to come and admire the "Pharaonic edifice" that Ouattara has built for them. Government ministers and security forces leading the populations of Abidjan organized televised fitness sessions on the bridge in the days leading up to its inauguration. Religious leaders were transported to the bridge to bless it. The epic inauguration of the HKB Bridge occupied the news and was the topic of demagogic ramblings for days and weeks; that is, until the edifice was put to the test by the country's first rainy season. On February 10, 2015, less than two months after the government-led ecstasy, a 45-minute downpour rendered the bridge impassable. Two days later, a second rain completely drowned it. A week after that, as the rain finally receded, the bridge revealed several structural fractures and potholes. The bridge of pride became the bridge of shame. The Ivorians rechristened it "the Drunk Bridge," sometimes "N'Zuebeach." They found it better to laugh at the misfortune that dealt them such a bad hand than to cry. Once again, they had been swindled by a French multinational in collusion with their political leaders.

This is the kind of deceitful, one-sided cooperation that, as president, Gbagbo had set about to overhaul. Gbagbo's FPI prided itself in being a Pan-Africanist party committed to dignity, independence, and fair wealth distribution through social programs, organic development, decentralization of economic power, that is, against any kind of monopoly of state resources, especially by foreign conglomerates. In order to unshackle the Ivorian economy from French multinationals' monopoly, Gbagbo's social engineers had devised a program called Refondation (renewal or reconstruction). One of Refondation's pledge was to proceed by competitive bidding in awarding contracts, and to cooperate with any economic actor that was willing to be a partner in good faith rather than a cutthroat speculator inclined to breaking any sovereign law in order to make a profit, as has usually been the mode of operation of the French multinationals doing business in Côte d'Ivoire.

Refondation was a political, economic, and social rejuvenation project that was meant to identify and correct the structural flaws of the Ivorian society. Such a resolve implied that, thenceforth, some reassessing was going to take place; that the political pressure exerted by France on politicians in Côte d'Ivoire to cede all contracts to France by circumventing conventional procedures regulating commerce in democratic and law-abiding societies should be stopped; that from then on, in order to be awarded any deal in Côte d'Ivoire, French multinationals would have to openly compete against other multinationals (American, British, Canadian, Chinese, Japanese, South African, etc.). As soon as he was elected in 2000, President Gbagbo had naively trumpeted his determination to do away with the old, opaque ways of operating. He had publicly announced that in the new round of negotiations for contract renewal and attribution to take place in 2004, the rules of competitive bidding would apply. He had also announced that some companies of national strategic importance would be nationalized. These measures spelled economic disaster for France. In an open competition, not only would French multinationals have very little chance of maintaining the privileged position they had thus far enjoyed in Côte d'Ivoire, but also they would have much difficulty securing new contracts against other, more competitive, multi-nationals.

Given Côte d'Ivoire's economic situation at the time Gbagbo took office, it would appear that any aspiration for political and economic autonomy was excessively pretentious and that Refondation's socialist project was utterly unrealistic. A politics of waste and maladministration in the previous forty years had left the country heavily dependent on international aid and on loans from the World Bank and the IMF, of which France had strategically put itself in the position of underwriter. Furthermore, the previous praetorian government's bad relations with the Bretton Woods institutions had led the international financial establishments to sever ties with Côte d'Ivoire. To implement any program in Côte d'Ivoire without having France's support was thus deemed impossible, much less to develop any socioeconomic platform by jeopardizing the interests of France's multinational corporations. In 2001, in order to circumvent the obstacle of France's improbable blessing, Gbagbo's first Finance Minister, an indisputably expert economist by the name of Paul-Antoine Bohoun Bouabré, initiated what he coined *le budget sécurisé* (the secured budget), a budget that would not be dependent on external resources. Here is how Bouabré explained the secured budget of 2001: "This budget is 'secured,'" Bouabré explained, "in the sense that it only takes into account the country's own resources, thus excluding any external support. I want to clarify that for us, this concept reflects normal practice ... a budget that relied on the resources that we controlled and which were not subjected to the vagaries of external partnerships."[1]

Bouabré's secured budget was enhanced by a program of reduction of gov-

ernment expenditures and fight against corruption and tax evasion at the customs. The success of Bouabré's unconventional budgetary wisdom seduced the
international financial community. Faced with the irrefutability of such an efficacious administration, the World Bank, which had cut ties with Côte d'Ivoire
during the previous administration, returned to doing business with the country,
unconditionally. In 2002, the IMF, the European Union, and the African Development Bank followed suit. With the return of the international financial institutions, Bouabré introduced the *budget d'assainissement* (the clean-up budget),
meant to, on the one hand, clean up the state public finances, and, on the other
hand, restore clean, sincere relationships between the government of Côte
d'Ivoire and its economic partners. The clean-up budget, which cut down the
external debt to 4 trillion CFA francs from over 6 trillion CFA francs, was to be
followed by the *budget de relance* (the recovery budget) in 2003, and the *budget
de normalisation* in 2004. "It was an ambitious program carved to the dimension
of Côte d'Ivoire's economic potential," Bouabré proudly explained, one which
was to move the country from a 3 percent negative growth rate in 2000 to positive
rates of 3 percent in 2002, then 4.5 percent in 2003, and 5 percent beginning in
2004.[2]

Refondation was working to the chagrin of Paris and to the satisfaction of
the Ivorian masses. The republican institutions, such as the Economic and Social
Council and the National Assembly, which had collapsed after the 1999 military
coup d'état against the Bédié administration, were restored by Gbagbo. In July
2002, Gbagbo organized the first departmental elections in the country, which
led to the creation of 1,287 communes, 95 departments, and 496 sub-prefectures.
Each one of these new departments was outfitted with a substantial budget to
conduct the implementation of the vast program of guaranteed education until
age 16, empowerment of women, electrification of rural zones, and access to
potable water that Gbagbo had initiated in the framework of Refondation. In
December 2004, Gbagbo pushed for the passing of a law that guaranteed journalists free speech and shielded them from any prosecution in the exercise of
their profession. All these democratic measures did not shelter Gbagbo from a
coup, for the economic program of Refondation was not necessarily profitable
to France.

The Hexagon was losing both steam and esteem in Côte d'Ivoire. French
multinational companies could no longer be guaranteed privileged access to contracts in the country. In a competitive bid, a South African Company had
snatched the contract for the construction of a new airport in San Pédro, in south-
west Côte d'Ivoire, which French company Bolloré had hoped would go its way.
Refondation's anticorruption campaign was making it difficult for French companies to bribe state officials for lucrative contracts. Paris had no intention of
letting good governance prevail to the detriment of France's interests in the

wealthiest French-speaking nation in sub–Saharan Africa. Furthermore, if left unchallenged Côte d'Ivoire's audacity could become infectious, for there is no doubt that other African countries whose development was delayed by France's neocolonial interventions were observing to see how Paris would react. They, too, could, given a chance, reassess their unhealthy relationship with Paris. The future of Françafrique was being played in Côte d'Ivoire. And France, as is well known, was not going to allow it, as Senegalese lawyer Koureyssi Bâ remarked so perceptively: "[France] never compromises when its interests are at stake, and whatever party or group of parties are in power in Paris.... France's African policy remains unchanged. It is characterized by lawlessness, shrewdness, and violence, all served with unequaled cynical refinement."[3] Laurent Gbagbo, Paris's most annoying killjoy, had to be stopped. So, Gbagbo was never given a chance to fully implement his program of Refondation past 2002. Dramane Ouattara, who since 1999 had tried several coup attempts to be president, was waiting in the ante-chamber of political power. He was going to be the Trojan horse for France's imperialist design in Cote d'Ivoire, for as Koureyssi-Bâ remarked, "France can always rely on the servile devotion of its puppets and its good little service Negroes, who do not care about their legacies and who always respond present when they are needed to drive the dagger in the back of a rogue brother who dares say no to the master."[4]

Ouattara "must succeed. He has the blessings of the Fund"

Dramane Ouattara had an ax to grind with President Gbagbo. He had never accepted the way Gbagbo came to power. He felt robbed of the opportunity to realize his greatest dream, that of being president of Côte d'Ivoire, and he was determined to strike Gbagbo's government. This he unequivocally told the newly elected mayors of his party in December 2001, before a panel of journalists: "We will not wait 5 years to go to the elections. After all, in some countries, there are coups d'état, and people get used to the situation after a while. We have monarchies in the world, and people accept that a person who has not been elected represent the country in its totality."[5]

Indeed, by his own admission, Gbagbo came to power in "calamitous" conditions. His election to the presidency of the Republic of Côte d'Ivoire was precipitated by established resentment between the political actors of the country, which, in the end, disqualified two of the major contenders to the Ivorian presidency and left him to compete against the leader of a praetorian regime, whom the populations were eager to get rid of. On December 24, 1999, President Bédié had been deposed by the Ivorian military. The coup d'état, which was later claimed by General Robert Gueï, was by all indications carried out on behalf of Bédié's archrival Ouattara.

Ouattara Contra Bédié

Bédié and Ouattara had not been on good terms since the death on December 7, 1993, of the first president of Côte d'Ivoire, one called the father of Ivorian independence, Félix Houphouët Boigny. At the time of President Houphouët's passing, article 11 of the Ivorian constitution had set provisions to address the question of succession. The constitution stipulated that in the event of a power vacuum in the presidency of the republic by death, resignation or absolute impediment of the president, the functions of the president of the Republic would be temporarily exercised by a person chosen in the National Assembly by the president of that assembly. The interim president appointed by the president of the National Assembly would become ipso facto president of the Republic, with the rank, powers and privileges attached to the title. As the president of the National Assembly, Bédié had the legal prerogative of appointing somebody from within the institution that he presided over to fill the presidency vacuum. However, before Bédié had decided, Ouattara, who was Houphouët's prime minister at the time, made an appearance on national television to proclaim himself the rightful successor to the presidency. Determined to counter what he saw as a constitutional coup d'état in the making, Bédié, too, made an unscheduled appearance on national television to announce that as the constitutional heir he intended to fulfill his responsibility as successor to the president of the Republic. Dramane Ouattara would have carried on the power struggle with Bédié had he received the backing of the army chiefs, who, instead, advised him, in no mannerly terms, to conform to the country's constitution and step aside. So Ouattara withdrew to his former position at the International Monetary Fund as Deputy Director to IMF Director Michel Camdessus.

Nevertheless, for Paris, through the voice Ouattara's former boss Michel Camdessus, Ouattara had a messianic duty to fulfill in Côte d'Ivoire: "Ouattara is the last chance for Côte d'Ivoire.... He must succeed. He has the blessing of the Fund. All we hope is that there are no political problems just getting in the way of his efforts."[6] In fact, more than being the last chance for Côte d'Ivoire, Ouattara was believed to be the last prospect for the maintenance of Françafrique in Côte d'Ivoire. He was Houphouët's handpicked heir for the continuation of the Houphouëto-Foccartian order, to use this coinage by Marcel Amondji. And this is why, had no political problems gotten in the way of France on the day of Houphouët's death on December 7, 1993, France would have succeeded in imposing Ouattara on the Ivorian people.

It was not for lack of trying, nevertheless. Hours after Houphouët's announced death, the French media had anointed Ouattara his successor. French paper *France Soir*—which a fortnight earlier had caused a barrage of protests from Party Démocratique de Côte d'Ivoire (PDCI) members of parliament by suggesting that whatever happened to bedbound President Houphouët the country was safe in the hands of Ouattara—could now bask in its optimistic prediction. On December 8, 1993, one could read this headline in big letters on *France Soir*'s front page: "After the Death of Côte d'Ivoire President Houphouët Boigny Explosive Succession: The Prime Minister at the Helm." On December 9, Alain Frilet of *Libération* suggested that Bédié's filling the power vacuum was the result of an unconstitutional coup de force, a self-proclamation contrary to constitutional procedures: "Alassane Ouattara denies the legitimacy of Henry Konan Bédié, who proclaimed himself president on Tuesday."

Could the French media be blamed? Had not, as so discernibly noted Amondji, Houphouët himself prepositioned Ouattara to carry on the work he had started as the continuator of Françafrique in Côte d'Ivoire? Having placed Ouattara at the top of the ruling party (PDCI), ahead of such contenders as his longtime associate Philippe Grégoire Yacé, first president of the National Assembly, replaced in 1980 by Bédié, or president of the National Assembly Bédié, Houphouët had then disabled the supreme court by pushing its president, Lanzeni Coulibaly, to resign under never-investigated and never-proven allegations of misappropriation of public funds. Left without a president, the supreme court could not convene to constitutionally attest to the power vacuum and allow the president of the National Assembly to assume the presidency, thus leaving Prime Minister Ouattara to retain his powerful position long enough to create a constitutional crisis that would precipitate him to the palace.[7] So, determined to push Bédié over, Ouattara made a move that elsewhere would have been regarded as an act of high treason: he invited the French authorities to reinterpret the Ivorian constitution with an eye towards his usurpation of power.[8] This would not be the last time, as we shall see later. In fact, on December 7, 1993, France had even toyed with the idea of staging a coup d'état to make Ouattara Houphouët's successor.

Houphouët, who had been bedridden for months, first in France, then in Switzerland, was announced to have died in his bed in Yamoussoukro, on December 7, 1993. The date was significant. It was Independence Day in Côte d'Ivoire. So, December 7 naturally allowed for massive military parades, and, incidentally, for some military blunder by some hotheaded soldiers that could hijack the constitution, and—oh, supreme coincidence of all coincidences!—demand that in the "constitutional confusion" Dramane Ouattara be entrusted with the task of putting the house in order:

Officially, it is December 7, 1993, in his family home in Yamoussoukro that Houphouët died. But it is not impossible that he died actually in the Swiss clinic where he had been admitted from a hospital in Paris, or even in Paris, before being evacuated to Switzerland.... The choice of that date, a national holiday, a day of military parades in the compound of the Presidential Palace located in Plateau, was obviously not due to chance. There is at least some evidence that in Paris some people knew in advance that this would be the day that Houphouët died.... All prospective players have not yet accepted their role. This is particularly the case with Prime Minister Alassane Ouattara whom France would like to see remain in office at least for the transition.... The story does not say who had chosen December 7, or how it was chosen in preference to any other date. Why 7, and not 6 or 8 of December, for example? Why December and not November? Mystery! ... However it is not difficult to guess who would benefit the most that it be the day when Chief of Staff Robert Gueï, who was not hostile to Ouattara, would have inside and around the palace, legally, enough men and weapons to possibly take control in order to install his favorite.[9]

There was mistrust of, and hostility towards, Ouattara, even within his own first party, the PDCI. As prime minister, his disastrous austerity program had failed the masses. His unbridled economic liberalism, uncontrolled privatizations, and unethical, business-like management style, which sold off the country's economic assets to his wife's friends, had met with opposition both outside and inside his party. As the president of the National Assembly Bédié had led a group of PDCI members of Parliament in open protest against Ouattara's self-righteous economic liberalism that sold off state strategic companies to foreign entities with very little regard for the state's security. The distrust and utter hostility that most Ivorian politicians and the general populations of Côte d'Ivoire harbored against Ouattara constituted a steep hill for Paris to climb in instating him. The fact that he had very few allies even within his party undermined Paris's project to impose Ouattara on the Ivorian people. He had neither the support of the militaries nor that of the politicians, and even worse, he had turned the populations against him. So, in 1993, the constitution had to be respected willy-nilly. Bédié became the new president of Côte d'Ivoire, and Ouattara and Paris licked their wounds, resolute to come back and fight another day.

The Bédié-Ouattara conflict had weakened the Democratic Party of Côte d'Ivoire (PDCI), of which both men were influential members. The internal conflict had widened a schism present since the early 1990s, when a revolutionary bloc within the PDCI voiced the urgent need to instill in the party a more vivacious democratic spirit. Georges Kobena Djéni was the leader of that emerging trend. Soon after Bédié's inauguration, Djéni had demanded that an extraordinary congress be organized to elect the new leader of the PDCI. The PDCI Extraordinary Congress, which took place on December 27, 1994, was hijacked by Bédié, who admitted no other candidacy but his own and prevented some members, including Djéni, to take the floor in order to speak their minds. The masquerade that led to the election of Bédié as president of the PDCI split the party for good. On June 27, 1994, Djéni and some dissenting members of the PDCI officially filed for the creation of the Rassemblement des Républicains (RDR). On September 27, 1994, Djéni's Republican Party became legal. The new party drew many dissatisfied members from the PDCI, Ouattara among them. On September 15, 1995, when Bédié, who had been appointed to complete Houphouët's remaining two years, decided to organize a new presidential election, for which office he declared himself a candidate, Djéni asked Ouattara to be the candidate of his newly created RDR. Ouattara seized the occasion despite the fact that this time, again, his prospect of becoming the president of Côte d'Ivoire seemed unlikely. His candidacy could not fulfill the requirements set forth by the electoral commission.

Actually, on November 24, 1994, one year before the 1995 election, Bédié's PDCI, which held the majority vote at the National Assembly, had voted to modify the electoral code to prevent African residents of non–Ivorian origin from voting in the presidential election. For Ouattara, the devastating part of the new electoral code was that it also required all candidates to the presidential election to prove that they were Ivorian, born of two Ivorian parents. Bédié's decision to change the electoral code was prompted by his belief that France was strongly determined to intervene either softly or militarily in favor of Ouattara. Some land reforms he had undertaken had angered the rich French landowners in Côte d'Ivoire. The country was home to a large immigrant population from the neighboring countries of Mali and Burkina Faso, many of whom had come to Côte d'Ivoire attracted by the generously fertile lands of the country's rural zones. These immigrants—farmers and charcoal makers for the most part—had several violent encounters with the autochthonous populations, who accused them of illegally occupying their lands, setting fire to the forests, or deforesting the Ivorian classified forests and natural parks. To remedy the recurrent landownership conflicts, Bédié initiated a land reform that prevented the sale of land to foreigners. The Burkinabe and Malians—who saw in Bédié's reform a pretext to dispossess their compatriots of lands on which they had been working for many years— found support within the rich French landowner community, the members of which had acquired large portions of land in the southern part of the country, often in dubious conditions and with no legal contracts indicating the length of the leases of lands that they had nonetheless hoped to pass on to their children.[10] Ouattara had positioned himself as the avenger of the Malian and the Burkinabe communities and as the defender of French interests in Côte d'Ivoire. And Bédié understood that sooner or later the immigrant African and French communities would rally for Ouattara and against him.

Therefore, not only did Bédié, through an identification program he initiated, decide to limit voting rights in the presidential election to Ivorians only, but he also made entry into the presidential race possible only for candidates who could demonstrate that both of their parents were of Ivorian origin and who could prove that they had never renounced the Ivorian nationality and that they had continuously lived in the country for a minimum of five years. This officially eliminated Ouattara from contention: Ouattara's parents were from Burkina Faso (former Upper Volta). Ouattara admitted in a signed correspondence to the Supreme Court of Côte d'Ivoire that as a young man he was awarded a scholarship reserved for students of Upper Volta to study in the United States. Furthermore, in 1968, Ouattara was hired at the IMF under a quota reserved to Upper Volta, and he had worked in various African financial institution as a representative of Upper Volta citizens. On August 8, 1984, on page 21 of an article entitled "Monsieur FMI," Béchir Ben Yahmed, the editorial manager of *Jeune Afrique*, reported that, starting November 1, 1984, the Africa Department of the IMF would have a new director by the name of Dr. Ouattara, a man from Upper Volta, to replace Zambian Justin B. Zulu. The article emphasized that Ouattara was born in Côte d'Ivoire of immigrant parents from neighboring Upper Volta.[11] And the IMF's own internal memo noted Ouattara's Upper Volta nationality. So Bédié's electoral code revision excluded Ouattara from the presidential race. Ouattara's own demonstration of his eligibility was a confusing tale of nomadism that did little to clear all suspicions about his nationality. In fact, the more he explained, the more Ouattara confused the issue:

> I am an Ivorian and have been an Ivorian since I was born in Dimbokro in 1942. In addition, my father was born in Dimbokro around 1888 and my mother, a native of Gléléban (Odiénné), was born in Dabou, in 1920. They are Ivorian by birth.... For family reasons, I did part of my studies in Burkina Faso, at the time Upper Volta. After graduation, I got a U.S. scholarship under the aid to Upper Volta; so I went to the United States with a Voltaic passport. This does not call into question my rights and duties as an Ivorian.... I served as vice-governor of the BCEAO for Upper Volta for two years.... I did so as the result of an agreement between President Houphouët and the Voltaic authorities.[12]

A noteworthy fact was that, in his endeavor to reverse Bédié's electoral code, Dramane Ouattara had the support of Laurent Gbagbo, the leader of the Socialist Party (FPI), whom Ouattara, in his own suppression of democratic expression, had jailed in February 1992, just two years after Gbagbo's party was legitimized. In a September 1995 joint open letter, Ouattara's RDR and Gbagbo's FPI denounced the revised language of the electoral code, which they decried as "aimed at destroying the multi-ethnic social fabric of the Ivorian nation. If nothing is done immediately to minimize the impact of this devastating electoral code," the letter warned, "the foreseeable consequences will be extremely dangerous for the survival of this multi-ethnic West African nation of 14 million inhabitants with 4 million Africans of non–Ivorian origin."[13] Gbagbo went even further. In his strong support of Ouattara, whose candidacy was rejected by Bédié's electoral committee, Gbagbo's FPI joined the RDR in boycotting the 1995 presidential election. However, Ouattara performed a gesture that was blatantly contrary to Gbagbo's conception of sovereignty. In his desperate undertakings to have his candidacy retained, Ouattara invited France to meddle in the internal affairs of Côte d'Ivoire, a sovereign country. Once more, as he did in 1993, Ouattara called upon France to rewrite the Ivorian constitution in his favor:

> I appeal today to France, which has an important role in Côte d'Ivoire, because of a shared history, because of the defense agreements, which have to do with the security of Côte d'Ivoire, because of the currency, the CFA franc. France cannot remain indifferent to the situation in Côte d'Ivoire. France must do something…. I therefore appeal to President Chirac, to Prime Minister Lionel Jospin. These next few days, when I return to Paris—I am currently in Libreville—I will meet with the mediator, Bernard Stasi. I ask him to mediate in the matter with the Ivorian authorities.[14]

By so doing, Ouattara confirmed Bédié's suspicion that he was the plaything of France. Once more, as in 1993, Paris assessed the situation and determined that trying a coup de force on behalf of Dramane Ouattara would not be wise.

Ouattara's 1993 attempted constitutional coup was still fresh in the collective memory. Recollections of his catastrophic economic and social management had not yet faded; tales of his alleged illicit enrichment were still fresh; but above all, the brutality of his government during the time he was prime minister had left scars on the collective consciousness that had not completely healed. Ouattara's premiership was tyrannical. On June 17, 1991, as Houphouët's prime minister, Ouattara had ordered a violent punitive expedition against a student protest on the campus of Yopougon. Colonel Robert Gueï, his Army Chief of Staff, was the engineer of the Force d'Intervention Rapide des Para-Commandos (FIRPAC), the special, rapid commando force that led the bloody expedition that resulted in the arrest, torture, and rape of several students. Thumbing his nose at the investigative commission that had recommended Colonel Gueï be severely sanctioned, Ouattara promoted him instead to the rank of general. General Gueï, who would later pick up his party membership card at the headquarters of the RDR, would become instrumental in the Ivorian political scene, as we shall see later. In 1992, still under Ouattara's order, General Gueï arrested and incarcerated more than 200 political opponents, among whom were Laurent Gbagbo, his wife Simone and thirteen other major opposition leaders who were taking part in a protest march. Gbagbo and his wife were sentenced to a two-year jail term but ended up spending only six months in jail. Such a wide repressive net cast in the ranks of the opposition had never taken place before Ouattara's appearance on the Ivorian political scene. The people retained of Ouattara the image of a tyrant in the making. In order for France to make Dramane Ouattara an acceptable

president, his image needed time to be embroidered somehow, and Bédié's, perhaps, defaced. As Gbagbo and Ouattara were out of contention at the 1995 election, Bédié was elected with 96.44 percent of the votes against Francis Wodié of
the Parti Ivoirien des Travailleurs (PIT).

International critics, and French faultfinders particularly, made themselves
the mouthpieces of the opposition, especially of the RDR, suddenly describing
the Ivorian political and economic climate as disastrous, denouncing, in the foot-
steps of Amnesty International, daily repressions, predicting rampant poverty
and a looming famine, condemning the revision of the constitution and the identity politics of *Ivoirité*, recalling the street demonstrations, the untimely strikes
in the universities, and the misappropriation of a European Union's 18-billion
CFA francs donation. As noted Philippe David, Bédié was constantly cited in
the news as a villain: "'Radio-Sidewalk' has not hesitated to more directly accuse
[President Bédié] himself and his two sons of abusing their privileged position,
while in 1996, the president had launched a crusade for rigor, honesty, civility
and 'clean hands' in the public administration."[15]

The period between 1995 and 1999 was marked by frequent tensions
between pro–Bédié and pro–Ouattara factions. In October 1995, Bédié decided
to replace General Gueï, the Army Chief of Staff, whom he perceived as being
still too close to Ouattara. Bédié appointed him Minister of the newly created
Ministry of Civic Action and of the Reintegration of the Youths to the Rural Sector, then later Minister of Youth and Sports. Finally, in January 1997, Gueï was
dismissed and retired. Bédié was not comfortable with Gueï's loyalty to Ouattara.
He still remembered Gueï's insubordination when in 1993 the general refused
to repress a protest by Ouattara's RDR and Gbagbo's FPI. And as the 2000 presidential election was approaching, Bédié had deemed imperative that Gueï should
be cut from the Ivorian defense force, upon which he had too much influence.

In spite of the precautions Bédié took to ensure continuance of his political
power, he would not have a chance to vie for the 2000 presidential election. On
the night of December 22, 1999, he was deposed. A protest by a group of young
soldiers demanding unpaid bonuses turned into a successful coup d'état that had
Bédié fleeing the country. Yet, a few hours before, on December 22, 1999, an
unsuspicious and confident Bédié was deriding Dramane Ouattara, who had fled
to exile: "Who are these people," Bédié scoffed, "who call themselves Ivorian on
even days and on odd days say that they are not Ivorian? Are there not enough
Ivorian personalities in the political parties who have the requisite qualities to
be valid candidates to the presidential election?"[16] In 1999, the electoral code
that had barred Ouattara from the 1995 election was still in effect, and the
Supreme Court of Côte d'Ivoire had required of all candidates running for the
presidential election that they should include in their dossiers proofs of their
Ivorian nationality such as a national identification card and a certificate of

nationality. Ouattara filed his papers, then traveled to France. On September 8, 1999, in a communiqué read on national television the Justice Ministry expressed doubts on the authenticity of Ouattara's documentation of Ivorian nationality:

> The newspaper *Le Patriote* in its issue 24, dated Tuesday August 3, 1999, has published an identity card established in the 9th Precinct of Marcory Police, under the number 109/00868/82 of April 19, 1982, on behalf of Alassane Ouattara, making him a presumptive Ivorian citizen for at least since that date, while 8 months later the daily *Fraternité Matin* in its issue 5455, dated December 27, 1982, reported a ceremony held in Abidjan, on Wednesday December 22, 1982, at which Mr. Alassane Dramane Ouattara received from Mr. Abdoulaye Koné, Minister of Economy and Finance of Côte d'Ivoire, a decoration of the National Order of Côte d'Ivoire to the rank of Knight as a Voltaic executive working at the BCEAO, at the same time as Ivorian Patrice Kouamé. Moreover, it follows from the police archives of the 1st Precinct of Abidjan Plateau that on October 22, 1990, Mr. Alassane Ouattara, Chairman of the Interministerial Committee, was established an identity card number 101/00946/90, whereas, as indicated above, he was supposed to already own one. The brief review of the various documents above, and many others not mentioned here, uncovered several inconsistencies. So, the Office of the Prosecutor of Abidjan has instructed the Director of the Judicial Police to open an inquiry regarding the sincerity of the papers.[17]

Outfitted with his newly acquired papers, Ouattara was able to obtain a certificate of nationality signed for him by Epiphane Zoro-Bi, a judge in Dimbokro, a small town about 260 kilometers from Abidjan. On November 29, 1999, a judge in Abidjan invalidated Alassane Dramane Ouattara's identity card and certificate of nationality and launched an international arrest warrant against him for forgery. Judge Zoro-Bi was suspended and fled the country with his rumored 50-million francs payoff by Ouattara for the invalid certificate of nationality. Ouattara remained in Paris and called on his followers in Abidjan to take to the streets to demand that his candidacy be retained. In France, the media and government officials did not beat around the bush in their support for Ouattara. French Foreign Affairs Ministry Spokesperson Anne Gazeau-Secret said, "This decision, like others that already hit leaders of Ouattara's party, is not satisfactory from the point of view of democracy; neither does it promote a peaceful atmosphere for election preparations."[18] On December 24, 1999, Bédié was toppled.

Here Comes the Housecleaner!

The coup that toppled Bédié on the night of December 24, 1999, would later be claimed by Gueï, the Army Chief of Staff that Bédié had retired under suspicion of collusive association with Ouattara. He had come to "clean the house," he insisted. Power did not interest him, he claimed. He was called by the

higher imperative of rectifying the social injustices committed by Bédié and putting the country on the road to democracy. In fact, he had been forced by the
young soldiers who conducted the coup to lead the country lest his wife be killed
he claimed in defending himself. His job done, within the following six months
he would give back power to the civilians and return to his retirement, Gueï
promised. In fact, this was the scenario written by France: Gueï was expected to
later relinquish power to a civilian government, but a government headed by
Ouattara. Actually, the French authorities fell short of congratulating General
Robert Gueï for getting rid of Bédié, the tormenter of Ouattara. Four days after
the coup that toppled Bédié, French Minister for Cooperation and Francophonie
Charles Josselin all but justified the military coup as a logical outcome of Bédié's
exclusive politics, and especially as an expectable consequence of his harassment
of Ouattara and his followers:

> We had warned the government, the head of state and his government against what
> appeared to us like drifts, errors in stewardship ... particularly the debate on "ivoir-
> ité" and hardening the candidacy requirements ... appeared to be aimed at prevent-
> ing the candidacy of Mr. Ouattara. Add to this the recent events that have, again,
> further deteriorated the climate, such as the imprisonment of the leaders of Mr.
> Ouattara's party, the RDR. The arrest warrant issued against him, the speech last
> Wednesday in the National Assembly, which was proof that there was no change in
> the attitude of those in power. The situation was somehow blocked.[19]

In other words, the political and social situation in Côte d'Ivoire was
blocked because Ouattara's candidacy was blocked. The fate of the country was
summed up in the fate of Ouattara regarded as a messianic political actor. And
a coup d'état was the most logical solution to undo the gridlock. On January 3,
2000, Bédié, who had found refuge at French 43rd Marine Infantry Battalion in
Port-Bouët, a few hundred meters from the Houphouët Boigny International
Airport, fled Côte d'Ivoire, and, via Lomé, arrived at his private apartment on
rue Beethoven, in the luxurious 16th arrondissement of Paris. His plane must
have crossed paths with Ouattara's as Ouattara, who had been in exile in France,
arrived in Abidjan, triumphant. In an interview given to BBC a few days later,
Ouattara enthusiastically praised the military seizure of power as not a coup but
a people's revolution: "This is not a coup d'état. This is a revolution supported
by all the Ivorian people. The previous regime was a dictatorship. So the changes
that have taken place have helped to liberate the country and given the prospect
to build a democracy." Ouattara was not the only one to praise the coup d'état.
In a naive move, Laurent Gbagbo, too, breaking from his democratic principles,
had let his emotions get the best of him and had rejoiced to see Bédié fall by way
of coup d'état. Referring to what he read in history as positive coups, such as the
1974 Portuguese coup (the Carnation Revolution), which occasioned the independence of Mozambique and Angola, Gbagbo expressed his delight: "This coup,

we approve it completely. There are times when military interventions advance democracy. In African countries, or countries with obvious dictatorship, military coups are not necessarily bad things. Sometimes, they are steps towards democracy."[20] Was Gbagbo aware that in the minutes following the coup against Bédié, Ibrahima Coulibaly (IB), the sergeant who led the military operation and a former bodyguard of Ouattara's children, had called General Gueï with this urgent message?

> My General, President Bédié has divided the Ivorians; he has created xenophobia and *Ivoirité*.... We are coming to fetch you.... We want you to put in the heads of the Ivorians that foreigners are at home here ... [and] there should not be exclusion in matters of candidacy. All those who want to be candidates must register and must participate in the competition. The Ivorians are free to choose their president. If they want a Vietnamese, their choice must be respected.[21]

In other words, if the people wanted a Voltaic, their choice must be respected. As Gbagbo would very soon come to realize, Dramane Ouattara was the man for whom the coup d'état was undertaken. General Gueï was a mere pawn, a seat-warmer.

Ouattara Contra Gueï

Upon seizing power, General Gueï set up a provisional government, the Comité National du Salut Public (CNSP). On December 27, Gueï suspended the Ivorian constitution, whose electoral code was not advantageous to Dramane Ouattara, and established a Commission Consultative Constitutionnelle et Electorale, or CCCE (a constituent assembly), to be in charge of writing a draft constitution to be submitted to a referendum for a vote, for the purpose of creating "the necessary conditions for the establishment of a true democracy for the organization of fair and transparent elections for the return to normal constitutional life." The overriding question in the project was that of the eligibility for the presidency, precisely that of the nationality of the candidates to the presidency. Arguing on the basis of Ivorian cultural diversity, General Gueï had personally intervened in the debate to request that the word "and" in the proposition that required the mother *and* the father of any candidate to be Ivorian be replaced by the word "or," so that the Ivorian nationality of one *or* the other of the candidate's parents be sufficient to ascertain the candidate's Ivorian nationality. The RDR was jubilant. Dramane Ouattara was back. This was a very significant victory for Dramane Ouattara, who had up to then argued that the 1998 electoral code was expressly written to block his candidacy.

However, two months after the publication of the new language of the electoral code in the Official Journal of the Republic, General Gueï intervened again.

His consultations with the populations in the country's heartland, he claimed, had shown clearly that throughout Côte d'Ivoire the people were in favor of the first electoral code; the populations wanted a president whose nationality raised no doubt at all, because emanating from two Ivorian parents. So article 35 of the new draft constitution retained the coordination "and." The final language of the electoral code of the 2000 constitution, which was submitted to a referendum, on which the political parties freely prepared their members for a "yes" or "no" vote, and for which Alassane Dramane Ouattara's RDR publicly called on its members to vote "yes," while, according to some observers, secretly asking them to vote "no," thus read as follows[22]:

> The candidates in the presidential election must be at least forty years old and no more than seventy-five years old. They must be of Ivorian origin, born of a father and a mother themselves of Ivorian origin. They must never have renounced Ivorian nationality. They should never have acquired another nationality. They must have lived in Côte d'Ivoire continuously for five years preceding the date of the elections and have totaled ten years of effective presence in Côte d'Ivoire. The residence requirement specified in this section does not apply to members of diplomatic and consular representations, persons designated by the State for a post or a mission abroad, international officials, and political exiles.

The population adopted the new constitution with an overwhelming 85 percent of the votes. Little, if anything, had changed from the previous language of the electoral code contained in article 9 of the 1998 constitution that so much angered the members of the RDR and the international community. The previous constitution read,

> The candidates in the presidential election must be forty years old at least and seventy-five years maximum. They must be Ivorian by birth, whose father and mother themselves are Ivorian by birth. They must have lived in Côte d'Ivoire continuously for ten years prior to the election date. They must never have renounced Ivorian nationality. The candidates for the Presidency of the Republic holding other nationalities are only eligible if they expressly waive and formally renounce their foreign nationalities at least twelve months before the date of filing the application; and if that waiver is formally accepted by the Government of the foreign state. The residence requirement specified in this section does not apply to members of diplomatic and consular missions and persons designated by the State for a post or a mission abroad.

So then, the contentious language in Article 9 of the 1998 constitution, which was judged unfavorable to Dramane Ouattara and which helped Ouattara, his international backers, and part of the Ivorian opposition rationalize the putsch against Bédié, remained unchanged and reappeared in Article 35 of the new constitution. Whatever issue one may have with the contents of the new constitution, as has been noted by critics, its legitimacy could not be contested: "It was thought up and written by Ivorians. It was prepared by a constituent assembly which had been established partly by democratic means, and, above all, it was adopted by referendum."[23]

In effect, only weeks after the coup against Bédié, Gueï's relations with Ouattara had begun to deteriorate. Compelled to quickly relinquish power to civilians by France and the opposition parties, and particularly by Ouattara, who in the absence of Bédié saw the Ivorian presidency as an entitlement, Gueï, the self-proclaimed "housecleaner," had turned increasingly distrustful and had hardened his stance. He who was to be the regent of Ouattara's throne in the absence of Ouattara decided, after all, to permanently occupy that throne by running for the 2000 presidential election. In 2000, the soldiers that had deposed Bédié had warned that Gueï would meet Bédié's fate if he tried to betray them[24]—that is, if he bypassed the script given him by those who were resolute to see Dramane Ouattara at the helm. A number of events, among which was Gueï's dismissal from the government of national unity of Ouattara's ministers on May 18, 2000, had weakened the Gueï-Ouattara bond. The split was consummated on the night of September 17–18, when the soldiers that were at the forefront of the 1999 coup that put Gueï in power attempted to overthrow him in a coup that came to be known as the "plot of the white horse." That night, General Gueï's private residence in the affluent Abidjan neighborhood of Indénié was attacked by a group of soldiers. Gueï was not at home, but two of his guards were killed, fifteen were seriously wounded, and his white horse had its throat slashed in a manner that was said to be typical of Muslim rituals. Among the thirty people arrested in the aftermath of the failed coup were low-ranking soldiers (Chérif Ousmane, Issiaka Ouattara, aka Wattao, Oumar Diarrassouba, aka Zaga-Zaga, Souleymane Diomandé, aka La Grenade, etc.), as well as high-ranking officers (General Palenfo, General Coulibaly), all close to Ouattara and all principal participants in the coup d'état against Bédié. The series of arrests that followed the "plot of the white horse" prompted many soldiers close to Ouattara, especially those originating from the northern Muslim part of Côte d'Ivoire, to go into exile in neighboring Burkina Faso. These soldiers would later change the political landscape of Côte d'Ivoire with a series of armed interventions that would culminate in a ten-year rebellion.

As Gueï decided to vie for the supreme power, he understood that his chances of winning against France's horse was to eliminate that horse altogether—to make it irrelevant in the Ivorian political landscape for good. For that, all he had to do was to maneuver to keep the electoral code untouched; and he had succeeded through the democratic referendum, which, whatever one could think of it, further functioned as a referendum on Ouattara himself. The passing of the 2000 constitution by more than 85 percent of the votes meant that the masses were not ready to accept anyone with dubious nationality as their president, since it was clear in the collective consciousness that the candidate whose Ivorian nationality had posed problem and pervaded the political debates throughout the years was Dramane Ouattara. Gueï, like Bédié, was set on proving that Ouattara was a fraud.

On September 12, 2000, Gueï's lawyers disclosed some information on Ouattara's past, which they contended proved that he had not been truthful about his nationality. They published copies of documents dating as far back as 1966, revealing Ouattara's marriage to an American citizen by the name of Angela Davis. On the marriage certificate, Ouattara had declared that he was a citizen from Upper Volta. The certificate also bore the fact that Ouattara's mother was deceased, which contradicted his most recent statement to the electoral committee that his mother was a living eighty-year-old Ivorian woman by the name of Hadja Nabintou Cissé. Furthermore, Gueï produced a 1978 bank account document and a 1980 property sale certificate on which Ouattara declared himself to be a citizen of Upper Volta. For Gueï, all these discrepancies were enough to show that Ouattara was a forger. So, the Supreme Court of Côte d'Ivoire rejected Ouattara's candidacy to the 2000 presidential election on the ground of his dubious nationality. The contestations by the RDR led nowhere. Ouattara, once again, was out of contention. Bédié's candidacy was rejected for "obvious" reasons: He was "a dictator" who would not be permitted to run the country anymore.

In 2000, the political parties that had hitherto formed a Republican Front with the RDR to boycott the 1995 election, all chose, that time, not to side with Ouattara, and took part in the election. At the October 2000 election, Gbagbo was the main opponent to run against Gueï. Other candidates were Mel Théodore of the Union Démocratique Citoyenne (UDCI), independent Nicolas Dioulo, and Francis Wodié of the Parti Ivoirien des Travailleurs (PIT). Two days after the 2000 vote, on October 24, 2000, as the ballot results were coming in, Gueï ordered a stop to the vote count, dissolved the National Electoral Commission under the pretext that its incompetent members had not prevented obvious cases of frauds, and proclaimed himself the winner of the election in the first round with 52.72 percent against 41.2 percent for his rival, Gbagbo. However, because the vote count was being directly communicated to each candidate's headquarters by their respective assessors in the voting stations, Gbagbo's headquarters was able to establish that based on two-thirds of the polls reported, Gbagbo was ahead with 63.85 percent against 34.3 percent for General Gueï. So, Gbagbo, too, claimed victory from his campaign headquarters and appealed to his followers to take to the streets in order to stop Gueï's attempt at forceful seizure of power:

> Today duty calls you. I demand that all the militants stand up against the imposture. I ask that in all the towns of Côte d'Ivoire and in all neighborhoods, Ivorian patriots take to the streets until the law is recognized and until Gueï backs down. From this

moment, I declare the transitional government dissolved. It no longer has a purpose. Consequently, all our comrades who were in it are freed of their obligations vis-à-vis Robert Gueï.... I am the head of state of Cote d'Ivoire now.

Responding to their candidate's call, Gbagbo's supporters marching towards the Presidential Palace armed with slingshots and rocks met Gueï's army in the streets in a violent confrontation that raised outcries in the diplomatic community. On October 25, as the army and the gendarmerie finally started to rally to Gbagbo, Ouattara, who had hoped that the crisis would last long enough to cause a reshuffling of the cards and the organization of a new election—with him as a contender—called on his followers to meet Gbagbo's supporters in the streets, for, as he put it, "the power was in the street to be seized by the people who really wanted it." More than 300 civilians died in the clash, which lasted until October 26, before the security forces were able to control the situation. When the final vote count was published, the electoral committee declared Gbagbo the winner with 60 percent of the vote against 33 percent for General Gueï. Ouattara never accepted the legitimacy of Gbagbo's election and would spend the ensuing years undermining President Gbagbo's administration. In his subversive endeavor, Ouattara had the support of the international community.

"Gbagbo was terrifying"

From the very first hours of his presidency, Laurent Gbagbo had been defending himself against an unfair international media, particularly a biased French media that over the years had internalized an image of Dramane Ouattara as the martyrized American-educated functionary from the International Monetary Fund. Former French Ambassador to Côte d'Ivoire Gildas Le Lidec would later admit the following:

> The press played a pro–Ouattara role. That is undeniable. But already the French officials were pro–Ouattara in their minds. Ouattara presented better than Gbagbo. Ouattara was good because he had been an international civil servant; he spoke perfect English ... [and] somehow, it's true, Ouattara was a little formatted ... [and] certainly journalists helped fuel hatred against Gbagbo and drove pro–Ouattara feelings. Gbagbo was terrifying.

President Gbagbo was terrifying because he was different. He disrupted the stereotypes reserved to the African heads of states with whom Euro-American officials were used to dealing. He was not quick to say his number of yeses, not prompt to fall in line without weighing his country's interests first. He was highly intelligent and independent. His extraordinary insights on what is at stake in Africa and his profound knowledge of African politics and world history put him a step ahead of his peers.

By his intellectual education and his political upbringing, Laurent Gbagbo was a maverick president in Africa and an unconventional interlocutor by Euro-American standards. Professor Laurent Gbagbo has no American education. Most of his education, apart from a few years in France, he completed in Côte d'Ivoire. A very street-smart individual, he is neither a habitué of the felted lounges of high finance or a regular guest at palace balls. His experience is organic, acquired over forty years in the trenches of grassroots politics fighting for the birth of democracy against the monopartism of Houphouët Boigny, one of the African presidents most adulated by the Euro-American establishment. Gbagbo's language is simple, direct, and close to the people. He is what in Ivorian parlance is known as "*un enfant du terroir*," that is, a local child. From the perspective of the West, politicians like him are seen as wielding too much influence over the people, which can neutralize any attempt by the West to wrestle them. They are called populous and demagogic, and they are believed to be fighting a war sixty years obsolete, the anticolonial war, while time has now come to fall in line with the new political craze called globalization.

On several levels, Laurent Gbagbo was a gatecrasher, and in October 2010 the fact that he was elected the president of Côte d'Ivoire had not settled in well in some circles. For Dramane Ouattara particularly, this was a hard reality to live with, especially in such circumstances—that is, as the outcome of an election from which he, the darling child of France, who had come to see himself as the messiah, was barred. In fact, it would seem that all the major presidential hopefuls in Cote d'Ivoire had a profound disdain for Gbagbo. This is certainly the only thing upon which Ouattara, Bédié and Gueï could agree. From their respective standards, Gbagbo was not of the kind of dough that made a "good African president." And they were right. Gbagbo's political journey made him different. He was not anointed. While in Africa most presidents had come to power by way of coup d'état, had inherited their posts from their president fathers or had been sponsored by imperialist interests, Gbagbo is a self-made political figure, one who rose to power from very modest beginnings.[25]

A Militant Upbringing

Laurent Gbagbo was born two months before the victory of the Allied Forces, on March 31, 1945, in Kédio-Babré, in the commune of Gagnoa. His father was Zèpè Gbagbo Koudou Paul, from the village of Mama in the commune of Ouragahio. Laurent Gbagbo's grandfather Gbagbo Libi, a resistant to colonial invasion, was killed in 1912, leaving his pregnant widow to fend for herself. After the birth of Laurent Gbagbo's father, his grandmother went to live with her mother in the village of Garahio. There, she met Zèpè Vabiè, whom she married and who adopted her young son, Koudou Paul. The adopted son, having the name of his adopted father added to his, was thus called Zèpè Gbagbo Koudou Paul. Young Zèpè Gbagbo Koudou Paul received a Christian education at a Catholic school. Later, as a young adult, he volunteered in the colonial army in 1940 and was deployed to France to help liberate France from German occupation. In 1941, he was captured by the Germans and days before being sent to a Nazi camp, he escaped. After a long and exhausting walk in the unfamiliar woods, he collapsed at the doorstep of a French couple, only to regain consciousness days later on a bed at Saint-Raphael Hospital in Fréjus. Demobilized, Zèpè Gbagbo Koudou Paul returned to Côte d'Ivoire, where he met his wife and Laurent Gbagbo's mother, Lélé Gado Marguerite, from the sub-prefecture of Ouragahio. Of the four children they had together, only two survived, Laurent Gbagbo and his sister Jeannette.

A railroad worker on the Réseau Abidjan-Niger (RAN), Koudou Paul was very active in the fight for the rights of the railroad workers. Laurent Gbagbo's father was the one who first instilled in his son a sense of social justice, which was later reinforced at Saint-Dominique Savio Seminary of Gagnoa, which Laurent Gbagbo attended from 1958 to 1962. After seminary, Gbagbo attended the prestigious Lycée Classique d'Abidjan from 1962 to 1965. In 1964, at the age of 19, a year before completing his baccalaureate degree, Gbagbo's father was arrested by the Houphouët regime for allegedly plotting to topple the government; and Laurent Gbagbo, the eldest son, would have dropped out of school to take care of his family had not his mother persuaded him to go back to school. In 1966, after a year spent at the Université d'Abidjan, Gbagbo obtained a scholarship to study Greek and Latin at the University of Lyon, after which he returned home to register at the Université d'Abidjan in the Department of History and Geography. In 1969, he was back in France to earn his masters in history, which won him a teaching post at his old grammar school, the Lycée Classique d'Abidjan.

A year into his first appointment in March 1970, Laurent Gbagbo was arrested and held at the military camps of Bouaké and Séguéla for allegedly teaching subversive materials to his students. In the meantime, to further punish Gbagbo, the Houphouët regime had his French wife, Jacqueline Chamois, and their infant son, Michel, repatriated to France. Gbagbo would be incarcerated for three years. Once released, he was deemed too dangerous to be around students, so he was assigned a desk job at the Institut Pédagogique de Cocody. From there, he managed to enter the Institut d'Histoire d'Art et d'Archéologie Africain (IHAA) to prepare for a doctorate in history. In 1979, Laurent Gbagbo successfully defended his doctoral dissertation in history at the Université Paris VII, and in 1981 he became the director of the IHAA. Gbagbo's tribulations under the Houphouët regime did not stifle his enthusiasm to move Côte d'Ivoire along the path of democracy. Gbagbo took his political fight underground and with a group of friends, including his future wife, French professor Simone Ehivet, he created the Front Populaire Ivoirien (FPI). In 1982, Gbagbo went into exile as the regime was about to arrest him again. After six years in France, Gbagbo returned to his country to bring his party out of clandestineness, to be the first opposition party to challenge Houphouët Boigny's Parti démocratique de Côte d'Ivoire (PDCI). Being the major opposition party also made the FPI the main target of the regime's harassment.

Laurent Gbagbo had a clear vision for making Côte d'Ivoire a democratic state committed to the social well-being of its citizens. Over the years, faithful to his belief that political actors have the responsibility, using their political parties as pedagogical tools, to educate the masses, Laurent Gbagbo not only published his vision for a democratic society in a number of books, but he also undertook to directly interact with the Ivorian populations and explain his political and social programs for a better Côte d'Ivoire. In that perspective, He visited more than 9,000 of the 11,000 population centers of Côte d'Ivoire to share his ideas for a better society. Laurent Gbagbo is the father of the multiparty system in Côte d'Ivoire. It is his thirty-year struggle for democracy that had led to President Houphouët's surrender of the one-party system and opened up the possibility for other political organizations to be recognized.

On the other hand, Gbagbo's pathfinding struggle had made him many enemies, even among those who advertise themselves as partisans of democracy. In Europe, the nostalgic of the old "Africa of kings and informal dealings" resented Gbagbo, to whose struggle for a multiparty system they imputed the political instability of Côte d'Ivoire. Had Gbagbo left the old system unchallenged, they argue, there would be no bitter party-based contestation for power, and, therefore, no armed conflicts. Former French president Chirac is of this opinion. According to French Ambassador Le Lidec, Chirac once told Gbagbo, "What have you done of this once-beautiful country? Houphouët must be rolling over in his tomb." A sentiment that is echoed in the heartfelt lamentation of an Ivorian journalist who wrote in the June 21, 2005, issue of the government paper *Fraternité Matin*: "[T]here can be no development without democracy? What has that thing [democracy] given us in the last fifteen years? Almost everywhere, we witness endless conflicts. Africa itself, kills, literally as well as figuratively, her own children in the name of a quest for democracy that awakens primitive instincts that we thought forever removed from our rhetoric; which, alas, again, the Ivorian news profusely serve us on a daily basis." This analysis is, for some critics, pathetic and erroneous. As Macaire Etty so appropriately points out, although conflicts in Africa have intensified, beginning in the early 1990s, it would be simplistic to impute those conflicts solely to the advent of the multiparty system on the continent. The sense of stability that had prevailed in Côte d'Ivoire between 1960 and 1990 was less the consequence of the one-party system than the result of the total commitment Houphouët made to protect the interests of France. In return for his commitment to fight tooth and nail for safeguarding France's interests in his country, Houphouët was protected by a French military presence in Côte d'Ivoire. In fact, rather than being a factor of stability, what monopartism guaranteed was the opposite of stability:

> The one-party regime, in its very principle, cannot guarantee peace in a country, let alone development. The one-party system is the antithesis of freedom and change. It is an anti-progressive and anti-human regime. Let us remember the damages the one-party regime has caused in our country: embezzlement of public funds, mismanagement, megalomania, corruption of conscience, tribalism, etc. And anyone who dared to criticize the monarch was demonized and considered the enemy of the nation. His fate was imprisonment, torture, exile or death: Gbagbo, Mockey, Zadi, Memel Fote, Kragbé Gnagbé, Ernest Boka, the Sanwi people, the Guébié people, etc. All these people have suffered the worst treatment. But Houphouët, covered by the Foccart network, has not been harassed by either the UN or any human rights organization.[26]

Since multipartism necessarily implies recognition of dissent, contradiction, negotiation and arbitration, multipartism might seem antithetical to harmony and tranquility, which are believed to be the hallmarks of monopartism, especially as, sometimes, the various protagonist blocs or parties in a multiparty system do engage in violent rhetoric and even physical confrontations. For the nostalgic of feudal African societies, the one-party regime provides a false sense of security; it offers the image of an undisturbed, unified community harmoniously led towards a collective objective or Promised Land by an all-powerful sage, a Moses-like patriarch. In fact, in Côte d'Ivoire, as a presumed descendent of legendary Queen Abla Pokou, Houphouët had enjoyed that image for a long time and has held an almost transcendent power through his mythologized ethnic origin (Baoulé), which in turn had helped rationalize the single-party state of which he was the protector until challenged by Gbagbo. The concept of multipartism fractures the ideal of perfection, security and unity as purported to be safeguarded by Houphouët's monopartism. As the principal agent of multipartism, it is, thus, Laurent Gbagbo who ruptures the harmony of the Ivorian nation-state.

From the very onset of his struggle for democracy, Gbagbo had been tagged as arrogant and disrespectful, especially towards Houphouët. There is footage of Houphouët and Gbagbo in a meeting that had drawn much indignation against the latter. In 1990, pressed by recurrent political dissents, a reluctant Houphouët had finally agreed to meet with the Ivorian opposition leaders. The film of the gathering aired by state TV (RTI) showed Gbagbo sitting in a chair, facing Houphouët, with his legs crossed high. The recording, played over and over in the following days, made national news and was commented on as evidence of

Gbagbo's disrespect towards the father of the nation. Gbagbo's posture was inter-preted as an insult to God. Multipartism was an affront to God; and to punish the people of Côte d'Ivoire, God had the curse of division, sectarianism, and eth-nocentrism descend on them through the one who introduced multipartism.

Ouattara's Worn-out Discourse of Victimology: "They don't want me to be president because I'm a Muslim and from the North"

The image of President Gbagbo that his detractors wanted to stress to the international community was drawn out of a beaten discourse of victimology that had preceded his presidency. Truly, if the Côte d'Ivoire that Gbagbo inherited was artificially divided on ethno-religious grounds, it was not of Gbagbo's doing. Ouattara and Bédié created the chasm in the Ivorian society with their protracted hostility founded on ethnic and religious bases. In 1991, on the first anniversary of Dramane Ouattara's premiership, an enigmatic group of Ivorian intellectuals from the northern region of the country issued a pamphlet titled *Le Levain de l'insurrection* (The Seed of the Rebellion). The leaflet, which they distributed in the country's mosques as well as in selected gathering places mostly frequented by northern Muslims and which they also published in sympathizing papers, invited the men and women of the northern regions of Côte d'Ivoire to under-stand and to act upon Ouattara's appointment to be President Houphouët's prime minister not as some ordinary occurrence but, rather, as a special rupturing event in Ivorian politics—an event to seize upon as the seed of an insurgency to come, which would result in the advent of a Muslim president from the North.

Ouattara was Côte d'Ivoire's very first prime minister, and to the authors of the pamphlet his appointment, especially at a time when Houphouët was in poor health and had little control over the country's affairs, was opportune. It was a rare chance to witness the coming to power of a son of the Muslim north as president, an opportunity not to be wasted. The authors of the pamphlet knew that it would be a steep constitutional hill for their hero to climb, but it was a fight they would wage with arms if necessary. And so, the document prepared the northerners to the fight for political power by rousing them with past deeds of their epic ancestors:

> The Northern Charter to its sons at the 4 corners of Côte d'Ivoire, to its native sons. Intellectuals, illiterate, officials, officers, soldiers, workers, merchants, our voices sound the gathering of a United North, strong, credible, full partner, and arbiter of future situations within a renovated, equitable and coherent Ivorian ideal.... Alas-sane Ouattara needs the support of the citizens ... and especially the support of his people, all races of the northern community to which he belongs ... to help him

carry out his mission, whose success will inevitably lead to the path of succession. History, they say likes to repeats itself.

While the Ivorian constitution stipulated clearly that in case of death of the president of the Republic, the issue of his succession was the responsibility of the president of the National Assembly, the Northern Charter, which promoted Ouattara as Houphouët's spontaneous successor, was an unmistakable invitation to subversion of the constitution. Nevertheless, in December 1993, when President Houphouët passed, the military officers from the northern regions were not successful in imposing Ouattara. Was it because they were not ready yet? That President Houphouët's death had come earlier than expected, or because they had little support in the army? In any case, the army officers blocked Ouattara's attempt at power seizure and accompanied National Assembly President Bédié on national TV to make himself available to the country and in accordance with the constitution accept to carry on the duties of the president.

The short constitutional crisis helped Bédié identify the leaders within his party whose loyalty to him was at issue and to start a methodical purging of the PDCI. Most northerners within the party were found disloyal, and Bédié dishonored them and snubbed them out of the PDCI. Two hundred sixty-seven Northerners would later join Djéni Kobena's newly formed RDR and, in 1995, would solicit Ouattara to be their candidate to the presidential election. Speaking in Malinké at a ceremony held in Odienné, north of Côte d'Ivoire, the former Minister of State and Minister of Economy in the Houphouët government, Lamine Diabaté, justified his and many northerners' withdrawal from the PDCI and warned of a rebellion to come:

> They said that we were coward. Of what should we be afraid? Our forefathers were not afraid to occupy this region. This region was seized by means of gun and powder. We don't want to be with these people anymore. Here's what they did to us in the PDCI: First, they disrespected us, then the disdain and the lack of consideration. They treated us like animals.... They organized a denigration campaign. They insulted Alassane, his father, his mother and us. It was with guns and powder that our fathers conquered this land. We are not afraid of them.... Today they do to our brothers what the colonists used to do to us. The PDCI has decided to practice a politics that will take us directly into a civil war. We ask you to renew your trust in us by adhering to the RDR, which is the framework of our most profound aspirations for liberty, justice and equality. Have no regrets. The true PDCI died with Houphouët Boigny. Today's PDCI is the Party for the Destruction of Côte d'Ivoire.... They do not want to hear the muezzin's prayer call. They do not want Islam and Muslims. They send the military in mosques. If we accept this then we are not Muslims, then we are bastards.

In 1995, when the Supreme Court of Côte d'Ivoire rejected Ouattara's bid to the presidency on the basis of his "dubious nationality," he dug deep in the ethnic and religious rhetoric of the Northern Charter to explain his ineligibility. During an interview with French television TV5, Dramane Ouattara declared, "They don't want me to be president because I'm a Muslim and from the North"; thus further driving a wedge between the northern region of the country and the other regions and between the Muslims and the other religious communities of Côte d'Ivoire.

The puzzling result was that with his notorious complaint Ouattara—who as prime minister had instituted, in a country that knew not such a thing before, one of the most dreaded devices of harassment against the immigrant populations of Mali and Burkina Faso, the Ivorian Resident Card—had suddenly condensed all that was African north of Côte d'Ivoire as well as all that was Muslim in the world. The elimination of Alassane Ouattara from the presidential race became for many observers the hierarchization of the Ivorians before the law.[27] So then, any wrong done to Ouattara—either proven or unproven—became automatically a wrong done to any of the five million immigrants coming from countries north of Côte d'Ivoire and to any Muslim in the world. Equally, any justice rendered him could be interpreted as justice rendered to all the Muslim populations in the world and all the suffering immigrants in Côte d'Ivoire. Besides being figured as a martyr in Côte d'Ivoire, Ouattara also became the poster boy of the new Euro-American wave of thinking, for which the "hip cause" to embrace was the cause of "the suffering Muslim." And the Euro-American media, and academia so fond of exotic causes, could not print enough of Ouattara's inspiring story, could not wait to pounce on Bédié, the tormentor of the Muslims and of the immigrants of whom Ouattara was the epitome:

> The country's Islamic communities are subject to a great deal of Islamic discrimi-
> nations.... Muslim citizens often are treated as foreigners by their fellow citizens,
> including government officials, because Muslims are members of northern ethnic
> groups that also are found in other African countries from which there has been
> substantial immigration into the country. Many Muslims are northerners and tended
> to support the presidential candidacy of Ouattara.[28]

Cornered, indicted from all parts, Bédié made an ingenious recuperation. He appropriated for himself the concept of *Ivoirité*. The coinage was the brainchild of some Ivorian scholars who had originally intended it to express the national consciousness, the collective will of the people, who have chosen to live in a brotherly way together on the Ivorian soil and together share the same sufferings, the same joys, and the same hopes. In 1997, Bédié adopted the word as the basis of a societal program that would coalesce the various ethnic groups and social substrata of the Ivorian society into a strong stratum. For the more than sixty ethnic communities of Côte d'Ivoire, Bédié wanted Ivoirité to be a signifier of identification, the social glue that would bond them together by instilling in them a stronger patriotic fiber and consequently a stronger attachment to the state and its institutions as embodying the sum total of all individual nationalistic expressions.[29] However, as the accusations against Bédié intensified, Bédié's supporters turned reactive and the concept of Ivoirité as used by the PDCI quickly turned ideological and divisive. One of the PDCI's most bellicose heralds of the exclusivity of the concept was writer and journalist Venance Konan, who in a number of callous articles published between February and September 1998 in the government paper, *Fraternité Matin,* directly attacked Dramane Ouattara's integrity and challenged him to prove his Ivorian origin:

> Ouattara claims to be an Ivorian. Maybe this is true. But it is a fact that at one time in his life, he carried the nationality of Burkina Faso. Was he Ivorian first, then Burkinabe before returning to being Ivorian? Is it because one of his parents was Burkinabe? If that is the case, his tie with that country must have been strong enough for him to claim its nationality. Why should the Ivorians take the risk of entrusting their fate to a man whose patriotism is not exclusively Ivorian? In the name of what principle? Did he take the Burkinabe nationality simply because it allowed him to go to the IMF and the BCEAO? If this is the case, then he is an adventurer whose patriotism fluctuates according to his interests. Why should the Ivorians take the risk of entrusting their fate to a man whose nationalism varies with the circumstances? In the name of what principle? ... Is being a racist and a xenophobe to take a minimum of precautions so that our country does not fall into the hands of adventurers?[30]

Gbagbo had no interest in perpetuating the ethno-religious posturing between Ouattara and Bédié that had disrupted the fragile equilibrium maintained among the 60 ethnic groups in the country and transformed the political parties into ethnic and religious rallying grounds. If Ouattara's RDR and Bédié's PDCI could count on their respective huge constituencies of Malinké and Akan for membership, Gbagbo could not rely solely on his Bété fellow citizens to staff his FPI. Compared to the Malinké and the Akan, the Bété were a minority. And so, very early in his political struggle, either strategically or by moral conviction—and the latter undoubtedly, given Gbagbo's life story—Gbagbo resisted any temptation that may have existed within his party to regionalize the FPI, and he transcended the limited confines of ethnic and religious appurtenances and stretched his arms to all of his fellow citizens, regardless of where they came from or of which god they worshipped.

In fact, as has been noted by observers, Gbagbo's break with the system that existed before was admittedly a break with a political culture that he and his party members had qualified as tribal, predatory and turned toward the exterior. Gbagbo understood well that the task at hand was to demystify some stratifications within the Ivorian society inherited from colonial times as well as imposed by geographical and cultural specificities, for it is undeniable that an economic system inherited from colonization as well as some cultural mores had maintained the northern regions of Côte d'Ivoire in a state of backwardness. While the other regions of the country, endowed with generous yearly precipitations, had immensely benefited from the colonial export crop economy based on coffee, cocoa, palm oil, rubber, and tropical fruits plantations, the dry north, not propitious to a variety of export crops, had generally lagged behind. Furthermore a syncretism of Islamic and Animist esoteric tradition (the *Poro* rites) had undermined much of the effort undertaken by President Houphouët (construction of roads, schools, sugar factories, cotton processing factories, introduction of cotton and sugar fields) in the 1970s to develop the North.[31] The northern regions of Côte d'Ivoire remained largely unschooled and underdeveloped and continued to be drained of its youths who migrated to southern towns where their limited education usually could guarantee them jobs only as subalterns (house domestics, plantation workers, carriers, truck drivers, and the like).

Though many northerners were highly educated and had attained positions of prominence in government and in the public and private sectors, their success has been drowned out by the prevalent narrative of northerners as uneducated plebeians, a discourse that preceded Gbagbo's election. It is paradoxical, however, that Laurent Gbagbo—whose fight for democracy and multipartism had given a voice and political platforms to the northern elites hitherto taken for granted within the PDCI, as Lamine Diabaté himself had acknowledged—should be indicted for ethnocentrism by a northern elite committed to putting Ouattara into the presidency at any cost. In fact, what the northern elites reproached Gbagbo most for was that he had given no indication he was going to reform the constitution and remove from it the language that prevented Ouattara from being a candidate and thus realizing the northerners' ultimate aspiration of having one of their sons in the palace. "The rejection of Alassane Dramane Ouattara's candidacy to the presidential and legislative elections increased the resentments of the Muslims. Henceforth, Islam functioned as both a rallying superstructure and a locus of resistance to exclusion."[32]

So, in 2002, a little over one year after President Gbagbo was inaugurated, a second version of the Northern Charter was published, this one more belligerent than the first one and openly calling for the North to prepare for war against the government of Côte d'Ivoire. The second Northern Charter, titled *The Precursory Signs of the Partition of the Country*, accused Gbagbo of continuing the politics of Ivoirité instituted by Bédié and adopted by Gueï. It expressed the Northerners' exasperation with the "Blakoros" (the uncircumcised non–Muslims) and the "Boussoumanis" (Bushmen, southern forest dwellers as opposed to northern Sahel dwellers) and refused to let Gbagbo take credit for work that, in their opinion, Ouattara had accomplished as prime minister, that of jumpstarting the Ivorian economy in the early 1990s: "Alassane Ouattara … is an authentic

Ivorian from the North ... [and] it would be inconceivable that Alassane pull the chestnuts out of the fire and another enjoy them." Since 2002, the northern Muslim elites had sealed Gbagbo's fate. He would not be their president. He had to be toppled.

Gbagbo Must Go

On the day that Gbagbo was being sworn in, October 26, 2000, the leaders of the RDR invited a team of local and international journalists to a macabre scene behind the walls of the Maison d'arrêt et de correction d'Abidjan (MACA), in the suburb of Yopougon. Ouattara's RDR was denouncing an alleged carnage perpetrated by an alleged death squad operating under the orders of Gbagbo. On the scene, 57 stripped and piled-up corpses were said to have been executed by the gendarmes who had pledged allegiance to Gbagbo a day earlier. These corpses, according to the RDR, were all members of their party; they were said to be Northerners and mostly Muslims. The RDR insisted that an election such as the one that took place in October 2000—the organization of which was based on an unfair electoral code in which Ouattara did not participate and which was stained with so much blood of Ouattara's supporters—was naturally invalid and needed to be started over on the basis of a more inclusive electoral code. However, at his investiture, which was attended by the diplomatic corps in Côte d'Ivoire and the leaders of all the political parties (among which were the PDCI, the UDCI, and the PIT), except the leaders of the RDR, President Gbagbo deplored what the country of his childhood had come to be. He lamented the many Ivorians who fell during the violence that preceded his investiture, and he expressed the gratitude of the whole nation towards them: "May they find in our hearts," he declared, "the eternal gratitude of the entire nation." Then he went on, as if speaking directly to the leaders of the RDR, who were still contesting the results of the election and asking for a new vote: "We will not rewrite another constitution and we will not do another presidential election." Nevertheless, Gbagbo invited the leaders of all the parties to join him in the constitution of a government of national unity that would help heal the profound wounds of the country. Laurent Gbagbo had taken too lightly Dramane Ouattara's determination to be president by all means necessary. Ouattara had hundreds of soldiers committed to him, and he was going to use them against Gbagbo, just as he did against Bédié and Gueï.

In 2000, during the Gueï regime, hundreds of Ivorian soldiers who were on the run had found refuge in Ouagadougou, Burkina Faso, where Burkinabe President Blaise Compaoré had unrolled the red carpet for them. In fact, during the night of September 18, 2000, some of the soldiers who had overthrown Bédié and delivered power to General Gueï had attempted to depose the latter, too. Their grievance with Gueï was that the general-president had betrayed them. In fact, Gueï had been courted by the RDR after he had fallen in disgrace with Bédié, whom, as the Army chief of staff, he had supported in 1993 against Dramane Ouattara. When Bédié forced General Gueï into early retirement in 1997, the RDR of Ouattara saw an opportunity to rehabilitate the fallen shrewd general. In his little village of Kabakouma, General Gueï received the constant visits of RDR leaders and of some French officers, among whom was a fellow graduate of Saint Cyr, French Army Chief of Staff General Bantégeat. On one of his private trips to France "to visit old pals from Saint Cyr," General Gueï was officially greeted at the Elysée (French presidential palace), at Hôtel Matignon (the official residence of the French prime minister), and at the Quai d'Orsay (the Ministry of Foreign Affairs), a circumstance which had attentive political observers predict that Gueï was being prepared to play a significant future role in Ivorian politics.[33] They were right.

On December 24, 1999, Guei reappeared on the Ivorian political scene as a proxy president on behalf of RDR leader Ouattara. However, Gueï, had not lived by the agreed-upon scenario, which was for him to hand over power to Dramane Ouattara in a sham election after six months. Habituated to palace life over time, General Gueï had decided to run for the 2000 election, a decision the soldiers had hitherto solicited him to make to lead their coup, Northerners for the most part saw it as an act of treason. So they decided to get rid of Gueï. However, Gueï had been forewarned of the coup by a turncoat soldier, and he had prepared to ambush his assailants. Many of the attackers were killed, wounded or captured. Those who were lucky to escape fled to Burkina Faso, where Sergeant-Major Ibrahim Coulibaly (IB), a shunned guard of Gueï's who was sent on a penance assignment to the cold Ivorian embassy in Ottawa as a defense attaché for having unequivocally expressed more loyalty to Ouattara than to General-President Gueï, was awaiting them after he had deserted from his Canadian post. The number of Ivorian defectors in Ouagadougou was augmented by more soldiers from northern Côte d'Ivoire committed to Dramane Ouattara, who could not bear to serve under President Gbagbo.

During the night of September 18–19, 2002, about 650 Ivorian deserters attacked the cities of Bouaké, Korhogo and Abidjan. These soldiers were among those who had previously participated in the 1999 coup against Bédié that made Gueï president. Determined to see Dramane Ouattara in the presidency of Côte d'Ivoire, they launched a deadly attack against the defense forces of the country while Gbagbo was in Rome to meet Pope John Paul II. From Italy, Gbagbo politely declined French president Jacques Chirac's hasty offer for political asylum in Paris, shortened his Vatican visit, and returned to his country to organize a response to the attack. The rebels had estimated that their operation would last just a few days. They had hoped to seize power in a matter of minutes with shock and awe, force Gbagbo to exile, and put in place a new government. However, inexperience and disorganization plagued their plans and they found themselves under the firepower of the Ivorian Defense Force (FANCI), which, past the first moments of surprise, retook control of the situation and in a matter of hours were on a sweeping operation to eliminate the last pockets of the rebellion. It was then that the commander of the French army in Côte d'Ivoire requested a cease-fire so that he could evacuate the French citizens and a few American nationals living in Bouaké.

During the 48 hours allotted the French army, things changed dramatically and the rebel forces obtained reinforcement through the French authorities. Three Antonov-12 planes flew from Franceville (Gabon) to supply the rebels in armaments. Other planes and trucks brought in weapons and mercenaries from Liberia and Sierra Leone, and the rebel force, which was previously estimated at a little over 600 troops, grew to 2,500 mercenaries armed with Kalashnikovs and other weapons that had never been part of the Ivorian armory. The French army also supplied the mercenaries with sophisticated logistic and communication equipment that kept them aware of the movements of the Ivorian defense troops. Once the rebels were well-reinforced, the French army then retreated gradually, leaving the rebels in charge, with Eastern Europeans mercenaries as technical advisers. After the rebels were well positioned, Paris then activated the international pressure machinery through the United Nations to obtain a resolution entrusting France with a peacekeeping mission in Côte d'Ivoire.[34]

At the United Nations, the usual tergiversations, posturing and delaying were going on. In Côte d'Ivoire, the situation was worsening. The rebels were multiplying their fronts not just in the northern part of the country (Bouaké, Korhogo, Katiola, Odienné), but also in the western part (Man). They were recruiting more mercenaries from Samuel Doe's civil war troops as well as mercenaries from the RUF in Sierra Leone. In the occupied zones, the rebels' indiscriminate killing or raping or both of thousands of children, elderly people, and women led to a mass exodus toward Yamoussoukro (the political capital in central Côte d'Ivoire) and Abidjan (in the South). The rebels' claims were not clear at the beginning. They did not have an articulate leader or spokesperson capable of expressing clearly their grievances. After weeks of unclear and contradictory statements, they finally found a voice through Soro Kigbafori Guillaume, a former student association leader, who settled on accusations of ethnocentrism and xenophobia against the Gbagbo regime, the same charges that had been leveled against Bédié and Gueï. Ouattara's supporters, led by France, were principally accusing Gbagbo, as they did Gueï and Bédié before him, of hating foreigners in general and Muslim Northerners in particular.

The motive of tribalism and xenophobia which the rebels put forth as the main justification for their failed coup transformed into protracted rebellion was opportune, but it was not credible. The Ivorian long experience of peaceful multiethnic cohabitation belied the claim of ethnic and religious exclusion that the rebels brandished. The motivation must be something other, which the statement of marginalization was only dressing up. Furthermore, the rebels were too well-equipped and their logistical support too sophisticated for their war to be the mere expression of the despair of an ostracized ethnic group. Again, the Ivorian experience, up to the rebellion of 2002, was a successful story of multicultural coexistence. Indubitably, the rebels had big financial support by strong interest groups that had much to gain in destabilizing Côte d'Ivoire. What were these interests? In the early months of the rebellion, when information was still scarce, President Laurent Gbagbo had understandably argued that Burkina Faso's Blaise Compaoré was not innocent in the attempt at destabilizing Côte d'Ivoire:

> If I am told that a banker fled Côte d'Ivoire and is living in a villa in Ouagadougou, I can understand. But when I am told that a corporal fled the Ivorian army and that he lives in a villa in Ouagadougou, I understand a little less.... I do not know [who financed the rebellion], but it required a lot of money and at least the complicity of Burkina, if only a passive one.... This at least we know. It is obvious that [the Ivorian deserters] were housed and maintained by the Burkinabe government. This is obvious. We have known it for a long time. But was it [Compaoré] that financed them? This, I do not know.[35]

Indeed, the sophistication and sheer volume of the military and logistic equipment that was supplied to the rebel forces left no doubt about the financial power of their sponsors and on the lucrative yield that those who bet on the destabilizing operation could be expecting.

Speculating in wars could be very profitable, and one economic actor in Côte d'Ivoire, to whom the destabilization of the country had been so opportunely profitable, was Anthony Ward's multinational cocoa bean speculating company, Armajaro, the company for which Dramane Ouattara's 35-year-old stepson, Dominique Ouattara's son, Loïc Folloroux, was the director of the Africa division. In an article available on the Internet as the last paper written by Franco-Canadian journalist Guy André Kieffer before his mysterious disappearance, Armajaro was explicitly accused of disbursing $50 million towards the destabilization of Côte d'Ivoire in order to profit from a disturbance of the world's cocoa bean supply and its ensuing price hike on available stocks. It was clear from the standpoint of Armajoro's executives that Ouattara at the helm of Côte d'Ivoire would give them better control on affecting the price of cocoa beans on the world market. In fact, soon after Ouattara was "recognized by the international community" as the president of Côte d'Ivoire, from his hideout of the Golf Hotel he banned the export of cocoa. Ouattara's exhortation to coffee and cocoa exporters that they should suspend all exports in order to economically asphyxiate the Ivorian economy and force President Gbagbo to resign rang as suspicious in some milieus.

In effect, at the time, the Ivorian authorities, while remaining very prudent and refusing to specifically index anyone by name, had all the same denounced that a close relative of Ouattara's had bought and stocked a significant quantity of cocoa beans, waiting for a possible shortage of the precious beans on the international market to make a huge profit. Ouattara's decision—oh divine coincidence!—did in effect allow his stepson's company to make tremendous profits on 240,000 tons of cocoa (an impressive 20 percent of the Ivorian production and 15 percent of the world's stock) that his company had purchased ahead of the ban, in July 2010.[36] The fact that the political, economic, and social effects of the 2002 failed coup were still very much lingering in 2010, and had even worsened, might give the impression that no peace effort had been undertaken. Yet, only the contrary is true. Nevertheless, the testing quest for solutions to end the Ivorian rebellion would prove that, indeed, strong stakeholders were pulling the strings behind the visible part of the crisis, who had other objectives than the reunification of the country and peace for the Ivorian people.

Laurent Gbagbo Seeking Peace Desperately

Since the rebel attack on Côte d'Ivoire, the road to peace had been tortuous, uncertain, and often humiliating. Speaking to the Ivorian people on national TV, on February 7, 2003, President Gbagbo hardly hid his frustration with the interminable meandering in his quest for peace:

> Since September 19, 2002, as you know, Côte d'Ivoire was attacked unfairly. It was a coup. The coup failed. [The assailants] settled in Bouaké, where they created a cyst. And the failed coup turned into an armed rebellion. Since then, to obtain peace for my country, I have been going from country to country, from capital to capital: Accra, Dakar, Bamako, Lomé, and Paris recently.... The road to peace is difficult to find. It is not an easy path. It is not a six-lane wide asphalt road. It is a track that is sometimes rocky, sandy, and thorny.

On October 17, 2002, a month after the forces of the Northern Rebellion attacked the legally elected government of Laurent Gbagbo, the Economic Community of West African States (ECOWAS) managed to obtain a cease-fire agreement between the belligerents. On October 31, 2002, discussions between the Ivorian government and the rebels, which had started on October 24 under the auspices of Togolese president Gnassingbé Eyadéma (whom the ECOWAS had solicited to broker a peace deal between the Gbagbo government and the rebel forces), succeeded in securing a commitment by the MPCI, the newly created rebel party, to recognize the territorial integrity of Côte d'Ivoire, to respect the country's republican institutions, and to abstain from committing any violations of human rights. That agreement lasted only a few hours, with the government's insistence that the rebels disarm and the rebels' demand that President Gbagbo resign. Upon ECOWAS's demand that France play a greater role in finding a solution to the Ivorian civil war, French Foreign Affairs Minister Dominique de Villepin arrived in Côte d'Ivoire on January 3, 2003. After he consulted with the belligerent parties, the rebel leaders and all the leaders of the Ivorian parties agreed to meet a few days later in France for a solution-finding forum, the Linas-Marcoussis Roundtable.

From Linas-Marcoussis to Avenue Kléber

Of all the thorny paths traveled by the people of Côte d'Ivoire in their quest for lasting peace, Linas-Marcoussis was probably the most trying. Between January 15 and 23, 2003, on the invitation of French president Jacques Chirac, all the leading protagonists of Ivorian politics—the civil war main belligerents as well as the political party leaders—met at a rugby training camp in the Paris suburb of Marcoussis to hammer out a peace deal. Besides the fact that the choice of the place—the training site for an intense contact sport, in a European town more than 3,000 miles from Abidjan—was a deplorable metaphor for the objective of the meeting, the Roundtable of Linas-Marcoussis would also be the locus of the defilement of the Ivorian constitution and the site of humiliation of those among the Ivorian people who held dear their constitution.

Since the 2002 ceasefire and the establishment of a buffer zone between the rebels in the North and the loyalists in the South, the rebellion had branched out into several armed subgroups that were conveniently present at the Marcoussis Roundtable. In anticipation of future political portfolios distribution, as is often the case in the governments of "national unity" that post-crisis situations birth in Africa, but mostly to get the upper hand in any eventual peace negotiation, the rebellion had split into three political organizations, each insisting to be represented by an independent spokesperson. Hence, besides the representations of the traditional political parties, Henri Konan Bédié for the Parti Démocratique de Côte d'Ivoire (PDCI-RDA), Francis Vangah Wodié for the Parti Ivoirien des Travailleurs (PIT), Alassane Dramane Ouattara for the Rassemblement des Républicains (RDR), Theodore Mel Eg for the Union Démocratique et Citoyenne (UDCY), Paul Yao Akoto for the Union pour la Démocratie et pour la Paix en Côte d'Ivoire (UDPCI), Innocent Kobena Anaky for the Mouvement des Forces de l'Avenir (MFA), and Pascal Affi N'Guessan for the Front Populaire Ivoirien (FPI), there were also the offspring of the rebellion, the Mouvement pour la Justice et la Paix (MJP), the Mouvement Patriotique de Côte d'Ivoire (MPCI), and the Mouvement Populaire Ivoirien du Grand Ouest (MPIGO), respectively represented by Gaspard Déli, Guillaume Kigbafori Soro, and Félix Doh. Chairing the roundtable was a condescending French constitutional lawyer, Pierre Mazeaud, flanked by Senegalese judge Keba Mbaye and former Ivorian prime minister Seydou Diarra.

On January 23, 2003, the political organizations present in Marcoussis signed what came to be known as the Linas-Marcoussis Agreement. Among the propositions made by the Linas-Marcoussis Agreement was the constitution of a "government of national reconciliation," to be led by a prime minister of consensus picked at the roundtable. The government was to be composed of representatives nominated by the parties at the roundtable, a government whose ministerial portfolios would be equally distributed among the protagonists. It was agreed that upon taking office, aided by ECOWAS forces and the French forces, the government of national reconciliation would oversee the disarmament of all the belligerent forces and carry out the restructuring of the army. All recruits enlisted after September 19 were to be immediately demobilized, and the Government of National Reconciliation was to ensure the reintegration of soldiers from all backgrounds through the program of Disarmament, Demobilization, Repatriation, Resettlement, and Reintegration (DDRRR). Furthermore, the Government of National Reconciliation was to take the necessary steps for the release of, and amnesty for, all military prisoners detained for violation of state security and to extend this measure to soldiers living in exile. The amnesty law would, under no circumstances, exonerate people who had committed serious economic crimes and serious violations of human rights and international humanitarian law. The identification process was also to be suspended and, what was most important, Article 35 of the Ivorian constitution related to the double condition of eligibility to the presidency—that both parents of the candidate to the presidency be of Ivorian origin—was to be modified so that only one of the parents would be required to be of Ivorian origin. Thus, the new language was to read as follows: "The President of the Republic is elected for five years by direct universal suffrage. He can be re-elected only once. The candidate must enjoy his civil and political rights and be at least thirty-five years old. He must have exclusive Ivorian nationality. His father or mother must be of Ivorian origin."

Soon after the parties at the Marcoussis Roundtable signed the Marcoussis Agreement, held hands, and sang "L'Abidjanaise," the national anthem of Côte d'Ivoire, another conference was being held, that one, with the appearance of a mini summit, at the Center for International Conferences, at Avenue Kléber in the 16th arrondissement of Paris, from 25 to 26 January. It involved President Gbagbo, President Bédié, President Chirac, President Bongo of Gabon, United Nations Secretary-General Kofi Annan, former prime minister Dramane Ouattara, and rebel chief Guillaume Soro. That meeting was preceded a day earlier by a discussion between the main heads of delegation present at Marcoussis at the Quai d'Orsay, under the auspices of French Foreign Affairs Minister Dominique de Villepin. The January 24 conclave was to endorse the Marcoussis Agreement and decide on the name of a prime minister of consensus. As was to be expected, the protagonists could not agree on a single name, each insisting that its nominee was the best. Bédié proposed Kablan Duncan, who had been his prime minister between 1993 and 1999. Dramane Ouattara suggested the number two of his party, history professor Henriette Dagri Diabaté and the wife of Lamine Diabaté, the staunch supporter of the Northern Charter. Gbagbo proposed Essy Amara, the interim president of the African Union Commission, arguing that Essy Amara had the potential of reunifying the various tendencies in the country because he had served as Foreign Affairs Minister in the governments of presidents Houphouët and Bédié, he was a Muslim, and his wife was a Christian. Without explicitly putting his own name forward, Guillaume Soro argued that the post of prime minister should fall to his party, the MPCI, because about 60 percent of the country was occupied by his rebels. Every nomination seemed to generate some criticism, except that of Professor Dagri Diabaté, in whom no one seemed to have found any fault, which de Villepin understood as a consensus nomination.

The next day, however, at the Kléber Conference, Chirac announced that Gbagbo had proposed another name, that of Seydou Elimane Diarra, who was present during the Marcoussis Roundtable as an observer. Diarra had also been General Gueï's prime minister. Soro would accept Gbagbo's choice on the condition that the crucial cabinet posts of defense and interior should be awarded to his party. Bédié protested. Chirac scolded Bédié: "They are the ones who have the weapons. Not you."[37] Prime Minister-elect Seydou Elimane Diarra was to draft a final agreement to be signed the next morning by all the participants at the Kléber Conference. He never did. For reasons that remain mysterious, nothing was signed at Kléber. Once at home, President Gbagbo would play on this legal blunder.

In Côte d'Ivoire, the Marcoussis Agreement was met with massive public protests. In some quarters of Abidjan, people even rioted against French interests. France was perceived as a conspirator that, in spite of existing defense agreements with the state of Côte d'Ivoire, had sided with the rebels who attacked the republican institutions of the country. Many Ivorians decried the Marcoussis Agreement as an unfair assault on the constitution of Côte d'Ivoire. For critics of the Linas-Marcoussis Agreement, the Marcoussis Roundtable, which was prefaced with declarations of respect for the constitution, actually ended up trampling the constitution by legitimizing a rebellion against a constitutionally elected government. Those who swore by the Ivorian constitution, the legalists, would not accept any agreement that stripped the president of his executive prerogatives guaranteed in Article 41 of the Ivorian constitution, such as his role as Supreme

Leader of the armed forces and his privilege to appoint a prime minister of his choosing. The army and police chiefs wrote a letter to President Gbagbo expressing their refusal to serve under any defense or interior minister coming from the ranks of the rebellion and protested the fact that the chapter of the Marcoussis Agreement concerning disarmament recommended that the regular army of Côte d'Ivoire, too, should be disarmed. Many criticized the proposed ministerial portfolio distribution as a recipe for stultification. The rebellion had split into three organizations and would therefore hold majority ministries in the new government, wielding tremendous power and with its natural ally, Dramane Ouattara's RDR, would constitute a coalition of saboteurs of the political and social missions of the government.

The Linas-Marcoussis Agreement had wanted to rewrite the Ivorian constitution to satisfy Ouattara as well as those who, by their own admission, had attacked the republican institutions of Côte d'Ivoire to deliver him the presidency. Furthermore, a sizeable segment of the Ivorian population was distrustful of the French army for its proven open support of the rebels and were not comfortable having French military advisers supervise the disarmament and demobilization process and the restructuring of the national army. Marcoussis, they argued, fulfilled through juridical shortcuts what the Kalashnikovs of the rebels had failed to achieve. The Ivorian government, which was not a signatory of the Marcoussis Agreement, immediately declared that it was not bound to it, and on National TV, professor of public law and Interior Minister Yao N'dré declared the Marcoussis Agreement "null and void."

On the other hand, critics such as French law professor Jean Du Bois De Gaudusson offered to those who clung to the argument of the inviolability of the constitution that it is not always that strict application of the law offers solutions to societal issues. Therefore, it is essential sometimes, as it was in the context of the Ivorian crisis, that political solutions be found, which would then be given juridical force by the law. Thus, he wrote, the modification of Article 35 at the Marcoussis Roundtable was to be viewed from the perspective of a political solution waiting to be conferred juridical force: "Under these conditions, it is now to the law and to the jurists to recognize ... that they have come to a dead-end, that not every problem can be solved by the pure logic and on the sole field of the law ... and that the time of legal agreement with political contents has returned."[38]

Gbagbo was a staunch defender of the Ivorian constitution, a position that he had held from the very first days of his political struggle. Now he was confronted with the task of reconciling a frustrated population with a solution it found intolerable because it was anticonstitutional. Secluded in the Presidential Palace, Gbagbo observed the population's venting for days, to the chagrin of the international community. On February 7, 2003, after two weeks of intense manifestations, Gbagbo finally decided to speak to the Ivorian people. In his communication broadcast on national television, he addressed the main contentious issues, such as the violation of the Ivorian constitution, the disarmament of the Ivorian defense forces, the appointment of rebels at key ministerial posts, and the ambiguous role played by France since the inception of the civil war, and precisely at the Marcoussis Roundtable and at the Kléber Conference. Gbagbo, in his posture of Pan-Africanist, deplored the fact that a solution could not be found in Africa and that resolution of the Ivorian crisis had to be outsourced to France: "We went to Paris because we have not found a solution in Africa. This is our drama." Despite contracting out to France the search for a solution to the Ivorian crisis, it did not seem to have helped much. In fact, Gbagbo admitted, Ivorians had good reasons to be suspicious. There was an attempt to substitute the Marcoussis Agreement for the Ivorian constitution, an endeavor to damage the republican institutions and to transform the system of government of Côte d'Ivoire from a presidential system to a parliamentary one, a machination which he vowed he would never allow:

> The most salient aspects of the Marcoussis Agreement are the parts of the text that are in contradiction with the Constitution of Côte d'Ivoire. In the text of Marcoussis, the Prime Minister is irremovable until 2005. This is contrary to the Constitution which says that the President appoints the Prime Minister and terminates his duties. [The Marcoussis Agreement] tried to convert our presidential system into a parliamentary system. But we are not in a parliamentary system; we are in a presidential system. The text of Marcoussis will not be considered an extension of the Constitution (*une constitution plus*). Each time there is a contradiction between the text of Marcoussis and the Constitution, I will apply the Constitution.

Thus, Gbagbo reassured everyone, the army, the police, and the gendarmerie would not be disarmed. Seizing on the absence of a signed document binding him to the gentlemen's agreement of the Kléber Conference, as well as the absence of any official government representative at Marcoussis, Gbagbo declared that Marcoussis was a meeting of private entities that did in no way involve the government. He would confirm Seydou Diarra as his prime minister, but he would neither surrender him his executive powers nor accept any ministerial portfolio distribution agreed upon in Marcoussis as a fait accompli: "Let us not say that such and such ministry belongs to such and such party. Ministries are assigned when the president of the Republic by the powers you gave him in electing him, powers guaranteed by the Constitution, signs a decree appointing the government of the Republic. I have appointed no government." Nevertheless, Gbagbo continued, the Marcoussis Agreement was a good beginning. Though it was flawed, it was a well-intentioned document from which a quest for lasting peace could start, a medicine to try with hope: "That said, the Marcoussis text was written in the spirit of finding a peaceful solution to our current crisis...

Therefore, I invite you, dear compatriots, to accept the spirit of the Marcoussis agreements and therefore the Marcoussis Agreement as a basis.... So let us try this drug. If he heals us so much better. But if he does not heal us, we will try another medication."

While the Ivorian Defense Forces seemed to have softened their rhetoric and were willing to accept the rebels in the government as long as the rebels were not given the defense and interior portfolios, for the young Ivorian patriots led by the charismatic Blé Goudé it was out of the question that the rebels should have any part in the government. As for the rebels in Bouaké and Man, they were threatening to resume war if Seydou Diarra's proposed government was not conformed to what was agreed upon in France. Colonel Michel Gueu averred, "If there is no hope, nothing will prevent us from obtaining by means of our weapons what Gbagbo promised us in Paris." The reality was that Gbagbo's government had signed nothing and made no promise in Paris. They were not present at Marcoussis, and at Kléber Avenue in Paris no document was ever signed. Chirac and de Villepin knew that; yet in Paris the Chirac government accused Gbagbo of dishonesty, painting him as a man who would not hesitate to renege on his own signature—an image that the French media, known to always espouse the editorial line of its government, abundantly distilled in the news. In defense of Gbagbo, Boga Sivori of Ivorian daily *Notre Voie*, a paper close to the FPI, noted on February 5, 2002, that it was instead Chirac and Villepin who were being deceitful for wanting to attribute to Gbagbo a contract he never signed:

> French Foreign Minister Dominique de Villepin and his band of racketeers have been trying in vain to make people believe that President Gbagbo refuses to implement agreements that he has signed in Paris.... President Laurent Gbagbo and his government were not invited to Linas-Marcoussis. They are therefore not part of the agreements that came out of this meeting. The second phase of the Summit took place from January 25 to 26 at the Avenue Kléber.... At this meeting in which President Laurent Gbagbo took part, no agreement has been signed between the head of state of Cote d'Ivoire and other heads of state.... At most, President Laurent Gbagbo, being shamelessly pressured by Chirac, issued a decree appointing a prime minister in the person of Mr. Seydou Diarra; which is absolutely within his powers.

On February 24, after nearly one full month spent in France, Seydou Diarra arrived in Côte d'Ivoire with a list of his prospective post–Marcoussis government appointees in his pocket. A group of students sat on the tarmac of the Félix Houphouet-Boigny Airport to prevent his plane from landing. For them he was "the Prime Minister of coups d'état." Earlier, he had met with Soro Guillaume in Paris to discuss the rebels' role in the government and had promised, among other cabinet posts, the sensible Ministries of Defense, Interior, and Justice, respectively, to Gueu Michel (Rebellion), Louis Dacoury Tabley (Rebellion), and Henriette Dagri Diabaté (RDR). Laurent Gbagbo—true to his conviction that as the elected president of the Republic and in accordance with the prerogatives afforded him by the constitution he had the last word on the composition of the government—rejected Prime Minister Diarra's first list, not without a note of sarcasm: "His mission is to conduct consultations to quickly form a new government. He showed me his work. I looked at his handwriting, illegible, and I asked him to continue to talk to all parties. This is the price of peace. He must take the time to talk and convince. I'm here to give him directions."

The rebels threatened to march on Abidjan if anything less than what was promised them in Paris was offered them. Insisting that he made no promises, Gbagbo dared them. France pretended to be holding them back. Gbagbo urged Seydou Diarra to send him an acceptable list. Diarra threatened to resign if he kept being undermined by all sides. Finally, after much posturing on each side, the prime minister nominated in Paris at Avenue Kléber, in the 16th arrondissement on February 25, 2003, and appointed by decree at the Ivorian embassy in Paris on February 26, had his government formed in Accra, Ghana, on March 8 and communicated to the people in Yamoussoukro, Côte d'Ivoire, on March 13, 2003. Composed of 23 cabinet members, Seydou Diarra's government of National Reconciliation had still no representation in the contended ministries of Defense and Interior. The Ministry of Economy and Finances went to Bohoun Bouabré, father of the secured budget (FPI), and the Ministry of Foreign Affairs went to Bamba Mamadou (PDCI). There were ten ministers for the FPI, seven for the PDCI, seven for the RDR, seven for the MPCI (the major rebel party), two for the UDPCI, two for the PIT, one for the UDCY, one for the MFA, and one for the MJP and the MPIGO (two minor rebel parties). Thus, Dramane Ouattara, for whom the rebels took up arms, ended up with a majority of posts (15) in the Government of National Reconciliation. Nevertheless, Ouattara's RDR and the three rebel parties made no appearance at the first council of ministers of Diarra's government presided over by President Gbagbo on March 13 in Yamoussoukro. For them, it would have been too much of an honor done to Gbagbo. Ouattara had one more jab to throw, one more handful of mud to throw Gbagbo's way, before allowing his party's executives to take their seats in the government. The world must remember that Gbagbo was a killer and he himself an eternal victim. "As you know many executives of the RDR, including those appointed as members of this government of national reconciliation, are presently outside the country in view of the many executions and killings of which our activists were victims in the recent months," Ouatarra declared as a justification for boycotting the first council of ministers. This tergiversation was the first of many more to come that would cripple the peace effort.

The Ouagadougou Peace Agreement (OPA)

After all efforts at resolving the Ivorian crisis and reunifying Côte d'Ivoire had failed, Laurent Gbagbo, cognizant that one of the sticking points was Burkinabe President Blaise Compaoré, had decided that perhaps Compaoré should be entrusted with the task of resolving the dispute between his government and the rebel forces, that perhaps then the African sponsor of the Ivorian rebellion should be put in a situation such that he would put his cards on the table and clearly state the necessary conditions for disentangling the conflict and allowing the reunification of Côte d'Ivoire. So, on January 23, 2007, President Gbagbo solicited President Compaoré in the latter's role as chairman of the Economic Community of West African States to negotiate a peace agreement between his government and the rebel forces. Compaoré would have to be either straightforward with the protagonists, put forth the rebels' true grievances, some of which were his, too, broker a definitive peace deal, and be remembered as a successful chairman of the West African states organization or he would have to continue to be two-faced, publicly show his bias, and be remembered as a failed ECOWAS chairman. Gbagbo was rather hoping for the former alternative. After consulting the different parties involved in the conflict, Compaoré accepted the mission. From February 3 to March 5, 2007, two delegations, one conducted by Mr. Désiré Tagro, Special Adviser to President Gbagbo, and the other conducted by Mr. André Dacoury-Tabley, Deputy Secretary-General of the Forces Nouvelles, met in the Burkinabe capital of Ouagadougou under the aegis of Compaoré. Under what came to be known as the Ouagadougou Political Agreement (OPA), the parties decided to work on achieving several goals.

The first one was the identification of the general population through public hearings, with an eye towards outfitting them with birth certificates and identification cards. One major grievance that the Burkinabe president had explicitly expressed since the mid–1990s, especially at the time when Ouattara's nationality became an issue in Ivorian politics, was that many people born in Côte d'Ivoire of Burkinabe parents had neither birth certificates nor identification papers because they were never declared by their illiterate parents; these people were now being harassed or refused land ownership in Côte d'Ivoire with the alleged rise of xenophobia since Ouattara had decided to run for the Ivorian presidency. In fact, one of the slogans being chanted by the supporters of the rebellion was "we want our identification papers," as the leaders of the rebellion had stated that the goal of their fight was to obtain identification papers for all the supposedly disenfranchised northerners. Soro Guillaume had once proposed this: "Give us our identity cards and disarmament will be as easy as child's play." Likewise, Chérif Ousmane, another leader of the rebellion, insisted, "We will lay down our arms when our identity problem is solved, not before. This is not negotiable. We want identity papers in exchange for our weapons. Any other proposal is not negotiable."[39] The identification process was to satisfy these grievances. The second goal of the OPA was the commitment by the belligerent parties to quickly organize open, democratic, and transparent presidential elections, which essentially made overtures to all candidates, including, and especially, Dramane Ouattara. The third goal of the OPA concerned the merging of the loyalist army, the Forces Armées Nationales de Côte d'Ivoire (FANCI) and the Forces Armées des Forces Nouvelles (FAFN) in order to arrive at an army that would reflect unity and national cohesion. Among the objections that the rebel forces had raised against the previous army was the infamous discrimination against ethnic Northerners and Muslims, which had been the rehashed justification for the coups against Bédié, Gueï, and now Gbagbo. That sentiment had been expressed by Chérif Ousmane in an interview: "In the army of Côte d'Ivoire, people were judged by their ethnic origin or religious affiliation. Because my name is Chérif Ousmane, people called me a pro–Alassane, a man I knew only through TV, like everyone else."[40] The task of unifying the two belligerent armies was entrusted to a Centre de Commandement intégré (CCI) (Integrated Command Center) led by the army Chiefs of Staff from the two forces (General Philippe Mangou for the FANCI and General Soumaïla Bakayoko for the FAFN). Among other responsibilities, the CCI would also administer a program of disarmament of the belligerent forces, their demobilization and their reintegration into public life, secure the public hearing program, secure the elections, and protect the free circulation of people and goods throughout the country. The fourth goal of the Ouagadougou Peace Agreement was the restoration of the authority of the state, which was to happen through the redeployment of public administration and public services in the country and following the suppression of the buffer zone separating the loyalist south and the rebel north. It was agreed that a police force of 600 people to be trained by the United Nations would ensure the security of the prefectural and technical services deployed by the government. None of these goals could be said to have been reached. The rebels and the international community's hidden agenda was to remove Gbagbo from power, and the various agreements passed with the government of Abidjan were nothing but delaying tactics. Although the conditions propitious to fair and open elections were not in place and 60 percent of the country was still occupied by armed rebel forces, the international community insisted that a presidential election should be held as a means to end the gridlock.

CHAPTER 6

Côte d'Ivoire: The International Community Hiding No More

After many delays due to a number of logistical glitches and partisan posturing by all sides, the presidential election set for 2008, then 2009, finally took place in 2010. The Marcoussis Agreements had proposed that Article 35 of the Ivorian constitution be modified to allow Ouattara to run for the presidential elections. President Gbagbo, whose government was not a signatory of the Marcoussis Agreements, continued to argue that he would not caution a trampling of the Ivorian constitution. Gbagbo's resolve was seen by many as the sticking point in the negotiations to find a solution to the Ivorian crisis. To help the negotiation advance without making Gbagbo lose face before the patriots who had thus far applauded his determination to safeguard the constitution, President Thabo Mbeki of South Africa urged his Ivorian counterpart to avail himself of Article 48 of the Ivorian constitution to exceptionally, and only for the 2010 elections, allow Ouattara to be a candidate. In effect, Article 48 allowed the president of the Republic, when the institutions of the Republic, the independence of the nation, the integrity of its territory or the fulfillment of its international commitments were under a serious and immediate threat, and the regular functioning of the constitutional public authorities is interrupted, to take exceptional measures required by the circumstances and inform the people, after consultation with the president of the National Assembly and the Constitutional Council. With Gbagbo's authorization through Article 48 of the constitution, Ouattara was able to run an open campaign on the entire Ivorian territory, without restriction.

No Adequate Conditions for Democratic Elections

Since the 2002 rebellion against his government, Gbagbo had eluded all the traps set on his path by the international community. He had not succeeded, however, in having the rebels disarm before the election as was agreed upon in

127

the Ouagadougou Peace Agreement. And that would be his biggest mistake. He had put too much faith in an international community set on getting him out of power and which had never intended to disarm the rebels. In an article titled "What the World Got Wrong in Côte d'Ivoire," published in *Foreign Policy* magazine, President Thabo Mbeki of South Africa, who from 2004 to 2006 had been designated by the African Union as a peace broker in the Ivorian conflict, deplored the United Nations' and the international community's insincerity and incompetence in pushing for the October 31 election in Côte d'Ivoire when they knew very well that adequate conditions were not set for it to take place satisfactorily, and that the rebels' refusal to disarm before the elections would irremediably lead to disaster:

> Everybody concerned should have probed very seriously the critical question: Would the 2010 elections create the conditions that would establish the basis for the best possible future for the Ivorian people? This was not done. Rather, the international community insisted that what Côte d'Ivoire required to end its crisis was to hold democratic elections, even though the conditions did not exist to conduct such elections. Though they knew that this proposition was fundamentally wrong, the Ivorians could not withstand the international pressure to hold the elections. However, the objective reality is that the Ivorian presidential elections should not have been held when they were held. It was perfectly foreseeable that they would further entrench the very conflict it was suggested they would end.[1]

In effect, in the rebel-held areas, the armed rebels would not allow Gbagbo's campaigners to promote their candidate. Laurent Gbagbo's campaign took place mainly in the West, Southwest and Abidjan region, avoiding the rebel-held north. Ouattara concentrated much of his campaign in the North and in Gbagbo's strongholds, and Bédié campaigned in the central and southern parts of the country, staying away from the rebel-held zones. In other words, during the campaign for the October 2010 presidential first run, the north remained Ouattara's exclusive zone, where none of his opponents was allowed to campaign and no support for his adversaries was to be publicly demonstrated.

Consequently, the October 31 election was fraught with blatant irregularities. Despite documented massive fraud, ballot stuffing, voter intimidation and violence in the rebels' strongholds, the official ballot counts gave Laurent Gbagbo 38.04 percent and Ouattara and Bédié, respectively, 32.07 percent and 25.24 percent. In the international community, where it had been hoped the irregularities would help Ouattara defeat Gbagbo in the first round, the strong support that Gbagbo garnered, though not enough to spare him a runoff, was alarming. It was clear indication that given a fair campaign in the rebel-held regions and in the absence of voter intimidation in the North, Gbagbo could largely win reelection. The plan, henceforth, for Ouattara and his international community was to walk resolutely and without qualms into fraud and deceit.

According to the report of the African Union Observer Mission on the Presidential Election in Côte d'Ivoire, in the rebel stronghold, the election runoff of November 28, 2010, was a grand display of raids, arsons, rapes, beatings, arbitrary imprisonments, murders, fraud, and exercises in mathematical impossibilities. The report presented by Head of Mission Joseph Kokou Koffigoh states, among other irregularities, that in the town of Korhogo, the day before the election, Laurent Gbagbo's representatives were forbidden by the rebel forces to enter the city, and the representatives of Gbagbo that were already in the town were forbidden to enter the polling stations and were robbed of their properties and identity documents. The report further states:

> [It] is a fact that in the entire district of Korhogo, serious cases of murders, death threats, intimidation, confinements, and physical assaults were perpetrated against [Gbagbo's] activists and representatives by New Forces [rebels] and the RDR activists. For example, one of [Gbagbo's] supervisors, Mrs. Coulibaly Sita, was savagely beaten then illegally detained before being murdered after denouncing irregularities she recorded during the polling process in her area of duty.

The report went on to document more cases of beatings and acts of arsons throughout the rebel-held northern areas. In many cases, Gbagbo's representatives, who had been detained during the polling process and were unable to observe the election process, were forced under threat of death by RDR activists and New Forces to sign the minutes of the fabricated vote tallies. As reported by Gbagbo's Bouaké District Campaign Director N'Goran Kouassi Pierre,

> On November 28, 2010, during the ballot process, the representatives of the LMP [Gbagbo's coalition party] candidate, as well as their activists and sympathizers, were subjected to death threats, physical acts of violence, intimidation and other criminal acts from elements of the New Forces. As an example, we can consider the eviction of the representatives of the LMP candidate who were turned away one after the other from 147 polling stations located in this town…. In all polling stations, the minutes of the closing of the polls were signed either in the absence of the representatives of the LMP or by themselves under arms constraint.[2]

The fraud and ballot stuffing in the North were so flagrant that on some minutes the total vote counts largely exceeded the entire population of the areas and in many other areas candidate Gbagbo had not a single vote, not even the votes of his own representatives. These were violations so flagrant that in its own communiqué, the Economic Community of West African States (ECOWAS) recognized that serious irregularities prevented citizens from freely expressing their votes:

> ECOWAS is concerned with the renewal of tension which, since the second round of the presidential election on 28 November 2010 seemed to have marred the serene atmosphere at the conclusion of the electoral process. Consequently, ECOWAS

recalls the incidents that disrupted or prevented citizens from expressing their voting rights, particularly in some areas in the north of the country, which are to be vehemently condemned and culprits involved in such acts sanctioned in accordance with the laws of the land.[3]

The ballots in the northern areas of Côte d'Ivoire were utterly rigged and absolutely unreliable. It would have been impossible to reorganize the elections in the North, with heavily armed rebels that were unwilling to lay down their weapons to allow the civilian administration full control of the electoral process. In fact, even some African Union elections observers had been attacked and detained and were released only after intervention by the United Nations.

Bicephalism at the Head of the State

A few weeks after they had denounced the undemocratic nature of the November 2010 Ivorian elections, the African regional organizations changed their tunes and were clamoring, along with a biased international community led by France, the United Nations and the United States, that the Ivorian presidential election took place in optimum conditions and that to consider Gbagbo's demands to review it would set "a grave precedent" for democracy. On December 2, 2010, Mr. Youssouf Bakayoko, the president of the electoral commission, speaking from the Golf Hotel, the headquarters of Ouattara's campaign, flanked by the American Ambassador to Côte d'Ivoire and in the conspicuous absence of all the other members of the commission, declared Ouattara the winner by 54 percent against 46 percent for Gbagbo. On December 3, 2010, the Ivorian highest authority for its part took its responsibilities.

In effect, after invalidating the results of 7 regions of massive fraud (Bouaké, Korhogo, Ferkessédougou, Katiola, Boundiali, Dabakala, and Séguéla), the Constitutional Council proclaimed Laurent Gbagbo the winner of the November 21, 2010, presidential election with 51 percent against 49 percent for Ouattara. On December 4, 2010, Gbagbo and Ouattara were inaugurated presidents separately at a few hours' interval, the former by the Constitutional Council, the latter by the international community. The first was tagged the "President of the Ivorian people," and the second the "President recognized by the International Community." On November 5, 2010, Gbagbo chose economics professor Gilbert Marie Aké N'gbo to be his prime minister. The same day, Ouattara chose rebel chief Guillaume Soro as his prime minister. In a sudden volte-face, the African Union, whose own election observers had recognized that the votes in the North were unreliable, sided with the United Nations, France, and the United States, declared Dramane Ouattara the winner of the election, and dug in for a war against President Laurent Gbagbo. As the tension mounted against him and the international community prepared for war, Gbagbo remained inflexible on his claim that only a vote recount could convince him that he had lost the election.

As far as the international community was concerned, a vote recount was out of the question. It was either war or Gbagbo's resignation. With two governments claiming legitimacy, one at the Presidential Palace and the other one at the Golf Hotel, Côte d'Ivoire was henceforth on the road to a long-drawn-out constitutional gridlock. Nevertheless, from that moment onwards there began an arm wrestling between, on one side, incumbent President Laurent Gbagbo, who believed that he was robbed of his victory, and, on the other side, France, the United Sates, and the United Nations, which were determined to "put the proper leader back in place" by all means necessary. These three entities, by the voice of Choi, had rejected the Constitutional Council's decision and certified Bakayoko's results. From then on, the Ban Ki-Moon administration; Susan Rice; American Ambassador to Côte d'Ivoire Philip Carter III; French Ambassador to Côte d'Ivoire Jean-Marc Simon; and French Ambassador to the United Nations Gerard Arnaud had made among their highest priorities the departure of Gbagbo and the forced enthronization of Ouattara. From then on, the troika (France, the UN, and the U.S.), either directly or indirectly, through the United Nations Security Council, through the African regional organizations, and through the world financial institutions, initiated a number of measures intended to isolate Gbagbo by strangling his administration, diplomatically, financially, socially, militarily, and constitutionally.

The African leaders' disingenuousness was chilling. As they sided with France, the United Nations, and the United States against their own professed principles of independent thinking and political decision-making, the African regional organizations had proven once more that, contrary to what they openly propounded, they were in reality a mere sound box for a troika that had already decided that Dramane Ouattara would be "the President-Recognized-by-the-International-Community" no matter what the consequences could be for the Ivorian people—and even for the wider world the United Nations, France, and the United States had been lecturing about "democracy." Even more chilling than the way the African leaders had outsourced their decision-making abilities was the way the United Nations, France and the United States so unashamedly trampled their own professed democratic principles in order to carry out their political heist in Côte d'Ivoire.

The Constitutional War

On March 9, 2012, in an interview with *Morning Joe*'s Joe Scarborough, either by mere incompetence or in a crisis of uncontrolled debit of candor, Susan

Rice raised some serious questions on the 2010 Ivorian presidential election and validated President Gbagbo's point that a recount was in order to settle the question of which candidate really won the election. In any case, Rice had confessed that a vote recounting was not warranted because the president that the people had really elected in Côte d'Ivoire was a *different* president from the one that the United Nations wanted; and therefore, the United Nations had to intervene *militarily* to put the *proper* man in place:

> The Russians will tell you that they are not in agreement with externally orchestrated or externally prompted regime change. They fear that this is a pattern that they have seen in different places and they go as far back as Côte d'Ivoire; which is a different circumstance, because *the people* [of Côte d'Ivoire] had *elected* [Gbagbo] a *different leader* and the UN *stepped in* and said that the election had been manipulated, and *the proper leader* had to be put back in place and [the UN and France] accomplished that through protection and *military force*.[4]

In fact, Rice was admitting that in Côte d'Ivoire the international community had succeeded in a constitutional coup d'état. A leader was elected by the people who was not the leader the international community wanted; so the UN had to overstep its authority of neutral broker and intervene militarily to put the proper leader in place. Nowhere in the world had such a blatant trampling of a sovereign country's constitution by outside forces taken place before. This constitutional war on Côte d'Ivoire was a première. The conspiracy was overwhelming. Its perpetrators were powerful and had a crushing power they were determined to use to reach out for their goal. The "proper leader" was not the preferred leader for the United Nations alone. He was the common "proper leader" for the United Nations, France/EU, and the United States. And the troika's strategy to put the "proper leader" in place in Côte d'Ivoire had corrupted all democratic rules known to civilized societies.

On Wednesday, December 1, 2000, Mr. Youssouf Bakayoko, president of the Ivorian Independent Electoral Commission, appeared on channel 1 of national television and declared that the provisional results of the presidential elections would be proclaimed on time to meet the constitutional deadline of midnight. So, the Ivorians glued themselves to their TV sets, waiting to know whom they had elected as their president. Around 1:00 a.m. however, some African foreign diplomats in Côte d'Ivoire were anonymously alerted that Mr. Bakayoko was meeting in the IEC office with the American Ambassador to Côte d'Ivoire, Philip Carter III. So, the African diplomats rushed to the IEC office to enquire about the nonconforming meeting taking place an hour after the constitutional deadline. And indeed, they did find Bakayoko and Carter in the office. To their inquiry about the purpose of the meeting, Bakayoko explained:

We have been able to consolidate the results from about 15 regions. No consensus has been reached yet concerning the remaining 4 regions. At 9:00 p.m. yesterday, we had agreed to make a declaration to the press in the presence of all the commissioners of the IEC … [and] *incumbent Laurent Gbagbo is winning in the regions whose results have been consolidated.*

According to the African diplomats, a very perturbed Carter III "awoke Ouattara at the Golf Hotel at 2:00 a.m. and asked him how he could be in bed at such a crucial time." The puzzled diplomats left Bakayoko, who had promised to make a televised declaration on national television at 9:00 a.m. Bakayoko did make his declaration. It was not on national TV but in front of the cameras of French television France 24. It was not from the headquarters of the IEC but from the campaign headquarters of Dramane Ouattara, at the Golf Hotel. Bakayoko was not with the other commissioners but all alone. It was not the result he had announced to the African diplomats and which annoyed Ambassador Carter III but a different result, which declared Dramane Ouattara the winner of the Ivorian election. The imposture was exaggeratedly flagrant. This was a constitutional coup d'état against President Gbagbo, and the French and American ambassadors were its principal engineers. Laurent Gbagbo would not have it:

> The French and the American ambassadors created the crisis. They fetched Youssouf Bakayoko, the President of the Independent Electoral Commission, and drove him to the Golf Hotel, which was the Headquarter of my opponent. And over there, while he was outside the constitutional deadline and all alone, which is serious, Bakayoko announced that my opponent was elected. And from then on, the French and the Americans said that it was Ouattara who was elected. This is what we call a conspiracy.[5]

At a January 7, 2011, public relations breakfast at which he was questioned by journalists on the ambiguous role he played on the infamous day of result publication, U.S. Ambassador Phillip Carter III tried to offer a fairy tale explanation about how he ended up with IEC president Youssouf Bakayoko at the headquarters of Dramane Ouattara, in front of French TV France 24 to announce the fabricated results that elected Dramane Ouattara. A toddler caught with his hand in the cookie jar could have offered a better defense. That day, a United States ambassador displayed a less-than-bright performance:

JOURNALIST: Why did you escort the President of the Independent Electoral Commission to the Golf Hotel?

CARTER III: This accusation is completely false. I was visiting Mr. Ouattara…. I was surprised to see that Mr. Bakayoko was at the Golf Hotel. It was a surprise to me. I took advantage of the situation to ask Mr. Bakayoko what he was doing there. He told me that he was having difficulty making his declaration

... I then asked [Bakayoko] what he was going to do. I proposed to Mr. Choi (the UN Representative) that the announcement be made at the UN headquarter. He refused for fear that it should affect the impartiality of the United Nations. Mr. Bakayoko made his announcement, but I have nothing to do with it.

SKEPTICAL JOURNALIST CHARGED ON: You are surprised to see Mr. Bakayoko at the Golf Hotel; you propose that the results be announced at the Hotel Sebroko (the UN's headquarter); Mr. Choi refuses. How do you feel now that the results have been announced from the campaign HQ of an adversary?

CARTER III: This is good question, but frankly, I don't know why he [Bakayoko] did that. He recently explained himself in the press. He found a site at the Golf Hotel. I don't know why. You have to ask this question to Mr. Bakayoko himself.

JOURNALIST: Don't you think that Mr. Gbagbo has legal ground to contest the fact that Mr. Bakayoko announced the results at the headquarter of Mr. Ouattara?

CARTER III: It's a question of political opinion. For me, the issue about the Independent Electoral Commission and the Constitutional Council is a little outdated. You have institutional problems that ought to be addressed, because they create much confusion here. With a certification of the United Nations, the result of this election is obvious ... [and] you have an institutional crisis, but this is an Ivorian question. The smooth running of the election has been certified by the United Nations. This is what matters most to us.

Indeed, Dramane Ouattara was proclaimed the winner of the presidential election, by Youssouf Bakayoko, in the absence of the other commissioners of the IEC, from the campaign headquarters of Dramane Ouattara, flanked by U.S. Ambassador Carter III, French Ambassador Jean-Marc Simon, and UN Representative Choi Young-Jin, outside of the constitutional deadline and in front of a foreign TV camera—and that was all that mattered as far as the troika was concerned. For Gbagbo, it was not the end of the matter. He was the legally elected president of Côte d'Ivoire, unless a vote recount supervised by impartial international observers decided otherwise.

The Financial and Economic War

The EU/France-UN-U.S. troika had decided that the matter of the election was settled and that Gbagbo should be stripped of his financial and economic anchorage, and that economic and financial power should be transferred to Dramane Ouattara so as to precipitate Gbagbo's surrender. Although the troika was actually the entity pulling the strings, Gbagbo's financial isolation was to be first staged from within Africa, in order to give it a semblance of organic legitimacy. Central Bank of West African States (BCEAO) Governor Philippe Dacoury-Tabley had resisted all pressures and intimidations to get him to pledge allegiance to Ouattara; for Dacoury-Tabley, the Central Bank's mission was essentially financial, and so it should remain. The institution should not be used as political pressure tool. Consequently Dacoury-Tabley continued to honor Gbagbo's signature at the West African Central Bank, allowing the Gbagbo government to pay retiree pensions and civil servant salaries and thus foiling ONUCI representative Choi's hope to see 60,000 unpaid soldiers and 140,000 starving civil servant families turn against Gbagbo and his associates.

On January 22, 2011, at a summit in Bamako, Mali, the heads of state of the West African Monetary Union (UEMOA) recommended that Dacoury-Tabley be fired from his post of governor of the BCEAO and gave Ouattara authority to appoint a new governor. Ouattara appointed Burkinabe Jean-Baptiste Compaoré to replace Dacoury-Tabley, a clear wink towards Burkinabe president Blaise Compaoré, since it was tacitly understood from the creation of the bank that Côte d'Ivoire, as a majority stakeholder, would have priority right over its governorship. In fact, since President Houphouët's death, and especially during the Ivorian crisis, Blaise Compaoré had argued that this gentlemen's agreement should be abandoned to make room for a rotating governorship. Gbagbo had been a fierce opponent of Compaoré's proposition. With the nomination of Burkinabe Jean-Baptiste Compaoré, Ouattara was signaling to the Burkinabe president that he intended to reward him for his support. In Abidjan, Gbagbo's camp condemned the dismissal of Dacoury-Tabley as a political precedent susceptible of destroying the financial aspirations of the West African Central Bank and started floating the idea of Côte d'Ivoire leaving the UEMOA zone to create its own currency. Before his dismissal, Dacoury-Tabley had allowed the disbursement of between 60 and 80 billion CFA francs, which had allowed Gbagbo enough cash to pay salaries for two months to come. Furthermore, Gbagbo had seized operations of the BCEAO subsidiaries in Côte d'Ivoire, appointed a team of young, savvy economists and kept bank activities alive. Gbagbo's move drew an immediate outcry from Paris. In a declaration that completely ignored the psychological and even physical violence the financial war against Gbagbo exerted on the Ivorian populations, French Foreign Affairs spokesperson Bernard Valero tried to pass off the victimizer as the victim:

> France reaffirms its condemnation of all forms of violence and threats against financial institutions and economic operators in Côte d'Ivoire and all form of violence and threats against civilians…. The forces loyal to Laurent Gbagbo threaten economic operators and occupied the Ivorian agencies of the Central Bank of West African States. This has caused a major crisis of cash and the impossibility for banking institutions to continue their activities in a safe environment.[6]

Gbagbo's government continued to pay salaries, and the populations continued to see President Gbagbo as the one battling for their well-being. On the other hand, Ouattara's efforts to undermine Gbagbo by punishing the population—as well as the international politicians' constant referral to Ouattara as "the President recognized by the 'international community,'" a euphemism for "imperialist powers"—further alienated him from the general population. Exasperation and impatience with Gbagbo's political elasticity and his ability to overcome any obstacle put in his way started to overwhelm the international community that had "recognized" Ouattara as president, a sentiment of frustration which then–French foreign affairs minister Michèle Alliot-Marie expressed when she urged the European Union states to be more tenacious in their banishment of Gbagbo: "We must keep the pressure or increase it, by the fact that the only acceptable bank signature for the Ivorian government is now that of Ouattara."

Starting February 14, 2011, most international banks operating in Abidjan, such as BNP Paribas's subsidiary International Bank for Trade and Industry (BICICI), Société Générales's subsidiary SGBCI, Citibank, Access Bank, Standard Chartered Bank, Bank of Africa, the Regional Stock Exchange (BRVM), and others, citing a hostile atmosphere, abruptly interrupted their services in Côte d'Ivoire without any warning given to their clients, without the three-month advance notice, thus paralyzing economic activities in Abidjan and leaving entire families cashless and fearful for their future. The days that followed saw panic-stricken clients rush to their banks only to see the doors locked with nobody to answer their questions. On February 17, 2011, after a council of ministers, the Gbagbo government announced the nationalization of the renegade banks, in order to ensure the continuity of their operations, to preserve jobs and to guarantee citizens and economic operators' access to their assets, which assets were not the property of those banks: "Faced with this serious breach, the President of the Republic His Excellency Laurent Gbagbo, taking his responsibilities vis-à-vis his people and the economic actors, and after review by the Council of Ministers, issued a decree authorizing the State of Côte d'Ivoire to take control ... of these banks."

The Societal Crisis

A key strategy adopted by the France/EU-UN-U.S. troika in its attempt to force Gbagbo out of power was to upset the societal balance in Côte d'Ivoire by financially weakening the sector of the population that, by and large, still supported him, even if that strategy led to pauperizing these people. Two hundred thousand families, of which 60,000 were soldier families and 140,000 civil servant families, depended on government salaries. The troika had decided that these 200,000 Ivorian families should be starved to force them to accept Dramane Ouattara as their president. Without money to pay the Ivorian civil servants and soldiers, Gbagbo could not be assured of their loyalty. According to the United Nations Special Representative in Côte d'Ivoire, South Korean Choi Young-Jin, the salaries of these family providers should be frozen to get them to turn against Laurent Gbagbo: "If Gbagbo cannot pay them," he triumphantly announced at a briefing, "that should end the crisis." Thus, the United Nations mission in Côte d'Ivoire, whose mandate specified the protection of the civilian populations in imminent danger, was suggesting that entire families should be starved into accepting Dramane as the president of Côte d'Ivoire. This, as the crisis continued, would prove to be even lighter punishment on the populations of Côte d'Ivoire, compared to what the troika had in store for them.

The Troika's Racialogical Embargo on Food, Medicine, and Equipment

Each year, Côte d'Ivoire spent at around 300 billion CFA francs for its needs in medicine, which principally came from Europe and 80 percent to 85 percent of which was shipped by sea. On February 10, 2011, in order to negatively impact Gbagbo's popularity and force the Ivorian president to give up power, the EU/France-UN-U.S. troika had decided to interrupt medicine supply to Côte d'Ivoire. All EU ships sailing to the two major Ivorian ports of Abidjan and San Pédro were ordered to turn back or were redirected to other African ports, where their cargos destined to the Ivorian governments were seized. This blockade on Ivorian imports affected the supply of food and other goods to Côte d'Ivoire, and, what is most important, it disrupted the supply of medicine to Ivorian pharmacies, hospitals, and health care centers. The devastating effects of the blockade had prompted the UNICEF representative in Côte d'Ivoire, Agostino Paganini, to sound the alarm about the looming shortage of essential medicines in the treatment of malaria, one of the most devastating diseases in Africa, of which, even in the best conditions, according to UNICEF, 7 children die every hour in Côte d'Ivoire.[7] "We have already been told that general pharmacies are short of drugs against malaria…. This shortage could soon affect other essential medicines. If we do not act quickly to send these drugs, patients may be forced to discontinue the treatments prescribed by doctors and nurses, including basic antibiotics."[8] On March 15, 2011, Médecins Sans Frontières (MSF) denounced on its official Web site the troika's blockade, which had further aggravated the difficulty to care for the vulnerable and the wounded at a time when armed conflicts were raging in Côte d'Ivoire: "In order to influence the political crisis, the international community has imposed trade and financial sanctions which, added to transportation difficulties, cause shortages of medicines and medical equipment. In several parts of the country, health facilities lack basic drugs and also treatments for chronic or acute diseases, especially for renal dialysis."[9]

The odious blackmail that the troika had exerted on the people of Côte d'Ivoire in 2011 was a first performance. It had never been witnessed anywhere else in the world and at no time in the history of mankind before this. Even in the worst situations, be they from natural disaster or war, the first human instinct had been to run to the rescue of the weak and vulnerable with food and medicine. In Iraq, while Saddam Hussein's government was under siege, a 67-billion-dollar fund was set aside to supply the Iraqi civilians with food and medicine (the infamous oil-for-food program). At the very moment when Ivorian children, women and elderly were being refused medicine, the same troika that had imposed a drug embargo on Côte d'Ivoire was furious that in war-torn Libya, Gaddafi was delaying international drug-loaded trucks entering his country. In February 2011, the International Committee of the Red Cross had appealed for the world to come up with 4.7 billion euros to help the Libyan people, and the Red Cross itself had pledged medicine and medical personnel to Libya. On August 28, 2011, Great Britain had guaranteed 3 million pounds in emergency aid for Libya and had channeled medicine and a surgical team through the Red Cross to help the Libyan people.[10] The next day, the European Commission announced in Brussels that it had deployed a multisectorial team of humanitarian experts to coordinate through a newly established Tripoli office medicine, food, and drinking water to be expeditiously delivered to the vulnerable populations of Libya; and the European Commissioner for International Cooperation, Humanitarian Aid, and Crisis, Kristalina Georgieva, had not strong enough words to express the EU's compassion for and solidarity with the helpless population of Libya:

> My major concern now is for the civilians in Tripoli. Our field experts are assessing the humanitarian situation and the fast-evolving needs in Libya's most populated city. In their initial findings the experts point out the shortage of emergency healthcare provision and the disruptions of drinking water supply. We are working with our humanitarian partners who are doing a tremendous job in a very difficult context. We have allocated €10 million to support their emergency humanitarian operations. We are fully committed to ensure that the basic and most urgent needs of the population are met as swiftly as possible.[11]

By contrast, in Côte d'Ivoire, human decency was put on its head. In its attempt to choke Gbagbo and force him to surrender power to Dramane Ouattara, the U.S.-UN-France coalition, along with the European Union members, had agreed that a blockade on medicine to Côte d'Ivoire was called for. In other words, unless Dramane Ouattara presided over the destiny of Côte d'Ivoire, the country's 20 million civilians could die in silence and with the indifference of

Sarkozy, Ban Ki-Moon, and Obama. On February 20, 2011, health care professionals in Côte d'Ivoire organized a sit-in in front of the office of the World Health Organization (WHO) in Abidjan to protest what they called a "crime against humanity." Their outcries found no attentive ear in the U.S., in the European Union or at the United Nations. While the average Ivorian had no other alternative but to die waiting for the troika to lift the deadly embargo, Ouattara and his associates (Mabri Toikeusse, Djédjé Madi, and Soro Guillaume, among others) had taken several trips to France, Morocco and Senegal to have themselves and their family members treated. The so-called "Ivorian elite" who wanted to lead the Ivorian people were hypnotized by their hatred and contempt for that very people. These Ivorian elites, who were claiming to have in their heart the well-being of their people, were in fact making themselves accomplices of an international community that viewed Côte d'Ivoire as the locus of its racial supremacy affirmation; for, indeed, the embargo on drugs that the international community had imposed on Côte d'Ivoire was nothing but racism disguised under the appearance of politics. It was unfortunate that black elites had elected to take part in this contravention to human decency. In the racial logic of the U.S.-UN-France troika, the children of Libya and Iraq were entitled to welfare, even in the most difficult situations. The black-complexioned children of Côte d'Ivoire could be left to die, unless "the proper leader," the leader chosen by the troika, was put in place. Such was the thinking of the time.

The Diplomatic War

On January 22, 2011, the spokesperson of the government of Abidjan announced that French Ambassador Jean-Marc Simon was no longer in Côte d'Ivoire as an official interlocutor of the Ivorian authorities: "We have put an end to the accreditation of the [French] ambassador. He is now considered an unemployed, ordinary French citizen, who is no longer an interlocutor for us." Gbagbo's decision had come in retaliation of a decision made earlier by the international supporters of Ouattara to expel his ambassadors and recognize only those appointed by Ouattara. On December 29, 2010, Quai d'Orsay spokesperson Bernard Valero had announced that from the perspective of France, the European Union and the United Nations, the new president of Côte d'Ivoire was Dramane Ouattara, and only ambassadors named by him would be recognized: "The European Union adopted a concerted approach last week: only the ambassadors appointed by President Ouattara will be recognized by the European Union.... Similarly, the UN General Assembly recognized the validity of the powers conferred on the new delegation of Côte d'Ivoire to the UN by the legitimate Ivorian authorities."[12] So, Dramane Ouattara, heeding the insistence of France, the

European Union and the United Nations that he should appoint new diplomats replacing those loyal to Gbagbo, had named, among others, Youssoufou Bamba as his new Ambassador to the United Nations to replace Alcide Djédjé, Aly Coulibaly as his new Ambassador to France in replacement of Pierre Kipré, and Daouda Diabaté in Washington, D.C., to replace Charles Yao Koffi. In the European capitals and even in the United States, throngs of Ouattara's supporters besieged the Ivorian embassies and ejected Gbagbo's ambassadors from their offices, and in some cases their official residences.

The Ambush

The troika had hoped that the Ivorian Defense and Security Forces (FDS) would turn against President Gbagbo. It was not the case. Most Ivorian Defense and Security Forces had remained loyal to Gbagbo. Consequently, the rebellion adopted a method of urban guerrilla warfare, whereby the police forces and the militaries were identified even when they were not on duty and savagely killed in the streets and in their beds. The aim was to instill fear in the defense forces with cruel methods and cause them, if not to switch sides, at least to abandon their posts.

Since 2002, the rebellion had been flooding several densely inhabited quarters of Abidjan with insurgents disguised as shepherds, mechanics, security guards, iron workers, etc. They had arrived by bus or by train, in small inconspicuous groups, with their weapons and ammunitions hidden in ordinary suitcases or bags. During the month of Ramadan (the Muslim month of fasting), in the overcrowded quarters of Abobo, Adjamé, Attécoubé, Yopougon, Gobelet, Remblais, Koumassi, and others, weapons, hidden in sugar boxes and rice bags as alms for breaking the fast, had been discreetly distributed to selected families. To hide their meetings from the authorities, the insurgents had used mosques not only as war rooms to discuss their strategies but also as hiding places for weapons, a strategy that some dissenting Muslim leaders such as Imam Idriss Koudouss, the chairman of the National Islamic Council (CNI), had denounced after weapon caches were uncovered by the authorities on January 25, 2011, and on March 4, 2011, respectively in Yosséhi and Banco 2, two quarters of the populous city of Yopougon: "For the sake of God, let us get back to our primary vocation; which is to lead our brothers and sisters to God. Let us not act in ways that can create suspicion." By January, the whole of Abidjan was infiltrated and pockets of insurgencies were targeting loyalist soldiers, police forces, their families, and anyone sympathizing with Gbagbo's government—that is, any civil servant ignoring Dramane Ouattara's call for civil disobedience against the government of Gbagbo. In late December 2010, from his headquarters at the Golf

Hotel, where he was being protected by French and United Nations troops as "the elected President recognized by the International Community," Ouattara had ordered a general work stoppage throughout the whole of Ivorian territory. Ouattara's call for civil disobedience met with very little approval. "The ports of Abidjan and San Pedro, home of the biggest cocoa exports, [operated] smoothly. Even in Abobo, a stronghold of [Dramane], life [went] on."[13] Hence, it had been decided that terror should be the dissuading force and that the suburb of Abobo should be the epicenter of the terrorists that operated under the moniker of "Commando invisible."

"This is not peacekeeping. This is war making"

"This is not peace making. This is war making" are the terms that Oklahoma Republican Senator James Mountain Inhofe used on the United States Senate floor to decry the role that the United Nations in Côte d'Ivoire (UNOCI) played between March and April 2011. As it happened, on March 30, 2011, the UN Security Council adopted UN Resolution 1975 (2011), which, among other provisions, authorized the United Nations mission in Côte d'Ivoire to use force to protect civilians in danger of violence by armed groups and to prevent heavy weapons being used against civilian populations: "The Council stressed its full support given to UNOCI, 'while impartially implementing its mandate, to use all necessary means to carry out its mandate to protect civilians under imminent threat of physical violence, within its capabilities and its areas of deployment, including to prevent the use of heavy weapons against the civilian population.'"[14] The UNOCI did use its mandate. The problem was that it did not use it impartially, precisely because the UNOCI was an unfair participant in the Gbagbo-Ouattara dispute.

As is well known, the United Nations has no army of its own. It depends on contract soldiers from member countries. In Côte d'Ivoire, the essential of the UNOCI military support came from the Licorne Force, a French contingent deployed in Côte d'Ivoire in 2002, in the early months of the first Ivorian civil war, to supposedly secure the separation line between rebels and government forces and "prevent a humanitarian crisis." In Côte d'Ivoire, the French forces had already defined themselves in several sinister events between November 6 and 9, 2004, such as the bombardment of the entire Ivorian army's aerial fleet, the massacre in front of the Hôtel Ivoire of Ivorian civilians who had constituted a human shield to prevent the French army from marching on Gbagbo's residence, and the massacre of Ivorian protesters on the Houphouët Boigny and de Gaulle bridges. The French Licorne Force, the armed branch of the UNOCI, which had already killed more than 60 civilians in Côte d'Ivoire, according to the

International Federation of Human Rights (no more than 20, retorted the French Defense Minister Alliot-Marie), was going to seize upon United Nations Resolution 1975 (2011) to not only openly arm Ouattara's rebels but also to directly fight Gbagbo's Forces de Défense et de Sécurité (FDS).

Indeed, pressured by the international community to step down and cede power to Dramane Ouattara, President Gbagbo had eluded most of the sanctions exerted upon him and was still insisting that he would give up power only if a vote recount by independent international assessors determined that he had lost the election. President Gbagbo's proposition of vote recount was gradually being considered by some African leaders, among them former and current South-African presidents Thabo Mbeki and Jacob Zuma, former Ghanaian president Jerry Rawlings, Angolan president Dos Santos, and Zimbabwean president Robert Mugabe, and the idea was being rumored to be adopted at the upcoming 16th Summit of the African Union held in Addis-Ababa, Ethiopia. French president Nicolas Sarkozy and UN Secretary-General Ban Ki-Moon made an appearance at this gathering of African heads of states, determined to quash any recommendation of recount. In a declaration he distributed to the international press on Sunday, January 30, 2011, ahead of the summit, UN Secretary-General Ban Ki-Moon contended that "to recount the vote will be a grave injustice and will establish a problematic precedent." And so, Ban Ki-Moon urged Dramane Ouattara to forge ahead and start forming his government. Secretary-General Ban Ki-Moon must have awakened from a long slumber not to know that in many places, including the United States, Afghanistan, and Haiti, when there was uncertainty in the vote recounting was the method chosen to find the truth instead of floundering in distrust. Obviously, for Ban Ki-Moon, the quest for facts was antithetical to the principle of democracy. Clearly the fate of Côte d'Ivoire had already been decided by the Ban Ki-Moon-Sarkozy-Obama troika, and Ban Ki-moon was just relaying the troika's message.

Only one day after the adoption of UN Security Council Resolution 1975 (2010), on March 31, 2011, a group of Dramane Ouattara's rebel forces, outfitted with brand new uniforms and all-terrain vehicles and heavily armed, rolled into Abidjan from their northern enclaves of Bouaké, Man, and Korhogo. Others would follow. Their movements had been carefully prepared in advance. On 20 January 2011, the United Nations mission in Côte d'Ivoire had established an important logistical and military platform established in Bouaké and was making daily rotations between Entebbe, Uganda, and Bouaké, where the rebellion had established its headquarters. According to French journalist and writer Leslie Varenne, who had spent six months investigating the Ivorian crisis, French special forces had supported the advance of the pro–Ouattara troops from the North to the South in February. This was part of a larger Franco-American ploy to deliver Abidjan to Ouattara's rebels:

On April 2, the Elysée convened a war council. Participants included Admiral Guillaud, Chief of Staff of the army, General Puga, special chief of staff of Nicolas Sarkozy, Alain Juppe, foreign minister, Gerard Longuet and his defense colleague. The same evening, an army regiment left for Abidjan with several cargo planes bringing war materials. On April 4, France, supported by the UN, dropped its first bombs. Forces loyal to Ouattara then tried several times to take Gbagbo's residence. In vain…. Until the bombing of April 11. French tanks then entered into action to secure access to the residence to the rebels. The end of the story is known.[15]

The rebel's descent into the government-held zone of Côte d'Ivoire would prove apocalyptic: 800 civilians from the Wê ethnic group of West Côte d'Ivoire presumed to be supporters of Gbagbo were executed by Ouattara's militiamen. Entire families were completely wiped out. Tens of thousands more people were mutilated, raped, or chased out of their villages and expropriated. The "massacre of the Wê" was for the troika a mere collateral occurrence in the necessary installation of Dramane Ouattara. Yet it would be unconscionable that history should write off the unspeakable atrocities suffered by this people, as have been written off too many exterminations of dark and brown peoples.

A Word on the Massacre of the Wê

The extermination of the Wê by Ouattara's militias was systematic. It was a programmatic elimination of a people whose supposed allegiance to Gbagbo was seen as the ultimate sin but it was also the programmatic elimination of a people whose very fertile lands had been coveted for decades. The Wê have been the epitomic victim of Ouattara's and the United Nations' partiality in the Ivorian war. Their fate was nightmarish. The fate of the Wê is that of an ethnic community run out of its villages, its fields, and its places of worship by a coldblooded ethnic militia supported by the saintly trinity of Sarkozy, Obama, and Ban Ki-Moon. It is the fate of thousands of children, youths, women, and elderly people from an autochthonous community in the west of Côte d'Ivoire who have been mercilessly butchered by ethnic legionnaires, legionnaires who then occupied the homes, the lands, and the fields of their victims with the blessing of the UN-U.S.-France troika. Those of the Wê who escaped the ethnocide were rounded up and parked in a refugee camp administered by the United Nations, just a few yards from the places that used to be their villages and which have now become the dwelling places of new settlers brought in by the tribal legionnaires. And from across the place that used to be their homes, the Wê looked in the eyes of their executioners each day. And their gazes were unbearable to their executioners, who felt the stares of their victims and feared for a future of possible retaliation. Haunted by what their victims might do someday, the ethnic militia concluded that its work had yet to be completed. So, on July 20, 2012, Ouattara's tribal militia, escorted by the Forces Républicaines de Côte d'Ivoire (FRCI) attacked the UN refugee camp of Nahibly and butchered and burned more Wê people, under the indifferent watch of the United Nations mission in Côte d'Ivoire, whose mandate, according to UN Security Council 1975 (2011), was also "to protect civilians under imminent threat of violence." As of today, more than 3,000 Wê have been killed by Ouattara's ethnic militias, and the lucky ones, for the most part strangers, evacuees, and refugees on their own land, live in constant fear of violence by Ouattara's northern militia.

Since the July 20 murderous incursion against the Wê refugees, the United Nations' mission in Cote d'Ivoire and Ouattara's government have been engaged in a game of accountability ping pong: For the UNOCI number two officer, Arnauld Akodjénou, the security of the Nahibly camp should have been the responsibility of Ouattara's army, the very tribal army that was repeatedly cited by several human rights organizations for carrying out carnages on the Wê, the very army that escorted the barbarous throng into the camp on July 20. For Ouattara's Defense Minister Paul Koffi Koffi, the camp was to be secured by UNOCI, the organization that saw the necessity for its being built. This apparent lack of responsibility elucidation between the Ouattara regime and the United Nations mission in Cote d'Ivoire is actually the well-thought *pièce maîtresse* of the logic of organized chaos which, under the guise of ignorance of clear directives, gives Ouattara carte blanche to implement his political program based on what he unapologetically names *rattrapage ethnique*, a sort of Hitlerian cleansing project meant to privilege people of a certain ethnic background and eliminate those who do not fit the criteria of ethnic selection. Ouattara's privileged ones are the Malinké populations from northern Côte d'Ivoire, from whose bosom he has been claiming appurtenance since the 1990s, despite evidence to the contrary.

The sickening complicity between Ouattara and the UNOCI has been abundantly documented. It is now no secret that the UNOCI had supplied weapons and logistics to Ouattara's militias during the Ivorian crisis; some blue berets were even caught on camera fighting alongside Ouattara's army. In the thrust of this repulsive collusion, the UNOCI had certainly conceded to Ouattara that the circumstances were not appropriate yet for a full-fledged hands-on society, that a necessary level of human rights abuses and praetorian violence were needed to rid the country of remaining "pro–Gbagbo fanatics." This today could explain the UNOCI's participation in the various raids on the western countryside, presumably undertaken by the FRCI to rid the country of Liberian mercenaries still fighting for Gbagbo, raids that have actually served as pretexts for "disinfecting the West" of its Wê agitators, to use a disturbing allegory by Ouattara's party leader Amadou Soumahoro.[16]

So, this act of barbarity perpetrated against the Wê was not a chance occurrence. It was an act that fit within Ouattara's Hitlerian scheme, the aim of which was to exterminate the Wê and colonize their lands with new populations. In doing so, Ouattara had hoped to reward one of his greatest sponsors, Burkinabe dictator Blaise Compaoré, by making Burkinabe immigrants the custodians of the fertile cocoa belt of Côte d'Ivoire that has been the traditional dwelling place of the Wê people. Being the custodian of productive lands and of a seaport had always been the dream of Compaoré, who had never hidden his desire to annex the Ivorian seaport of San Pédro as a war trophy in the early 2000s. Furthermore, Compaoré had accused all the Ivorian governments up to Gbagbo's of mistreating migrant workers from his country and putting in place land reforms that would never make his compatriots landowners in Côte d'Ivoire. Dramane Ouattara had promised him that under his presidency things would change, provided he obtained his help for toppling Gbagbo. Compaoré trained Ouattara's rebel forces in Burkina Faso, armed them, and sent Burkinabe mercenaries to fight in the northern rebellion. A Burkinabe bike mechanic turned warlord, Ouodraogo Rémi, aka Amadé Ourémi, had recruited thousands of fighters for Ouattara's forces and had been one of the most brutal commanders of Ouattara's army. A key player in the Duékoué massacres, Ourémi was equipped by Ouattara's commanders and given specific orders on where to operate. His field of operation was Duékoué, which he colonized after massacring the local populations.

In May 2013, after going rogue, Ourémi was brutally arrested by his former associates. During his first interrogation by a judge, he made some revelations incriminating several FRCI commanders. Ourémi stated that he led an armed group during the carnage of Duékoué and that his troops received their uniforms, weapons, and orders from Commander Losseni Fofana, aka Loss. Ourémi admitted that he fought alongside Lieutenant Coulibaly, former commander of the city of Kouibly and now in charge of the Tabou area, and Lieutenant Dramane Traoré, then head of the city of Bangolo, and Lieutenant Nadia Koné, under the direct orders of the commander Losseni Fofana.[17] A UN Security Council report published on October 13, 2014, sounded the alarm on Ourémi's illegal expropriation of the Wê communities and the Ouattara regime's unwillingness to rectify the injustice taking place in the Wê region:

> [S]ince the post-electoral crisis, a considerable amount of land in the west, where people were perceived to support the electoral hold-up of Laurent Gbagbo after his defeat against Alassane Ouattara, has been occupied by nationals from Burkina Faso, Guinea and Mali. *The new occupants claimed that the lands were the prize for their support to Mr. Ouattara during the post-electoral crisis.*[18] The best-known case is the occupation of the Mount Peko National Park by Amadé Ouremi and his 24,000 Burkinabe loyalists, who started exporting cocoa illegally planted and cultivated in the occupied area. Since the arrest of Mr. Ouremi by Ivorian authorities in May 2013, FRCI has not cleared Mount Peko of the aforementioned occupants. This

situation exasperates the local autochthone communities, which accuse FRCI elements and command structures of being accomplices with the occupants and sharing revenues from illegal cocoa production.[19]

Ouattara was not willing to remove the illegal occupants for the simple reasons that first, he had a promise to keep to Compaoré, and, second, Ourémi's 24,000 Burkinabe recruits, along with the occupants coming from Guinea and Mali, outfitted with forged documents, had helped him stuff the ballots and intimidate voters in 2010 and could still be helpful in 2015. Incidentally, only one year after the political crisis that witnessed the deaths of hundreds of thousands of Ivorians, Ouattara's government announced, in June 2012, that the Ivorian population, which was around 20 million before the war, had increased to 26 million in spite of the war: a six-million increase in population in only one year, and after so many deaths!

Actually, this fanciful indicator reflected the millions of Burkinabe that Ouattara and Compaoré had smuggled into Cote d'Ivoire before and after the 2010 presidential elections, which have recorded the most flagrant cases of massive fraud ever documented in recent history. In some areas where Ouattara scored more than 98 percent, the number of voters surpassed the actual population counts. Having blatantly cheated against Gbagbo, Ouattara has later cheated during the 2011 legislative elections against the other parties of the RHDP bloc with whom he had hitherto entered into an alliance to "defeat" Gbagbo. As the RHDP alliance is falling apart in the months leading to the 2015 presidential elections, habituating the Ivorian people to a six-million population increase that can make a difference in 2015 is, a priori, a winning strategy by an incumbent determined to win at all costs. Six million potential voters who nevertheless must be rewarded for their services, for whom fertile lands must be found. In order to accommodate these substitutes, Ouattara's parliament was considering a land reform whose language would stipulate that the land belongs to the one who enhances it. From this perspective, a running Wê, a hiding Wê, a Wê that has surrendered his land for fear of being butchered, is an absent Wê and certainly not a Wê that is enhancing his land; whereas a present immigrant working on the Wê's ancestral land is an immigrant that is enhancing the land. The land belongs to the one who enhances it, not to the one who flees from it. Ouattara's programmatic extermination of the Wê people seems to have only started. As Human Rights Watch reported, the extreme violence during the postelection crisis has forced hundreds of thousands to seek refuge in neighboring countries or elsewhere in Côte d'Ivoire. A large number of displaced people have returned home to find their land occupied or sold illegally, circumstances that violate their property rights and their rights as refugees returning home. In mid–2014, more than half of returning refugees were homeless, according to the United Nations High Commissioner for Refugees (UNHCR).[20]

Ban Ki-Moon's unwillingness to protect the Ivorian civilians, the fact that the United Nations mission in Côte d'Ivoire had even supplied weapons to, trained with, and fought alongside the very brutal militiamen who were massacring the Ivorian civilians belied the United Nations' professed impartial mandate. In fact, Choi Young-Jin was deep in the conspiracy to impose Ouattara without clear evidence of his having won the 2010 Ivorian presidential election. Gbagbo was right to protest that Choi had lost credibility in Côte d'Ivoire, that the ONUCI representative was no longer impartial, and that between Choi and him, there needed to be another neutral mediator: "In Côte d'Ivoire, the UN and its leader have shown their partiality. But the United Nations should be an impartial force. These forces are now partisan, one wonders what they are still doing there."[21] What the Special Representative in Côte d'Ivoire to the Secretary-General of the United Nations was still doing in Côte d'Ivoire, despite obvious evidence of his bias towards Ouattara, was finishing the job he had started since he arrived in the country under pretense of neutrality. In fact, Choi had stated in a video briefing to the Security Council that he had been pressured by U.S. Ambassador Susan Rice and French Ambassador Arnaud to certify the winner of the election even before the Ivorian Constitutional Council had made a declaration, a strange idea of impartiality that did not escape the sharp analytical eye of Matthew Russell Lee of Inner City Press: "You said that you were not under pressure, but I heard in your Security Council briefing that you gave on video [in closed session] that Ambassadors Rice and Arnaud were very forceful on you on the day of the certification, saying that you should certify even before the [Ivorian] Constitutional Council. Can you confirm that? Does that not constitute pressure?"[22]

The UNOCI-France-U.S. Triad was not impartial in the Ivorian election. They had a clear agenda to make Ouattara the president of Côte d'Ivoire no matter what the voters had decided. To "put the proper leader back in place," this troika had tolerated, and in the case of France and the United Nations, participated in egregious crimes against humanity. As noted former French Ambassador to Côte d'Ivoire Gildas Le Lidec, it is strange that President Laurent Gbagbo is the one being judged at The Hague for crimes against humanity. Nicolas Sarkozy is the one that should be judged for crimes against humanity for his actions in Côte d'Ivoire. Far away, indeed, is the day when a Euro-American leader will be brought to court for atrocities he has committed in Africa. In spite of having a black man of recent African heritage in the White House, the prospect of justice for Africa has never been as improbable as today, and the United States had never been as eager to go on destruction orgies in Africa as today.

Too Far in the Kaisermarsch

In the United States of America, the only sensible official voice that was heard on the Côte d'Ivoire crisis was that of Republican Senator James Mountain

Inhofe of Oklahoma. An indefatigable advocate for the manifestation of truth in the Ivorian presidential election, Senator Inhofe had gathered proofs of Dramane Ouattara's massive frauds as well as evidence of France's and the United Nations' deceitful maneuvers and had lobbied Senator John Kerry, chairman of the Senate Foreign Relations Committee, and U.S. Secretary of State Hillary Rodham Clinton, as well as the Obama administration, to push for a vote recount or a new presidential election. Senator Inhofe knew that, along with the U.N. and France, his government was deeply implicated in picking the "proper leader" in Côte d'Ivoire against the will of the Ivorian people. On April 7, 2011, on the U.S. Senate floor, Senator Inhofe pressed the case of the Ivorian people:

> I have been concerned about what is happening in Cote d'Ivoire, in West Africa. I am very close to the situation. I have had occasion to be there over the last few years nine different times…. I was familiar with the election that came around, so I have been on the floor talking about what I believe should happen there, that we should call for a new election. Unfortunately, the United States and our State Department— I will be very critical of them—have joined with the United Nations and with France in taking the side of Alassane Ouattara from the north who was the challenger, who has been challenging this administration now for at least 10 years that I know of. I got a scathing reply from the Ambassador to the United States from France. I am not going to read it. I am not going to enter it into the *Record*. It doesn't make any sense. I only wish to respond to a couple of things in that letter…. In fact the Independent Electoral Commission did not fulfill its constitutional mandate to announce the final provisional vote tallies within three days. It announced them almost 16 hours after it was constitutionally mandated to report them to the Constitutional Council. And it is my understanding, that it is the Constitutional Council of Cote d'Ivoire and not the Electoral Commission which certifies and declares the winner of presidential elections. It seems that this election was not carried out in accordance with the constitution of Cote d'Ivoire. In addition, there is evidence of massive electoral fraud in the rebel held north. I submitted this evidence in two letters to Secretary Clinton and am awaiting a response to these specific allegations. The evidence submitted to Secretary Clinton includes tallies of precincts where, in the first round of voting, President Laurent Gbagbo received multiple thousands of votes, but in the second round he received zero votes. I also submitted an electoral document showing official regional electoral returns, where it shows Ouattara receiving a total 149,598 from one of five northern regions. But when the total is officially reported in the "total vote" column, Ouattara receives 244,471; a difference of 94,873 votes. From all the evidence I now have gathered, I am convinced that it is mathematically impossible for President Gbagbo to have lost the election by several hundred thousand votes. And if a similar amount of fraud exists in the other four regions of the rebel-held north, Gbagbo is actually the winner of the presidential election.[23]

Senator Inhofe was preaching in the desert. His audience had made its choice. The Obama administration had gone too far in its support of Sarkozy's clamor for war against Gbagbo, and Obama could only keep moving forward in his *kaisermarsch*.

"History will never record that Gbagbo was a fugitive"

President Laurent Gbagbo once said, "History will never record that Gbagbo was a fugitive. If Gbagbo must fall, he shall fall in the house where he works." In December 2010, President Obama offered President Gbagbo, who has a PhD in history and geography, a teaching job at a university in Boston if he recognized Ouattara as the winner of the 2010 Ivorian presidential election and surrendered power to him.[24] President Gbagbo refused and instead promised to leave the presidency if a vote recount concluded that he had lost. Four months later French and United Nations helicopters were shelling Abidjan. Gbagbo was at the place where he worked, at the Presidential Palace, when French soldiers blew up a tunnel linking the Presidential Palace to the French embassy in Abidjan—a tunnel which had been in existence since the time of Houphouët and which Gbagbo had had blocked with concrete—and captured Laurent Gbagbo, his wife Simone Gbagbo and some of their close friends and relatives. Days earlier, as his residence was being besieged by international troops and an attack was all but imminent, Laurent Gbagbo had asked those who wanted to leave the palace to exit it while it was still possible. His wife and his mother, among others, decided to remain by his side.

On April 11, 2011, after two weeks of shelling of the Ivorian Presidential Palace by the French troops, when the French soldiers finally captured the Gbagbo couple and delivered them to Ouattara's rebels, the world saw on live TV a hatred-filled throng of Ouattara's rebels and supporters submit the representative of Abobo and the first lady of Côte d'Ivoire to the most degrading abuses. Simone Gbagbo had offended France with her persistent criticism of French neocolonialism. She had offended Ouattara with her criticism of his politics when he was prime minister and with her criticism of his alleged collusion with the neocolonial forces. It was unbecoming of a woman, of an African woman, for that matter. She had to be put in *her place* through violent humiliation: Ouattara's supporters beat her, pulled her hair, tore her clothes, denuded her, and groped her in every fold of her being. This treatment to which Simone Gbagbo was submitted on live TV, and which Sarkozy saw as well-deserved, has made many in Africa wonder what the world reaction would have been had it been applied to Dramane Ouattara's white wife or to any white woman.

Yet again, politicians are known to not answer hypothetical questions. Simone Gbagbo was guilty of many things, and most important, she was guilty by association with her husband, who had offended President Obama. So, in the United States of America, the "country of human rights," the public torture of Simone Gbagbo, a woman, a mother, and a first lady, had hardly caused a shudder. The official stance was that Simone Gbagbo's savage treatment by Ouattara's supporters was well-deserved. Her husband had had the nerve to disrespect the president of the United States of America; in these circumstances, all our pompous discourses on the sanctity of women's rights could be tossed in the cauldron of ideology. She is either with us and deserves the protection guaranteed to women, or she is against us, and in this circumstance has no right to human rights and any harm done to her is therefore justified. For the Obama administration, Mrs. Gbagbo fit in the latter case; and to prove it, Obama sent his top women officials, UN Ambassador Susan Rice and Secretary of State Hilary Clinton to Abidjan, in indefectible support of Mrs. Gbagbo's tormentors, while Professor Simone Gbagbo was still being tortured in the jails of Ouattara. Who was this woman that so intrigued and worried the political establishment?

Simone Gbagbo: The Iron Lady

Laurent Gbagbo had created many disturbances in Ivorian politics. One of the intolerable disturbances that democracy as championed by Gbagbo ushered in the Ivorian society was the rise of women in politics. And one of the women whose political journey had little to envy compared to Gbagbo's own was Simone Ehivet, whom Laurent Gbagbo married on January 19, 1989, after he divorced his first wife. Simone's incorruptibility, her moral fortitude, and the unwavering conviction with which she held to her political ideals won her the sobriquet of "Iron Lady," an epithet, which, in the Ivorian political and social context, was laden with derogative connotations. The term "Iron Lady" as attributed to Simone generally means that she is a failed woman, one who has dared to intrude in a domain usually reserved for men—that is, the field of politics. And it is precisely for the very reasons she is loathed by her critics that Simone Ehivet Gbagbo is proud of herself. In fact, she is proud of having traveled a path opposite those traveled by most of the women that gravitate around the Ivorian politicians. She particularly does not trust Dominique Ouattara, who resents her, too. She dislikes Dominique's opportunism and the way she has landed on the front burner of the Ivorian political scene, through several questionable passageways.[25] Simone Ehivet Gbagbo is proud of her own journey, however difficult it has been. She is a self-made woman, comfortable in her role as an active decision-maker in her country. "Far from being a figurehead, like the wives of African leaders who do their shopping in luxury stores during official trips, [Simone] has her own office in the presidency and her own agenda. Money is not her thing, even if evil tongues accuse the Gbagbo couple to have stolen more than all their predecessors combined. Simone does politics, from evening to morning."[26]

Though Simone Gbagbo is best known on the international scene as the wife of President Laurent Gbagbo, she is much more than a mere first lady, which, for all sorts of reasons, sometimes even contradictory reasons, has won her comparison with Hilary Clinton.[27] Simone Gbagbo is an elected political official of Côte d'Ivoire. Voted in 1995 to represent the populous District of Abobo at the National Assembly, Simone has also served as the vice president of the institution. Her political posts Simone has earned after long years of formative activism and personal sacrifices, which has anchored in her a fundamental faith in due process that no intimidation can shake. On March 2, 2015, she demonstrated her moral endurance and political principle. After almost five years of torture in the dungeons of Dramane Ouattara's ruthless regime, while her jailers thought she had been mollified and brought to the point where she would finally admit the legitimacy of their power, Simone Ehivet Gbagbo, unperturbed, made the following statement to the judges of the kangaroo court that put her on trial:

> Who won the elections in Côte d'Ivoire? That question has yet to be answered. Alassane Ouattara is the President of the Republic. That is a fact! But he did not win the elections. We should be guarded not to distort the history of our country.... Alassane Ouattara is President of the Republic.... We must accept it. Côte d'Ivoire needs to move forward. But if it must advance, we must do so in the truth. Do not return the knife in the wound. Alassane Ouattara has not won the elections in Côte d'Ivoire.[28]

Born on June 20, 1949, Simone Gbagbo was the second child of a large family of 18 children. Her activism and the harassment that came with it started early in her life, when, as a 17-year-old student at the Prestigious Lycée Classique d'Abidjan, she was arrested for denouncing the politics of President Houphouët Boigny. In 1972, as a student at the Université d'Abidjan, she was a member of an underground think-tank (Cellule Lumumba) animated by her Marxist linguistics professor, Bernard Zadi Zahourou. It was there that she met a young history professor who had just been released from jail for his political activism, Laurent Gbagbo, whom she would marry years later and with whom she would have twin daughters. Simone's meeting with Laurent Gbagbo at Cellule Lumumba introduced her to a group of Gbagbo's friends (Aboudramane Sangaré, Emile Boga Doudou, Assoa Adou, Pierre Kipré, Pascal Kokora, and others) who met secretly for discussions towards the creation of a political organization that would come to life as the Front Populaire Ivoirien. The legitimation of the FPI in 1990 did not spare Simone further harassment from the Houphouët regime. As Houphouet's prime minister, Dramane Ouattara would have Simone Gbagbo incarcerated briefly in 1990, then for a longer period in 1992. Savagely beaten and tortured in prison to the point of once being thought dead, Simone would later confess that her jailers had "dishonored" her during her incarceration. This, as we saw, was only the defeminization of politics, in order to return to an orthodox way of doing politics in Africa whereby women nod and implement but take no initiative of their own. After all, this is Africa, the sempiternal continent of "gender inequality" that so fascinates exotic image hunters. Politics had to be defeminized in order to preserve this pristine image. In April 2011, the treatment given to the Gbagbo couple, which was either explicitly or implicitly approved by Paris and Washington, was also to punish them for perverting politics in Côte d'Ivoire, precisely for feminizing politics with the propagation of multipartism. Not only had Gbagbo feminized politics, which was, to his detractors, a serious sin, but, even graver, he had also injected sincerity into politics, a most unpardonable betrayal.

A Man of Integrity

The day Laurent Gbagbo was inaugurated president of Côte d'Ivoire, he gathered his children and spoke to them:

> This job, I will do it with honor. I will make sure that you are never told that your Father stole a single penny. I will make sure that none of you who bear my name is ashamed of it. I will make sure that no one points a finger at any one of my children, saying: 'this is the son of the thief or the son of the traitor.' But you, the only legacy I leave you, understand it today, is my name. Whatever happens to me sooner or later, I have no account abroad. I have no home abroad. The only legacy I leave you is my name. Be worthy of that name, because that name is clean. If it were not clean, I would have been crushed by my opponents throughout my struggle. This is my faith and this is my way. Because I believe that it is through this path that young Africans can have a revival. My role is not to accumulate money. My role is to help young people earn money for a living. This is the meaning of my struggle.[29]

Throughout his presidency, Gbagbo kept repeating to his fellow countrymen and to the international community that he had only his salary to live on, his Ivorian house to live in, and a single bank account in Côte d'Ivoire to save money and draw money from. Gbagbo published his bank account number and invited anyone willing to verify it with the bank to do so. In Africa, a continent known for the kleptocratic inclinations of its elites, such a declaration could seem purely declamatory. However, in the case of President Gbagbo, it has turned out to be genuine, so far.

On December 14, 2011, the defense team of President Laurent Gbagbo of Côte d'Ivoire, who is presently incarcerated at the International Criminal Court at The Hague to be judged for crimes against humanity following the 2010–2011 postelection crisis in his country, introduced a request for financial assistance from the court. They argued that their client was indigent and therefore not able to pay for his defense. The request was greeted with much incredulity, especially coming from an African head of state. Radio France Inter (RFI) sardonically wrote, "So then Gbagbo is indigent? This, an investigation by the ICC will determine soon."[30] On December, 28, 2011, the judges of the International Criminal

Court had determined that Gbagbo was indigent and needed assistance from the Court to pay for his defense: "[A] preliminary examination suggests, a priori, that the petitioner does not have sufficient resources to support all or part of the costs of his legal representation before the court." Therefore, the ICC committed to retain one lawyer, one legal assistant, and one clerk and to reimburse up to 76,000 euros in expenses already incurred by Gbagbo's lawyers, while pursuing investigations of rumored stashed money by President Gbagbo. On May 15, 2012, in an article published online under the title "*Côte d'Ivoire: plus de 700 millions FCFA sur un compte de Laurent Gbagbo*" (More Than 7000 Million CFA Francs in a Bank Account Owned by Laurent Gbagbo), *Jeune Afrique* suggested that President Gbagbo was not as needy as had been claimed by his lawyers and that he could afford his 1.3-million euro defense bill at the International Criminal Court.[31]

Thanks to the Ouattara regime, *Jeune Afrique* had identified a bank account, opened at the Société Générale de Banques en Côte d'Ivoire (SGBCI) by the financial services of the Ivorian presidency in late October 2000 on Gbagbo's behalf, which held exactly 741,071,364 CFA francs (approximately 1.13 million euros). The *Jeune Afrique* "scoop," which was published after six months of intense international investigations led by teams of sleuths from the United Nations, France and Côte d'Ivoire determined to find Gbagbo's alleged concealed treasures, was in fact not a scoop at all. The bank account in question was the very one Laurent Gbagbo had publicly disclosed over the years. The money in the account came from his 14,642-euro monthly salary of the last ten years. That account had been disclosed to the International Criminal Court by Gbagbo's lawyers as frozen by the Ouattara regime, along with the account of 400 members from Gbagbo's party, and therefore not accessible by their client. The regime that froze Gbagbo's account could not ignore its existence; and the fact that the existence of that account was communicated by that very regime to *Jeune Afrique* as a "revelation" certainly indicated participation in an effort to further sully Gbagbo's reputation. It did not work. On the matter of his finances, Gbagbo was, for the time being at least, found to have no fault, to the dismay of the Ouattara regime.

Gbagbo Is No Bozo

Gbagbo was a nonconforming African president whose outlook on his duty was different from those of most African presidents present and past. In a June 6, 2006, interview with French daily *France Soir*, Laurent Gbagbo once tried to explain why most African heads of state were shy in denouncing Konan Bédié's concept of Ivoirité that had permeated the Ivorian electoral code, culminating in the protracted rebellion that had crippled his presidency since 2002. In the process, Gbagbo derided Gabon's president Omar Bongo, who, while posing often as "the wise man" of Africa, as a moralist, had enshrined in his country's constitution an electoral code that was even more restrictive than Bédié's:

> No African state has condemned the Constitution because their own constitutions are marked with the seal of nationalism and written in the same way. Look at Gabon: Father Bongo likes to give lessons, but he is a joke! To be a candidate in the presidential election in Gabon, one must be Gabonese for at least four generations. Since I have been President, I have never introduced a piece of legislation like Bédié's on *Ivoirité*.

Gbagbo's "insult" met with the indignation of the Gabonese, who on June 12, 2005, organized a huge march from the Foreign Affairs Ministry to the Presidential Palace of Gabon to show support for their president and ask a public apology from Gbagbo. Bongo took the occasion to jab at Gbagbo—though he had promised to respond to Gbagbo's affront—not from Gabon but from France, standing on the steps of the Palais de l'Elysée on the occasion of a two-day visit he would be paying soon to his "good friend" Jacques Chirac. By vowing to respond to Gbagbo from France rather than from his own country of Gabon, Bongo intended to emphasize to his protagonist that he, "the joke," was the relevant one, the one who had access to world leaders, while Gbagbo "the sage" was the irrelevant one, the one who was ostracized by world leaders. And Bongo's naïveté very much proved Gbagbo's point.

Underlying the two-man dispute lay a larger conflict; the Abidjan-Paris arm-wrestling, the nationalist-imperialist clash, of which Gbagbo and Bongo were the respective proxy agents. The Gabonese president was the quintessential illustration of the kind of African elites that Gbagbo would argue needed to be decolonized in a process that irremediably implied the termination of France's exceptional privileges in French Africa and the diversification of Africa's partnership. Bongo was of the African elites who secured France's exceptional prerogatives in Africa and prevented changes from happening; Bongo was of the old guard of African leaders who were particularly adored and propped up by the Euro-American leadership, not for the brilliance of their ideas for the betterment of their continent, but precisely for their shortsightedness, their off-the-cuff and comedic approach to governing, and their inability to cogently articulate Africa's pressing issues at world summits, all of which sustained the Occidental sense of intellectual superiority and exceptionalism. The imperialist West can gleefully point to these incompetent leaders and declare that they are the best brains Africa has to offer the world, which, therefore, justifies the continued expatriation of decision-making power from Africa to the Euro-American world. On September 15, 2005, at the United Nations General Assembly, Bongo offered the world the kind of incomprehensible rambling that for decades made him the African darling of the Euro-American world:

> Ehhhhh.... The papers disappeared [frantically searching in his speech pages], forgive me, oooooh.... Well, then I am going.... I said.... Mr. Chairman, Ladies and Gentlemen, there are things that were said, but that one does not do. Gabon has perhaps strengths, but I heard the President of Venezuela talk and talk.... He said many things, but I cannot say the same. I am just saying that we have created parks and national parks are those available to all who want to come and invest in Gabon. With us, there are many other countries called the countries of the Congo Basin ... since we have created these parks, since we have been talking about the biosity (he meant biodiversity), nobody came. Now, what do we have as wealth.... Oil.... Oil, there is enough.... What else? Forest! It seems that there are environmentalists ... it seems that you cannot touch the forest.... So we created the park ... and these parks is tourism, it is ecotourism. That's why we talk of Gabon first since it is my country ... and then my colleagues in the Congo Basin, we demand ... we will appeal to the whole community, for the funder to address this issue, and make at home what you have done with us in the context of tourism, because you need it ... the forest, carbon ... and the Kyoto agreement is there. This is why I invite you all to come to the park.

The average reader may not have understood anything in Bongo's longwinded incoherence. However, for the Euro-American leadership, the message was clear. What it meant was the following: Here is a corrupt, clueless African head of state with whom we have been doing extremely profitable business for the last thirty-eight years, and with whom we would rather continue to do business for many more years to come. Let us insure him a very solid and long tenure in his country, lest one of the perceptive nationalists that have been humiliated by his four-decade long display of utter ineptitude and dishonesty should take his place, one who could then reconsider the sincerity and the legitimacy of the contracts that we had signed with him. And so, in order to discourage anyone from challenging Bongo, Euro-American leaders made him indispensable to his people, invited him repeatedly to official visits, patted him on the back and congratulated him deliberately in front of international cameras for his people at home to see, publicly pretended to seek his "invaluable" counsel on African affairs, presented him as a wise conflict resolution expert, and, outfitted him with a strong military base, so that he should understand, at the same time, that the tranquility of his nights held less to his being an African nationalist and a renegade—insofar as for the Euro-American imperialist power these two terms amount to the same—than to his insuring that his overall politics worked at protecting the interests of the Euro-American imperialist power. Having properly secured his imperialist masters' interests in Gabon, Bongo, his family, and his associates were allowed to plunder the country's resources until his death in 2009.

Anointed to carry on his father's reign unopposed, Baby Bongo (Ali Bongo) is well on his way to honoring the tradition of ineptitude. On September 24, 2013, at the United Nations General Assembly, like a cherub, his head peacefully resting on the right shoulder of a French diplomat—this should serve as a beautiful metaphor of how France takes care of her dutiful children—Ali Bongo, the proud son of his father, slept through President Obama's foreign policy speech. Ali Bongo needn't worry. Just as was customary during his father's forty-two-year corrupt rule, a French adviser would fill him in on what he had missed when he was in Morpheus's embrace, and, in the process, prescribe for him the steps to take next in defining the foreign policy of Gabon. Father Bongo, by his excesses and his incompetence, was just symptomatic of a pervasive disease in African politics, conveniently cultivated by the Euro-American imperialist power. The Gbagbo-Bongo dispute was finally settled at the 34th African Union Summit of Peace and Security, in Sirte, Libya, thanks to the mediation of Muammar Gaddafi. The Libyan Guide was certainly laughing up his sleeve. Gbagbo had said loudly what he certainly was thinking low. Gbagbo was in his club, the club of the proud sons of Africa who, like Paul Kagamé of Rwanda, Dos Santos of Angola, and Mugabe of Zimbabwe, resented the African leaders who by their moral indolence enabled the perpetuation of the West's superiority complex and economic and human genocide in Africa, African elites who were, absurdly enough, often referred to as the sages of Africa.

He Burnt His Bridges with Europeans and His Peers in Africa

Gbagbo's criticism of Bongo was an attack on the old guard of corrupt African leaders whom he saw as failed representations of African elites and away from whose traditions he was resolute to steer clear. During a congressional appearance, Mike McGovern—who passes for an "expert" of Ivorian politics for having "spent a total of nine months in Côte d'Ivoire, most of it scattered over a 17-year period," who does not particularly have a soft place in his heart for Gbagbo, and who wrote a book replete with untruths and fabrications on the Ivorian crisis—had at least a sensible explanation of why Gbagbo was treated differently from other African presidents, though McGovern thought he had detected moral insufficiency where in fact moral competence was to be extolled: "Gbagbo was treated differently because he had burned his bridges with Europeans but also with his peers in Africa"; for, indeed, as far as his relation with Europe was concerned, it was rather with an oedipalized relation with Europe, laden with the scent of abusive Europe, especially colonialist France, that Gbagbo had decided to break. And as to his relationship with his West African peers, what Gbagbo abhorred much in them was their slave mentality, their complex of inferiority, that has made them agents for the conservation and perpetuation of imperialist domination in Africa. In Gbagbo's appreciation these mentally affected African leaders are no different from the African kings of yesteryear who sold millions of their own people to Europe and the Americas to be used as slaves. Though today's mentally enslaved African elites do not traffic in people, they do, nonetheless, participate in the depreciation of Africa's human potential by plundering and selling off cheaply African resources and by being complicit in the destabilization of the African continent that sends millions of Africans embarking on flimsy, unsafe migrant vessels on stormy seas, hoping to reach European "heavens." In a recent interview, Chadian leader Idriss Deby Itno addressed the matter of African leaders' psychological entrapment and their responsibility in the underdevelopment of the continent, and he urged African journalists to be relentless in denouncing the accomplices of Euro-American interventionism and empire-building ambitions.

To affirm, as McGovern has in front of the United States Senate Foreign Relations Committee, that Gbagbo has met the fate that befell him because he had burnt his bridges with his Euro-American and West African counterparts is an unequivocal testimonial that Gbagbo had broken with good governing practice in the Euro-American world as well as West Africa. At this point of the study, we have clearly demonstrated that the Euro-American world order characterized by economic and human genocide is far from constituting good practice. The Euro-American governing practice is in fact among the most wretched practices—if not the gloomiest practice—ever thought up by human intelligence. Gbagbo was right to be distrustful of the Euro-American deadening way of doing politics. What then of the good West-African practice that McGovern faults Gbagbo for having refused to duplicate and carry on? Perhaps, a cursory examination of what has become habitual governing method in West Africa should illuminate this debate.

In a candid conversation with two French journalists, Nathalie Schuck and Frédéric Gerschel, which was later transcribed in a book the title of which is revelatory—It Stays Between Us, Right? Two Years of Confidence by Nicolas Sarkozy— former French president Nicolas Sarkozy was caught criticizing President François Hollande's military intervention in Mali and in the Central African Republic in terms that gave away his own criminal, at best immoral, involvement in Côte d'Ivoire in 2011: "There was improvisation in Mali and in the Central African Republic. I'm not saying that we should not have intervened there, but I still do not understand what we were going there for. Mali is made up of a desert, mountains, and caves. When I see the care that I put into intervening in Côte d'Ivoire.... We removed Laurent Gbagbo, and we installed Ouattara without any debate, none."[32]

Sarkozy had always denied any French direct military involvement in the bombardment of Abidjan and in the capture of President Laurent Gbagbo on April 11, 2011. In this short, unfiltered declaration, Sarkozy was admitting at least three things: First, that under his orders, the French army had directly intervened in Côte d'Ivoire to remove President Gbagbo by force and install Dramane Ouattara; second, that it was a carefully premeditated coup d'état; and third, that the motivation for the coup d'état was economic—that is, that France had a good reason to intervene in Côte d'Ivoire, precisely because, unlike the rocky desert of Mali, Côte d'Ivoire was lush with cocoa, coffee, timber, cotton, all sorts of tropical fruits, and abundant with oil, diamonds, gold, and more. Thus, two years after he had claimed that France was in Côte d'Ivoire under the aegis of the United Nations to enforce "Democracy," French president Nicolas Sarkozy was confessing that in Côte d'Ivoire he was just a vulgar buccaneer raiding a country for its resources. And who helped him fulfill his goal in Côte d'Ivoire? The very West African heads of state whose practices Mike McGovern saw as deserving duplication and perpetuation.

Sarkozy's African Tirailleurs

Indeed, in late 2010, presidents Goodluck Jonathan of Nigeria, Abdoulaye Wade of Sénégal, and Blaise Compaoré of Burkina Faso, three of McGovern's exemplary West African presidents, had decided to give French president Nicolas Sarkozy an early Christmas present. Sarkozy had been eagerly looking for a good pretext to go to war against Gbagbo's government; these West African heads of state handed it to him on a silver platter. They urged Sarkozy to help support a military intervention against President Gbagbo, who had been insisting that a ballot recount be undertaken by the international community to determine who, of he and Ouattara, had really won the 2010 presidential election. Only in Africa would African heads of states invite an external military force to wage war on another African country in a postelection dispute when war could be avoided by a simple vote recount. In fact, Jonathan and Compaoré even wrote an impatient letter to Sarkozy insisting that he intervene as early as possible. Sarkozy, in a deceitfully cautious tone, replied to this request favorably through a communiqué by the Elysée: "The head of state [Nicolas Sarkozy] expressed his gratitude to President Jonathan for the ECOWAS' resolute commitment to the rapid restoration of peace and stability in Côte d'Ivoire, in accordance with the will of the people expressed during the presidential election." The absurdity of this declaration was that the will of the people expressed in the presidential election was not known yet; it was that which was still at issue and which could be clearly elucidated by a vote recount; it was that which Sarkozy did not want to know, because neither he nor President Obama or United Nations Secretary-General Ban Ki-Moon wanted a recount.

Sarkozy had carte blanche from McGovern's exemplary West African leaders. He could now go to war against an African country with the blessing of Johnathan, Wade, and Compaoré. Pondering over the international community's muscled intervention in the Ivorian crisis, Achille Mbembe and Célestin Monga asked this most relevant question: Is the use of military force by neighboring or foreign states to resolve postelectoral conflict in a sovereign country justified in law?[33] If so, then what democratic criteria must first be fulfilled by the countries that send their troops to foreign independent nations? Indeed, how much democracy existed within the very nations that were so eager to send troops to Côte d'Ivoire to resolve the electoral dispute between Laurent Gbagbo and Dramane Ouattara? The troika whose intervention was effectuated through the presence on the terrain of French and UN troops, the troika of whose duplicity we have spoken at great length but which, nevertheless, we shall never tire of denouncing, a troika that wants to pass for the moral compass of the world, that promotes principles of democracy during the day but at night becomes a buccaneer of the worst kind, a cutthroat of the most despicable type, a supporter and financier of the vilest dictators—what moral legitimacy can such an entity have? Mbembe and Monga continue:

> What value should be assigned to the legal requirements proclaimed *urbi et orbi* by the international community on a continent where its principles, its passion, its firmness and sanctions are applied differently depending on the country and time, that is to say, inconsistently or arbitrarily? Specifically, what legitimacy can claim a former colonial power, which in the day, embraces, supports, funds, arms and awards repugnant commendations to autocrats and at night ... maintains military bases in countries at war while posing as moralizer and pontiff of democracy? ... The Western states—even those that constantly blather about freedom, human rights and democracy, but never hesitate to trample them under their feet whenever it comes to Negro lives—by their unwavering and multifaceted active or silent support lavishly given since 1960 to unique party regime corporals and other kleptocrats in civilian clothes ... have killed any credibility they might have had.[34]

And the black tirailleurs of this corrupt international community, how credible could they be when they served such crooked masters? More precisely, how much commitment to democracy did Jonathan, Wade, and Compaoré—the three African heads of states who signed on to be the troika's first tirailleurs in the wee hours of the Ivorian crisis—have? Who were really McGovern's superlative leaders from whom Sarkozy obtained blessings to wage war against an African country?

Goodluck Jonathan: Bad Luck for Nigeria

The first responsibility of any democratic nation's army is to secure the integrity of its territory and the security of its citizens. Goodluck Jonathan's alacrity to take his army into foreign places to restore peace and order would make one think that in his own backyard of Nigeria Jonathan had maintained peace and stability and was poised to fight any aggression, both from within and from without, capable of perturbing the serene existence of the Nigerian people. In fact, only the contrary can be true. Jonathan has turned out to be a brutish president outside of Nigeria, but a pathetically weak one at home, a head of state incapable of guaranteeing peace and security to the Nigerians. Jonathan's cowardly leadership has shown most in his fight against Nigeria's terrorist group Boko Haram, a group of radical Islamic fighters who have vowed to fight "infidels" as represented in anything they see as being associated with Western education and way of life.

On the afternoon of Wednesday, January 7, 2015, a group of Islamic terrorists attacked the Parisian offices of the French satirical paper *Charlie Hebdo* and killed 12 people and wounded 11 others. The same day, a statement from the office of Nigerian president Goodluck Jonathan expressed solidarity with the French nation: "The President believes that the cowardly and ignoble attack by violent extremists is a monstrous assault on the right to freedom of expression." Jonathan's manifestation of solidarity with the French nation would have remained a normal occurrence had the Nigerian leader shown the same concern for his own people. The night of April 14 and 15, Islamic terrorist group Boko Haram abducted about 270 girls from a boarding school in the city of Chibok, in the state of Borno, Northeast Nigeria. For two weeks, the Nigerian president uttered not a peep on the tragedy, tried even to hush it up as if it never happened. When disturbed Nigerians decided to march in order to raise world awareness about the fate of the abducted girls, the first lady of Nigeria, Patience Jonathan, who had no official position in the country, whose freedom-of-speech-championing husband would not hesitate to lament any attack on freedom of expression in France, threatened the protesters and went so far as to order the arrest and detention of two of the leaders of the march.

In fact, Boko Haram, which had started its violent campaign of suicide bombings and raids in 2009, had killed more than 4,000 people in Nigeria. And the Nigerian leader's response each time had been less than tepid, which had led the British paper *Economist* to accuse him of callousness: "For the past few years, President Goodluck Jonathan has publicly shrugged off the deaths of thousands of people … portraying them as the unfortunate but unavoidable result of a fanatical insurgency for which his government cannot be blamed."[35] On January 3, 2015, Boko Haram attacked the Nigerian towns of Baga and Doron Baga. The Nigerian army placed the death toll at 150 people, when several independent sources estimated the killed to be no less than 2,000, another telling example of what Nigerian lives really meant to Jonathan and his army. President Jonathan was the Supreme Leader of one of the largest armies in Africa, certainly the most brutish and the most corrupt army on the African continent. During his tenure, Johnathan has proved to be deserving of Nigeria's corrupt defense force.

Goodluck Jonathan, whom Emeka Thompson, a Nigerian Internet commentator, once characterized as "corrupt, incompetent, and not fit enough to manage a lemonade stand," had continued the tradition of his predecessors, which was to pocket the country's oil revenue together with army officers in the hope that in the coups d'état-prone country his tenure would not be militarily interrupted. The consequence of this maladministration was that it perpetuated lower-rank soldiers' frustration and led to their refusal to fight for their people. In fact, in their fight against Boko Haram, hundreds of Nigerian soldiers had surrendered their weapons and crossed into neighboring Cameroon. For Hilary Clinton, President Jonathan's corrupt dispositions were directly attributable to the Nigerian army's deficiency. As she stated, "The government of Nigeria has been in my view somewhat derelict in its responsibility towards protecting boys and girls, men and women in northern Nigeria over the last years.... They have squandered their oil wealth, they have allowed corruption to fester and now, they are losing control of parts of their territory because they wouldn't make hard choices."[36] Incompetent Jonathan was certainly not an example to emulate in West Africa, whatever critics of Gbagbo such as McGovern may think. In fact, Gbagbo was right, if he really had, to burn his bridges with Goodluck Jonathan, the corrupt leader that bad luck gave the people of Nigeria. All of Sarkozy's three African tirailleurs have been retired, Jonathan and Abdoulaye Wade beaten at the democratic ballots and Blaise Compaoré kicked out of office by public protests.

Abdoulaye Wade: A Slavering Megalomaniac

On February 24, 2015, speaking to a panel of journalists and a group of his party loyalists, disgraced Senegalese President Abdoulaye Wade, who had ruled Senegal for 12 years before being beaten in 2012 at the ballot box by his former prime minister Macky Sall, was captured on video with these disparaging words about his successor:

> He is a descendant of slaves ... [and] his parents were cannibals. His parents used to eat babies and were expelled from the village. It is gradually that they started relating to humans normally. You know if a child is rude, he will hear about the circumstances of his father's circumcision. That is, he will hear what he would rather not know.... If he wants, he can lock me up but that is the truth. Those who owned Macky Sall's family are still alive. He knows that he is their slave. I say it and I assume it, because you cannot always hide the truth. This insolence of Macky Sall is incomprehensible. It must be stopped because they say it is force that stops force; then it must be stopped by force. You can accept, you Senegalese, that he be above you,

but me, I will never accept that Macky Sall be above me. Never my son Karim will accept that Macky Sall be above him. Were we in other situations, I would have sold him as a slave.... Do not worry; nothing will happen. Macky Sall has no elements in the army. However, if he appeals to the army, I will do the same and we will see.

In the country of Gorée, the island where the edifices of the ugly commerce of slavery have been preserved as a reminder of a shameful episode of human history never again to be repeated, that an African elite, particularly a former president, would nostalgically summon up the time when it would have been possible for him to sell off one of his fellowmen as a slave was greeted with incomprehension and anger. For most Africans in general, that President Wade would revive and appropriate for himself racist epithets to discuss another African was immoral and unconscionable. Wade's odious video toured the social networks and generated countless replies, mostly of disapproval. For Aliou Tall, "Abdoulaye Wade, who sees himself as one of the greatest African intellectuals, corroborates the fanciful and extravagant clichés developed in philosophical works and colonial narratives about cannibalism in Africa. Racists can rub their hands with satisfaction."[37]

In order to better appreciate the exasperation that pushed President Wade to unleash such a string of insanities against the sitting president of Senegal, one must understand the future that Wade had carved for Senegal, a future whose fullest expression he allegorized in a 160-foot-high bronze statue standing on one of the two volcanic hilltops that tower over the city of Dakar. For the 50th anniversary of Senegal's independence Wade had commissioned a Monument of African Renaissance from the North Korean Mansudae Overseas Projects. Estimated to have cost 23 million euros, the statue, which from its plinth to its tip is a few meters taller than the Statue of Liberty, was inaugurated in early 2010. To those who criticized him for spending 23 million euros on a statue in a country that lacked basic facilities such as potable water, electricity, education and health infrastructure, President Wade rejoined that he built his monument with proper means, without drawing funds from Senegal's public coffers: "I never spent a cent from the budget for the realization of this statue. I told the Koreans that I had no money but that I could pay them with land.... People should not say that I wasted 23 million euros.... There is no public money in this. The cost is 23 million euros. But the value is three or four times that." Supposing that Wade's defense were right, that he financed his Monument of African Renaissance with no public money, one could still wonder how upon becoming president a Senegalese lawyer of no extraordinary means was able to acquire so much land as to compensate Mansudae Overseas Projects for 23 million euros worth of labor. In fact, as was later discovered, Wade had transferred 27 hectares of the most expensive public land around the Dakar airport to Mbackiyou Faye, a businessman of his friends, who sold the land to the Institut de Prévoyance Retraite du Sénégal

(IPRES), a public organization, which bought the land with public money, which money was then used to pay the North Korean constructor. So, finally, Wade's statue was paid for with public money. Nevertheless, Wade still insisted that the intellectual rights of the edifice were his and that he should personally pocket 35 percent of the benefits generated by the monument.[38] President Wade went so far as to send the police after small Senegalese artisans who sold miniature wood reproductions of the sculpture to tourists.

Wade's monument was in the image of a nuclear family. At the center was a strong, muscular father in a forward motion, carrying in his right arm, almost dragging her, an exhausted mother, whose dress a licentious wind pressed against her skin, revealing an uncovered right breast. On his right shoulder, the father was carrying an infant child, whose outstretched left arm was terminated by a firm index pointing to the horizon, as if to show the way. When the last piece of the statue, the head of the central figure, was finally placed on the edifice, it bore a striking resemblance to President Abdoulaye Wade. The muscular father dragging a woman and carrying a child on his shoulder that showed the way to the future was Abdoulaye Wade, the woman was Viviane Wade, and the child was Karim Wade. Thus was the renaissance of Senegal according to Abdoulaye Wade: A Senegal led by his son Karim after his own tenure. At the time of the unveiling, Wade was 84 years old. The statue was to reveal the new Senegal: One governed by his son Karim.

Wade's determination to have his son succeed him was no secret. On many occasions, President Wade had spoken about the exceptional intellectual qualities of his son and the fact that no one in the country was competent enough to accomplish the job that he assigned to Karim. Outfitted with a master's degree in finance from the Sorbonne and with an impressive experiential vitae of multiple internships in the U.S. and Great Britain as well as posts at UBS Warburg, DeBeers, and Texaco—though inflated, according to some critics—Karim Wade was certainly a very intelligent young man. But he was not the above-the-cut genius his father portrayed him to be, and certainly not the most intelligent Senegalese.[39] For Papa Wade, however, Baby Wade was promised to a presidential destiny that he, the father, ought to facilitate. Thus, one year after he was elected, Abdoulaye Wade appointed his son as his special adviser in the government of Prime Minister Souleymane N'déné N'diaye with the task of overseeing huge infrastructure projects such as the construction of a new airport and roads, the construction of the Integrated Economic Zone of Dakar, and the reform of the Industries Chimiques du Sénégal (ICS). Karim Wade's performance was publicly decried as being riddled with financial improprieties. Yet, in 2004, Baby Wade was given more responsibilities by his president-father, who appointed him president of the Agence Nationale pour l'Organisation de la Conférence Islamique (ANOCI), which made him the sole interlocutor to Arab and Middle Eastern countries. Under Baby Wade's supervision, ANOCI facilitated the acquisition of lucrative contracts by Middle Eastern partners. Dubai acquired the port of Dakar and the Dakar Economic Zone. A Sudanese and Kuwaiti operator by the name of SUDATEL acquired the third telephone exploitation license. Karim built for himself a strong Arab and Middle Eastern network of financial support and public exposure necessary for the fulfillment of his father's dream to see him run Senegal someday. On March 23, 2009, Karim attempted his first political bid as a candidate for the post of mayor of Dakar. He was soundly beaten. To punish the Dakarois for having snubbed his son, Papa Wade came to the rescue and two months later got Karim a cabinet post as Minister of State for International Cooperation, Territorial Development, Air Transport, and Infrastructure, a super minister with almost 50 percent of the government budget. The Senegalese, who derisively called Karim Wade the "Minister of the sky and the earth," would be even more stunned when, on October 4, 2010, Papa Wade added to his son's multiple portfolio the portfolio of energy. Nothing and no one could prevent Baby Wade's ascension to the Presidential Palace. No one? Not exactly!

Macky Sall, the president of the National Assembly, also had presidential ambitions, and he would not allow that Karim Wade be so easily promoted by his father as the future president of Senegal without an audit of the various responsibilities he had held since his entry into public administration. In October 2007, seeing the meteoric ascent of Karim Wade taking shape at the horizon, Macky Sall summoned him to a hearing before the National Assembly to elucidate his management of the ANOCI. Debates at the National Assembly are usually held in the national language of Wolof, which Karim did not speak well. Besides exposing the financial opacity in Karim's management of ANOCI, Sall was also planning to reveal Karim as not culturally impregnated enough to lead Senegal. Abdoulaye Wade went into an uninhibited furor against the president of the National Assembly, accusing him of disloyalty:

> Macky Sall has not complied with the procedure. When the Assembly wants to hear a member of the government or of the Presidency, it must first make a request to the Prime Minister or the head of state. And we are close enough for him to be able to give me a call and let me know. It's not so much the principle of calling Karim but the method that shocked me. Macky Sall is a weak character, very badly surrounded. Some of the people around him pushed him to summon Karim in this manner. He made a mistake and showed me one thing: He is not a statesman.[40]

President Wade insisted that Macky Sall return what he gave him, that is, the presidency of the National Assembly that Macky Sall acquired as an elected member of Wade's majority Democratic Senegalese Party (PDS). Macky Sall refused. In November of the same year, Sall was dismissed from his post as Deputy Secretary-General of the PDS by the party's steering committee. To force

Sall out of the National Assembly's presidency, MP Sada N'Diaye succeeded in pushing for a law that reduced the mandate of the president of the National Assembly from 5 years to one year, renewable, this allegedly to make sure that the end of the mandate of the president of the National Assembly does not coincide with that of the president of the country. In September 2008, the Sada N'Diaye Law was voted on and applied to Macky Sall, who lost the presidency of the National Assembly.

The same year, Macky Sall left the PDS and created his own party, l'Alliance pour la République (APR). In a bitter presidential campaign against Abdoulaye Wade, Macky Sall defeated Papa Wade in 2012 and pulverized the Wades' dream to see Baby Wade become president of the Senegalese nation. Even worse, Macky Sall did something that would have been impossible under Abdoulaye Wade's presidency: he gave the judiciary full independence to investigate the Wade family. In April 2013, the Senegalese justice arrested Karim Wade under suspicion of illegal enrichment. On July 31, 2014, Karim appeared before the Court for the Suppression of Illicit Enrichment (CREI) to be judged. On March 25, 2015, Karim Wade was found guilty, condemned to six years in jail and ordered to pay 209 million euros back to the state of Senegal. For Abdoulaye Wade, Macky Sall was the man by whom the collapse of the Wade dynasty came. For him, Wade had nothing but contempt and hence came former President Wade's insanities against President Macky Sall.

Though one can argue on the nature of the trial as to whether it was politically motivated or not, Karim Wade's wealth—evaluated at more than $1.4 billion held by a young man who had served only five years in public administration—said something about the Wades' conception of public and private property distinction or the lack thereof. Assuredly, Baby Wade, whose short tenure in government was, like his father's, replete with several financial scandals, had learned a few tricks from Papa Wade. Indeed, On September 24, 2002, when the northern towns of Côte d'Ivoire were under rebel occupation, the West African Central Bank's branch of Bouaké was attacked and its vaults completely emptied. And four days later, the branches of Man (west of Côte d'Ivoire) and Bouaké and Korhogo (north of Côte d'Ivoire) were attacked at one hour's interval. These operations were planned and executed by the leaders of the Northern Rebellion, Soro Guillaume—whom Abdoulaye affectionately called his son—and his lieutenants. The money, which the Central Bank's authorities evaluated in the hundreds of billions of CFA francs, made its way to Burkina Faso, Mali, and Senegal, where part of it was easily laundered and reinvested in these three West African countries' economies in real estate and hotel development and in restaurants. Some of the money also ended up in Brazil in the purchase of vast ranches.[41]

According to Amath Dansokho, a state minister in Macky Sall's government who was the leader of the Senegalese Parti de l'Indépendance et du Travail (PIT),

Abdoulaye Wade was directly involved in laundering the stolen money. In fact, on October 8, 2003, President Gbagbo and the Central Bank Governor, Ivorian Charles Konan Banny, lodged two separate complaints against X for the stolen money. In Senegal, Konan Banny gave a press conference at the bank's headquarters in Dakar, during which he publicly implicated the authorities of Senegal and expressed fear for his own life: "Maybe you will never see me again. They may kill me, but I inform you that we have a list. We have identified those who laundered the money from Bouaké and from Korhogo. In three days we will publish the list, and the whole world will be surprised that it is the higher authorities who are involved in this case." According to Dansokho, that list was never published because it was life insurance for Banny, who was signaling to Abdoulaye Wade and his accomplices that should anything happen to him the world would know that Wade had personally facilitated the laundering of the heist's money.

Abdoulaye Wade's eagerness to have Sarkozy's army remove Gbagbo from power was understandable. The prospect of President Gbagbo—who outfitted with the state means of investigation could prove the involvement of his West African peers in a string of criminal activities—remaining in the Presidential Palace was too terrifying a scenario to imagine. President Gbagbo knew that in his daily dealings with his West African peers he was wading in a pool infested with high-level corruption and that the less time he spent in their company, the better it would be. In fact, Gbagbo's persistence in maintaining that he only had one bank account and his insistence that anyone doubting his sincerity could have permission to check his account balance was intended to create a gap between his approach to state property and the approach of his West African peers, for whom the same claim of moral cleanliness could not be made. Should we blame President Laurent Gbagbo for keeping exclusively businesslike relations with such corrupt leaders as Abdoulaye Wade of Senegal and Blaise Compaoré of Burkina Faso, who so brazenly participated in the robbery of a bank in which the countries they governed were stakeholders?

The people of Senegal and Burkina Faso themselves seemed to have answered this question. If in Côte d'Ivoire president Gbagbo was violently attacked and defeated by a manufactured coalition from without, in Senegal and Burkina Faso, as the Ivorians like to say, "Wade and Compaoré have been regurgitated by their own peoples." For Senegal, the straw that broke the camel's back was Wade's attempt at tinkering with what Gbagbo had always claimed was the quintessential law of a democratic state—that is, its constitution. Against the constitution of Senegal, which Wade himself had amended to introduce a two-term limit, Wade, now 85, not only had decided to run for a third term but he had also, like a supercomputer, projected the outcome of the election, predicting exactly 55 percent of the vote for himself and a precise proportion for each one of the candidates in the first round. On January 27, 2012, when a team of judges in the pay of the Wade regime, after a twisted interpretation of Senegal's constitution, declared Abdoulaye Wade eligible for the February 26, 2012, presidential election, the Place de l'Obélisque immediately ignited with popular protests that quickly spread to the rest of the country. Wade's resolve to violently repress the demonstrations was met with a unified opposition determined to block his unconstitutional third term. In the anti–Wade coalition were three of Wade's former prime ministers; and Wade, who just a few weeks before was still being praised by his Western counterparts as "the Wise Man of Africa," saw his support quickly dwindle. In Paris, Foreign Affairs Minister Alain Juppé urged President Wade to make way for a new generation. For U.S. Department of State spokesperson Victoria Nuland, it would be wiser for "the Wise Man" to step down and preserve his legacy as a "democrat." At a daily press briefing in Washington, D.C., on January 27, 2012, she had these words for Wade:

> We do continue to believe that his decision to try to run for a third term as president does have the potential to jeopardize a lot of the achievements that he himself has made, including ushering in new constitution with a two-term limit for presidents. So he's had two terms, he supported a constitution with two terms, and we want to see him be a leader in paving the way for a new generation of African leaders and solidifying his own stature as a democrat in this way.[42]

As Wade felt "the betrayal" of his erstwhile friends, he suddenly remembered the sacrosanct principle of African countries' sovereignty and urged his Euro-American critics to essentially mind their own business: "The Senegalese people [are] a free people. [They] will decide if I have two mandates or three mandates or four mandates or five mandates…. This must be a question for the Senegalese people to decide and not for foreigners from France or the United States."

The problem with the servile African heads of state is that they have an extremely limited reading of historical events. They never learn from Africa's 600-year relation with the imperial powers. Looking at and listening to them, one cannot help but think of this scene in the film *Coup de Torchon*, where Philippe Noiret, in the role of a French colonist, tells Friday, his African lackey, who does not understand why after so many years in his service his master would give him the same treatment he gives to the other blacks, "You see, Friday, you have kissed too many white asses, and you wouldn't understand!" President Abdoulaye Wade would not understand why, after so many years in the service of his Euro-American masters, they would treat him as they treated President Gbagbo. Wade would not understand, and neither would Blaise Compaoré of Burkina Faso, who felt betrayed by France.

CHAPTER 7

Côte d'Ivoire: The International Community's Panglossism

On Sunday, May 20, 2012, Susan Rice arrived in Abidjan. The following day, she met with Dramane Ouattara and his prime minister, Jeannot Ahoussou, who satisfied her with reports of enhanced security, improving refugee issues, progressing disarmament of militias, and the prospect of local elections by year's end. Then Rice supposedly met with "leaders of the opposition parties" and members of the National Assembly. The reality was that the key opposition leaders were either dead, in exile, on the run or in jail. Ouattara's seizure of power on April 11, 2011, was accompanied by a wide ethnocide conducted by his northern militias, which targeted non–Muslim populations from the western, eastern, and southern parts of Côte d'Ivoire. In fact, Rice's visit to Côte d'Ivoire was sandwiched between several carnages that seemed to matter very little in the grand scheme of ideological positioning. Diplomatically, the aim was to support and prop up Dramane Ouattara as the constitutional leader of Côte d'Ivoire, and no talk of human right abuses by his troops was to be allowed to derail this enterprise. Yet, it was not from occasional crimes that the people were suffering in the hands of Ouattara's militias, but from planned, programmatic exterminations.

Exactly two months after Rice's satisfied visit to Côte d'Ivoire, on July 20, 2012, Dramane Ouattara's ethnic militia, escorted by the Forces Républicaines de Côte d'Ivoire (FRCI) and traditional northern Dozo hunters, stormed the Nahibly UN refugee camp where 5,000 people from the Wê community (around 2,500, according to official numbers) who had been driven from their homes and lands found shelter under the "protection" of UN peacekeepers. There, under the impassive gaze of UNOCI troops, Ouattara's militias set fire to the camp, destroyed 90 percent of the camp infrastructure, killed 13 refugees and injured dozens of others. Video evidence of the attack that circulated later on Facebook showed that not only was the Nahibly refugee camp attack planned by the FRCI-Dozo coalition, but also that the barons of the RDR, the local authorities, and the UN peacekeeping forces were privileged spectators of the massacres. Those who were in charge of the populations stood aside and watched the whole attack as if they were at the movies. In the video, the U.N. peacekeepers, the FRCI, and the prefectural authorities stayed back, impassive, watching RDR militiamen armed with clubs and machetes butcher the Wê refugees in a circle of fire.[1] In a scathing report published on July 29, 2013, Amnesty International indicted Dramane Ouattara's militias for the massacre of Nahibly and charged his government with enabling the summary executions of people perceived to be supporters of Gbagbo. Amnesty International also accused the government of stalling investigations on the carnage and faulted UNOCI police for not fulfilling their mission of protection:

> The attack at Nahibly raises concerns similar to those that emerged in the March–April 2011 widespread and systematic attack directed against the civilian population in the Duékoué area. In both cases, members of the FRCI and the Dozo militia attacked a group of people belonging to the Guéré ethnic group, which is widely perceived to support the former President Laurent Gbagbo. In both cases, the military and police attached to the United Nations Operation in Côte d'Ivoire (UNOCI) and posted near or at the site failed to protect the people targeted in the attack. Similarly, in neither of these two cases did the Ivorian authorities take immediate action to suspend from duty any military personnel allegedly involved in the attacks or end the de facto policing and security role played by the Dozo militia. Finally, in both instances, there has been virtually no progress towards accountability even though inquiries have been opened … impunity still prevails, denying victims and their relatives the possibility of establishing the truth and obtaining reparation.[2]

In the U.S., this carnage was treated as epiphenomenal. A little over four months after the July 29, 2013, Amnesty International report was published, at the Human Rights First Annual Summit held on December 4, 2013, in Washington, D.C., Susan Rice, now Obama's National Security Advisor, was gleeful about her role in Côte d'Ivoire: "In Cote d'Ivoire, we worked through the United Nations to arrest spiraling violence and enable the duly-elected leader of Cote d'Ivoire to take office after a despot stubbornly refused to cede power."[3] Rice, who counted among her proudest accomplishments, her "Turtle Bay–led campaign to take down Ivory Coast's former leader, Laurent Gbagbo, after he refused to accept an electoral defeat,"[4] continued to take for granted her interpretation of the results of the Ivorian elections, while the very question of the outcome of the 2010–2011 elections in Côte d'Ivoire was still at issue and remained unresolved, while it was precisely Gbagbo's insistence that the issue be resolved in the most peaceful and democratic way, that is, vote recount, which had angered the Obama administration and prompted an ego-bruised Obama to give his go-ahead to Sarkozy's military operation.

President Gbagbo had decided that the transfer of power, thought, and responsibility from Côte d'Ivoire to the metropole that had hitherto defined the

France-Africa relation and made Ivorian governments nongovernmental organizations at the sole service of France's interests with no regard to the interests of the Ivorian people had to come to an end through political, economic, and social purgative Refondation. Had he succeeded, this would have meant a slash in the dividends of French multinationals and a certain deficit in France's economy. Sarkozy needed Obama's support to see to completion a protracted ploy started by Chirac in 2002. Obama needed some backbone, which at home he was accused of lacking, even after the fall of Gaddafi. Obama could get his spine and strengthen Susan Rice's résumé. So to war Sarkozy and Obama went against Gbagbo under the pretext of freeing the world of an illegitimate president, an assassin and a killer-of-his-own-people worthy of the International Criminal Court. Sarkozy, Obama, and Ban Ki-Moon would have made the world believe that in Côte d'Ivoire all was for the best in the best of all possible worlds had the truth not caught up with them.

A Most Imperfect Mise-en-Scène

On March 3, 2011, four months after the unresolved presidential election in Côte d'Ivoire that saw President Gbagbo and rival Ouattara each claim victory, the news of nine women allegedly shot by Gbagbo's troops in the populous suburb of Abobo sent shockwaves throughout the media. These women were allegedly targeted with live ammunition by Gbagbo's crowd-control police while they were marching to the Presidential Palace to seek his resignation. The Western media, and especially the French media, profusely relayed the "news" of Gbagbo-the-African-dictator-that-would-not-hesitate-to-slaughter-his-own-people. French president Nicolas Sarkozy, UN secretary Ban Ki-Moon, and American president Barack Obama characterized the "massacre" as the straw that broke the camel's back. Gbagbo had crossed the red line that human decency would not tolerate. He could no longer be a party to any political negotiation. His forced removal was henceforth the order of the day. This new, harsher, and firmer rhetoric in the Ivorian crisis was enthusiastically applauded by those who had been lamenting the international community's sluggishness in removing Gbagbo.

On April 11, 2011, the international community, led by France, the United Nations, and the United States, kept its word, shelled Abidjan, and forcefully arrested President Gbagbo. On November 29, 2011, Gbagbo was deported to the International Criminal Court to be judged for "crimes against humanity." On February 20, 2013, the prosecution team of the International Criminal Court, led by the first substitute to the prosecutor, Eric McDonald, assisted by Maria Berdennikova, Krisztina Varga, and Florie Huch, presented its "Document Containing the Charges" (DCC) against President Gbagbo. The prosecution's case rested essentially on four elements: (1) the alleged violent repression by Gbagbo's forces of a march to the national TV station (RTI) organized on December 16, 2010, by members of the Rassemblement des Houphouëtistes pour la Démocratie et la Paix (RHDP) (the coalition of opposition parties established in 2004 against Gbagbo in the aftermath of the Marcoussis Agreement), a repression which the prosecution alleged was planned and coordinated at the highest level of the military hierarchy; (2) the alleged killing by Gbagbo's Republican Guard and Gendarmerie of seven women in the populous suburb Abobo during a March 3, 2011, protest march organized by Ouattara's supporters to demand that Gbagbo resign (the alleged "Abobo Massacre"); (3) the alleged bombardment on March 17, 2011, by Gbagbo's army of the Siaka Koné Market, in Derrière Rails, a quarter of Abobo, which according to the prosecution caused 25 deaths and around 40 wounded; and (4) the alleged abuses (arrests, rapes, and murders), jointly perpetrated by the police and the young patriots faithful to Gbagbo, in mid–April in the Doukouré and Mamie Faitai quarters of Yopougon in what came to be referred to as "the Battle of Yopougon."

As Gbagbo's defense team, led by Emmanuel Altit, assisted by Jennifer Naouri, Natacha Ivanovic, and Assistant Professor Dov Jacobs of Leiden Law School, started to deconstruct the prosecution's DCC, it became clear that in its haste to condemn President Gbagbo, and convinced that it had the backing of the international community, the prosecution team did not thoroughly and professionally investigate the facts constitutive of the DCC. Instead, the prosecutor presented an amateurish, sloppy, and imprecise DCC that was more a compendium of allegations and biased articles fed him by the Ouattara camp than it was the result of serious work by a professional investigator seeking to get to the bottom of things.

Had the prosecution investigated the accusations thoroughly, it would have discovered, as most Ivorians did, that as time passed, the story of the "Abobo Massacre" started to show serious holes. Videos of the march had surfaced on social media, which suggested that the story of the seven women killed was a cinematic production gone wrong. One video, particularly, showed one of the alleged victims of the purported attack getting up at a moment she was supposed to play dead and being ordered in Malinké language by a man on the scene to "lie back down, because [the scene] was not over yet." Evidently, Dramane Ouattara had arranged for a fake attack of civilians by the Defense Forces of Côte d'Ivoire to be manufactured for the purpose of affecting world opinion and precipitating a military action against President Gbagbo. This, Gbagbo's defense team at The Hague was able to show on February 25, 2013, before the judges of the International Criminal Court. The account of a former member of the Commando Invisible, a leader in the theater of operations in Abobo, explained the deception. The infamous march was not a spontaneous march. It was organized from the Golf Hotel (where Ouattara had established his headquarters and whence he was challenging Gbagbo's government), by order of Ouattara. The goal was to create empathy towards Ouattara's camp in the international community by presenting Ouattara's supporters as the victims of a brutal regime. A carefully rehearsed mise-en-scène with paid actors, the act was finally performed on March 3, 2011. What the international community witnessed on TV were bleeding women strewn on the ground in a chaotic mêlée, alleged victims of deadly rockets launched by the loyalist troops against a peaceful demonstration. The real story, however, was something else, as one of the scenarists explained:

> We had coordinators giving instructions to some women. We had some of our invisible commandos shoot warning shots. While some women simulated the march, several militiamen, firm supporters of Dramane, armed with rockets and Kalashnikovs, hid in the crowd. They had received their weapons from Imam Sidiki from the Marley Quarter Mosque. They were to shoot the loyalist troops in case the event was to be secured by Gbagbo's forces. And as there was no presence of security forces, seven women were designated to simulate the attack. Each of them was to receive 100,000 CFA francs. All the coaches and participants were to receive 50,000 CFA francs. And all have received their money at the mosque of Marley Quarter, at the Roundabout of Banco, at Derriere Rails. So while some women pretended to walk, others were lying down. We poured sheep blood on them. This was how our technicians made a fake film to look like reality. That artwork was presented on TV and put on the head of Gbagbo.

Ouattara and his international backers almost had the world fooled. Unfortunately for them, Ouattara's mise-en-scène was a badly produced piece; and, as is the case with every badly fashioned piece, it contained major defects.

In this case, however, the flaws had fatal consequences. The armed militiamen that Ouattara hid among the women ended up, either by mistake or by design, killing their own actors. Gbagbo's defense team's evidence in support of this proposition was an undated video of a march of women that took place on the same route as the march of Abobo. Both the defense and the prosecutor agreeing that no other march of this kind took place in Abobo, it is easy to ascertain that the video was in fact from the infamous march that made international news. In the film, young men in civilian clothes who were armed with rocket grenade launchers and firearms were among the protesters, which corroborated the Commando Invisible leader's account that Ouattara's operatives had the march infiltrated by armed militiamen.

As noted by Gbagbo's defense team, all happened as if the prosecution was not interested in discovering the truth about the "Abobo Massacre." While it would have been more instructive for the prosecution to try to understand who fired on the marchers, from where, and with what kind of weapons, in fact the prosecution conducted not a single ballistics test, did not even bother to go on the scene of the event, questioned neither the loyalist forces nor any member of the Commando Invisible; it only satisfied itself with exhibiting the manufactured video as evidence that one of Gbagbo's tanks fired a heavy weapon into the crowd of protesters, killing seven women. Had the prosecution been more professional, it would have discovered that, while a heavy caliber round fired from a tank does indubitably leave a sizeable impact on its landing site, there was, curiously, not a single crater that would suggest the shot or shots that killed the women came from a tank; none of the alleged victims were autopsied, and the bodies were mysteriously "disposed of." Indeed, a serious investigation would have taught the prosecution that on the very day of Gbagbo's arrest, orders were received from Ouattara to quickly get rid of the bodies of the victims of the "Abobo massacre," while good judgment would have demanded that the victims be autopsied for Gbagbo's implication in their deaths to be unequivocally established. Instead, five victims were precipitately buried in a mass grave and another victim was buried separately in the Banco Natural Park. Why was Ouattara so quick to get rid of the bodies at the very moment when, in total control of the state power, he could have calmly conducted a full and accurate investigation on the matter, and, as was his keenest wish, establish Gbagbo's indisputable guilt? Obviously, the victims' bodies carried evidence, or the lack thereof, that Ouattara would rather not see disclosed, evidence that would have cleared President Gbagbo and incriminated Ouatarra instead. In fact, in its zeal to expeditiously send Gbagbo to the pillory, the prosecution included in the DCC videos of postelectoral violent acts in Kenya that Ouattara's operatives had given them as showing acts commissioned by Gbagbo in Abobo, Côte d'Ivoire. The manipulation was monumental!

In fact, as the prosecution's own witness stated, on March 3, 2011, Abobo was no longer controlled by the loyalist forces. An urban guerrilla that ambushed and tracked the loyalists and anyone associated to them down to their residences and assassinated them in the streets and in their beds had the loyalists surrender Abobo and six police stations out of the seven that the city counted. Law enforcement forces were concentrated in only one police station in the city of 1.5 million people. Overtaken by the Commando Invisible, Abobo was a lawless zone where several rival rebel groups vied for power. The populations of Abobo, whenever possible, fled the town to take refuge under the protection of the Ivorian Defense Forces (FDS), the very forces that the prosecution alleged were targeting the populations. Of the rival groups in Abobo, Ibrahim Coulibaly's (IB) Commando Invisible was the most powerful and occupied the city and used the population as a vast human shield. IB, who had been infiltrated in Abobo by the United Nations and France in order to undermine Gbagbo's forces, was as well-equipped as the National Defense and Security Forces (FDS).

After the capture of President Gbagbo by the UN and French forces, the rivalry between Ibrahim Coulibaly's and Guillaume Soro's forces, which had started in the early 2000s, went a step further. IB insisted that it was his work in Abobo that occasioned Gbagbo's fall and claimed that he deserved a bigger share of the loot as well as a high position in Ouattara's administration. He was eying the position of Army Chief of Staff. IB's regular, reckless declarations on foreign television stations took on the appearance of blackmail. He was quickly perceived by Ouattara as a loose cannon in a rebellion that had come to power by stepping over hundreds of thousands of deaths since 2002. On April 27, 2011, after IB was convinced by the United Nations to lay down his weapons and discuss with Ouattara's defense minister (Guillaume Soro), the leader of the Commando Invisible and his lieutenant, Félix Anoblé, were ambushed and assassinated by Soro's forces. In his resentful ramblings, Ibrahim Coulibaly was certainly going to give away privileged information on the Abobo operations, and certainly on the controversial "Abobo Massacre," of which he was one of the coordinators. Dramane Ouattara and Guillaume Soro had IB killed and buried with his secrets—though some people had stated that Ouattara had wanted IB captured alive.[5] The prosecution's sloppy job and failure to substantiate its accusations against President Gbagbo, Professor Jacobs argued, demanded that the DCC should be rejected. In any judicial trial this would be possible. However, the trial against Gbagbo was no judicial trial. It was political. As noted François Mattei, whose conversations with President Gbagbo at The Hague have come out in book form, Gbagbo is a political prisoner at The Hague despite the international community's efforts to present him otherwise:

> I cannot dissociate the fate of Laurent Gbagbo, who is at the ICC today, from the state of affairs of the Franco-African relations that are misguided and are hidden from public view…. Gbagbo was going to make the system collapse. The fact that he was going for the creation of an Ivorian currency, the fact that he would not renew the defense agreements, the fact that he did not come to the celebration of the fiftieth anniversary of Independence in Paris, during which Nicolas Sarkozy gathered all the French-speaking African heads of state made him a pariah. France had wanted him gone for a long time.[6]

The International Criminal Court Is a Plantation Court

France, the United Nations, and the United States' seditious project in Abidjan has further corrupted the International Criminal Court, which has had a serious credibility problem since its inception, and which many critics view as a Western political pressure tool to extend Western imperialism in the world. Today, as renowned Pan-Africanist and fighter for the freedom of Africa from the shackles of neocolonialism Laurent Koudou Gbagbo is sitting in a "white" prison at the International Criminal Court at The Hague after an eight-month detention in a concentration camp in northern Cote d'Ivoire, the ICC difficulty in substantiating the accusations against him gives credence to the belief that the International Criminal Court is a Plantation Court run by a lynch mob at the service of the imperialist powers. No one, not even President Gbagbo's white captors, are really convinced of the crimes of which he is being accused. The truth is that President Gbagbo is being punished for daring to look the white imperialist in the eyes and tell him that the white program of rape and plundering of the African continent will take place only over his dead body. So, the "superior" men came with their "superior" morals and, with the help of those African collaborators who cannot forgive God for having made them in the color of the devil, who cannot wait to have the gates of white bliss opened to them, shackled President Gbagbo and took him to this 21st-century Plantation Court they call the International Criminal Court.

For indeed, apart from victimizing the victims and rewarding the victimizers, what justice has this Plantation Court, allegedly created to prosecute individuals for genocide and other crimes against humanity, ever really rendered Africans? Whatever happened to President Mitterrand of France, who organized, trained, armed, and transported the perpetrators of the Rwandan genocide? Whatever happened to President Chirac of France, who orchestrated and supported the killing of tens of thousands of Lissouba's supporters in Congo? Whatever will ever happen to presidents Chirac and then Sarkozy of France, whose military forces killed thousands of Ivorian civilians in 2004 and in 2011? We surmise that no Western leader, no matter the scale and violence of his crimes on Africans, will ever be tried in this Plantation Court system they call the International Criminal Court. President Gbagbo's arrest, the most theatrical capture of an African freedom fighter since the capture and elimination of Patrice Lumumba, is meant to quash any African outrage about the plunder of the continent by the unscrupulous West, to serve as an example of white justice to any African nationalist opposed to the West's predatory projects in Africa. If the so-called International Criminal Court is really looking for criminals and human rights abusers in Cote d'Ivoire, it is Alassane Dramane Ouattara, this puppet of international finance, whose protracted rebellion has killed more than 100,000 civilians in Côte d'Ivoire since 2002, who ought to be interpellated. For this Plantation Court called the International Criminal Court to deserve some semblance of credibility, it is Ouattara's special police, with its daily lot of documented kidnappings, rapes, killings, and extra-judiciary assassinations, that ought to be brought to justice. But most of all, for real justice to ever take place, it is those for whom Ouattara works, the Western heads of state and financial interests that funded his war on the people of Côte d'Ivoire, who ought to be interpellated.

This, however, will never happen as long as Ouattara continues to enable the transfer of the Ivorian geological and agricultural resources to the First World. The illegal capture and incarceration of President Gbagbo in a white jail has historical precedence. Toussaint Louverture of Haiti died in a white jail. Samory Touré of West Africa died in a white jail. King Behanzin of Dahomey died in a white jail. Their crimes? They opposed the rape of Africa by the ravenous Occident. Their captures were also facilitated and applauded by some Africans. Each time an African freedom fighter is arrested by the white world and Africans applaud, each time the African continent is plundered of its natural and human resources and Africans applaud, Africans give a standing ovation to the Gobineauian and Levy-Brhulian Aryanist theses of black inferiority and cerebral ugliness, a cerebral ugliness that can be made responsible for all the ugliness of the world, even that which is openly perpetrated by white malice.

A Coalition of the Most Violent

Since 2002, in its effort to present the armed front against Gbagbo's government as unified and rational, the international community had tried to glaze over bitter and violent internal dissentions within the rebellion. The truth is that Ouattara—"the democrat" imposed by means of heavy artillery upon the people of Côte d'Ivoire by the United Nations, France, and the United States on April 11, 2011—does keep a good company of friends, so good that often he must eliminate his friends or get them to eliminate one another so that he can sleep more soundly. With the assassination of IB, Guillaume Soro was henceforth rid of his archrival within the rebellion and wielding tremendous military power over Ouattara. That is why, though Ouattara, too, could breathe more easily with the death of IB, it was not too certain that he was better-off. Perhaps he would have wished that IB and Soro had eliminated each other. Indeed, though sandwiched between two armies—those of IB and Soro—glaring at each other and at him, too, Ouattara had the benefit of counterbalancing IB's influence with Soro's and vice versa. With IB dead, Ouattara was totally at the mercy of Soro, a man with overweening ambitions and as ruthless as Outarra who would not hesitate to take Outarra's place if the occasion presented itself. With Soro's assassination of IB, Ouattara lost a counterbalance to Soro's fear-provoking clout.

The IB-Soro rivalry dated back to the early days of the rebellion. In 2002, after the failed coup against President Gbagbo was transmuted into the protracted Northern Rebellion, Guillaume Soro was chosen by the leaders of the insurrection to be their spokesperson. Soro had been a charismatic leader of the Fédération Estudiantine de Côte d'Ivoire (FESCI), and among the group of mostly uneducated, scruffy ragtag fighters French Foreign Affairs Minister Dominique de Villepin had advised upon his first visit in Bouaké to cut their beards and clean up in order to appear less Islamist, less frightening to Western opinion, Soro's youth and oratory skills were seen as invaluable assets. The youthful and somewhat educated persona of Soro could change the image of the rebellion, it was hoped. And indeed, by 2003 the rebellion had been laundered and freshened up. It had adopted the statutes of political organization and branched into three political parties, the MPCI, the MPIGO, and the MJP, with an army, the Forces Nouvelles (New Forces) (FN). Its soldiers had been showered with new equipment and vehicles, as well as shiny uniforms, by France and the United Nations. En route to Marcoussis, via Senegal, Guillaume Soro had received from President Abdoulaye Wade his first suit and a crash course in diplomacy and negotiation skills[7] he used efficiently to legitimate the rebellion in the eyes of a very hostile Ivorian population and snatch a few cabinet posts from President Gbagbo.

Guillaume Soro had successfully parleyed his role as spokesperson of the rebellion into that of the chief of the rebellion, a title that IB, who had been at the forefront of all the military fights in the string of military coups against Bédié, Gueï, and Gbagbo, believed should be naturally his to carry. Although Soro was not very fond of President Gbagbo, it was undeniable that Gbagbo helped Soro tremendously in the fight for positioning that opposed Soro to IB. In fact, the more Soro negotiated with Gbagbo, the more exposure Soro garnered, the greater aura it conferred him, and the more it estranged IB and made him irrelevant in the Ivorian political landscape. After the Linas-Marcoussis Conference and the Kléber Summit, Soro's influence was on the rise, to the chagrin of IB. Ibrahim Coulibaly decided that the only way for him to recapture his rebellion would be another rebellion against Guillaume Soro, who had all but pushed him aside. On August 25, 2003, while he was in a meeting with a group of his partners in a Parisian hotel, IB was arrested by the French authorities and incarcerated for "terrorism" and attempting to derail the peace efforts in Côte d'Ivoire. Freed a month later, IB nonetheless remained outside of his country while Soro continued to marginalize him.

In December 2003, in order to keep IB relevant, one of his lieutenants, Corporal Kassoum Bamba (Kass), commander of the Bouaké Air Base, had claimed that Ibrahim Coulibaly (IB) was the president of the Forces Nouvelles and that no agreement with President Gbagbo would have validity unless approved by IB. During the night of June 20–21, 2004, Kass's forces were attacked by Soro's soldiers. On the morning of June 21, Kass's body was found mutilated and charred in a heap of smoldering destruction. Before Kass, Adama Coulibaly, another close associate of IB's and chief of the zone of Korhogo was ambushed and riddled with bullets on February 8, 2004, on order of Chérif Ousmane, another close associate of Soro's. The Soro-IB war had been merciless. In 2004, hundreds of

IB's soldiers were killed by Soro's forces while IB was in exile, and in 2009, IB had tried another coup against Gbagbo before being summoned by the Beninese authorities to leave Benin. IB had a bone to pick with Soro, and despite his collaboration with Soro's troops in his role as the leader of the Commando Invisible, he remained a constant headache Soro had decided to get rid of in the most drastic way. IB was executed in a manner that, though ruthless, has become routine for an autocratic regime that from the very first had chosen to rule by fear, and which, nonetheless, the Obama administration continued to certify as democratic. In fact, it would seem that one major criterion for social mobility in the world according to Dramane Ouattara is brutality.

The more brutal one is, the greater prospect one has of being promoted; and in a regime that has made *Rattrapage ethnique* its basis for development, the odds for promotion increase even for those who are able to combine ruthlessness with northern appurtenance, and preferably northern–Islamic ascendency. A cursory survey of Ouattara's proudest appointments verifies his overvaluation of cruelty as qualifying virtue. Indeed, in the framework of a vast program of administrative reshuffling he undertook a little over a year into his installation by the international community, Ouattara decided to appoint three new prefects in the sensitive regions of Côte d'Ivoire.

Hence, on September 26, 2012, Ouattara reached out to the most merciless warlords of the rebellion. He appointed Ousmane Coulibaly, better known as "bin Laden," to administer the city of San-Pédro, capital of the region of Lower-Sassandra. "Bin Laden," as his nickname attests, is an admirer of the legendary al-Qaida leader and a believer in Islamic fundamentalism and terrorist modes of operation. In Odienné, where he was zone commander, "bin Laden" had established a vast racketeering system and a profitable network of illicit diamond and gold trafficking. After his ruthless reign as zone commander in Odienné, the town where Simone Gbagbo was being held before her trial in Abidjan, "bin Laden" had been in charge of the security of Yopougon, in the District of Abidjan. In 2011, as commander of the Anti-Riot Brigade in Yopougon, Ousmane Coulibaly, aka "bin Laden," tortured and executed many civilians. In 2012, he directed "Operations Cleansing" in Dabou. There, too, "Bin Laden, racketeered, tortured, and murdered several civilians. According to Human Rights Watch Ousmane Coulibaly aka 'Bin Laden'" had very close ties with Charles Taylor and Liberian mercenaries. Human Rights Watch, Amnesty International, and International Crisis Group have all accused Ousmane Coulibaly of serious crimes against humanity (torture, summary executions, sexual abuses, etc.) in the city of Man and its surrounding area. However, for Dramane Ouattara, "bin Laden's" ruthlessness was a prerequisite for being a superlative administrator. And so, satisfied with "bin Laden's" résumé, Ouattara promoted him prefect of the San Pédro area on September 26, 2012.

Ouattara's second nomination on that day was Tuo Fozié. Appointed to be the prefect of Bondoukou, capital of the Zanzan Region, Fozié was previously head of the unit responsible for the FRCI fight against racketeering. Tuo Fozié had been a recruiting agent for the rebellion. A close associate of Ibrahim Coulibaly (IB), but also one of those who deserted him first to join his rival faction within the rebellion, Fozié was among those who attacked Abidjan in the first minutes of the rebellion and left the capital in a bloodbath as they were retreating. Tuo Fozié is the "success story" of the rebellion, though Exhibit 1 of how armed insurgencies have kept Africa in a state of backwardness, to the delight of the Euro-American imperialist powers that finance them and profit from Africa's instability. Outfitted with only a third grade education and incapable of correctly formulating the simplest idea, Tuo Fozié was proposed by the rebels to be the Minister of Youth and Civic Service in the post–Marcoussis government of 2003. Fozié had been a fierce combatant in the rebellion. By Ouattara's standard, he had proven that he could also be a great administrator; after all, the job at hand was to subdue the population through fear, and Fozié was good at that.

Ouattara's third new prefect was Commander Koné Messamba, the former director of the paramilitary forces of the FN. Ouattara chose Messamba to be the prefect of Guiglo, in the western region, along the Liberian border, in the Middle-Cavally region. Reports by Amnesty International, the International Committee of the Red Cross, and the International Federation of Human Rights cite Tuho Fozié and Messamba Koné for serious human rights abuses. Messamba, like Fozié, is an illiterate Ouattara named for his propensity for brutality. After their nominations, Ouattara sent his unschooled war criminals to the French military camp in Port-Bouët to learn the rudiments of administration. As a French officer explained, they showed up with personal scribes to take notes for them; the officer added, as if to justify this incongruity, "Should we leave at the head of the new Ivorian army some unskilled corporals, or should we provide them with skills? Like it or not, without these guys it would be the reign of anarchy [in the country]. We are only helping the legal Côte d'Ivoire. Besides, it was President Ouattara who asked us to do the job."[8] They could have fooled us. The fact is that it is the reign of anarchy in Côte d'Ivoire, precisely *because* of "these guys." "These guys" brought anarchy to the country with their bloody insurgency, and "these guys" have been sustaining anarchy with their politics of ethnic and religious cleansing. Nevertheless, it is incomprehensible that France, which armed and supported the rebellion of "these guys," should rationalize their presence as indispensable to democracy and stability in Côte d'Ivoire. It is the height of cynicism for France to pretend that it is helping bring stability in Côte d'Ivoire while it is France that helped destabilize the country in the first place.

Uncontrolled Controlled Bungles

France's cynicism can be of disconcerting morbidity. One of the events that precipitated America's hostility against Gbagbo's government and helped consolidate France's coalition against Gbagbo in the years to come took place in the rebels' stronghold of Bouaké. In effect, a year after the Marcoussis Agreements that had seen the composition of a "government of national reconciliation" in which the rebels were fully integrated, little progress had been achieved in disarming the rebellion, reunifying the country, and restoring full civilian administration on the entire Ivorian territory. In spite of enormous sacrifices consented to by the authorities of Abidjan, the rebel leaders continued to taunt the legal authorities. In fact, the rebels had established a parallel administration in the northern and western regions of the country, with their own taxation system networks, and were siphoning the agricultural and geological resources as well as racketeering in the population through a plethora of occult passage fees on the northern roads.

So, in early November 2004, President Gbagbo decided the time had come to end the partition of the country and halt the bleeding of the Ivorian economy by taking decisive military action. He set about weakening the rebels' positions with airstrikes and had the infantry move in next. He called on President Chirac to inform him of his intention. According to former French Ambassador Gildas Le Lidec, a furious Chirac scolded Gbagbo like a master would a schoolchild. In an audition he gave in his jail cell at The Hague, Gbagbo described his conversation with Chirac as being very hard:

> [Chirac] asks me what I am thinking. He is shocked that my army wants to attack the rebels. I say "don't you think it's normal? These people stifle us, do not respect the agreements." I add that he did nothing to disarm them. Our conversation was very hard. I do not know who hung up first but it was very hard. I learned later that Barnier [French Foreign Minister] told Chirac that he had gone too far; that he did not have to talk to me like that.[9]

Chirac's paternalistic posture and his evident bias in favor of the rebels reinforced Gbagbo's resolve to take his responsibilities as the leader of a sovereign country. On November 6, 2004, two Ivorian Sukhoi 25s flown by two Byelorussians pilots, Barys Smahine and Yuri Sukhos, assisted by Ivorian Lieutenant-Colonel Ange Gnanduillet and Lieutenant Patrice Oueï, took off for Bouaké and heavily bombarded the rebels' positions, weakening their military infrastructures. Around 1:30 p.m. the planes made a second round in Bouaké, then one of them circled the French military camp established on the ground of Lycée Descartes once. On its second pass, it dropped its rockets on the camps, killing nine French soldiers and one American humanitarian worker and wounding 39 other people.

Immediately, and quite understandably, all fingers pointed at President Gbagbo as having ordered the killings. After all, it was his plane and his army, and it was now no secret that he had launched Opération Dignité, whose objective was to end the protracted rebel occupation of the North and reunify the country. Nevertheless, did Gbagbo actually order the attack on the French camp? What would he gain by making such a move? When passions quieted down and coolheadedness returned, the facts started to tell another story. It became increasingly clear that the victims of the Bouaké bombing were all the collateral damages of a sinister ploy by the French authorities to indict and attack Gbagbo and operate a regime change. The Bouaké attack was supposed to be a controlled blunder attributable to Gbagbo. Unfortunately, the plot did not work as planned, and the controlled gaffe eluded its planners. Years after the attack on the French camp, those who really sought to understand how it happened, such as Jean Balan, a lawyer representing 22 of the victims in the bombing, were unambiguous in charging the French authorities with orchestrating the airstrike. Mr. Balan's difficulty in getting the French authorities to cooperate in resolving the issue, crossed with his own findings, led him to conclude that the Bouaké attack was a conspiracy by the Elysée to use French soldiers as pawns in a macabre game to justify a war against Gbagbo: "I accuse the political authorities of the time of sabotaging the investigation by all means possible. The victims are nothing but the collateral damages of a very dangerous and ill-managed game by the French president [Jacques Chirac] to set his scores with Laurent Gbagbo."[10] After having questioned hundreds of witnesses ranging from low-ranking soldiers to generals who had been subpoenaed by two judges of the Military Court of Paris and later by Judge Sabine Kheris of the District Court of Paris, Balan confidently stated, "The facts are established today. The attack against the French camp was deliberate, but the deaths were not intentional. The objective was to find a reason to get rid of Gbagbo…. Today, no one denies the evidence. They just try to avoid the question or obstruct justice."[11] Like Balan, French General Henri Poncet, who was in charge of the French operations in Côte d'Ivoire at the time of the event, stated unambiguously that the deaths of the French soldiers were an orchestrated bungle by the French authorities which did not go as planned. The expression General Poncet used before a judge of the Army Court was that it was "a manipulated blunder." For French pilot Jean-Jacques Fuentes, the Byelorussian pilot of the Sukhoi that fired the rockets on the French camp had received contradictory orders directly from the Elysée asking him to shift targets and hit the French camp instead.[12]

The French authorities, as the investigations revealed, were closely informed of the itinerary and objectives of the operation. Gbagbo's army Chief-of-Staff, General Mathias Doué, kept the French authorities au fait of the details of Opération Dignité to ensure that the airstrikes would not cause any French casualties.

On November 6, 2004, at the time of the strike the officers' mess was supposed to be empty, and the French authorities bet on a strike without casualties, which would be good enough pretext, all the same, to pin down Gbagbo. Unfortunately for them, nine French soldiers and one American humanitarian worker, unaware of the deadly game of chess being played by the French authorities, had unexpectedly taken refuge under the porch of the mess. The French authorities' attempt to obstruct the emergence of truth on the matter started in the very hours that followed the attack. Upon their landing in Yamoussoukro, rather than being arrested by the French soldiers that guarded the airport, the Byelorussians were instead surreptitiously put on a bus with 15 other of their compatriots working as mechanics for Gbagbo's army—whom General Poncet had arrested and was hoping to question—and exfiltrated out of the country towards Togo. In Abidjan, General Poncet was ordered by his superiors in Paris to let them go free. In Togo, the mysterious travelers' suspicious behavior alarmed the Togolese Interior Minister, who ordered their arrest and immediately contacted the French intelligence services representative in Togo. For ten days the Togolese Interior Minister had the suspects in custody. He understood that Paris wanted nothing to do with them. So, he too let them leave and never heard from them again. When the French Foreign Affairs Minister-become-Interior Minister, Dominique de Villepin, was questioned by the judges on the issue he simply acted dumb and explained that he knew nothing about the affair, absolutely nothing. For Balan, it is as if de Villepin had suddenly never heard of Côte d'Ivoire: "He knows nothing, nothing at all. Listening to him, it is as if he had never heard of Côte d'Ivoire." French Defense Minister Michèle Alliot-Marie justified the release of the suspects by the fact that there existed no international warrant allowing France to question them, to which the victims' lawyer retorted as follows: "Michèle Alliot-Marie lied deliberately ... [and] the case would have been quickly resolved if from the beginning the French authorities had allowed justice to run its course. The juridical context existed." And, indeed, the context for questioning the suspects existed. French law had three arsenals for bringing them to justice:

> First, the Pelchat law of April 14, 2003, which represses the activity of mercenaries. Secondly, Article 65 of the Code of Military Justice provides that are amenable to the Army Court all perpetrators or accomplices of an offense against the French armed forces. Finally, Article 113-7 of the Criminal Code states that French criminal law is applicable to any crime committed by a foreigner outside the territory of the Republic when the victim is a French national.[13]

Were the French authorities really interested in finding the truth, they could have activated any one of these juridical arsenals available to them and retained the suspects for questioning. Instead, they put the suspects on a bus and maneuvered to get them out of Africa.

The fact that the original plans went terribly wrong did little to curb the French authorities' intention to remove President Gbagbo from office. Au contraire, in the hours following the manufactured attack, in a sinister turn of events the bungled controlled bungle gave the French authorities even greater justification to carry on their seditious endeavor. In Yamoussoukro and in Abidjan, French soldiers executed Chirac's order to destroy Côte d'Ivoire entire army's planes on the ground, a decision that undermined the Ivorian Defense Force's ability to defend its territory from the rebellion and strengthened the latter's position. On the night of November 6, a human tide of angry young patriots decided to walk to the French army camp in Port-Bouët to protest the French army's destruction of the Ivorian defense infrastructures. Over the two bridges that link the northern suburbs of Abidjan to the southern suburbs, French helicopters were positioned, waiting for them. As the first wave of the crowd reached the middle of the bridges, they were greeted with live rocket fire. Many died of bullet wounds. Many panicked and jumped to their deaths. To this day, it is difficult to know how many people perished in the savage attack.

On November 8, in the heat of the popular protests against the French army's carnage on the young patriots, a convoy of French tanks coming from Bouaké was supposedly sent to Abidjan to secure the Hôtel Ivoire, a location where French citizens were said to be gathering for imminent evacuation. The Hôtel Ivoire is the tallest and most unmistakable building in Abidjan. It is located on Boulevard Latrille, one of the largest boulevards of the Ivorian capital, in the affluent suburb of Cocody. Allegedly the tank convoy "got lost" and, coincidentally, ended up in a much smaller street, right in front of the gates of President Gbagbo's official residence. The fable of the "lost regiment" was another manufactured blunder by the Chirac regime, whose aim was to remove President Gbagbo and find a "convenient" substitute, the international community's poster boy, that is, Dramane Ouattara. While Ouattara was patiently waiting for the plot to be fully cooked up, Gbagbo's prospective temporary replacement, army Chief-of-Staff Mathias Doué, was said to be in one of the lost tanks, ready to take over. Doué, it was expected, would briefly take power after the coup, put in place a transitional government and within six months organize a presidential election that would result in Ouattara's landslide victory. It was to be a repeat of Gueï's regency, but this time with a tightly guarded result by the French authorities. Doué was going to do what Gueï refused to do. He was going to put Ouattara in the Presidential Palace.

This nth plan to topple Gbagbo failed. On November 8, 2004, thousands of young patriots, who had been alerted of the rolling tanks from Bouaké, had sensed the coup in preparation and had formed a human barrier to protect the Presidential Palace. Evidently their suspicion was right, given the final destination of the regiment. However, the French army would not retreat without satisfying its thirst for Ivorian blood as, once again, at the Hôtel Ivoire, the French army shot and killed scores of young Ivorians without the international community's uttering a peep. Years later, the explanation to cover the attempt to remove President Gbagbo would be a rosary of incongruities. In May 2010, Michèle Alliot-Marie stated under oath to Judge Sabine Kheris that the column of tanks that "lost its way" and ended up in front of the Presidential Palace was going to secure the residence of the French Ambassador, which was contiguous to Gbagbo's residence. Her statement was contradicted by General Poncet and the officer whose mission was to guide the column. While General Poncet explained that the French guide panicked and got lost on his way to Hôtel Ivoire, the French guide stated that, indeed, he got lost on his way to Hôtel Ivoire, but not because he panicked. His GPS instruments panicked and gave him false information. It was General Poncet's deputy, General Renaud Malaussène, who finally stopped the runaround and told the truth about the events of November 6–8, from the attack on the Bouaké French military camp to the story of the "lost tanks":

> There was a political project in place to install Ouattara and get rid of Gbagbo, who was an intelligent, cultured, and refined man, who had weathered many crises, and who, deep in his heart, loves France…. I am convinced that it was not Gbagbo's intention to kill any French soldier. Someone in his entourage took that initiative without his knowing…. I believe that the presidential camp fell in a trap.[14]

The political project to put Ouattara in Gbagbo's place finally succeeded on April 11, 2011, because a spineless Ban Ki-Moon and a weak Obama in search of gumption blindly followed Sarkozy in his illegal Ivorian adventure. Today, Gbagbo is sitting at the International Criminal Court under false accusations while in Côte d'Ivoire a dictatorship propped up by the international community is festering in the Ivorian social fabric.

There is an indispensable level of vigilance that is required of the readers of the Ivorian crisis, lest they should be misled by those who have commissioned it, especially by France, whose latest efforts have been deployed in rewriting history, in passing for the redeemer, while, in fact, France is the foe. Yet, for a moment, Sarkozy had the world fooled, had the world believing that the attack against Gbagbo was the sole initiative of the rebel forces, that the French troops the cameras captured leading Gbagbo in protective gear minutes after his arrest were his protectors, and that the installation of Ouattara in Côte d'Ivoire was the outcome of a democratic process. It did not take long, however, for major actors of the war on Côte d'Ivoire to become talkative. And it is the French Ambassador in post in Abidjan at the time of the event who, contradicting Sarkozy's statements that Paris had nothing to do with the shelling of the Presidential Palace and the capture of President Gbagbo, would spill the beans on Radio France Inter, on April 11, 2012, at the one year anniversary of the war:

When the FRCI have tried to approach the residence of Laurent Gbagbo, they encountered an extremely high resistance because there was absolutely insane movements around the residence and all the crossroads of Cocody; so the FRCI found themselves in difficulties. In the morning, they were unable to cross the lines after suffering many losses in material but also in human lives. So at that point decisions have been made to end this tragedy.... And therefore the intervention of the Licorne force was made at that time to open the axes and allow the FRCI to advance towards the residence of Cocody. And so the order was given to deploy the Licorne Forces in Cocody.

The attempt at freedom failed in Côte d'Ivoire, less because of the French innate superiority than because of internal moles that worked at weakening the struggle. For days a small army of young Ivorian militaries, with rudimentary weapons, held back a coalition of French, UN, and rebel armies. However, as the inquiry of Gbagbo's defense team would reveal later, key officers who had Gbagbo's trust— the army Chief of Staff Philippe Mangou and Chief of Gendarmerie Edouard Tiapé Kassaraté—had been selling weapons to the rebels all along. It is the internal betrayal of the higher-ranking officers that allowed the defeat of the Ivorian patriots.

For a moment, indeed, the international community and the corrupt African leaders who genuflected before it had us almost fooled, had us almost convinced that we had missed something, that we had slept through the erection of new democratic principles which, since the 2000 American vote recount in the Bush versus Gore electoral contest made vote recount a heresy. Actually, we had not slumbered through any change at all, as only a few months later the very harbingers of "no way, no recount!" were calling for vote recounts in order to settle their own electoral disputes. First, it was Raila Odinga, the declared loser of the 2013 Kenyan presidential election, who would not admit defeat until a vote recount had decided that he had lost. Could that be true? Was not Odinga among the fiercest detractors of President Gbagbo in 2010? Was not Odinga one of the loudest voices to call for an international army to dislodge President Gbagbo from his palace and deport him to the ICC rather than go through the more peaceable process of vote verification? Odinga must have considered himself a very exceptional human being to believe that his verity applied only to others, not to him. As he was stirring the muddy pond of ethnic conflicts, suggesting in hardly veiled terms that a refusal by the election commission to recount the vote could "agitate [his] supporters," he must, indeed, have been very assured of his extraordinary global relations to think that any trouble he generated would indubitably be placed entirely on the shoulders of Mr. Uhuru Kenyatta, his rival. Could Odinga be blamed for thinking that he was special, for displaying such self-sufficiency? Had not President Obama, on his behalf, inserted his bias into the Kenyan election when his Assistant Secretary of State, Jonnie Carson, a month before the March 4 contest warned Kenyans that there would be hell to pay if they reelected President Uhuru Kenyatta? "We live in an interconnected world ... and people should be thoughtful about the impact that their choices have on their nation, on the region, on the economy, on the society and on the world in which they live. Choices have consequences." The Kenyans had an answer for Obama and his preferred horse in the Kenyan presidential race: "Alone in the polling booth, more than six million Kenyans said to themselves: 'I'm an African and a Kenyan, I don't need anyone out there telling me who or what to vote for.'"[15] They reelected Uhuru Kenyatta.

Time Is, Indeed, the Second Name of God

President Laurent Gbagbo used to say that time is the second name of God. In November 2012, time vindicated him: that, indeed, vote recounting was no heresy, and that, to the contrary, the very politicians in Paris who had pilloried him for requesting a vote recount would be eating their own words. At the time when Nicolas Sarkozy was shelling Gbagbo's Presidential Palace to punish him for demanding a vote recount, the French dweller of the Hôtel Matignon (the official residence of the French prime minister) was François Fillon. By November 2012, Sarkozy had been defeated by François Hollande, and his party, the UMP, was in search of a new chairman. The November 21 election that pitted François Fillon against Jean-François Copé to that effect saw the former accuse the latter of fraud, and demand, against all French democratic principles as rewritten in the Ivorian case, that the election results be reviewed. And for a moment, we thought that the United Nations, the United States, the European Union, and Papua New Guinea would form a coalition to freeze Fillon's and his associates' assets, ban any exports from and imports into France, and bomb the Elysée into good sense. It did not happen. We were told that a vote recount was one way to arrive at determining who really won the election. Vote recount was good for France but not for Côte d'Ivoire.

The Euro-American World Has Decivilized Itself

In 1950, the Martinican poet, political leader, and founder of the Negritude Movement Aimé Césaire could not know to what extent his words were far-sighted when he wrote, "The hour of the barbarian is at hand. The modern barbarian. The American hour. Violence, excess, waste, mercantilism, bluff, gregariousness, stupidity, vulgarity, disorder ... be careful! American domination—the only domination from which one never recovers. I mean from which one never recovers unscarred."[16]

Europe, indeed, has decivilized itself, degraded itself, and awakened itself to buried instincts, to covetousness, to violence, to race hatred. It is regrettable that America should seek to become the heir of Europe's 600-year-old affliction. It is unfortunate that America should choose to scoff at Putin's insightful warning on the perils of the belief in the myth of exceptionalism, this virus of self-importance and conceit that is more destructive to the bystander whose properties the disease carrier covets than to the carrier himself, but which, nonetheless, does not spare its carrier, the coveter of other people's chattels. The Euro-American belief in the myth of exceptionalism has decivilized Europe and America. Out of the malady of exceptionalism Europe came raping and pillaging Africa until she turned her degenerate morals on her own children, until that fine day when she woke up to find her depravity turned against her own children, in her own backyard.

Today, a terrorist organization in the Middle East, determined to convert the whole planet to its vision of the world, has decided to take no prisoners; and while the Euro-American moralizers revel in their righteousness and condemn the other's savagery, nevertheless, the similarity between the terrorists' approaches and the Euro-American's modes of operation in the world, and in Africa particularly over the last 600 years, is confounding. More deplorable than America trying its best to catch Europe's disease—exceptionalism—it is regrettable that Obama, this American president of African descent in whom the people of Africa had placed so much hope for the reconstruction of America's troubled past with Africa, should be the most destructive hit man of the Euro-American world in Africa the 21st century has so far witnessed. For America, Obama has not been tough enough. For most Africans, Obama has been ruthless, one of the most brutal American presidents with whom the Black Continent has had the misfortune to deal.

In Libya, Obama Was Rambo on a Mission

In spite of what some of Obama's supporters had characterized as a "victory" in Libya and a vindication of Obama's toughness, Obama was still getting no respect; he was still not getting credit for gumption. The length of the operation against Gaddafi (six months to defeat Gaddafi's troops), which some overzealous conservatives criticized as a result of Obama's "Limited Engagement" strategy, led his critics to characterize him as leading from behind. In fact, Sarkozy's hyper agitation made him appear as the leading authority behind the war against Gaddafi, which left no doubt when, at the conclusion of the war, Senators John McCain and Lindsay Graham toasted the French and the British and continued to beat on Obama for being a reluctant warrior in Libya. Yet, the scarred face of

Libya today is Exhibit 1 that in Libya Obama was not a reluctant warrior. In Libya, Obama was Rambo on the mission of asserting American exceptionalism; and during that mission, Obama took no prisoners. Obama's prowess in Libya could not erase America's suspicion about him.

When Obama—by his own admission—was touched by the counsel of Pope Francis to be considerate of other peoples' feelings, he found it important that the Christian West be cautioned about its conflation of Christian faith and self-important claims to superior ethics, Civilization, and truth. And he found it imperative that the Christian West be reminded that its own history is littered with violence. Obama's opportunity for historical examination presented itself on the occasion of a February 3, 2015, event, when the world learned that a Jordanian pilot captured by ISIS (an Islamic extremist organization seeking a state of its own in the Middle East) had been burned alive in a cage. The event drew outrage in many places, especially in the United States, and it caused a resurgence of Islamophobia and Arab bashing in some milieus. Already, with the executions of Western citizens by the terrorist organization and the carrying out of terrorist attacks in Australia and in France in the name of ISIS, Muslims had been under scrutiny in the Western world, and some politicians had distinguished themselves in leading the frenzy. As an example, in Texas the date of January 29, decreed by the Council on American-Islamic Relations to be "Texas Muslim Capitol Day," a day for Texas lawmakers "to provide training on political activism, especially for students, show support for civil rights and Muslim-Americans, and educate lawmakers on those topics," was tainted with bigotry. On that day, Texas Republican lawmaker Molly White instructed Muslims in Texas to "renounce Islamic terrorist groups and publicly declare their allegiance to America and [American] laws." This and other events, which some observers identified as a clear demand for apostasy disguised in refutation of terrorism, prompted some Western leaders to be on the lookout to diffuse any scapegoating. Obama, who in his Cairo speech had promised to defend Muslim faith whenever it was under attack, was among those leaders; and two days after the Jordanian pilot was burned by ISIS militants, Obama had these words for his fellow Americans:

> Humanity has been grappling with these questions throughout human history. And lest we get on our high horse and think [violence in the name of religious faith] is unique to some other place, remember that during the Crusades and the Inquisition, people committed terrible deeds in the name of Christ. In our home country, slavery and Jim Crow all too often was justified in the name of Christ.... So this is not unique to one group or one religion. There is a tendency in us, a sinful tendency that can pervert and distort our faith.... And, first, we should start with some basic humility. I believe that the starting point of faith is some doubt—not being so full of yourself and so confident that you are right and that God speaks only to us, and doesn't speak to others, that God only cares about us and doesn't care about others,

that somehow we alone are in possession of the truth. Our job is not to ask that God respond to our notion of truth—our job is to be true to Him, His word, and His commandments. And we should assume humbly that we're confused and don't always know what we're doing and we're staggering and stumbling towards Him, and have some humility in that process. And that means we have to speak up against those who would misuse His name to justify oppression, or violence, or hatred with that fierce certainty. No God condones terror. No grievance justifies the taking of innocent lives, or the oppression of those who are weaker or fewer in number.[17]

Obama's words created a tremor of discontent not only among conservatives but also among liberals in the United States. The demands for historical amnesia did not wait long to pour forth.

So They Say We Should Forget

Reacting to Obama's speech on Christian barbarity, conservative commentator Charles Krauthammer confessed to Sean Hannity that he "was stunned that the president could say something so at once banal and offensive.... The present issue is Muslim radicalism and how to attack it." Remarking that "the story of the Crusades is over," the commentator complained that "everything [Obama] does is to ... to hold us back and to essentially deny the gravity of what's happening [today]. And that's why today he had to compare [ISIS's brutality] to the Crusades and to the Inquisition, which is simply astonishing."[18] Directly interpellating Obama, Krauthammer railed, "Mr. President, the Crusades were 800 years ago and the Inquisition 500 years ago."[19] Lawrence O'Donnell of MSNBC's *The Last Word* could not understand Obama's eagerness to reach back 800 years, 1000 years into the history of Catholicism to establish some moral equivalence between the West and the Orient.[20] Radio talk show host Mark Levin simply repudiated Obama as fit to be the president of the United States:

This man is a nihilist and a narcissist and an extremist.... Mr. Obama ... ironically you brought up slavery in the United States. And what's ironic about it ... is if Abraham Lincoln took [your] position, it would have been something like this. Lincoln saying we've had slavery on every continent in every country since the beginning of mankind. The Egyptians enslaved the Jews, the Romans enslaved Christians. Slavery is almost a human natural act, is it not? And Lincoln would say, following [your] argument, don't get on your high horse.[21]

Between Levin and the host of *Morning Joe* on MSNBC, Joe Scarborough, it was difficult to say whose outrage was the more apoplectic. For Scarborough,

it's unbelievable, the moral equivalency. The President having to go back 700, 800, 900 years? You see this when you have people that somehow want to paint a broad brush. "Uh, yes, radical Islam is bad but look what Christianity does." Really, you have to go back 800 years to a Crusade which, by the way, most historians say, Christians launched in response to years and years of Muslims taking over their former land ... feel the need to go back 800 years? This stupid left-wing moral equivalency.... You don't have to go to the other side, "oh, and Christians are bad, too." There is such a desperate plea for some reason on the left to do that, for some people on the left.... No, no, it's not okay. It's not okay for this president. You almost have to ask the question, where did he go to church? Where would he get such ideas from?[22]

What Scarborough's question was suggesting was, as has been propagated in many places, that Obama was not a Christian, that his politics contradicted any claim of Christianity. What we saw instead was the contrary, which is that Obama had constantly claimed that he was a Christian, that he was raised as a Christian, and that his politics were inspired by his Christian faith. In fact, while Americans were clamoring for higher ethics, they were paradoxically transfixed on *American Sniper,* a film glorifying extreme, savage violence in the name of superlative Christian values, a film which, for the *New York Times,* however violent the movie might be, was illustrative of America's moral virtue and commitment to good versus evil in a world that has gone astray: "'American Sniper' ... reaffirms Mr. [Clint] Eastwood's commitment to the themes of vengeance and justice in a fallen world. In the universe of his films—a universe where the existence of evil is a given—violence is a moral necessity, albeit one that often exacts a cost from those who must wield it in the service of good." The archetypal place where things had fallen apart—which, incidentally, the *New York Times* made no allusion to in its review of who was really responsible for making things fall apart, for transforming an otherwise not-so-perfect society, and we dare challenge anyone to show us a perfect society, into hell on earth—was Iraq, the country of unequivocal human as well as spatial dissipation, where noble Christian American righteousness faced unprincipled Muslim evil with indispensable ruthlessness, the country where *Christ* must do his duty of saving humanity, no matter how much suffering it required of him:

> Iraq, where [the hero] served four tours of duty, racking up 160 confirmed kills. He approaches his work with steady nerves and a clear conscience, banishing the doubt and fatalism that afflict some of his comrades and buttressed by the unambiguous depravity of his enemies. These are people who use women and children as suicide bombers, who mutilate and torture anyone who opposes them, who ambush American Marines in the street.... Remorse is out of the question, which is not to say that Chris doesn't suffer.[23]

A superlative patriotic and pro–American family movie, which, in the words of *New York Times'* Brooks Barnes, has appropriately and overwhelmingly conquered the hearts of ordinary Americans while an out-of-touch intellectual community had its gaze turned elsewhere, slobbering on movies of insignificant merit: "While America's coastal intelligentsia busied itself with chatter over little-seen art dramas like 'Boyhood' and 'Birdman,' everyday Americans showed up en masse for a patriotic, pro-family picture that played more like a summer superhero blockbuster than an R-rated war drama with six Oscar nominations."[24] What, then, is this adulated, "patriotic, pro-family film that so entranced everyday Americans?," asked Noam Chomsky. According to the famous American linguist and social critic:

> It's about the most deadly sniper in American history, a guy named Chris Kyle, who claims to have used his skills to have killed several hundred people in Iraq.... Kyle's first kill was a woman who apparently walked into the street with a grenade in her hand as the Marines attacked her village. Here's how Kyle describes killing her with a single shot: "I hated the damn savages I'd been fighting.... Savage, despicable, evil—that's what we were fighting in Iraq. That's why a lot of people, myself included, called the enemy savages. There was really no other way to describe what we encountered there...." He regarded his first kill as a terrorist—this woman who walked in the street—but we can't really attribute that to the mentality of a psychopathic killer, because we're all tarred by the same brush insofar as we tolerate or keep silent about official policy.... Now, that [sniper] mentality helps explain why it's so easy to ignore what is most clearly the most extreme terrorist campaign of modern history, if not ever—Obama's global assassination campaign, the drone campaign, which officially is aimed at murdering people who are suspected of maybe someday planning to harm us.[25]

And indeed, Obama's politics—though criticized by neocons as being far below the standards of the West's general politics and as disappointing as they can be to the most bellicose wing of the confrontational society that the West is—actually falls within the West's politics of domination by all means, even leads the West's politics of hegemony, which is itself supported by the Euro-American Judeo-Christian belief that the West *incarnates* truth itself. The Euro-American world has outclassed any other society known to man in its taste for iron and blood; and Western Europe, led by its daughter America, is not ready to be overtaken. The West's inhumanity is performed at an industrial level. America's warmongers should not worry about Obama failing them, for he is really and truly a son of America, chosen by America to carry on America's tradition of hubris and condescension. And Obama applies himself very well to his task. America should not be afraid of Obama's skin complexion. His mind and his soul are entirely devoted to implementing the most violent brand of Americanism. To borrow these words from Civil Rights icon Harry Belafonte, "[Obama] has only listened to the voices that shout loudest, and it's all those reckless right-wing forces. It's almost criminal."[26]

Africa Got Played by Obama

"Almost criminal" is an understatement. We might even argue that, anxious to comfort America, keen on easing America's fear that he might be a wrench in the works, Obama has gone far and beyond the call for proving himself, exhibiting toward African leaders the same contempt and patronizing attitude that he is shown at home by white racists. It is not America, even less the West, that Obama has disappointed. It is Africa that Obama has disillusioned. And, on June 28, 2013, as Nelson Mandela was taking his last breaths of air in a Pretoria hospital where Obama was scheduled to call on him, about 200 South African union workers and students wanted to drive home their dissatisfaction with a man upon whom Africa had placed so much unmet expectation. As deplored Khomotso Makola, a 19-year-old law student, "We had expectations of America's first black president. Knowing Africa's history, we expected more. He has come as a disappointment, I think Mandela too would be disappointed and feel let down."[27] Rudy Giuliani laments,

> I do not believe ... that [Obama] loves America.... He doesn't love you, and he doesn't love me. He wasn't brought up the way you were brought up, through love of this country.... This is an American President I've never seen before.... I do not detect in this man the same rhetoric, the same language, the same love of America that I detect in other American Presidents, including democrats.... I have doubts about his emotion, his feelings, his attitude, and the way in which he developed.

We are tempted to ask in whose name do you think Obama goes around destroying the world? In whose name has Obama condoned the destruction of Egypt, Libya, and the Côte d'Ivoire if not in the name of American exceptionalism? Have no fear, Rudy! Disown him not, for, as said David Axelrod, "Barack Obama knows who he is." He is a proud son of America. Obama is a proud product of American exceptionalism. Obama does love America. It is rather Africa that Obama does not love. However, is one to love exclusively one part of oneself and disdain the other? Can one who is both African and American love America if, and only if, one is able to disdain Africa?

As for us, we have always been wary of the Obama fever that had seized the world in 2008. From the very first, many intellectuals of African descent had assumed that Obama would be good for Africa because of his ancestry. We had refrained from falling prey to this *politics of color*, though we had hoped, just for the sake of Africa, that the Obamanians would be right. Without being anti–Obamanian, we found the circumstances of Obama's rise to power to be too cosmetic and his campaign speeches to be too dramatically crafted to have any bearing on the *real*. Besides, as well-intentioned as Oprah Winfrey might be, we found her show to be less than a reference platform for anointing world policy makers. So, we remained pessimistic. And when President Clinton remarked that "the whole thing looked like a fairy tale," we tended to agree with him while still wishing to be proven wrong. Nevertheless, as time passed, we started wondering, among other things, whether President Obama had a perceptible African policy. We desperately looked for something concrete to point to, beyond Obama's speeches or the exegetical exercises of Obamanians, that would give us the full measure of the American president's genuine interest in the development of the African continent. And many of the Africans who prayed for his election, who cried tears of joy at his inauguration, are also waiting to see genuine gestures of encouragement. But time is passing, Obama is now a year to the end of his second term, and nothing positive is happening for Africa. Of course, President Obama had given a memorable speech in Accra in July 2009, had hosted a lunch for two dozen African leaders and greeted young African "leaders" in Washington. Of course, he had honored a Zimbabwean women's group with the Robert H. Kennedy Prize for Political Courage. Of course, as U.S. Ambassador to the United Nations, Susan Rice had trotted around Africa and, as Secretary of State, Hillary Clinton had almost toured the continent. But do these routines amount to a clear African policy? In fact, when submitted to scrutiny, Obama's actions run counter to Obama's declared policy for Africa, and they counter his faith in diplomacy such as that rehearsed by Secretary of State Clinton in front of the Senate Foreign Relations Committee on January 13, 2009:

> The president-elect has made it clear that in the Obama administration there will be no doubt about the leading role of diplomacy. One need only look to North Korea, Iran, the Middle East and the Balkans to appreciate the absolute necessity of tough-minded, intelligent diplomacy—and the failures that result when that kind of diplomatic effort is absent.... President-elect Obama has emphasized that the State Department must be fully empowered and funded to confront multidimensional challenges—from working with allies to thwart terrorism to spreading health and prosperity in places of human suffering.... We will lead with diplomacy because it's the smart approach. But we also know that military force will sometimes be necessary, and we will rely on it to protect our people and our interests when and where needed, as a last resort.[28]

War is the antithesis of diplomacy. War does not spread health and prosperity in places of human suffering. And in Africa, Obama has not led by diplomacy. In Africa, Obama has been a warlike president whose bellicose politics has spread misery and suffering to the most vulnerable. It would be gravely dishonest to pretend that after the passage of Obama's war machines in Libya, Egypt, and Côte d'Ivoire, these countries are better off than they used to be. No honest mind can say that Obama has brought democracy to Libya, Egypt, and Côte d'Ivoire or that the daily violence and human rights abuses in these countries since Obama's intervention indicate democracy.

President Obama's stance on the Ivorian crisis belied his pledge to *strengthen democratic institutions* in Africa. Obama's support of rebel chief Dramane Ouattara— whose renegades have massacred more than 100,000 civilians since 2002 and who after failing to seize power by force openly cheated in a theatrical presidential election and declared himself president against the decision of the Constitutional Council—contradicts the American president's promise to see democracy prosper in Africa. President Obama's surprising silence on—and perhaps acquiescence to—the European Union's embargo on medicines to Côte d'Ivoire during the electoral crisis contradicts his propounded stance on a *healthy African continent* free of diseases. In fact, his resounding silence on the issue undermines great efforts started hitherto, such as President George Bush's Emergency Plan for AIDS, to which Obama had even reduced funding. President Obama's siding with the European Union's decision to blockade Ivorian agricultural exports disagrees with his commitment to *empower African populations*. On a continent where 70 percent of the people make their living in the agricultural sector, shutting off outlets for agricultural products was far from strengthening and empowering these populations. President Obama's support of France's will-to-economic-monopoly in Cote d'Ivoire belies his commitment to see an *economically strong Africa* that will not only have *ownership* of the resources of which it has natural custody, but also draw a decent profit from the exploitation of these resources. Abdul Karim Bangura is right to state that in Africa, and Côte d'Ivoire particularly, Obama's policy has been characterized by coercion and demonstration of brute force: "Just as he has done at home on lecturing African-Americans on their shortcomings but has done nothing significant for them.... Obama has done nothing substantive to point to in terms of Africa's economic development.... The power and coercion and world order paradigms seem to undergird Obama's foreign policy toward Africa in general and, consequently, Côte d'Ivoire in particular."[29] The truth is that even the most fervent African Obamanians have lost hope. Africa has stopped looking for concrete signs of President Obama's commitment to a strong African continent. President Obama's African policy is rigged with contradictions. A year to the end of Obama's second term, it is safe to venture that his record concerning Africa has been dismally disappointing. As Adekeye Adebajo said,

> The early luster of Obamania has ... clearly faded, as the realization has gradually dawned on Africans that even a powerful leader with close family ties to the continent cannot change 55 years of "malign neglect" of their continent by the U.S. The enduring continuity of U.S. foreign policy has trumped the early idealism of an extraordinary individual of African ancestry. Obama has not only failed to remake Africa, he has also failed to change the U.S. and the world.[30]

Let us put it less mildly and more urgently: Obama has failed Africa. He has failed Africa more than any American president before him. The harm against Africa condoned by Obama will take hundreds of years to be corrected.

Is there an explanation for Obama's disdainful and paternalistic posture towards Africans? Could it be that Obama was trying his best to run away from himself? Obama's constant mention that he is a "black" man, which needs no allusion, as it is so obvious on the face of it, sounds a lot like an attempt to persuade himself that black he is, too, although only white he has thought he was. African Union president Robert Mugabe of Zimbabwe has tried to offer the beginning of an explanation for Obama's warlike stance on Africa and his condescending attitude towards African heads of state. For Mugabe it all amounts to naiveté and self-hatred:

> I doubt that Barack Obama understands [the U.S.'s] grievance with us, whatever it is. I suppose in his case, it has a lot to do with being a black president in White House, a virtual prisoner enjoined to pander and dutifully mind white interests. He retires from office with an African curse, this man from whom so much was expected by our continent. But we know better that nothing much should be expected from him.[31]

Knowing how much perception contributes to election, and how much Africa's general "good feeling" about Obama has contributed to his election in the U.S., Africa "got played" is what Mugabe is saying.

Obama's paternalistic attitude towards Africa and African heads of state denotes sheer incompetence and shortsightedness. Obama, as has been noted, continues to see Africa in the old colonial prism of a continent that needs the U.S.'s saintly aid and guidance, but he should rather regard the continent as a partner.[32] Thus in Côte d'Ivoire, for instance, Obama's attitude towards Gbagbo has been something in the order of "I am the President of the United States, and I know better,"; which is not necessarily the case. In matters of struggle and sacrifice for democracy as well as in matters of political experience, Gbagbo's 30-year record is undeniably very strong, stronger than Obama's; and President Gbagbo's knowledge of the intricacies of African politics could have been an expert contribution to President Obama's foreign policy had the latter not already had a distorted idea of Africa and the Africans. Unfortunately, as noted Miniter so discernibly, "under Obama, the U.S. [has followed] France … when it [acted] at all."[33] Many of the African heads of state that have visited the White House since Obama first took office are far from possessing exemplary records on democracy and good governance. Yet, in the Ivorian crisis they have been precious counsels to Obama. What advice could they have provided—other than the ideas that have driven their own countries into moral, economic, and political maladministration? In fact, by comforting the catastrophic reign of these kleptocrats Obama did not help Africa. He further undermined Africa's democracy.

"He posed as a progressive and turned out to be counterfeit"

It is not only Africa that fell for Obama's beautiful fairy tale, his promise to turn things around and do politics a different way, that is, on the principles of fairness and reciprocity. America, too, black America particularly, was taken for a ride by Obama. At least, this is what Professor Cornel West thought"

> ... [T]he thing is he posed as a progressive and turned out to be counterfeit. We ended up with a Wall Street presidency, a drone presidency, a national security presidency. The torturers go free. The Wall Street executives go free. The war crimes in the Middle East, especially now in Gaza, the war criminals go free. And yet, you know, he acted as if he was both a progressive and as if he was concerned about the issues of serious injustice and inequality and it turned out that he's just another neoliberal centrist with a smile and with a nice rhetorical flair.... You would think that we needed somebody—a Lincoln-like figure who could revive some democratic spirit and democratic possibility.... It was like, "We finally got somebody who can help us turn the corner." And he posed as if he was a kind of Lincoln. And we ended up with a brown-faced Clinton. Another opportunist. Another neoliberal opportunist.[34]

Professor Cornel West's point is well taken, except that Obama is no Clinton. President Clinton would never have thought of exerting on Africa the destruction that Obama has ordered on the continent. Obama has been very bad luck for Africa and for people of African descent.

CHAPTER 8

We Shall Remember
as Far Back as Lumumba

Who wants to kill him?
Do you want to kill him?
Raise your hands if you want to kill him.
—FRANCK LUNTZ, American Political
Consultant and Republican Pollster

This is American political consultant and Republican pollster Franck Luntz conducting his signature survey on Sean Hannity's show on *Fox News*. Luntz has his own way of giving American politicians a very "sophisticated" assessment of America's opinion, a basis upon which they can safely conduct foreign policy. He seats a dozen or so "real Americans" on a television news set, of whom he excitedly asks, "Raise your hands if you want to kill [Bashar al-Assad]."[1] And American politicians can now sit back and watch Luntz's crowd, like exalted spectators at a coliseum's animal fight, offer their sentence. The more hands that go up from Luntz's focus crowd, the more substantiated is the proposition that Bashar al-Assad must die. To his credit, Luntz, at least, conducts a poll to take the pulse of the American nation. But what a poll! A straw poll that for him and the decision makers who use it as rationale for attacking foreign countries has scientific value. "The American people wanted it, and we followed the will of the American people," they can safely justify themselves. Killing foreign leaders on the basis of a straw poll is 21st century American foreign policy decision making at its best. How far we have travelled from the years of barbarity, when assassination of foreign leaders used to be the norm to settle differences! Truly, the antiquarian methods of the brutal forefathers have not evolved much. The Euro-American world unashamedly continues to perpetuate its barbarous technique of political and civilian assassinations, especially in Africa, while nonetheless claiming to hold the primacy of "Civilization."

Surprisingly, in responding to the accusations of inhumanity leveled against the West, some apologists in the Euro-American world are quick to rejoin that we shall turn the page, that "all this is ancient history already atoned for."[2] So Western apologists say we shall forget. To this we shall retort, "What then is new history and deserving of attention? Since we should have some minimum memory, since the human species is distinguished by its consciousness of having a memory, how recent should our memory be in order not to vex the West? How far back shall we forgive and forget the West's proclivity for assassinating Africans? Can our memory go as far back as the Rwandan genocide? As far back as the 2004 and 2011 butchery of Abidjan? Since we shall remember so as not to fall prey again, how far back would the West 'allow' us to remember?" We, the eternal victims of the West's proclivity for raiding, let us a least remember this, even if the West demands that we become amnesic; we shall, at least, allow our memory to wander as far back as the most recent rapine the Euro-American world has committed on Africa, as far back as Lumumba, and return as recently as to Gbagbo, the first for epitomizing the broken resistance of Africa to recolonization and the second for symbolizing Africa's shattered resistance to neocolonialism, both keeping alive the seed of Africa's ultimate freedom, nevertheless.

In fact, though 50 years apart, Ivorian president Gbagbo's and Congolese prime minister Lumumba's fates in the hands of the Euro-American imperial force are so strikingly similar that they deserve mention as case studies of the West's continuous endeavors to undermine total independence in Africa. Lumumba's and Gbagbo's mistakes were that the two men envisioned for their respective countries policies that were articulated around themes of anti-imperialism and total independence, two expressions which, especially when they are projected on a grand scale, on a continental scale, make the West cringe and immediately seek and support alternate leading figures, regardless of the abuses—human, economic, or other cruelties—that these alternate figures might have in stock for the people. Though the Gbagbo government of the 2000s never explicitly cited anti-imperialism as its overriding principle for governing, in the Euro-American world, its project of Refondation was nonetheless perceived as threatening to Western interests. It was a holistic program of development that proved successful in its beginning and would have lifted Côte d'Ivoire from the condition of indebted and broken country to that of successful and economically independent country had it not been wrongly construed as being anti–Western, principally anti–French business, and hence sabotaged by Paris. As is well known, imperial rules are distinguished by one principal feature: their externality, the forced outsourcing of *the power to make decisions* from local Third World populations to some power center in a remote Western capital (London, Paris, Brussels, The Hague or Washington).[3]

In digging into the foundation of the Ivorian society in order to correct the structural flaws that were slowing down or impeding progress and, thus, undermining the development of Côte d'Ivoire, the architects of Refondation, university professors in their great majority, came to the glaring realization that much of their country's woes derived from the abusive "partnership" France had enjoyed with its former colony since the latter proclaimed its independence on August 7, 1960. Refondation was thus sounding the end of France's illegal activities in Côte d'Ivoire. To undermine Refondation, and keep any hope of recovering France's exceptionalism in Africa, Sarkozy obtained the support of Obama, a lapdog but a powerful lapdog, nonetheless. Likewise, in the Belgian Congo, the Belgian authorities obtained the precious help of the United States for the elimination of Lumumba, the father of the Congo's independence whose nationalist bent they saw the West interpreted as hatred towards the Euro-American world.

The Congo Free State: The Plaything of a Crooked European Crowned Head

From whatever perspective one decides to look at it, today's Democratic Republic of Congo is the legacy of centuries of exploitation by the kings of Belgium, from Leopold II to Baudouin I, and later by America. Indeed, in 1875, Paris was the center of world geography. For years, tales of great explorers had been trickling down to Europe and the French Geographical Society had finally decided to showcase the exalting reports of the great adventurers, who, beyond the vast stretches of the oceans, deep into the jungles, in the realms unforgiving heat, humidity, diseases and "savage people," had brought to civilization the oddities of the Heart of Darkness. The Paris Conference proved very instructive to Belgian King Leopold II, who a year later organized his own Brussels Geographical Society conference, on September 12, 1876, at the Royal Palace. One of the illustrious attendees of Leopold II's conference was English explorer Henri Morton Stanley, who had been trying in vain to persuade the British authorities that annexation and investment in the Congo would be a highly profitable venture. For years, Leopold II had dreamt of possessing an overseas empire. Stanley's availability was too good an opportunity to pass. So, Leopold II convinced Stanley to work for his Association Internationale du Congo (AIC), a structure whose aim was to exploit the Congo for the Belgian king's benefit and which the king deceptively presented to the world powers as a philanthropic organization intended to eradicate Arab slavery in central Africa and bring development and civilization to the region. Thanks to Stanley's illegal land grabs on his behalf, Leopold II was well positioned to be the biggest European landlord in Africa in the days leading to the 1885 Berlin Conference, which decided on the sharing of Africa among the Western powers.

Indeed, although the Western powers were not totally taken in by Leopold's trickeries and knew somehow that the Belgian king's objectives were purely pecuniary, nonetheless, at the Berlin Conference they allowed Leopold II to become the sole owner of the Congo, a territory 95 times larger than his native Belgium, which had a population of 10 million inhabitants. The Belgians had no inclination for colonial adventure and the cost it might incur. So once "given" the Congo at the Berlin Conference, Leopold's next task was to persuade the Belgian parliament to sign onto his ownership of the vast central African territory. For that, the King of the Belgians used the sempiternal rhetoric of "superior" peoples' divine duty to import light and civilization to "inferior" peoples; and if in the course of it they could make some money and give work to the Belgian youth, so much the better:

> It is from here the light shines forth which for millions of men still plunged in barbarism will be the dawn of a better era…. Our cities are gorged with the products of the most diverse industries; nowhere will they find so great a market to absorb them. The most intelligent of our youth demands wider horizons on which to expand their abounding energy. Our working population will derive from the virgin regions of Africa new sources of energy and render more in exchange.[4]

Helped by his loyal friends, one of them Belgian prime minister August Beernaert, Leopold went on a vast campaign to persuade a Belgian people hesitant to engage in an onerous colonial enterprise that his initiative in the Congo would be strictly personal and would not require expenditures from Belgium. On April 21, 1885, the Belgian parliament was set to vote on a motion framed as "the King is authorized to be head of the State founded in Africa by the International Association of the Congo. The union between Belgium and the new Congo State will be exclusively personal." The first two words of the motion were amended to be "His Majesty Leopold II, King of the Belgians" in order to avoid the misunderstanding that any of Leopold's successors should be bound to his engagement in the Congo. On April 28, 1885, the Belgian parliament gave Leopold its unenthusiastic support to carry on his "personal" Congo adventure. Although Leopold would have liked Belgium to fully embrace the Congo enterprise and commit to the overhead that came with it, he nonetheless satisfied himself that there was no longer any obstacle standing in his way except that of raising the necessary monies for the task at hand. Soon after this, Leopold, who on March 20 had signed a transfer of responsibilities between him (as president of the International Association of the Congo) and himself (as King Leopold II, Sovereign of the Congo Free State), passed one of his first decrees: "Any unoccupied land is the property of the State," a decree that would have terrible consequences for the natives of the Congo. What it meant was that apart from the sites which were physically inhabited by the natives, the surrounding forests, which they considered as their game hunting and food and healing plants gathering grounds, and the surrounding waters that were their fishing basins were thenceforth interdicted to them, and any resources harvested on these grounds that were not collected on behalf of, and for the sole benefit of, the state would be considered illegally collected and thus offenses that were punishable:

> Native rights in land were ... confined to the actual sites of the town or village, and the areas under food cultivation around them. Beyond those areas no such rights would be admitted. The land was "vacant," i.e., without owners. Consequently, the "State" was owner. The "State" was Leopold II.... Native rights in nine-tenths of the Congo being thus declared non-existent, it followed that the native population had no proprietary right in the plants and trees growing upon that territory, and which yielded rubber, resins, oils, dyes, etc.[5]

In fact, in 1891, Leopold instructed the Congo Free State authorities such as the district commissioners to "take urgent measures as necessary to preserve for disposal by the State all products of the domain, especially ivory and rubber." Thus anyone caught selling or purchasing the territories' products from the natives could be charged with accepting stolen goods.[6]

Leopold needed money and could not afford to be less scrupulous on "his" properties. In fact, he needed to garner 25 million francs for the development of a railway system in the Congo without which the only partly navigable Congo River would make it extremely difficult for him to do profitable commerce. After gathering most of the monies from private national and foreign investors, the King of the Belgians obtained from a reluctant Belgian parliament the remaining 10 million francs to start works for the Chemin de Fer du Congo on July 31, 1889. However, Leopold was still haunted by the prospects of any financial incapacitation likely to douse his colonial endeavor; so, on August 2, he devised a stratagem that put to rest the question of the fate of the Congo in case of his passing and at the same time purposefully appealed to the vanity of the Belgian people to not let his Congo venture fail, which, after all, belonged to them, too. To the Belgian people who had been most unwilling to share the financial burden of the Congo, the King of the Belgians had this testament made public:

> The beginning of enterprises like those which have so much preoccupied me is difficult and dangerous. I have wished to carry its financial burden myself ... the wealth of a sovereign consists in public prosperity ... until the day of my death, I shall continue to have the same regard for national interest as has guided me so far in directing and maintaining our work in Africa. But if, without waiting for that, it pleases the country to contract more binding ties with my possessions in the Congo, I shall not hesitate to put them at its disposal.[7]

Leopold was, in other words, telling the Belgians, *It is your heritage. You had better make sure that it prospers.* The argument must have worked to perfection. In July 1889, on the 25th anniversary of his accession to the throne, Leopold II, King of the Belgians, was showered with praise for his vision and given a 25-million interest-free loan by parliament to continue his work in the Congo Free State. Still unsatisfied, Leopold would argue—against the clauses of the Berlin Conference, which had decreed the Congo a duty-free zone—that in order for him to effectively fulfill his resolve to free the Congo from slavery a colonial army should be raised, an army that needed money that could not be obtained unless he received additional revenue through taxes. And once again Leopold got his way and built his colonial army of tax collectors and law enforcers. Leopold's army, the *capitas,* was staffed with 5,000 natives supervised by European officers.

Instead of stamping out slavery in Central Africa as he promised he would, Leopold II used his army to transform the Congo Free State into a vast slave camp where 10 million Congolese toiled for the King of the Belgians in the most horrendous conditions, collecting rubber, ivory, and other commodities. Leopold's agents, who were incentivized with bonuses to bring in as much rubber as possible, arbitrarily instructed each village to fill certain quotas. The quota demands made on the natives were so egregious that villagers had to abandon their subsistence activities in order to tend exclusively to the needs of the state. Consequently, fields were left uncultivated and famine and death became the daily lots of the native Congolese. Those villagers who refused to comply with the state's orders were punished by mutilation (usually of the hands) or by death, and if they fled their wives or children were made to pay for them. Leopold's capitas, principally recruited among the fierce Bangala people, enforced his laws in the Congo Free State without any qualms, with cold-heartedness. As reward, Leopold's agents allowed the capitas to loot and rape women with impunity in the recalcitrant villages. The king's agents usually sent the capitas to repress villagers with whom they had no family ties and toward whom there was little chance they felt any compassion: "It was the policy of the Belgians to garrison the provinces with soldiers from another part of the Congo, who would not therefore have to take action against their own tribesmen."[8] In a report to the British authorities, British Vice-Consul Wilfred Thesier described how Leopold's system had affected the demographics of the Congo Free State. Villages that were hitherto prosperous were reduced to smoldering deserts by Leopold's agents:

> The rubber tax was so heavy that the villages had no time to attend even to the necessities of life…. [T]he company's armed soldiers stationed in the villages told me they had orders not to allow the natives to clear the ground for cultivation, to hunt, or to fish, as it took up time which should be spent in making rubber…. In consequence, their huts are falling to ruin, their fields are uncultivated, and the people are short of food … and dying off…. This district was formerly rich in corn, millet, and other foodstuffs … [and] now it is almost desert.[9]

Eventually, Leopold II's inhumane exploitation of the Congo came under harsh criticism by social activists, traders, and missionaries, among them black American clergyman and scholar George Washington William and English journalist E.D. Morel. William, who convinced himself that in Africa educated black Americans would be better treated and would have greater social mobility than afforded them in the United States, had hoped at one time to recruit educated black Americans to work for Leopold. William became disillusioned once he discovered the Congo Free State. Horrified by what he saw, William wrote an open letter to Leopold in which he indicted the King of the Belgians in a 12-point charge that he promised to deposit "with her Brittanic Majesty's Secretary of State for Foreign Affairs, until such time as an International Commission can be created with power to send for persons and papers, to administer oaths, and attest the truth or falsity of these charges." In his letter, William alleged the following:

1. In the Congo, Leopold has bitten more than he could swallow. Leopold's claim on the vast territory of the Congo is too ambitious. He actually lacks the means to implement order and develop the region in such a way that would improve the lives of the natives.

2. Leopold's government has instituted lawlessness, arbitrariness, injustice and murder as State policy.

3. Leopold's government has persistently engaged in breach of contracts it signed with black soldiers and machine workers.

4. Leopold's legal system in the Congo was prejudiced, deceptive and corrupt.

5. Leopold's governments and agents were continually committing against the natives excessive acts of cruelty and inhumanity that would not be conceivable in Europe.

6. Leopold's government was guilty of promoting prostitution and sex slavery, whereby individuals were paid to capture indigenous women or incarcerate them under false charges just for the purpose of sexually gratifying Leopold's white agents. Whenever children were born from these forced rapports, they would be considered government properties and thus, later, forced to work for Leopold.

7. Leopold's government forbade natives to trade while his agents were encouraged and rewarded to raid villages and seize villagers' goods.

8. Leopold violated the fundamental terms of the Berlin Act by which the Powers permitted him to acquire the Congo.

9. Leopold's government would arm villages to fight one another so that war prisoners could be utilized as forced laborers for Leopold. In the process, Leopold's government encouraged mutilation and cannibalism of natives by Bangala soldiers.

10. Leopold's government bought, sold, and stole slaves.

11. Leopold armed Arabs in territories where he had no jurisdiction.

12. Leopold, Stanley, and his agents have alienated the natives, who would therefore not respond spontaneously to their authorities or to any program they could put forth. Leopold's sanctimonious claims of improving the lives of the natives constituted an outright fraud. "Trade in the Upper Congo consists only of ivory and rubber. The first is old, the latter is poor." There was no real development taking place in the Congo that would benefit the natives. Consequently, "Emigration [could not] be invited to this country for many years.[10]

William did not live long enough to see his struggle vindicated. In 1891, he died of tuberculosis. Nevertheless, William's condemnation of King Leopold II's brutal regime in the Congo Free State went global. American Protestant missionaries denounced Leopold's system. Thus wrote Mr. Clark, "It is bloodcurdling to see the soldiers returning with hands of slain, and to find the hands of young children amongst the biggest ones.... [T]he rubber traffic is steeped in blood." In Belgium, the League for the Defense of Belgian Interests Abroad was created by Baron Wahis, Governor General of the Congo Free State, to fend off the harsh criticisms against the king led at home by pugnacious socialist Emile Vandervelde. In Great Britain, one of the indefatigable critics who battled to call attention to Leopold's callousness in the Congo was E.D. Morel, the founder of the Congo Reform Association. A journalist and founder of his own paper, the *West African Mail*, Morel started a publication campaign of the atrocities carried out on the native Congolese by Leopold's agents. Eventually, Morel's outcry reached the British House of Commons, which, in 1903 debated the issue with indignation and adopted a motion to ensure with the other powers that the clauses of the Berlin Conference were respected and that the natives of the Congo were treated decently. The British House of Commons also elected to conduct an official inquiry on the matter. Roger Casement, the British Consul at Stanley Pool, was designated to lead that inquiry.

On June 5, 1903, Casement left the lower Congo, where he was stationed, and headed for the Upper Congo with one porter and two dogs. Casement's investigations took him to various regions of the Congo Free State, where he interviewed Leopold's officials, his agents, and many missionaries. Casement also spoke extensively to the native populations of the Congo through interpreters, and he observed the interactions between the Europeans and the natives. Before Casement had started drafting his report, however, British Foreign Secretary Lord Lansdowne, as voted on by the British House of Commons on May 20, 1903, addressed a protest letter to the signatories of the Berlin Conference, including Leopold, in which he requested that another conference be held to assess King Leopold II's compliance with the clauses under which he was granted proprietorship of the Congo by the world powers. Lansdowne's mail angered Leopold. The King of the Belgians went on the offensive, offering British authorities a lecture on hypocrisy, reminding them that in the Congo he had done nothing that they themselves had not initiated in their African colonies, and pointing out that their own atrocities in Africa far exceeded the crimes of which they accused him in the Congo Free State:

> If the Congo State is attacked, England may admit that she, more than any other nation, has been the object of attacks and accusations of every kind, and the list would be long of the campaigns which at various times, and even quite recently, have been directed against her colonial administration. Has she not been blamed in regard to the long insurrections in Sierra Leone: to the disturbed state of Nigeria, where ... military measures of repression cost, on one single occasion, the lives of 700 natives ... and the conflict in Somaliland, which is being carried on at the cost of many lives, without however exciting expressions of regret in the House of Commons except on the score of the heavy expense![11]

As was to be expected, Leopold's reminding the British that they were worse than he could ever be and that before passing judgment on him they should clean their own backyard was ill-advised as far as Great Britain was concerned and did little to weaken the onslaught of criticisms against him. On the contrary, for Great Britain, which was the first country to have officially attacked Leopold, it became henceforth urgent that Leopold's abuses in the Congo be meticulously documented and exposed to the world.

By December's end 1903, Casement's report was ready and submitted to the British Foreign Office. The Congo Free State, as Casement described, reproduced the Manichean compartmentalization characteristic of any colonial administration: a world of Europeans, clean, opulent, and sanitized, and a world of natives, poor, decrepit and dirty:

> A hospital for Europeans and an establishment designed as a native hospital are in charge of a European doctor. The native hospital ... is, however, an unseemly place. When I visited the three mud huts which serve this purpose, all of them dilapidated and two with the thatched roof almost gone, I found seventeen sleeping sickness patients, male and female, lying about the utmost dirt. Most of them were lying on the bare ground.... [T]wo days later, the 19th June, I found one of them lying dead out in the open.[12]

The natives' condition was caused and maintained by an exploitative organization that drained all their efforts towards the well-being of the Europeans and left them very little, if any, energy to care for themselves. Speaking of the rubber chores they were submitted to, some villagers confided:

> It used to take ten days to get the twenty baskets of rubber—we were always in the forest and then when we were late, we were killed. We had to go further and further into the forest to find the rubber vines, to go without food, and our women had to give up cultivating the fields and gardens. Then we starved. Wild beasts—the leopards—

killed some of us when we were working away in the forest, and others got lost or died from exposure and starvation, and we begged the white man to leave us alone, saying we could get no more rubber, but the white men and their soldiers said: "Go! You are only beasts yourselves, you are nyama (meat)." We tried, always going further into the forest, and when we failed and our rubber was short, the soldiers came to our towns and killed us. Many were shot, some had their ears cut off; others were tied up with ropes around their necks and bodies and taken away. The white men sometimes at the posts did not know of the bad things the soldiers did to us, but it was the white men who sent the soldiers to punish us for not bringing in enough rubber.... We said to the white men, "We are not enough people now to do what you want us. Our country has not many people in it and we are dying fast. We are killed by the work you make us do, by the stoppage of our plantations, and the breaking up of our homes."[13]

Not only did the natives have little or no time to feed themselves, but they were also required to feed their oppressors. Thus in Leopoldville, for instance, where lived some 130 Europeans and 3,000 native government workers, the populations from the surrounding villages were compelled by the government to supply both the European and the workers with food at no cost, even though the native workers were required to purchase their food (essentially constituted of cassava bread and porridge) from government stores:

These demands for food-stuffs comprise fowls and goats for consumption by the European members of the Government staff at Leopoldville, or for passengers on the Government steamers. They emanate from the Chief of the post at Bolobo who, I understand, is required as far as he can, to keep up this supply. In order to obtain this provision, he is forced to exercise continuous pressure on the local population, and within recent time, that pressure has not always taken the form of mere requisitions. Armed expeditions have been necessary and a more forcible method of levying supplies was adopted than the law either contemplated or justifies.[14]

One district officer reported to Casement that in fourteen small villages that failed to fulfill their required quota, sixteen villagers were killed by the soldiers, of whom three were women and one was a boy. Furthermore, ten villagers were captured and held for a ransom of sixteen goats. A five-year-old boy who was among the hostages died at Bolobo before the ransom could be gathered.[15] In a brutally repressive system such as Leopold's in the Congo Free State, it should not be surprising that the harsh working conditions imposed on the natives depopulated the country:

Perhaps the most striking change observed during my journey into the interior was the great result observable everywhere in native life. Communities I had formerly known as large and flourishing centers of population are today entirely gone, or now exist in such diminished numbers as to be no longer recognizable. The southern shores of Stanley Pool had formerly a population of fully 5000 Batekas. These people some twelve years ago decided to abandon their homes, and in one night the great majority of them crossed over into French territory. Where formerly had stretched these populous natives African villages, I saw today only a few scattered European houses.

Casement, who had also crossed over to the French Congo, had spoken with these migrating populations as much as with those he encountered in the Congo Free State. The Casement Report corroborated most of the allegations made by his critics against King Leopold's administration in the Congo. Though the findings of the report showed little difference from what could be found in the colonies of France or England, for Great Britain, which had been waiting for it, the report was a much needed bombshell to be dropped on Leopold. The King of the Belgians, as Casement confided to Morel during the drafting of his report, was guilty of "grave maladministration and ill-treatment."[16] Upon reading Casement's report, Lord Lansdowne exclaimed, elated, "Proof of the most painfully convincing kind, Mr. Casement!"[17] Lansdowne had his evidence and would publish it. Nevertheless, the British Foreign Secretary suggested to King Leopold that he should conduct his own investigation of the evidence alleged in the Casement Report, a highly opportune occasion for the King of the Belgians to save face.

On July 31, 1904, Leopold appointed his Commission of Inquiry by decree. It was composed of Baron Nisco, the Italian president of the Court of Appeals at Boma in the Congo Free State, Swiss jurist Edmond de Schumacher, and Advocate-General of the Cour de Cassation of Brussels. As some argued, "the composition of the Commission was sufficient guarantee that the administration of the State would be looked at through friendly eyes," which was perceptible, given the contortions through which the commissioners went to qualify the testimonies of the native Congolese they interviewed:

It would be going too far to call the native a liar, but his notion of the truth differs from ours. Truth for the native is not what is or has been, but what ought to be—what he wishes, or what he thinks you desire or expect of him. He has only a vague notion of time, and cannot localize past events; it is very much to be feared that the Commission has not had before it evidence of the actual state of affairs in many districts.[18]

On many points, the report praised Leopold's administration in the Congo. It rejoiced in the advance of "civilization" in the heart of hostile nature, barbarism, cannibalism, and frenzied chaos:

The Commission cannot refrain from comparing the state of affairs now with what it was formerly, as indicated in the narratives of explorers. In districts that twenty-five years ago were plunged in the deepest barbarism, and which white men traversed with the utmost difficulty and at great risk ... a State has been organized in a marvelously short time, which has introduced into the heart of Africa the benefits of civilization.[19]

The commissioners found the imposition systems, including forced labor law, "justified … not merely by the ordinary taxation of European citizens, but by the existence in nearly every country in continental Europe of compulsory military service" and necessary for the continued development of the Congo Free State for the betterment of the native Congolese. The commission's only qualms with the imposition system was that it was a little excessive.

Nevertheless, the fact that the commission's report, which was available as early as March 1905, was made public only on October 30 of that year was indicative of the wrangling that took place behind closed doors to make the report more digestible to both the administration of the Congo Free State and to that of Belgium. In fact, the report had angered many people in the high spheres of the state and the kingdom as well as the Catholic missions, which it indicted for blindly serving King Leopold first and God second. The evangelical missionaries, on the other hand, were praised by the report as being the only people who truly had the well-being of the natives at heart and to whom the natives could go when they needed to be heard. To soften the blow on Leopold, his administration, and the Catholic missionaries, the commission's report was published without the minutes of the evidence submitted by the commissioners. Thus, from such efforts by the Commission of Inquiry to bend over backward in order to avoid bruising the reputations of the king, the king's administrators and the Catholic Church, the commission's condemnation of Leopold's system as guilty of "grave abuses" might appear extremely indulgent. Though carefully crafted in felted words, the criticisms contained in the report of Leopold's own Commission of Inquiry, which the king and his unconditional friends had hoped would assuage the dishonor brought onto the kingdom by his detractors, essentially reiterated the conclusions put forth by George Washington William and Roger Casement—that is, in the Congo Free State, the King of the Belgians was nothing more than an avaricious speculator and abuser of human rights and not the magnanimous sovereign he promoted himself to be to the native Congolese.

While Leopold had wished upon the publication of the Commission of Inquiry's damaging report to proceed by a *fuite en avant* with the appointment of another commission that would look into what reforms to bring to the Congo, within the kingdom support for the king's Congolese venture was collapsing. The sovereign of the Congo was being increasingly blamed for constituting the root source of the abuses in the Congo, principally through his decree that expropriated the native Congolese of their ancestral lands by stipulating that "any vacant land belonged to the State." That decree was an ugly affair in Leopold's administration of the Congo which his foes could not help criticizing, as evidenced by the report of his own "friendly" Commission of Inquiry:

Without contesting the legitimacy of the appropriation of vacant lands by the State, the Commission holds that the position of the native populations [in] the land system, depends entirely on the meaning attached to the words "occupied lands" "vacant lands"; and that if it wishes to prevent the principle of its lordship over vacant lands from being abused, the State must put its agents on their guard against a too-restricted interpretation of the term. In default of legal definition (and none exists), it seems to be generally agreed in the Congo that land "occupied by the natives," is limited to that on which they have erected their villages, or which they have brought under cultivation. Moreover, their right to dispose of the products of the soil is limited to that enjoyed before the constitution of the State. As the greater portion of the land on the Congo is not under cultivation, this interpretation gives the State absolute and exclusive property in almost all the land, with the result that it is free to dispose of all the products of the soil, to prosecute as a thief anyone who gathers any produce, as receiver him who buys it, and to forbid anyone to settle on the greater portion of the territory; it greatly restricts the area of activity of the native; rigorously applied, it prevents all expansion of the life of the native. It not only prohibits the removal of villages, but the native has even been forbidden to leave his village for a brief visit without a special permit; otherwise he exposes himself to arrest, to forcible return, and to punishment.[20]

Eventually calls for Belgium's annexation of the Congo became strident from socialists as well as conservatives; in a surprising volte-face, Leopold, who had pledged in 1889 that he would readily relinquish the Congo to Belgium whenever Parliament judged it appropriate, became reticent about doing so. In fact, to guarantee retention of his ownership of the Congo he went so far as to alter the will he had made to bequeath the Congo to Belgium.

Death of a Disconsolate Businessman

Leopold's resistance did little to dissuade the Belgian parliament mired in the scandal in which the kingdom was now wallowing. In March 1906, the Belgian parliament voted to annex the Congo. In an act of defiance the same year, Leopold founded three new companies in the Congo Free State whose profits would be directly deposited in the coffers of the state of which he was the sole proprietor: the Compagnie de Chemin de Fer du Bas-Congo, the Société Internationale Forestière et Minière du Congo, and the Union Minière du Haut Katanga were, respectively, meant to collect any monies coming from transportation, the forests and the underground resources of the Congo.[21] These, however, were the last convulsions of a disgraced, dying monarch and businessman. The previous three years had not been kind to Leopold; neither would be the years to come.

In 1908, after many debates on the actual terms of annexation, the Belgian parliament, which had already voted two years earlier to take over the Congo from Leopold, finally unburdened the Belgian monarch of his Congo Empire. The King of the Belgians had no choice. The onslaught of international resentment was too powerful for him and his defenders to withstand. Furthermore, for the Kingdom of Belgium, the Congo Free State had become an international embarrassment. The movement that mostly brought about the fall of Leopoldianism in the Congo was E.D. Morel's Congo Reform Movement. While Casement was drafting his final report to the House of Commons, he had urged Morel to create a movement that would bring down Leopold's system in the Congo Free State. "[Casement's] suggestions were concrete," wrote Morel. "If Leopoldianism was to be overthrown, an organization would have to be created, and I must be its creator. He would help."[22] So, in 1904, Morel created the Congo Reform Movement and stepped up his criticism against Leopold. As noted Nzongola-Ntalaja so discernibly, Morel's movement was in the early 20th century what such humanitarian organizations as Amnesty International and Human Rights Watch are in the 21st century.[23] Sympathizers of Morel's Congo Reform Movement were prominent figures whose criticisms of the Leopoldian system were long established, figures that included Casement, the Archbishop of Canterbury, African-American Reverend William Henry Sheppard, Samuel Lapsley of the American Presbyterian Congo Movement founded in 1891, Reverend William Morrison, a colleague of Sheppard's, American writer Mark Twain, and scholars Booker T. Washington and W.E.B. DuBois, among others.

The movement had several international chapters. American journalist E. Park headed the American chapter of the Congo Reform Movement. In Switzerland, René Claparède was at the helm; Pierre Mille organized the movement in France; and in Belgium, Socialist Deputy Emile Vandervelde supervised its actions. Morel's paper, the *West African Mail*, became the publication outlet of the movement, and several of the aforementioned scholars and activists contributed articles critical of Leopold to the paper. Furthermore, contributions and pictures came from various eyewitness sources in the Congo, which Morel gladly printed in *West African Mail*. The king's defense could not resist the pugnacity of such devoted activists. So Belgium took over the Congo from Leopold to appease world opinion and redress an increasingly tarnished image of Belgium.

The loss of his African Empire must have been unbearable to King Leopold. He had fought tooth and nail to retain his Congo Free State and had lost that battle in humiliation. A year after the Congo Free State officially became a colony of Belgium, Leopold's health started to rapidly falter. A few days before his passing, Leopold summoned Prime Minister Schollaert into his room for one last instruction. If he had lost his Congo, Belgium, at the least, should entertain every possible effort to preserve every inch of it: "If you yield an inch of the territory your old King will rise from his tomb to reproach you."[24] On December 13, 1909, Leopold passed away in a little pavilion on the palace grounds. The King of the

Belgians, we can see from his last will, must have felt betrayed and must have never forgiven his subjects for surrendering to international pressure and stripping him of his Congo Free State. In the last entry of his testament, written on November 20, 1907, a little over a year after the Belgian parliament voted to annex the Congo, Leopold had this recommendation for his subjects: "I wish to die in the Catholic faith which is mine. I do not wish any autopsy to be performed on me. I desire to be buried very early in the morning without any pomp. Apart from my nephew Albert and my household, I forbid anyone to follow my remains. May God protect Belgium and deign in his goodness to be merciful to me!"[25] Prince Albert ignored his uncle's testament and buried him with royal honors.

Belgium Takes Over and It Is Business as Usual

With the 1908 annexation of the Congo, King Albert I also inherited a colonial system of administration forged by his uncle Leopold II and on which it proved easier for him to rely than starting anew. Of course, soon after his appointment to the newly created Ministry of the Colonies, Justice Minister Jules Renkin had undertaken a few reforms. With annexation, a colonial constitution was adopted. La Charte Coloniale introduced some reforms to the Congo intended to correct the flaws of the previous regime and improve the daily lot of the native Congolese. The most notable changes contained in the charter were the restoration of the natives' rights to freely use and exchange products from their ancestral lands—which de facto ended the monopoly observed in the defunct Congo Free State. The charter also ended the arbitrariness of forced labor and replaced it with monetary taxation and a set number of hours of labor due the colonial administration (totaling 120 days per year per native Congolese). A few measures aimed at improving the health and social well-being of the native populations were also adopted by the charter.

However, because the Colonial Charter was designed by men who had financial interests in the Congo, it did little to usher in meaningful changes. In fact, the Minister of the Colonies and 8 of the 14 men who constituted his cabinet were direct appointees of the king, and they were in the Congo principally to guarantee that the dividends of the shareholders associated with the king's ventures in the defunct Congo Free State were not at risk. Leopoldianism was dead only theoretically. Practically, its substructure was strongly set, upon which the new, modern system of exploitation of the Congo was built. Just like the regime that preceded it (the Congo Free State), Belgian Congo made persistent demands on the natives to satisfy the agricultural and geological exploitation of the Congo by the Société Internationale Forestière et Minière (Forminière) and the Union Minière du Haut Katanga (UMHK). Huge commercial plantations and mining fields were created, and native Congolese were initiated into the techniques of extensive farming and mining for the voracious metropolitan markets. Timber was cut. Cobalt, copper, zinc, gold, iron, silver, and diamonds were mined at insatiable industrial scales. With the end of the monopoly system, the Congo became fertile ground for the major economic powers (Great Britain, France, Germany, Australia, the United States). Prominent names with ancient vested interests in the Congo were the Ryan and Guggenheim groups (involved in diamond mining) and the Rockefeller group (involved in industry, commerce, agriculture, and finance of public works).[26]

Until 1960, the Congo functioned as a source of wealth accumulation for Belgium, albeit not without any turbulence caused by a devastatingly abused native population whose subsistence economy was endangered by the demands of an exploitative capitalistic colonial system. In order to control the increasingly discontent populations that threatened agricultural and commercial outputs, the colonial administration, in a most unwise move, substituted local chiefs with salaried personnel. Misled by their belief that the more ruthless they were the stronger the authority they wielded, these manufactured chiefs actually further deepened the gap between the natives and the colonial administration and by the mid–1950s precipitated the Congolese's demands for full autonomy. One of the figures that emerged during that period of struggle for self-administration was Patrice Emery Lumumba.

CHAPTER 9

The Congo's Bumpy Road to Independence[1]

Patrice Emery Lumumba was thrown into politics by circumstances that were not of his making. Born on July 2, 1925, in Eastern Kasai, Lumumba was not destined for a political life. A student at a missionary school, his education would have predisposed him to excusing the colonial system of the Congo of which the Belgian missionaries were colluding agents. For some reason, however, Lumumba dropped out of school before he could complete his elementary school education and found himself involved in anticolonial political activism that put him on the blacklist of the colonial administration. Mainly an autodidact, Lumumba educated himself by reading extensively and by joining liberal discussion groups in Stanleyville (today's Kisangani). Quickly, Lumumba's charisma made him the chairman of the Association des Évolués de Stanleyville, an association of the westernized elites of Stanleyville, who were dedicated to redressing the inequities of the Manichean colonial system.

Political Organizations and the Challenge of Tribal Allegiance

In 1956, Lumumba founded a political party that he wanted to be different from anything that had so far been proposed by the Congolese évolués. Lumumba wanted his Mouvement National Congolais (MNC) to be reflective of the Congolese social makeup, which was not the primary concern of most of the political parties then. Indeed, the mid–1950s were a fertile period for political contestations in the Congo. The westernized natives had become bold in their demands for equal treatment, and political organizations were mushrooming. Nevertheless, most of the political platforms that had been offered were far from proposing an all-embracing national agenda. Their inclinations were principally ethnic and tribal. Of the political actors in the Belgian Congo, Joseph Kasavubu, Moïse Tshombe, and Jason Sendwe particularly were inclined to representing their tribes first and the rest of the Congo later. In 1945, Kasavubu was solicited by the Union des Intérêts Sociaux Congolais (Unisco) to be their spokesperson. The association, which boasted 15,000 members, was mainly frequented by workers with some education who had hoped that Kasavubu's charisma and training (he was a former theology student) would help better articulate their claims and give their movement greater exposure. However, soon after his arrival as Unisco chairman, Kasavubu redirected the association to further the agenda of his Bacongo tribe (whom he qualified as the "first occupants") against those of the Bangala. Later in 1950, when Kasavubu joined Edmond Nzeza-Nlandu's Association pour la Sauvegarde de la culture et des intérêts des Bakongo (Abako), he agreed with the movement's primary line of preserving the proud cultural and ethnic heritage of the prosperous agricultural and trading fifteenth century Kongo Kingdom that gave its name to today's Congo. It was only much later, in 1956 when he took over the chairmanship of the Abako, that Kasavubu started to timidly ascribe it a national agenda. Nevertheless, until the independence of the Congo, and even in the months following independence, Kasavubu had not shaken off Abako's early ethnocentric objectives, as he was hoping for a balkanized Congo where he could be left to rule as the all-powerful king of the Kongo people. Likewise, Moïse Tshombe's Confédération des Associations Tribales du Katanga (Conakat) drew its constituencies from the tribes of southern Katanga. Tshombe's Conakat constituency came principally from the Luanda and Yeke people of southern Katanga, who considered themselves the "original Katangese." Since its inception, the binding glue of the Confederation of Tribal Associations from the Katanga was ethnic supremacy. The Yeke had developed some aversion against the Luba-Kasai people who immigrated from the Kasai province in the north to work in the Katangese mines and who had done well in the mining business; and Jason Sendwe's Balubakat recruited its members from the Baluba people of northern Katanga.

Either for practical reasons or for his resolute belief in national imperatives, Lumumba assigned to his MNC a grander agenda, a national one. By going beyond ethnic and regional considerations, Lumumba was making a demystifying gesture not necessarily appreciated by some of his fellow Congolese or by the colonial administration. In fact, since the early days of the Congo Free State, some tribal stratifications had been artificially set and maintained by the colonizers, which, by the tasks they were chosen to complete for the colonial administrations, privileged some tribes over others and gave them a false sense of superiority. The colonial administration had used the intertribal hatred against the Congolese, and, as a result, the Bacongo and the Bangala particularly had been at each other's throats to own the title of supreme tribe. Lumumba's going beyond this petty squabbling might appear blasphemous to some Congolese, especially those from the Katanga regions, whose geologically rich lands, they assumed, must give them privileged status.

By the late 1950s, however, a new national, even continental, consciousness had emerged with the wave of African independences. Accra, the capital of newly independent Ghana, was the center of Pan-Africanism, where the first All African-People's Conference was taking place in December 1958. Either out of sincere conviction or a perceived need to keep the in-fighting going among the Congolese, progressive Minister of the Colonies Maurice van Hemelrijck, whose openness to the idea of the Congo's eventual independence had won him reprimands by the Belgian authorities, exclusively allowed Lumumba and two of his associates, Joseph Ngalula and Gaston Diomi, to attend the All-African People's Conference organized by Ghanaian president Kwame Nkrumah. In Ghana, Lumumba met with prominent leaders and advocates of Africa's emancipation, such as Guinean president Sékou Touré and Martinican activist Frantz Fanon, who by their respective engagements for anticolonialism in Guinea and Algeria had given the measure of what it took to be really free from imperialist oppression.

Actually, in 1943, Frantz Fanon had volunteered to fight in Europe to liberate France from German Occupation. To his fellow Martinicans who reproached him with fighting a war that was not his, Fanon replied, "Whenever the dignity and freedom of man are concerned, we are concerned, white, black or yellow, and every time they are threatened in any place whatsoever, I fully commit myself." However, Europe, France particularly, had betrayed Fanon's ideal in several places, most notably in Africa, and Fanon's commitment was henceforth to disenfranchise Africa from its greedy European oppressors. When the Algerian fight for independence reached its apex, Fanon, the Martinican, quit his French psychiatrist job and volunteered to fight with the Algerian Mujahidins (freedom fighters). For his strong commitment to the Algerian cause, Fanon was banned from Algeria by the French colonial administration. In Guinea, in 1958, Sékou Touré had refused de Gaulle's Loi Cadre (a decentralized administration that gave greater authority to local officials without giving them full independence) as a desperate attempt by France to save its African Empire, and he had demanded full independence for his country. In retaliation, France had destroyed any infrastructure that could not be taken to France and left Guinea destitute. For many Africans aspiring to independence, Fanon and Touré were the heralds of Africa's struggle, an imperative that was affirmed with the loudest conviction at the Accra Conference. Ghana was the epicenter of Africa's struggle for full autonomy. The Ghanaian national and African consciousness was becoming happily contagious. Lumumba was the pilgrim who had been to the epicenter of Pan-Africanism when it became evident that it could no longer be fashionable to think of the Congo in terms of an aggregate of tribes and ethnic groups. Many adepts of the national ideal joined Lumumba's MNC and made it one of the most important parties, if not the majority party, in the Congo.

Nevertheless, Lumumba was aware that the ideal of national autonomy with a unified Congo would be difficult to sustain, given the imperialist forces' primary strategy of dividing the countries they conquered in order to better subjugate their peoples. This was done in the Congo Free State under Leopold II, and Belgium, once again, was going to attempt a balkanization of Belgian Congo in order to undermine independence. Most important, Lumumba was convinced that Belgium would not easily surrender the rich mineral province of Katanga. He was right.

The Double Edge of Colonial Manipulation

A strong population of 34,000 white settlers lived in the Katanga in the late 1950s. These colonists were prospectors who at one time, as was the case with the *pieds noirs* (white settlers) in Algeria, had hopes of making the province of Katanga a white colony independent from the Belgian central authority. As independence neared inexorably, the white settlers decided to play the Congolese against one another, this time with the objective of making the province of Katanga a separate, independent state from the Congo, where, as was the case in South Africa, whites would constitute a privileged ruling class. For that, the settlers turned to the leader of the Conakat party, Tshombe. The Yeke "natural" constituencies of Tshombe's Conakat were made to believe that if they joined with the white settlers for an independent Katanga, it would be in their interest, for they would not have to compete against the Luba-Kasai for social status. Tshombe was fascinated by the idea, which intensified the Yeke's artificial hatred against the Luba-Kasai. For their part, too, in order to organize the defense of their interests, the Luba people from northern Katanga gathered under the banner of Jason Sendwe's General Association of Baluba People from Katanga (Balubakat), whose program was to have a separate country of Luba-Kasai people, away from the Katanga province. In the late 1950s, the Congolese struggle for independence was far from being a unified one. It was fraught with internal contradictions deliberately sustained by the colonial administration and the white settlers. The most difficult task Lumumba had at hand was to first reconcile these contradictions.

However, Lumumba's own MNC, which until 1959 was the only party to have eluded the malaise of tribal division, underwent its own internal partition. In July 1959, three of Lumumba's associates within the MNC did not bear well Lumumba's growing popularity. Albert Kalonji, Joseph Ileo, and Cyrille Adouala split the MNC and offered a version of it that was to look after the specific interests of the Luba people. They named their version of the MNC the MNC-Kalonji (MNC-K), as opposed to the MNC-Lumumba (MNC-L). In the Congo, the colonists' and the colonial administration's strategy of *divide and rule* created undesired effects. The proliferation of tribal fronts and the intensification of intertribal confrontations made it impossible for Belgium to fully control where the Congo was headed. The chaos stimulated in the colony by the colonial administration actually multiplied the sites of demands for independence, be it a balkanized one. Independence appeared imminent, which could either be won through armed struggle as in Algeria or through negotiations. For the Belgian authorities the responsibility for the imminence of the Congo's independence was to be impugned to Minister of the Colonies Hemelrijck, whose excessively reformist policy permitted the bourgeoning of so many sites of contestation.

Hemelrijck would later pay a price for his convictions. For many colonists, Hemelrijck was a "nigger-lover" and an anticolonial who was recklessly encouraging political advancement for the natives of the Congo. In fact, Hemelrijck held his conviction from Joseph van Bilsen, a Belgian professor at the Institute for Colonial Studies of the University of Antwerp who had published a thirty-year plan for the gradual emancipation of the Congo. Van Bilsen had argued that the Congo would need thirty years to create properly educated leaders capable of filling the void left by any eventual withdrawal of the colonial administration. Van Bilsen's thesis, which was dismissed by many radical critics in Belgium and in the Congo—among whom was Kasavubu, who on August 23, 1956, publicly rejoined with a more radical proposal of his own that fell short of asking full and immediate independence dismissed—nevertheless, seduced Hemelrijck. The Minister of the Colonies believed that a slow and controlled nationalism should be allowed in the Congo to avoid the eventual radicalization of the colony against Belgian rule. Among the Congolese who endorsed van Bilsen's plan were leaders of the Conscience Africaine, a group of moderate Catholic liberals. Among them was Joseph Ngalula, one of the Congolese who joined Lumumba's MNC and accompanied him to Accra. Hemelrijck's role was primary in preparing for the Congo's independence, even if not necessarily by his own volition.

By 1959 Kasavubu and Lumumba were battling not just against the colonial administration but also against each other. They were jostling for position and multiplying political gatherings for a show of force. On account of what he saw as privileged concessions made by the colonial administration to Lumumba (especially Himelrijck's granting permission to Lumumba to travel to Ghana), Kasavubu was getting restless and stirring up the political waters for recognition of his party's strength and relevance. So, when on January 4, 1959, Belgian authorities issued an interdiction to his Abako to hold a political gathering for failure to file the requisite papers, Kasavubu sent his party members to the streets in protest. The Colonial Police's (Force Publique) attempt to quash the Abako's demonstration resulted in many deaths among Congolese (50 by official estimations) and several wounded. The colonial authorities jailed Kasavubu and some of his associates. Kasavubu's rally was in fact a response to Lumumba's own. Indeed, the leader of the MNC had returned from the All African-People's Conference in Accra more radicalized than ever, but more popular, too, and he organized several political gatherings and was speaking for the Congo's autonomy. On December 28, 1958, Lumumba held a well-attended rally in Leopoldville that almost overshadowed the leader of Abako. It was mainly in response to Lumumba's powerful popular demonstration that Kasavubu scheduled his memorable January 4, 1959, gathering.

Then Lumumba rejoined to Kasavubu by animating an MNC congress in Stanleyville from 23 to 28 October 1959. Lumumba's conference ended with a riot as violent as Abako's January 4 demonstration and registered almost as many deaths. The colonial administration arrested Lumumba on November 1 and sentenced him to six-month's jail time. The irony of this interparty power struggle was that if the colonial administration had wanted the Congo's political parties divided and thus weakened, the competition between the parties had strengthened their faith in full autonomy for the Congo because what was henceforth at stake in their posturing was who was more qualified to speak for the independence of the Congo. Independence was hence the order of the day, and the various demonstrations to claim it reinforced the colonial administration's fear that the situation in the Congo was bound to end in one of two ways: a smooth transition to independence or war. Realizing that Belgium did not have the resources to fight a bloody, protracted war of the kind France was losing in Algeria, the Belgian authorities opted for negotiations with all the political organizations of the Congo.

So, on January 13, King Baudouin of Belgium announced Belgium's "firm intention without undesirable procrastination but also without undue haste to lead the Congolese populations forward to independence in prosperity and peace."[2] "Without undue haste" meant, as far as Belgium was concerned, that independence would be granted to the Congo not immediately but in five years. A document titled *Déclaration Gouvernementale* was drafted to that effect. It promised municipal elections as well as provincial elections with a bicameral house in 1960. Then, the Congolese would have until 1964 to decide whether they wanted full independence or partial autonomy, with Belgium retaining the control of the Congo's currency, defense, and foreign policy. This was a delaying strategy to give Belgium enough time to manipulate the Congolese political elites towards partial independence. Minister of the Colonies Himelrijck, who had developed too-good relationships with the Congolese évolués, was asked by his king to redeem himself in furthering that agenda. Once again, Himelrijck chose the sempiternal colonial method of ambiguity.

On March 13, 1959, Himelrijck managed to free the Abako leaders and, without even informing the families or any other political leader in the Congo, flew them directly to Belgium, where the king had hoped to have their privileged and influenced response to his proposed *Déclaration Gouvernementale* before their constituencies or the leaders of the other parties could have a chance to express their opinions on it. In Belgium, the three Abako leaders were given first-class treatment by the Belgian authorities. For three days, from March 13 to 16, Kasavubu, Daniel Kanza, and Simon Nzeza had secret meetings with Himelrijck about the best response to give to the *Déclaration Gouvernementale*. Himelrijck could not persuade the Abako leaders to wait until 1964 for full independence. Kassavu remained firm. It was independence now or total boycott of the colonial administration's political program. Belgium's tactics of postponement of independence created much suspicion, and each tribe started looking for a way to get out of the fragile Congolese union and ascertain its independence. If the Congo were to balkanize, with multiple tribes seeking independence on their own, Belgium could be faced with protracted war on multiple fronts. Brussels saw no other solution than to yield to the demand for independence. Himelrijck had failed his mission of obtaining the Congolese leaders' signatures of the *Déclaration Gouvernementale*. So, in September 1959, Hemelrijck, who was praised by some to be "one of the very few Belgian politicians able to keep a balance ... between the aspirations of the Congolese people and the financial interests of those who lived off the riches of the colony," was asked by his superiors to hand in his resignation.[3] Hemelrijck was replaced in the Congo by two Belgian officials, Auguste de Schrijver, for Congolese political and administrative affairs, and Raymond Scheyven, a rich Belgian businessman with stakes in the Congo, for economic and financial affairs.

The Brussels Table Ronde: Anticipation, Deceit, and Naïveté

The effort to delay the Congo's independence having failed, in January 1960 the Belgian authorities convened a roundtable in Brussels to discuss under which conditions the Congo would be granted its independence. The Brussels Round-table saw the participation of more than forty Congolese political organizations around the discussion table with the Belgian authorities. Lumumba was still in jail when the conference started, and the other Congolese leaders insisted that he be invited to the talk. Still wearing around his wrists the bandages used to hide traces of the torture he endured in captivity, Lumumba arrived in Brussels on January 26, 1960, to take part in the roundtable discussions. In Brussels, a timetable was established for the Congo's independence. It was decided that after some legislative elections set for no later than May 1960, the country would be granted full independence on June 30, 1960. Elated, the Congolese leaders rushed back home to campaign for the legislative votes that would determine the leaders of independent Congo.

Brussels appointed a Resident Minister by the name of Ganshof van der Meersch, a lawyer by trade, to oversee the Congo's transition to self-government. The idea was that even if the Congo was to be independent, it should nonetheless never steer away from Brussels' zone of influence. And in fact, van der Meersch was instrumental in selecting the leaders of the newly independent nation. It is he who arbitrated the appointment of Kasavubu as president and Lumumba as prime minister of the Congo. In fact, the legislative elections of May 30, 1960, gave Lumumba the largest number of votes. He captured 35 out of 137 seats; Abako gained 12 seats, the Conakat 8 seats, and the Balubakat seized 7 seats. However, because the MNC-L leader failed to capture the majority of votes and since the cumulative number of his opponents' votes largely exceeded the MNC-L's, compromises had to be found to appoint the new leaders of the country.

The arrangement that made Kasavubu and Lumumba respectively president and prime minister of the Congo was fraught with the very tensions that had always defined political parties in the Congo as ethno-cultural movements, and it would later serve to undermine the country's fragile independence. The negotiations that resulted in the choice of Kasavubu as president of independent Congo were full of maneuverings. Besides Kasavubu, another candidate, Jean Bolikango, a leader of the powerful Bangala tribe of the Upper Congo, was vying for the position. Bolikango had sought Lumumba's support for the presidency and had received a written promise from the latter in exchange for Bolikango's support for the government election. When it became clear to Lumumba that he could become prime minister only if, as Belgium wished, Kasavubu became head of state, he was ready to break his word on the promise made to Bolikango. Lumumba suddenly reversed his views on Bolikango, to the astonishment of some of his closest collaborators urging him to be good for his word, and he unexpectedly qualified the man he had hitherto praised as a man of his word and worthy of trust as a "pawn of Belgium and a protégé of the Catholics," for whom Lumumba had little consideration. So, Lumumba directed members of his party and other nationalist parties to vote for Kasavubu, to whom he had also promised support. In the end, Kasavubu was elected with 159 votes against 43 for Bolikango. Lumumba certainly knew, as many Congolese did, that Kasavubu was "lazy, cruel, and cynical," but what Lumumba did not know was that, as Antoine Kanza, a former collaborator of Kasavubu's, had tried to warn him, he had just maneuvered to elect a man "the pressure groups that distrusted [Lumumba] saw as ... a delaying agent, a shrewd politician, a lazy but ambitious man who would have the courage to get rid of him should the need arise."[4]

It was also a testimony to their inexperience and naïveté that the Congolese évolués' attention should be markedly focused on political positioning and nothing else, while the real future of the Congo was being decided elsewhere, in the economic arena, where Congolese leaders were so conspicuously absent. The Congolese leaders who were present at the Brussels Political Roundtable made no objection at all to Belgian authorities' proposal that economic and financial issues should be discussed at another roundtable, that one termed "Economic and Financial Roundtable." The Belgian authorities were well aware of the under-the-surface brewing rivalry between the party leaders and the high price that they tended to put on what political position they would occupy in the eyes of their constituencies when all was said and done. In fact, Brussels had insured that the atmosphere of the Roundtable would be propitious to massaging some egos and frustrating others. The first Roundtable was surrounded by a dazzling show of luxury and Belgian razzmatazz in the flamboyance of Brussels' Hotel Plaza, which could be enchanting and distracting at the same time for those who were allowed to enjoy it—and create bitterness and suspicion in those who were not permitted to benefit from it. The Hotel Plaza that hosted the Congolese attendees was a carnival site. Belgian fine chefs hustling and bustling to wait on their African guests, young Belgian girls being ushered into the attendees' rooms, journalists and autograph seekers waiting in line to see the political leaders—all this attention gave the Congolese évolués a false sense of importance and assurance. At least, for one month, the Congolese leaders naively trusted the very Belgian administration they had mistrusted for decades and all but gave Brussels carte blanche to determine the economic future of the Congo, as they rushed back home to campaign for the legislative elections. In Brussels, this Fanonian verity was given all its significance:

> As soon as the native begins to pull on his moorings, and to cause anxiety to the settler, he is handed over to well-meaning souls who in cultural congresses point out to him the specificity and wealth of Western values. But every time Western values are mentioned they produce in the native a sort of stiffening or muscular lockjaw. During the period of decolonization, the native's reason is appealed to. He is offered definite values, he is told frequently that decolonization need not mean regression, and that he must put his trust in qualities which are well-tried, solid, and highly esteemed.[5]

In Brussels, "the native" (yes, we shall not forget that such was his name and "primitive" was his epithet) was dazzled and forgot to pull his dagger against he who had for centuries treated him like a mere animal. In Brussels, the native believed its oppressor's honeyed words and let his guard down.

The Economic and Financial Roundtable that "sealed the fate of the Congo" finally took place in Brussels from April 26 to May 16. Most political leaders, except Tshombe, were absent. Belgian economic experts were left to discuss the economic prospect of the Congo with mere Congolese students who had very rudimentary understanding of the complex conventions they were agreeing to. "The Belgians laid the groundwork for transferring much of the enormous state portfolios in colonial companies to Belgium, through privatization, while leaving virtually all the public debt to [the Congo]."[6] On September 1, 1960, the Congolese realized the full consequence of this negligence when, in the chamber of representatives, Joseph Kasongo, the Congolese Speaker of the House, reported his last trip to United States in the following terms:

> We arrived in Washington where we were officially welcomed with a nineteen-gun salute; we were given rooms in the presidential guest house, where all important guests stay. On the day of our arrival we were received by the American secretary of state…. We took the opportunity of asking to become members of the World Bank and the International Monetary Fund…. We had also intended to choose this moment to ask for a loan. It was then that we discovered that Belgium had made a contract in the name of the Congo to borrow 120 million dollars…. We were told that of the 120 million dollars, Belgium had already received 79 million and was still to receive 41 million. We were told that we could not touch this remaining money, because Belgium had not yet given receipts to show how she had spent the 79 million she received. We were asked to pay back the advance. We replied that we had not had any of it, and were in serious financial difficulties which would make it impossible to do so. Belgium was supposed to have repaid 14.5 million dollars at the beginning of the previous August, but had not done so…. Both our wealth and our hard work had been exploited.[7]

The Congolese leaders fell victim to their own overvaluation of political power and social prestige against economic independence. Obviously, if Congolese leaders like Lumumba were pleased to be in the company of Pan-Africanists like Fanon and Touré, they had all the same given little consideration to this Fanonian proposition that decolonization had more to do with building a new society free of colonialism's moral vestiges than settling complacently on the throne of the former master. "While they neglected to protect the country's economic assets, the newly elected leaders were more concerned with enjoying the material benefits that colonialism and the color bar had denied them than with a radical transformation of the inherited system for purposes of meeting the people's expectations of independence."[8] The Congolese évolués easily gave credence to apologists of Belgian colonialism in their claim that for most Congolese independence "consisted of a common desire to take over the white man's job as a means of enjoying his higher standard of living."[9] For, indeed, many of the Congolese leaders displayed utter dereliction in the job at hand, which had a distressing effect on those who took their postindependence mission to heart:

> The first meetings of our Council of Ministers were unforgettable. Our discussions were of the most desultory kind. All of us were happy, or at least cheerful and satisfied, at being ministers. It was play-acting; some of it pure comedy, some nearer

to tragedy. We were ministers; we, the colonized, now had title and dignity; but we had no power at all about any of the instruments we needed to carry out the functions expected of us. We argued about offices, about suitable and available sites for them, and how they should be shared among us. We discussed the allocation of ministerial cars; the choosing and allotting of ministerial residences; arrangements for our families and their travel—some from the country into the capital; others from the African part of Leopoldville to what had been the European part. In short, we talked endlessly, laughed ourselves silly, and concluded by generally agreeing that the Belgian colonizers were to blame for all our troubles.[10]

Finally came the day so anticipated by all the Congolese: Independence Day, June 30, 1960. The guest of honor of the ceremony of "transfer of power" from Belgium to the Congo was Baudouin I, King of the Belgians. Though Baudouin had wanted to appear as a beloved "father" pleasingly betrothing his "children" to emancipation with guiding principles for success, earlier, on the eve of independence, an event had augured that Belgium had totally lost esteem in the Congo and would never again be welcomed in the country it had exploited for so long. On June 29, 1960, as a motorcade of Baudouin and newly elected Congolese president Kasavubu stopped in a main artery of Leopoldville for a ceremony of flag salute, a Congolese nationalist by the name of Ambroise Boimbo snatched Baudouin's scepter and ran with it. The man was later captured by the Force Publique and the king's scepter returned to him. For Boimbo, his gesture was one of defiance and self-affirmation. As a former soldier, he had learned that the baton of a leader was the symbol of his authority over his underlings. The Congo was independent. The King of the Belgians had no business parading in the Congo as a conqueror would in a conquered territory.[11]

A Congolese Leadership Rigged with Inexperience and Impulsiveness Facing a Morally Deficient Euro-American Power

The following day, Lumumba reiterated Boimbo's gesture to the satisfaction of many Congolese. To King Baudouin, who praised Belgium's actions in the Congo from Leopold's Congo Free State to Belgium's colonial administration as restorative and humanitarian, Lumumba rejoined that in the Congo, Belgium's economic gluttony had led it to perpetrate a holocaust that was still very much alive in the Congolese collective memory. Lumumba's impromptu speech, which drenched Baudouin's and Kasavubu's satisfied discourses with pessimistic prospects for the Congolese-Belgian future relationships, was immediately greeted in the Euro-American world as hostile to America and Western Europe. Of course, as noted a former minister in the Lumumba government, in the days following the independence of the Congo, labeling became a frequent practice: "We no longer hesitated to describe this or that colleague as reactionary or pro–Belgian; while others were labeled anti-colonialist, socialist, progressive or anti-imperialist—for they were almost always to be seen in company with Guineans, Ghanaians, Egyptians, Czechoslovakians or Russians."[12] In this name-calling exercise, Lumumba was tagged with the most lethal epithet western powers could attribute to anyone: that of communist, anti-white and pro–Soviet Union. Lumumba thus became the man to eliminate and Kasavubu the "right leader" to prop up.

From June 30, 1960, the Euro-American coalition spared no effort to get rid of Lumumba, and it mattered not that two hours after his impulsive rejoinder to Baudouin, at the reception dinner given in the honor of King Baudouin at the Palais de la Nation, Lumumba had regretted his previous outburst and gone through all sorts of humiliating contortions to repair the damage he had caused during his earlier speech, pledging to "pray with His majesty by the tombs of the pioneers and the statue of Leopold II, the first sovereign of the independent state of the Congo." This genuflection came too late. The dice were cast. "It was agreed all over the West the day after Lumumba's speech on June 30: it was the beginning of the end of this man as a politician"; Belgium and its allies could no longer be dissuaded that Lumumba "would foster Communist infiltration into the Congo. Therefore, they were determined that he be removed from power as soon as possible after June 30, and the Congo restructured on a federal basis, with the cooperation of Kasavubu, Tshombe and Kalonji."[13]

Tshombe had been contacted by the white settlers of the province of Katanga to secede from the Congo, and he had enjoyed the idea of being president of his own rich state. Now that Lumumba had clearly fallen out of grace, they reiterated their proposal to Tshombe and set about to put their secession plan in practice. On July 5, 1960, Belgian General Emile Janssens, in charge of the Congolese police, instigated a mutiny of his forces. The idea was to get them to revolt against Lumumba's government by pointing out that independence would not usher in better social conditions for them and that though the évolués had been living in luxury the African soldiers would still be living as subalterns in segregated barracks under the leadership of racist white officers. General Janssens obtained more than he had bargained for. The African soldiers not only revolted against the government, but they also attacked their white officers and the white populations and looted the white residences and businesses. On July 10, 1960, without consulting the Lumumba government, Belgian Minister of Foreign Affairs Pierre Wigny and Belgian Defense Minister Gibson ordered Belgians troops to land in Elisabethville to "protect the Western settlers and businesses." The following day, with the support of the white settlers in Katanga, Tshombe proclaimed the Katanga an independent state, inviting Belgium to "join ... in close economic community … to continue [its] technical financial and military aid; and also help us in reestablishing public order and security."

The Congo had fallen into chaos; worse, it was now a divided country, a division gladly sustained by Belgium. As for the Katanga, it was not independent as Tshombe had hoped, for the very Belgian officials who urged Tshombe to declare the mineral rich province autonomous, "in secret diplomatic messages, recommended all self-respecting states not to lower themselves to recognize a province which, though it called itself independent, had in fact returned to being a colony."[14] Given the United States' and the United Nations' indication that they would offer him no help in resolving the issue, Lumumba started courting the Soviet Union with the expectation that a looming threat of the Congo tipping into communism would prompt the Western bloc to be more supportive. On July 24, 1960, Lumumba took his case to the United Nations in New York. UN Secretary-General Dag Hammarskjöld was unquestionably the man of the West, and he did not appreciate Lumumba's cozying up to the Soviet Deputy Foreign Minister, Vasily Kuznetzov, and accepting an invitation to go to Moscow a few hours before he was scheduled to meet with President Eisenhower. This strategy proved damaging. The White House cancelled Lumumba's meeting, and a biased Hammarskjöld reproached Lumumba with losing the support of "the only ally the central Congolese government [could] count on, the only one that sincerely [supported] what the UN [was] doing in the Congo."[15] And what was the UN actually doing in the Congo other than supporting the politics of Belgium? Practically nothing.

Despite Hammarskjöld's assurance to the Congolese leaders that he was working for a positive resolution of the Congo crisis, the UN Secretary-General was actually working at fulfilling King Baudouin's program of recolonizing the Congo. Since Lumumba went rogue on June 30, 1960, and particularly with the violent rioting of the Congolese army and the ensuing massive exodus of the Belgians settlers, Brussels, through its ambassador in the Congo, Jean van den Bosch, had been exploring the possibility of finding a substitute for Lumumba. Justin Bomboko, who "throughout the Congo crisis … [had] kept in touch with Belgian emissaries," was slated for this post. Brussels had hoped that Bomboko, foreign minister in Lumumba's government and one of the moderate leaders ready to accept Belgium's protection, would be one of its puppet leaders for a confederated Congo rallied around Tshombe's Katanga. Belgium's crusade for federating the Congo was so well managed that it became a rallying cry for Belgians of all trades (politicians, journalists, missionaries) as well as non–Belgian Westerners with colonialist bent.

When after much delay the UN Security Council finally passed a resolution demanding the withdrawal of Belgian troops, it was in Leopoldville that the withdrawal actually took place. In Katanga, the Belgian troops remained in place. "The UN acted as a political but also military buffer between the Congolese government and Tshombe. Moreover, contemptuous of Leopoldville's sovereignty, UN leaders condoned the fact that Belgian administrators and advisers were staying on to build Tshombe's state. Belgian soldiers also had the right to stay: Changing into African uniforms, they could create a Katangese army."[16] This arrangement was wanted by Baudouin and Tshombe, and Hammarskjöld hinted that he supported it. Through a report of August 6, 1960, which he sent to King Baudouin, the UN secretary-general stated that the presence of UN troops in the Katanga should by no means be construed as having been prompted by Tshombe's intent to secede from the Republic of Congo.[17]

In fact, the decision to position UN troops in Katanga had first to gain Tshombe's approval, and when on August 10, 1960, the UN Blue Berets finally entered Katanga, Belgium breathed an air of optimism; it was henceforth evident, as the Belgian minister of African Affairs, Count Harold d'Aspremont Lynden, had expressed in a telegram to the King of the Belgians: "Katangese structures will be protected by UN troops and, in not too distant future, by Katangese troops under command of Belgian officers."[18] The reality on the ground confirmed collusion between Brussels and the UN. While the UN was propping up Tshombe's renegade regime, the democratically elected government of Lumumba was being financially constricted. Hammarskjöld insisted that any financial and technical assistance offered to Lumumba's government by any country should go through the United Nations and be approved by him, as chairman of a consultative committee he formed and which was composed of representatives at the United Nations of the countries that had contributed assistance to UN operations in the Congo, that is, Canada, Ethiopia, Ghana, Guinea, India, Indonesia, Ireland, Liberia, Mali, Morocco, Pakistan, the Sudan, Sweden, Tunisia, and the United Arab Republic (UAR).

This consultative committee under the auspices of Hammarskjöld had far-reaching authority; it was, in effect, a committee formed to "direct [the Congolese government] along the path it thought best for economic political and social life of the country and its people."[19] Clearly, Hammarskjöld was taking his orders from Belgium as a neocolonial power and from Washington as the leader of the Western powers and guarantor of American financial interests in the Congo. It is not clear whether Hammarskjöld had hardened and radicalized his position after bad treatment he received from Lumumba and his ministers or whether it had all along been his plan to play Belgium and Washington's game. One can only give Hammarskjöld the benefit of the doubt and surmise that the Secretary-General of the United Nations, this most prestigious institution, should be too rational a politician with too hard a shell to have international policy dictated to him by his mood. One should give Hammarskjöld the benefit of level-headedness and, thus, presume that his design for the resolution of the Congo crisis, however unfair and diabolical it might have been, was well examined, though skillfully concealed from even those who, like Thomas Kanza, the young Congolese minister delegate to the United Nations, had come to trust him at the peril of their lives. If Lumumba was awkward and politically inexperienced, Hammarskjöld was, in fact, coherently crooked.

In July 1960, the most loyal members of Lumumba's government had very strong suspicions as to where Hammarskjöld's dilatory method was taking the Congo. They were persuaded that the UN Secretary-General was cautioning the balkanization of the Congo. Lumumba's closest collaborators, led by Vice-Prime Minister, Gizenga, certainly receiving his orders from Lumumba, who was still in North America, decided to act. Their response was more impulsive than diplomatic. Understandably, they had been pushed to the edge by the West's insincerity and their inexperience had taken over. This was not an excuse. As leaders of an independent country, they were going to face multiple challenges, and coolheadedness under pressure ought to prevail. Unfortunately, the Congolese leaders elected to use Lumumba's signature strategy, the one he had employed against King Baudouin on Independence Day; they decided to publicly humiliate the United Nations Secretary-General. On July 30, 1960, at a dinner that was given in honor of Hammarskjöld, who had arrived days earlier in the Congo to appraise the conditions of any UN intervention, Gizenga relayed on radio a surprise speech in which he questioned the integrity of the United Nations Secretary-General and expressed his disappointment with the institution. Was that the move that tipped the balance against the people of the Congo and caused the UN to work in the corner of Belgium and the United States? As suggested earlier, one has to give the Secretary-General the benefit of rationality and conclude that he had only been paying lip service to Leopoldville's exigencies while secretly protecting Belgian and American financial interests. Protecting these interests dictated that Lumumba should be eliminated, especially in light of his increasing radicalization and unyieldingness, and sometimes, in light of his impulsive behavior since his return to the Congo from a globetrotting tour that took him to the capitals of some of the most vehement critics of colonialism.

In effect, before returning to the Congo from his failed New York trip, Lumumba had traveled to Montreal, and then to London, where he had met with the ambassadors of Tunisia, Ghana, Morocco, and Ethiopia. He then went to the nations of Algeria, Morocco, and Guinea, whence he arrived in the Congo "completely hypnotized" by the unmitigated anti-imperialist rhetoric his guests served him. Upon his return to the Congo, Lumumba found a country almost on its knees, in a more distressing state than he had left it two weeks before, a country that needed a strong leader with superlative abilities for negotiation. Unfortunately, negotiation skills were what Lumumba lacked most. On the other hand, the prime minister was not deficient in confrontational talent; and to prove it, he made a series of problematic decisions.

On August 8, 1960, Lumumba gave a speech that indicated in no ambiguous terms that the United Nations, its Secretary-General, the United States, and the Western powers were all corrupt entities; and without consulting a delegation he had earlier sent to the UN to make a case for his government, Lumumba declared a state of emergency, ordered the Belgian embassy to close and its staff to go back to Belgium, ordered Congolese students in Belgium to return to the Congo, and announced an independent African states summit to take place in the Congo on August 25. On August 15, Lumumba cancelled a tête-à-tête he was to have with Hammarskjöld just three hours before the scheduled meeting and from then on would communicate with the Secretary-General of the United Nations only through an exchange of fault-finding letters, which did nothing to improve his rapport with those people who, unfortunately, had real decision power over the future of the Congo. On August 17, Lumumba called a press conference in which he contradictorily denounced the incompetence of the United Nations, dismissed the institution as irrelevant, and yet asked for its help in solving the Congo crisis. Finally, on August 27, Lumumba put his threat of requesting help from the Soviets into effect. In preparation for the invasion of the renegade provinces of Katanga and Kasai and the unification of the Congo, Lumumba received aid from the Soviet Union in the form of military technical assistance, over 100 soviet military trucks, and 16 Ilyushin transport planes. Belgium, which "had done her best to make the West permanently uneasy at seeing Lumumba at the head of the Congolese government" and which had proclaimed all along that "Lumumba was a Communist, an anti-white, and an anti–Westerner," could now feel justified in its belief in the eyes of the Western alliance. The Russian presence in the Congo convinced public opinion in the Western community that "the Congo as governed by Lumumba was already more than half-way to being a Communist and anti–Western power"[20]; and if Lumumba's troops, which had started a successful invasion of Kasai and Katanga on August 31, 1960, were left to finish their operation of forced reunification, the whole Congo, and with it Western financial interests, could be irremediably controlled by Moscow. To prevent this from happening, a coalition of Belgian envoys, American diplomats, and unprincipled Congolese politicians prepared to stage a constitutional crisis that would topple Lumumba, even eliminate him.

The Americanization of the Congo and the Assassination of Lumumba

American Ambassador Clare Timberlake was working as liaison with the American financial interests to provide funds in support of Kasavubu. General Ben Kettani, the deputy to Carl von Horn, the UN force commander, in his capacity of UN military assistant, was conditioning the Congolese National Army to be more committed to Mobutu, who was under CIA influence, than to the Commander-in-Chief of the armed forces, Victor Lundula, who had been appointed by Lumumba and also was very close to him. Inside Lumumba's government, Albert Delvaux and Bomboko had been persuaded to defect. Also, Lumumba's military campaign in south Kasai would be used against him. Though strategically successful, the campaign against Kalonji was a humanitarian disaster, as it had caused the deaths of many civilians, especially in the regions of Mbuj-Mayi and Kasengulu. On September 5, in a bold and unpredicted move, using as his pretext the Kasai massacre, which Hammarskjöld had conveniently overstated as a genocide, Kasavubu announced the dismissal of Lumumba on Congolese National Radio. A few minutes after Kasavubu's declaration, Lumumba also went on national radio to dismiss Kasavubu as head of state. Two of Lumumba's ministers who countersigned Kasavubu's order of dismissal of the prime minister, as required by the Congolese constitution, or *Loi Fondamentale* were, as expected, Bomboko and Delvaux. Neither Kasavubu's order nor Lumumba's ever took effect, for the Congolese parliament annulled them and tried, with the help of the new special representative to Hammarskjöld, Rajeshwar Dayal, an East Indian, to resolve the crisis between the two leaders amicably. This was to no avail, for too much work had already been undertaken by those whose interests lay in the permanence of the Congo crisis.

Before Rajeshwar Dayal, who had replaced Ralph Bunche, arrived in the Congo, the American Andrew Cordier, acting as special secretary to the United Nations secretary-general/chairman of the consultative committee actually governing the Congo, had successfully managed to steer the affairs of the Congolese government in such a way as to strip Lumumba of any power and favorably position the Western coalition and their corrupt local informants (Tshombe, Kalonji, Kasavubu, Delvaux, and Bomboko). Cordier provided Kasavubu with Moroccan bodyguards; he disabled Congolese National Radio by removing a key piece from the broadcasting equipment; and he ordered the closure of all Congolese airports except the ones in Katanga, "where the Belgians were making the rules." Consequently, Congolese could only receive propagandist news from Radio Elisabethville and Radio-Makala, which were in the service of the Belgians, the white mercenaries, and the Kasavubu-Kalonji-Tshombe alliance. On September 12, 1960, the constitutional crisis was effective, as two Congolese delegations were sent to the UN Security Council to discuss the Congo crisis: a delegation led by Thomas Kanza, representing the Lumumba government, and another one, conducted by Justin Bomboko, representing Kasavubu.

Confusion in the Congo intensified, as it became difficult for the populations to figure out which government—Lumumba's or Kasavubu's—was actually running the country. This planned confusion by the Western coalition provided them the occasion to implement the coup that would finally rid them of Lumumba. Tshombe, his Belgian advisers, and General Kettani had already won the support of the Congolese National Army soldiers by bribing them heavily. The soldiers had not been paid since the beginning of the crisis and by then their only allegiance was to their growling stomachs. On September 14, the Congolese National Radio, until then disabled by Cordier, went on air to allow Joseph Désiré Mobutu to announce to the world that for the sake of the Congolese people he had decided to "temporarily neutralize" both Lumumba and Kasavubu until such time as the two leaders could come to their senses and decide to work for the good of the country and not for themselves. This was "not a military coup d'état," Mobutu insisted, "but merely a peaceful revolution; no soldier will be in power." Instead, the country would be run by a college of commissioners composed of university graduates and students. That college of commissioners was, curiously, to be led by Bomboko; and while Lumumba was confined in house arrest, "the apparently 'neutralized' Kasavubu presided over the swearing-in ceremony for the young commissioners, and continued to discharge his official functions such as receiving foreign envoys."[21] This is because Kasavubu, owing to his reputation of a coward and opportunist, had been doing what the Americans wanted him to do, while Lumumba had openly defied Mobutu's demand that he rally Washington. Indeed, as Kanza noted, "from 14 September, the Congo openly became a satellite country of the Western bloc."

Following Mobutu's "peaceful revolution," Congolese National Radio opened for good; airports reopened under the auspices of the United Nations; Russian diplomats and technicians were summoned to leave the Congo; and the military operations against Kasai and Katanga were stopped. From then on, "any representatives of other countries wanting to intervene there must first make sure they had the written or understood approval of Washington." The United States had started a progressive de–Belgianization and a slow Americanization of the Congo. Over time, the Belgians came to realize that they were no longer the masters in the Congo. A new sheriff was in town: America. The Belgians were thenceforth mere go-betweens that Washington still needed in its colonizing enterprise.[22] The Americans, in their colonization of the Congo, had decided to proceed more carefully, however.

For Washington, it was more prudent to work from behind the scenes— pulling the strings on known Congolese leaders with established constituencies who would act just as facades—than to be on the forefront. Of the two Congolese leaders needed for the American colonization of the Congo, Kasavubu was malleable, but Lumumba was inflexible and showed not the slightest hint of ever being bought. The former could stay; the latter had to be disposed of. The American decision to directly get involved in the possible elimination of Lumumba came on August 26, 1960, in the form of a telegram that Allen Dulles, the head of the CIA, sent to the CIA station chief in Leopoldville, Laurence Devlin. The telegram read, "We conclude that [Lumumba's] removal must be an urgent and prime objective and that under existing conditions this should be a high priority of our covert action," a decision for which Richard Bissell, the CIA deputy director for plans, would later provide more clarity: "[The CIA] had put a top priority ... on a range of different methods of getting rid of Lumumba in the sense of either destroying him physically, incapacitating him, or eliminating his political influence."[23] A CIA scientist, Sydney Gotlieb, was consequently ordered by his superiors to prepare a chemical composition that would be used against Lumumba. This plan would not be carried out. Lumumba himself would facilitate his own death. On November 27, 1960, refusing to take his friends' advice that leaving his official residence and the protection of the UN force could be suicidal, Lumumba eluded the UN guards and escaped from his residence in an attempt to rally his hardcore supporters in Stanleyville, where Gizenga had established the Nationalist government. Captured by the Congolese army on the banks of the Sankuru River, with two of his collaborators, Mpolo (minister of youth and sport) and Okito (vice president of the Senate), Lumumba was "beaten like a dog," taken back to Leopoldville, and paraded as a disgraceful and vulgar criminal by self-appointed "Major" Gilbert Pongo—a politician whose "hatred for Lumumba and Lumumbists verged on the paranoiac"—before being incarcerated in Thysville. Some of Lumumba's prison guards in Thysville were sympathetic to him. In fact, they had even threatened to set Lumumba free. So Lumumba's political opponents in Leopoldville, precisely Kasavubu, Mobutu, and Bomboko, decided that it would be wiser to transfer him to a "safer" location. Initially, Kalonji wanted the honor of having Lumumba sent to him at Bakwanga. The place was reputed to be the slaughterhouse of political opponents, and Kalonji wanted to kill Lumumba there on a public esplanade, cut his body in pieces, and feed it to the families of the victims of Lumumba's anti-secessionist campaign in Kasai. However, Munongo, Tshombe's strongman, wanted this honor to be reserved to the Katangese.[24]

In any case, because UN troops were stationed in Bakwanga, transferring Lumumba there could not be done inconspicuously. So, on January 17, 1961, Lumumba and his companions were transferred to Elisabethville in Katanga and delivered to his fiercest Congolese enemies, Moïse Tshombe and Godefroid Munongo, who tortured him in an inhabited house, the Villa Brouwez, before delivering him to the blows of Belgian and Katangese soldiers, who executed him and buried him in a shallow grave whence his body was removed one night and dismembered and burnt in sulfuric acid.

Lumumba had to be eliminated before the January 20, 1960, swearing-in ceremony of the new president, John Kennedy, as Kennedy could seek another resolution to the Congo crisis. The Americans were unnecessarily worried.

Kennedy was just another American president, committed to America's hubris and jingoism. In the Congo, there was no indication that Kennedy would have acted differently from his predecessor. In fact, had not Kennedy greeted one of Lumumba's local slayers in deferential terms? "General [Mobutu], if it hadn't been for you, the whole thing would have collapsed and the Communists would have taken over." Since Lumumba's death, all the actors of the Congo crisis have been involved in a comic contortion to prove their innocence. In a way, Lumumba's fate is like that of the Congo. Lumumba's body, like the body of his country, has been the theater of competing western as well as African interests that ultimately caused him to be cut into pieces. In this theater, Lumumba's crime is to have trusted the good faith of humanity and to have been an idealist of independence, often to the point of utter naïveté, to the point of inflexibility. Naivety, inflexibility, and political ineptitude are no crimes comparable to the genocidal impulses of the greedy West.

CHAPTER 10

There Shall Be Wars of Liberation

That until the philosophy which holds one race superior and another inferior is finally and permanently discredited and abandoned.... Until all Africans stand and speak as free beings, equal in the eyes of all men, as they are in the eyes of Heaven; Until that day, the African continent will not know peace. We Africans will fight, if necessary, and we know that we shall win, as we are confident in the victory of good over evil.

—EMPEROR HAILE SELASSIE, Address to
the United Nations, October 4, 1963

Now, we shall try to comprehend the violence carried out by the oppressed on their oppressors. To try to comprehend does not necessarily mean to condone. It does not necessarily mean to condemn either, since the violence of the oppressed, especially when the oppressor is totally shut off to understanding the illegality of his occupation and the inhumanity of his actions upon the oppressed, becomes the only means for the oppressed to reach out to freedom and self-government. There is, as Granvaud so rightly denounces, a Gaullist mythology in France, which has now taken root even among the French Republicans. This legend the French enthusiastically teach in their schools states that it is France that, from the time of the Brazzaville conference in 1944, gradually prepared its colonies for independence, to be finally "granted" in the early 1960s. It is a grotesque lie whose sole purpose is to perpetuate the colonial and racist cliché of the political immaturity of colonized peoples waiting to be delivered by their white masters. In fact, at the meeting of governors and senior colonial officials in Brazzaville, de Gaulle explicitly insisted that any idea of autonomy or any indication of the possibility for France's colonies to develop outside of France's tutelage as well as any question of self-government were out of the question.[1] Contrary to the disseminated fable of a magnanimous France handing independence to its colonies on a silver platter, in fact, de Gaulle never broke with the enduring master/slave paradigm.

Truly, at no time in the master/slave vile relation has the master decided, of his free will, independently of any fear of retribution from the slaves, to

233

surrender his capital, to free his slaves. The master would never have been a slave-owner in the first place had he one ounce of humane wisdom and democratic sense. It is never the good will of the master that frees the slave. It is the master's perpetual fear that one day a slave revolt might cause him to lose his own freedom, his own life, that convinces the master to loosen his grip on his human trafficking commerce. What frees the slave is the slave's determination to be free, which the master reads in the slave's eyes, in his songs, in his acts, and which the master recognizes will one day come to actualization. Unless faced with nationalists' determination for independence at all costs, the West would never, by its own volition, put an end to its abominable exploitation of the nationalists' countries. In fact, ideas that are often rehashed by the leaders of the oppressing countries are that nationalists do not need independence; that they are not mature enough for it; that they will not know what to do with independence; and that it will only be a wasted opportunity for them. Nationalists, the oppressing nations think, are better off under the oppressors' care than being independent. And to prove their point that Africans, "these overgrown children," are doomed to remain under their tutelage, imperialist nations like to point to the number of so-called independent African countries that have made independence a mockery. The West likes to take as evidence of Africa's immaturity and proof that independence has done more harm than good to Africans the thousand places ablaze on the African continent. But what the West does not say is that the West is not a stranger to the multiple arsons in Africa. In 1999, General Gueï, who had just toppled President Bédié's government, confidently declared to those among his detractors that were calling for France to sever diplomatic ties with his praetorian regime that they should stop being ridiculous, for no coup d'état in French Africa would be successful without France's backing.

In fact, a cartography of France's military bases on the continent seems to support Gueï's assertion that France is in on the destabilization of the continent. Indeed, the African continent is under siege by the French army: 2,800 troops in Mali, an intelligence base in Niger permanently staffed with 101 Special Forces, 950 men in Chad, 1,900 troops in Djibouti, 200 troops in the horn of Africa, 1,600 troops in Central Africa, 9,000 troops in Gabon, 250 troops in the Gulf of Guinea, 450 troops in Côte d'Ivoire, 350 troops in Senegal. But France is not alone in this uncontrolled militarization of Africa. The whole Euro-American coalition happily participates in this new form of colonization, for, indeed, the West's real motives for blanketing Africa with its military in this supposedly post-independence era differ not at all from its purposes for keeping hundreds of thousands of troops in Africa during the colonial days. These are armies of occu-pation whose objective is to maintain the West's hegemony in Africa by crushing any nationalist fervor. Speaking of the large French army in Africa, Granvaud notes, "The French army is one of the main instruments in the service of a policy aimed at maintaining the neo-colonial order from the 1960s. It ensures the defense and protection of countries and vassal leaders of France and symmetrically suppresses movements or destabilizes regimes that are opposed to the interests of the metropole."[2]

Now, if this is not sanctified international piracy, we challenge any Western leader or any citizen from any Western country to accept as absolutely *normal* the presence of a Third World army in his country working to influence economic and social policy in his country. Why are the West's military presences in Africa to be seen as normal when the reverse would not be? On what basis is this normalcy established if not on that of the right of the strongest, this most basic and animalistic right that in the 21st century should be regarded as belonging exclusively to the fauna than to the human race? The West has decided to keep Africa in a state of modern bondage through a cocktail of economic and military violence. While in the days of colonization the missionaries, with their corrupting churches and schools, preceded the military in maintaining the West's supremacy in Africa, today it is the West's corrupting financial institutions and greedy multinationals that precede military violence in keeping African nations in shackles.

It is quite an exceptional stratagem that the Euro-American power has set up for the purpose of reoccupying the African countries that have committed to determining the course of their respective developments away from the imperial motivations of Europe and America more than half a century ago. First, the Euro-American financial institutions (the World Bank and the IMF) and its multinational corporations enter the economies of Africa through some deceitful financial schemes (bailing out banks, investors and speculators and applying political pressure to open up markets to foreign investments); then they cause these African nations to be indebted to them and thus vulnerable. They then take over the economies of these nations and, like parasites, start syphoning these economies into the Euro-American economies, without shame, without scruples, just like any ordinary thief or burglar would do. The military intervenes when the attempts at economic and political takeover of the African nations are denounced and resisted by some nationalists, who propose alternative programs meant to recover and keep national control of their country's resources.[3] However, the Euro-American armies, conspicuously present in Africa, do not intrude right away. There is one more menu to be tried before their involvement, a menu which includes subversion of the political process, contact with and corruption of administration and business leaders, corruption of the national military, of the media, of trade unions, and of academics, and the stirring of ethnic and religious differences. When all this has failed, only then do the imperialist militaries move in to crush the nationalists. And when they do move in, the imperialist armies take no prisoners.

What the West fails to understand, however, is that the degree of the violence of the nationalists is attuned to the degree of the West's own violence. The West conveniently forgets that in 1832 one of its proudest war engineers in Algeria, General Savary, en route to systematically executing the whole Ouffas tribe, ordered, "I want some heads…. [B]ring me some heads. Plug all these punctured water pipes with the head of the first Bedouin you see."[4] The West conveniently forgets, the better to repeat it, that 10 years later, Lieutenant-Colonel de Montagnac instructed his soldiers in Algeria in this way: "All the people who do not accept [their] conditions must be razed. Everything must be taken, sacked, regardless of age or sex: the grass must no longer grow wherever the French army sets its feet."[5] And what of this despondent French soldier whose letter home confirms the application of Montagnac's methods? "The country of the Beni-Menasser is superb and one of the richest I have seen in Africa…. We have burned everything, destroyed everything … we devastate, we loot, we destroy the crops and the trees."[6] The West conveniently forgets and wants the rest of the world, too, to be selectively amnesic and to remember only what the West wants to be remembered as truth, for the West does not have just truth, but truth itself is embodied in the West, exults *RedState* editor Erick Erickson, who chastised Obama for lacking Christian gumption, "Christ himself is truth. When we [Americans] possess Christ, we possess truth. The President is a moral relativist."[7] And it is in the name of Christianity as the embodiment of the truth, and in its own name as the eldest son of truth, that the West has committed, and continues to commit, its virtuous massacres in the world.

To successfully represent itself as the carrier of truth, the West has developed a whole industry of expert centers for truth fabrication and dissemination meant, as notes Steven Ward, to "transform the abstract, ill defined, and unknown into the concrete, systematic and understood."[8] To make its truth far-reaching, sustainable, and universal the West indefatigably invests enormous resources such as financial capital, the construction of equipment, the collection, sorting and storage of data, the production of artifacts, the recruitment of allies, the forging of a network of knowledge creators. And when all goes as expected, a weak statement becomes fact, "not by showing that a particular position corresponds with the real, as in traditional epistemology, but by establishing strong allies and associational networks that are capable of resolving dispute over data interpretation, ending controversies, resisting the deconstructionist tactics of adversaries and spreading the word."[9] Finally, to be established in the masses required that the hard truth fabricated in the expert centers be softened, be half-digested, decrypted, made appealing and friendly. This, too, requires enormous means, such as a network of media resource services, television stations, computer connections, libraries, newspapers, conventions and conferences, educational institutions, and so on.[10] Truth is too often the truth of the West. Nothing is true until decreed by the West as true. Nothing has happened until exposed by the

West as being factual. History has left us some prime examples of the West's magical prowess at fact erasure and creation.

Before 1885 and in the years following the Berlin Conference, Germany had little interest in building an African empire. Bismarck's conference was less to secure a huge African colony for Germany than to impress on the European nations that Germany was the lead player in Europe after the 1870 Franco-Prussian war. In fact, Bismarck's offhand commitment to colonialism got him dismissed by Kaiser Wilhelm II in 1890. He was replaced by Leo Von Caprivi, who brought little change to Bismarck's opinion of "the less Africa, the better."[11] However, in the first years of the war, the Germans' general anticolonial sentiment was reversed. It was not that Germany became Africanophile, but that a nationalistic vigor reconsidered the need to *own* African colonies as a sign of stature. Furthermore, in those times of great need, the existing German colonies of Africa were supplying war materials not available in Germany, a war effort which a greater involvement in Africa could help further increase. This is why, in 1916, a pro-colonial demonstration organized in Germany won the endorsement of all the parties, including the Social Democratic Party, hitherto opposed to any colonial engagement.

So Germany began eying the colonies of Portugal in East and West Africa, the Belgian colony of Congo, the French colonies of West Africa, and even the British colonies of Africa. It was at this point that some German atrocities in Africa, up to then hidden, started coming out. To undercut Germany's colonial appetite, Great Britain decided to show the "civilized world" that Germany, by its past horrors, was unfit to possess and administer colonies in Africa. A written confession by German Colonial Secretary Bernard Dernburg, which for years was buried in the European dead archives, was suddenly "stumbled upon" by British troops in South Africa. Thus, suddenly "discovered," and selectively published in a 1916 South African Blue Book, the documents showed that between 1904 and 1906 German Colonel Lothar Von Trotha ordered the extermination of about 200,000 Hereros and Ovambos, "between half and two-thirds of German South-West Africa's entire indigenous population."[12] This was not news. Of course, the British government knew about the massacres by the Germans, chose to sit on the evidence, and only exhibited it when it served Great Britain's purpose; and it was only at that moment that the elements in the documents were allowed to be considered factual. At that moment, the documents "presented the British government with the perfect pretext for expressing outrage at a strategy to which it had previously turned a blind eye."[13] Needless to say, Great Britain, the great moralizer, has been hundreds of times more vicious in its colonies. In fact, as remarks Herman Merivale, "The history of the European settlements in America, Africa, and Australia presents everywhere the same general features— *a wide and sweeping destruction of native races.*"[14] Yet, hush! Who dares speak of genocide of any nonwhite race before the West has decreed that genocides were ever perpetrated?

The West has been, and continues to be, a mass killer in Africa at the same level as malaria or Ebola. And yet the West is stunned at the enormity of the nationalists' violence when the nationalists, having repeatedly been opposed callously in their attempts to claim their independence, finally choose to take up arms. The West does not understand the extent of the violence perpetrated by the nationalists precisely because the West does not understand the scale of its own savagery, barbarity with which it has become comfortable over time, barbarity which it has rationalized as clean, civilized, removed from itself, perpetrated onto faceless, nameless, emotionless, and strange peoples and thus tolerable, normal even. This tendency to relativize violence and morality has pervaded Western academia, and we, scholars in Western academia, naturally fall into the trap of not questioning it. Thus, for instance, in reporting the vengeful violence that ensued in the aftermath of the massacres by the French army of the Algerian protesters in Sétif, Guelma and Kherrata, Martin Evans seems to contrast two kinds of violence, of which the more horrific is when the killer looks his victims in the eyes. Writes Evans, "Over the following three days, 102 Europeans were killed. Much of it was crude face-to-face violence, followed up by ritualistic dismemberments where genitals were cut off and placed in the mouths of corpses, breasts slashed, throats slit and bellies disemboweled."[15] This violence—which though not the exclusive province of non–Western societies, as we have seen with the French in Algeria, as we have seen in the European torture chambers filled with imaginative gadgets for the grisliest and most interactive killings but which is too often attributed to non–Western societies—makes us cringe. Here, the number of the killed disappear behind the atrocious manner in which the victims are killed. From the Western perspective, one million invisible killed, where the killers' and the victims' gazes do not meet, would be less cruel than the death of a single disemboweled person. Why would the West not be truthful to itself and admit as loudly as American Republican presidential hopeful Ben Carson has said it: that when it comes to war crimes, the West is immune and should fear prosecution from no one, that American soldiers should go anywhere they please and butcher with no regrets or qualms:

> Our military needs to know that they're not going to be prosecuted when they come back, because somebody has, said, "You did something that was politically incorrect." There is no such thing as a politically correct war. We need to grow up, we need to mature. If you're going to have rules for war, you should just have a rule that says no war. Other than that, we have to win. Our life depends on it.[16]

The West will not admit it and will keep thinking of itself as having moved away from primitive killings where eyes meet and torments are felt. Today, the

West is proud to kill "surgically," from afar, from a safe distance, using a strategy which, regardless of how many are killed, still sanctifies the carnage with an aura of graciousness and civility. Today, with his drones, Obama has entered history as one of the greatest distance killers. His drone warfare, which has been denounced by Amnesty International as killing indiscriminately, was also criticized by some of his staunch supporters in the United States as being immoral and obscene. As Eugene Robinson wrote, "U.S. drone attacks in Afghanistan, Pakistan and other countries may be militarily effective, but they are killing innocent civilians in a way that is obscene and immoral. I'm afraid that ignoring this ugly fact makes Americans complicit in murder."[17]

How many "yellow" people died from the atomic bomb attacks in Hiroshima and Nagasaki dropped from 31,000 feet on cities still asleep? Some estimates say around 200,000. How many "brown" civilians died in Iraq as a result of the U.S.-led invasion? Half a million? And in Libya, under the Euro-American bombs? What is the price of a "black" person for the Euro-American coalition? Priceless? That the black is a man, too, and that in the 21st century human life is priceless? That we have come a long way and left behind us the time when a black man could be captured and sold like a workhorse on American plantations? Yet, not long ago the value of a black was estimated at a mere 28 cents. At least that is how much the Euro-American coalition thought the black was worth at the dawn of the 21st century, which still is better than what it used to be during the Triangular Trade but which also says much about where we stand as a human society.

It was on Wednesday, December 22, 2010, in Brussels, that the European coalition estimated a black person's life to be worth less than 28 cents. Something has changed, but not much since the time of slavery, when European slave dealers would round up black women, children and men, put them on ships to America and swap them for molasses, cotton, and tobacco. On that day in 2010 a small West African country, Côte d'Ivoire, was resisting another one of the European coalition's exploitative schemes. The European Union, under the veil of the United Nations, was poised to strike Côte d'Ivoire a severe military blow in order to keep the EU's privileged access to the country's agricultural and geological resources intact. On that day the European Union voted a €5-million budget to be earmarked for the inevitable humanitarian crisis that would be the projected outcome of a war it was actively preparing for the purpose of replacing a duly elected president with a docile subject of its own picking, a puppet leader prepared to help carry out the West's hegemonic policies in Africa. And while the European Union (France, Germany, and other European countries), along with the U.S., were all calling on their citizens to evacuate Côte d'Ivoire in anticipation of the war that they had planned and knew would be ruthless, they were at the same time voting a €5-million budget to assist neighboring countries (Mali,

Guinea, Burkina Faso, Liberia, and Ghana) in managing the unavoidable flow of Ivorian refugees that their savage war would generate. This was roughly 28 cents for each of the 20 million souls who lived in Côte d'Ivoire. And when the bombs finally fell on the country, how many people died? Does it really matter to the West, when one can still find "influential personalities" in the Euro-American world to defend these deaths in the name of "higher interests"? When one can still find influential thinkers to relativize morality? The West's violence is civilized. It is undertaken in the name of a higher cause. The nationalists' violence is uncivilized. It has no defensible cause:

> It is the difference in nature between a [Western] violence not just exaggerated, but mostly planned, coldly, by those who have the means to live humanely, and a disorderly [nationalist] violence, improvised, visceral, as it is, perpetrated by these unhappy crowds, for a few minutes or a few hours, who take their revenge on their own terms, on their typically inhumane and humiliating existence. Instead of machine guns whose [Western] carriers have the advantage of not seeing exactly who they reach, [the oppressed] have in their hands, knives, stones, spears, clubs or any other suitable objects and bottles ... and they are face to face with their enemy, vis-à-vis every day, ready to go after them in the heat of the action.[18]

In the case of Côte d'Ivoire, the oppressed, the nationalists, had nothing in their hands; bare-handed, they were resolute to be heard, to take their fight to the media through popular protests. And yet they did not escape the epithets that the West, blind to its own savagery, reserves for the other. Bare-handed, yet they did not escape cold butcheries. On November 6, 2004, a French reporter narrated his live footage of the callous butchery by the French army of bare-handed Ivorian protesters in the city of Abidjan:

> From our windows, we can see the protesters. It is 11:00 p.m. We can hear helicopters above the roof of our hotel. From the sky, the helicopters of the French army are shooting at the protesters. They are civilians. We can hear tracing bullets, loud grenades, and persistent machine gun blasts, causing panic in the crowd and forcing the protesters to retreat from the bridge. A few minutes later, the protesters return, but the helicopters are now positioned ahead of them and are shooting directly at the protesters again to cut their advance. Even isolated protesters are targeted. The few cars going south of the town are also shot at. As you can see the first car manages to get away, but the one following is not that lucky. The French helicopters made about thirty passages. For the four hours that the attack lasted, we did not witness a single protester shoot back at the French helicopters. Silence returned at about 3:00 a.m.[19]

These civilians must have committed some horrific act of lèse-majesté to be the targets of such a fierce airstrike by the French army. There must be a justifiable reason for the French army to be so callous and turn their heavy guns on unarmed Ivorian civilians. What then was the crime of the protesters that brought on them such heavy firepower from the French military? It was mere inexperience, the naïveté of believing that a country occupied for the last 600 years by military force could be freed overnight with bare hands and symbolic actions. On November 6, 2004, Charles Blé Goudé, the leader of the Young Ivorian Patriots, called on his followers to gather for a big sit-in at the front of the 43rd Marine Infantry Battalion in Port-Bouët, south of Abidjan, to protest the French army's abuses in their country, a symbolic gesture to signify to the French authorities in Paris the evident veracity that "Côte d'Ivoire was not a department of France and Abidjan not a district of Paris." For the young Ivorians born after the country's "independence," and who had never known the era of colonization, France's cavalier outlook on their country was inconceivable. In Côte d'Ivoire, as in most French-speaking Africa, the Hexagon had been acting as if it were in conquered territory. If for most of the older generation educated in the colonial system and fed with the belief that they were inferior to the French and, consequently, that France's arrogant attitude in its former colonies was to be expected, for the major part of the younger generation France's inconsiderate posture in Côte d'Ivoire was intolerable and needed to be answered with an appropriate rejoinder.

On November 4, 2004, after several failed efforts at arriving at a peace agreement with the rebel forces that had occupied the northern part of his country and pressed by his military and the population, President Gbagbo decided to reunify the nation by attacking the rebels' position in Bouaké, north of Côte d'Ivoire. During Gbagbo's Operation Dignité, a bomb allegedly fell on a French camp in Bouaké and killed nine French soldiers and two American civilians. In retaliation, before any investigation could situate the responsibilities, French president Jacques Chirac ordered the destruction by the French Army of the entire Ivorian air force. The indignation within the Ivorian population was immediate. On November 6, on national television, Blé Goudé sounded the rallying cry: "If you are eating now, stop. If you are sleeping now, wake up. All at the airport to free our country." Then Goudé, who had been accused of anti–French sentiment in the past, added this note of caution: "I am not asking you to go and attack the French who are at home now and have nothing to do with the situation that we are living."

Immediately in the hours that followed Goudé s appeal hundreds of thousands of bare-handed protesters started converging on Port-Bouët from the various suburbs of Abidjan. Those coming from the suburbs north of Abidjan had to cross the two bridges (Houphouët and de Gaulle). Helicopters of the French army were waiting for them there, with live ammunition. As bare-handed as the marchers were, for Paris they constituted a tremendous threat to France's position in Africa, as the French Ambassador on post at the time, Gildas LeLidec, would explain years later. The actions of the young patriots could have sounded the beginning of the rolling back of Françafrique. Goudé and his followers needed to be stopped. If General Poncet had not shelled the bridges, LeLidec insisted, "France would have been vanquished." The 43rd BIMA would have been over-taken by one million protesters, and it would have been the end of France's pres-ence in Côte d'Ivoire. "It would have been Dien Bien Phu all over again in 2004, in Côte d'Ivoire." On November 6, 2004, France was in the mind-set of not repeating its 1954 Indochina humiliation. Le Lidec's candor indicates one thing: The whole of France's operation in Côte d'Ivoire, indeed, the whole of France's operation in Africa, is constantly visited by the specters of past failures, is haunted by the necessity to recover and ascertain an exceptionalism that was lost during the decolonizing wars and perhaps even long before that. Like an addict incapable of kicking the habit that destroys him, France is hooked on the unhealthy rela-tionship it has built with Africa and hesitates to check itself into rehabilitation, "hesitate[s] to expurgate her bad habits of the past" and terminate Françafrique.

Indeed, of all the former empire building nations, France is certainly the nation that is the most disinclined to completely loosen its grip on the countries that were once part of its colonial empire; and of all the former colonies of France, Côte d'Ivoire is the nation in which France is the most disinclined to see its polit-ical and economic influence completely effaced. On that night of November 6, 2004, France had been more scared than at any other time in Africa. It is not difficult to imagine the end of the occupation, for the longer the imperialist coun-try stays the more the nationalists' hatred builds up. History has furnished us plenty of examples. The longer the occupation lasts the more the nationalists' hatred against the occupier builds up, little by little, until the day it cannot be contained anymore and boils over.

So one morning the West wakes up shaken and in total disbelief. It is under attack. In the middle of the night, while it was deep in its sweet dreams of the imbecile Master, sated and satisfied with the loot of the country it had taken over, the nationalists have decided to bring the violence it has taught them to its own doorstep, as true a circumstance as that chickens will come home to roost. The nationalists have attacked the West's positions. Though the nationalists did not have access to the same killing tools the West has, nonetheless, the magnitude of their savagery is incomprehensible to the West. And yet, things would have been quite different had the West understood the nationalists' simple message to do unto others what the West would like done unto itself. Dignity, reciprocity, equal rights—in other words, the right to self-determination. Here is what the nationalists wanted immediately, as true as their demands "reflect the imperative ... to be collectively recognized as entitled to being treated and viewed as equal, even if this equality is still only legal," leaving the economic and social demands to be won in the long term.[20] Instead of that, the West had for them the most despicable words: "niggers," "savages" and "primitives." Instead of treating the nationalists as equals, the West came firing machine guns and hurling grenades, resolute to delay indefinitely the freedom of the nationalists in the name of higher values, in the name of Judeo-Christian values, as it is too often that the West's pomposity and its claim of a cleaner conscience and a higher moral imperative is linked to a supposed higher faith: Judeo-Christian faith.

It is not a truism to affirm that an oppressed people shall fight for its freedom. Today, the countries under bondage at the time of Emperor Selassie's history-making speech at the United Nations have reached self-determination. Their freedom did not come from a stroke of "good will" on the part of the oppressor. Their respective paths to sovereignty were littered with humiliation, tears, and deaths. Today, as sovereign African countries, Angola and South Africa are able to give the West a taste of its own medicine. They are in a better position to apply to the West the same rules that the West has for so long reserved for Africans. Their respective experiences suggest that for the oppressed peoples to be free of Western occupation there shall be war, a war of liberation in which nations will have to take sides and ready themselves to put the lives of their citizens at stake to, on the one side, conserve their privileges as illegal occupiers of a country not theirs thousands of miles from their own coasts or, on the other side, regain their independences. This is a war in which there will be no mercy. It is one where the imperialist powers will have to line up on one side with all those countries and individual entities that choose to fight for them, and where the nationalists will also have to line up on another side with all the nations and individual entities that will elect to support their fight for freedom. In this war, as was the case in Algeria, there shall be no mercy. All the means will be necessary for attaining independence, for ejecting the occupiers and their local informants. This war of freedom is forthcoming, and the rapists of African children, women, and elderly shall come to terms with the fact that, unless they are disposed to dump their nuclear arsenal on Africa and blow the entire world up, conventional weapons will become available to the nationalists, whose resolve for freedom will never be surpassed by the imperialists' resolve for stealing, for he who defends his home and his family from a burglar-rapist has willpower that nothing can extinguish. For Africa to be liberated from its 600-year bondage, civil negotiations in felted salons and conference rooms have proven their irrelevance. It is now a return to Fanon that ought to be operated. Fanon's prescribed violence becomes relevant. It is more than needed, for mentally, economically, socially and politically, the African—the French African precisely—is still a colonized subject:

> National liberation, national renaissance, the restoration of nationhood to the people, commonwealth ... is always a violent phenomenon.... If we wish to describe it precisely, we might find it in the well-known words: "The last shall be first and the first last." Decolonization is the putting into practice of this sentence.... The naked truth of decolonization evokes for us the searing bullets and bloodstained

knives which emanate from it. For if the last shall be first, this will only come to pass after a murderous and decisive struggle between the two protagonists.[21]

There shall be a violent war, a war of extreme violence against the imperialist occupiers, by African nationalists, for negotiations only will not persuade the robber-rapist to cough up such a juicy morsel as the land of the other. Angola's, South Africa's and Zimbabwe's struggles do give credence to Frantz Fanon's philosophy that freedom acquired at the cost of high sacrifice cannot easily be taken away.

Indeed, it is all clear now. For Africa to be economically and politically free, there must, and will, be an all-out war, a war that will truly merit the designation of "world war." "World War 1" and "World War 2" had nothing worldwide about them. They were worldwide only insofar as the populations of the Third World countries were coerced into joining in. These two wars were European wars caused by European greed and barbarism boiled up to their highest degree. But there will be this time a true world war, a war of total liberation of the African continent from its greedy parasites that will oppose on one side an alliance of the Western imperialist countries and those satellite states that share their ideology of corruption and exploitation, and on the other side the African countries with all their allies who are fed up with six hundred years of the West's economic and human genocide. That Africa must wage an all-out war to free itself from the Western bully is no longer the rhetoric of some deranged radicals. It is not the language held by some harebrained idealist communists or crazy terrorists. It is the talk of the day, openly held from the slums of African capitals to the conference rooms of Europe and America. That Africa must meet the violence of the imperialist West with equal violence is no longer a shameful proposition. Frantz Fanon is no longer on the periphery of African emancipatory discourse. He is now at the center of it. And it is the utter ruthlessness of the West that has placed Fanon at the center of Africa's contemporary emancipatory strategy.

Now, we shall notice that most of the African countries that are free today are other than Francophone countries. This is because in these countries, the people took ownership of their freedom very early. They fought the invaders with ferocity. In Francophone Africa, however, the people satisfied themselves with the "good will" of the oppressor. Fanon was right to despair of the Francophone. Is it too late, however, as Fanon lamented? Not so. Fifty years after the French black thought that all was lost with the fall of Lumumba, a wave of self-consciousness started in Côte d'Ivoire that is slowly but surely gaining momentum. The fight for freedom should be fought. It will be labeled with the most despicable epithets by the very imperialists who merit these epithets. But name-calling shall not deter the fight for freedom. The hypocritical Euro-American imperialists had called our freedom fighters names before crawling at their feet.

Indeed, until July 2008—that is, before President George Bush had signed a bill that "absolved" Nelson Mandela—the late South African activist, freedom fighter, and president was on the U.S. terrorism watch list, alongside Osama bin Laden. On December 11, 2013, six years after being removed from America's blacklist and fifteen years after being awarded the Nobel Peace Prize, Mandela was being mourned by more than seventy heads of state and millions of ordinary people the globe over as an international hero, an icon of moral rectitude, justice, and human decency. Only humans can command such dramatic ethical acrobatics without laughing at their own folly. As hypocritical as the world military powers' sudden promotion of Mandela from purgatory to heaven might seem, this Occidental duplicity is far from being a novel occurrence. Too many times freedom fighters from the colonized world were shunned and led to physical exhaustion by imperialist powers only to be mysteriously rediscovered as heroes on account of the persistence of their ideas in the collective memory of their respective peoples, though after much of the "deleterious" corporal impetus of their fights have been effectively arrested by the Occident. The history of humankind is littered with the remains of Third World "villains" suddenly anointed "heroes" by Western historians immediately after their deaths and long after the resources of their respective countries have been pumped into the economic reservoirs of the Occident.

The Occident is deceitful. Its absolute right, dictated by its conservation instinct, is that it should be deceitful, the conservation instinct of a squid that is condemned to inhabit parts of the sea where resources are few and far between and which is resolute to scheme and steal on territories as far as it can spread its tentacles. The squid calls this rapacious adventure "globalization."

In the name of globalization, the squid has edified political (UN) and financial institutions (the World Bank and the IMF) and trained a plethora of informants to better crack the shells of the Third World. It is the absolute right of the squid, on account of its own survival, that it be duplicitous. We cannot hold it against the squid. What is lamentable, however, is that so many Third World actors, and increasingly young actors, have chosen to accompany the Occident in its scheme of elimination of Third World conscientious leaders, pillaging of Third World resources, and pauperization of Third World populations.

There is a level of partiality so contemptible that it turns the brains of those who indulge in it and of those who rationalize it into putrefied muck. For some pundits of the First World—victims of this kind of cerebral decomposition—righteousness cannot exist anywhere else but in the First World, and whatever actions the First World carries out against the Third World are necessarily justified. How can decent minds excuse any of the intimidations, coercions, and cruelties of which the First World has so far been the exclusive perpetrator and for which the estimable appellation of "embargo" has been found? On January 30,

2014, one such unconditional apologist and evangelist of this First World malady called self-righteousness, upon finding out that a surgeon he was interviewing had braved the Atlanta snowstorm and walked eight miles in the cold to reach his home, asked brave Dr. Hrykiwin—whose credentials out of intellectual indolence the apologist had not even bothered to properly research—if the brain surgeon would be his doctor. It was highly fitting that courageous Dr. Hrykiwin rejoined with this question: "Do you need brain surgery?" Indeed, our pundit could well be in need of one, given the agitation with which he had hitherto proselytized for the unilateral talking points of his ideological masters and clamored for the assassination of foreign dignitaries who did not share his ideology. We shall do him the honor of talking about him here only insofar as he is the symptom of a press that has become the sound box of America's imperialist enterprise.

On February 25, 2015, on CNN's *AC 360*, the host of the show, Anderson Cooper, offered the world one of his pathetic "journalistic" performances. Receiving a Libyan dissident who proudly claimed to have been part of a foiled coup d'état against Gaddafi in the past, the CNN host could not have greeted a national hero with that much slobbering. With Cooper, we learned that military coups and not democratic denunciations or pursuit of institutional rules were the way to egalitarianism. And when we thought to have seen the last of Cooper's senselessness he suggested, unreservedly, that Colonel Gaddafi, a foreign head of state, be assassinated by one of his guards, just as was Kabila of Zaire. This was not Cooper's first feat. On February 2, 2011, as the world was poised to witness the destruction of one of the greatest civilizations on the face of the earth through that ephemeral thing called the "Arab Spring," "Cooper and Co." missed a formidable occasion to provide Americans with great insights from inside Egypt, preferring, instead, to cast a very superficial and stereotypical look on the ongoing developments in Egypt. Why was CNN in Egypt if not to rise above very common observation, if not to offer greater scrutiny below what is happening on the surface? Indeed, in his attempt at an exegesis on a gradually growing countermovement against the huge crowd of protesters who were chanting for the resignation of President Hosni Mubarak, Anderson Cooper snickered that the crowd of "two hundred people" was a "rent-a-crowd paid" a few pounds by Mubarak to cause disruption by offering bogus support to the Egyptian sovereign. For the CNN journalist, after decades of ruling Egypt Mubarak had no genuine supporters in the country and could merely gather 200 people in his support. Perhaps had our ideological evangelist decided to hand his microphones to a few activists from the so-called rent-a-crowd, as he did so easily to many protestors among the "honest crowd," he would not have waited four years to discover that the "Arab Spring" was just a figment of the Occident's imagination, a flame that died as quickly as it was started but the destructive consequences of which will linger for a very long time.

Conclusion

Wherever the Euro-American power has set its feet it has left behind desolation, hunger, widows, and orphans. From Asia to Africa, passing through the Americas and Oceania, history is replete with evidence of the Euro-American destructive proclivity actuated in the name of exceptionalism, that is, the belief that one is endowed with innate disposition to do good only and to save others from themselves. In reality, what the Euro-American power practices as exceptionalism is the ability to go to faraway countries, throw one's military weight around, wreak havoc, and steal the countries' resources. This is the opposite of philanthropy. This is called piracy of the worst kind. And for the last 600 years, the Euro-American power has not diverged from its buccaneering ways. The Euro-American practice of attacking and robbing other nations has simply been "coutured," dressed up, under the gambit of globalization. While the earlier trend, from the 1885 Berlin Conference to the end of the second European war, was to go into foreign countries as lone wolves and raid their resources, the new trend, since October 1945, is to obtain permission to raid through the United Nations, this corrupt institution that represents itself as the custodian of the world nations' welfare.

Since its creation, whenever the United Nations organization has acted in the role of international justice broker in a dispute involving the Euro-American power and Africa as major stakeholders, the United Nations has shown partiality in favor of the Euro-American power. Though the evidence is plethoric, we have chosen to discuss a few of the most blatant cases of the Euro-American power and the United Nations' collusion. In the Congo, the UN has facilitated the Euro-American elimination of Patrice Lumumba, the installation of puppet regimes, the West's mainmise on the country's huge geological and agricultural resources, and the consequent pauperization of the local masses for over fifty years. In Libya, through a flurry of resolutions sponsored primarily by France and the United States and voted on by the United Nations Security Council, the West has succeeded in pulling one of the most profitable heists ever, pocketing, just in the first 6 months of the war on Gaddafi, about $77 billion of Libyan public money and leaving the country in total wretchedness. A metaphor for the Euro-American importation of democracy into Libya is the thousands of Libyan widows and children fleeing the country in flimsy boats. If the West has made Libya better for the Libyan people than it used to be under Gaddafi, then the question might be this: "Why are Libyans risking their lives fleeing the West-created heaven?"

Likewise, in Côte d'Ivoire, the United Nations has not only allowed the West to directly go to war against an elected government, killing thousands of innocent civilians, but in a move hardly witnessed elsewhere, the United Nations has actively taken part in the combat operations, using UN helicopters (partially bought by the people of Côte d'Ivoire as UN stakeholders) to indiscriminately shell Abidjan, a city of more than 2 million people. The goal was to install a president who would be more protective of Euro-American business than the nationalist who, against evidence to the contrary, was perceived as being hostile to the West.

On May 9, 2015, an eight-year-old Ivorian boy was found curled up in a fetal position in a suitcase at a border-crossing post in Spain. His parents had tried to smuggle him into Spain from Morocco. On May 11, 2015, in Philadelphia, a man from Côte d'Ivoire was found dead in a ship carrying cocoa beans from Côte d'Ivoire. He was a stowaway. These two events are metaphorical of what Côte d'Ivoire has become following the Euro-American propounded objective of saving the Ivorians from themselves by bringing them democracy packaged in Dramane Ouattara. Today, Côte d'Ivoire has become a poverty-ridden country, where 70 percent of the population live on less than a dollar a day, and a killing zone where governmental death squads roam free.

The Euro-American flag-waving jingoism that sows violence and misery in the Third World has left it no real friends in the world, and the list of its foes is growing. There will come a day when the Euro-American power will be completely isolated. Already, signs of the Euro-American isolation are appearing on the horizon. The West's instruments of coercion, such as the World Bank, the International Monetary Fund, the United Nations, and the International Criminal Court, are being challenged and will indubitably collapse. As an alternative to the financial institutions that the Euro-American power has traditionally used to pressure Third World countries into accepting their unfair conditions, the BRICS states (Brazil, Russia, India, China, and South Africa) have created the multibillion-dollar capital New Development Bank (NDB) headquartered in Shanghai, China, which is rapidly growing in membership. The allure of the NDB is its real investment in equality, which gives each member state one vote and no veto power to anyone, which is not the case with the Bretton Woods institutions. Moreover, the Kenyan people snubbing President Obama and the International Criminal Court to elect Uhuru Kenyatta as their president along with his deputy William Ruto, instead of America's favorite, Raila Odinga, is indication that the Euro-American bullying methods will not always work and that Africans, increasingly losing faith in the West, will find substitutes to the West's abusive institutions. In fact, African nations have already agreed on creating an African Court to prosecute "war crimes," as the term has been abusively used by the ICC to prosecute African leaders who do not sign on to the Euro-American exploitative policies in Africa.

The world is fast changing, and Africa with it. Soon, no nation will have exclusive license to dictate its rules to others or conventional military superiority, unless those countries with nuclear bombs are willing to annihilate the globe and themselves with it. Consequently, instead of thinking of the world as a movie that they can pause whenever it pleases them and press "play" whenever they want—to use this metaphor by Bahskar Chakravorti—Europe and the United States ought to catch up and write a new covenant with Africa, the custodian of the world's largest resources,[1] a contract based on mutual respect. Unless they want to be left behind, unless they want to become totally irrelevant to Africa and Africans, the United States and the European Union should put an end to their tradition of hubris and jingoism, nicknamed exceptionalism.

Chapter Notes

Chapter 1

1. Raphaël Granvaud, "De l'armée coloniale à l'armée néocoloniale (1830–1909)" (Paris), *Collections Dossiers Noirs* 23 (2009), 24.

2. Betsey Piettey, "Wachovia Admits Slave Trade Profits," http://www.workers.org/2005/us/wachovia-0616/ (accessed 1-11-2015).

3. For genocides of Indians in the Americas, see, among others, Bartolomé de Las Casas, *Brevisima Relacion de la Destruccion de las Indias* (London: Printed by J.C. for Nath. Brook, at the Angel in Cornhill, 1656).

4. See, for instance, Edward Paice, *Tip and Run: The Untold Tragedy of the Great War in Africa* (London: Weidenfeld & Nicolson, 2007) or Adam Hochschild, *King Leopold's Ghost: A Story of Greed, Terror, and Heroism in Colonial Africa* (Boston: Houghton Mifflin, 1998).

5. Though many have understood de Tocqueville as praising American exceptionalism, only the contrary is true. As T. David Gordon so perceptively noted, what Tocqueville was actually doing in his often-praised book was disparaging Americans as a plebeian people endowed with no inclination for the pursuit of intellectual matters such as art, literature, and science—an utterly unexceptional people.

6. See William Pfaff, "Every President Needs a War of His Own," http://www.williampfaff.com/modules/news/print.php?storyid=431&PHPSESSID=4bce6c3dd0877862ce81c30ae19f90a8 (accessed 1-2-2015).

7. See Steve Chapman, "Every President Is a War President," http://articles.chicagotribune.com/2012-05-06/news/ct-oped-0506-chapman-20120506_1_anti-war-candidate-air-war-barack-obama (1-2-2015).

8. According to the institute, "Nobel Peace Prize for 2009 is to be awarded to President Barack Obama for his extraordinary efforts to strengthen international diplomacy and cooper-

ation between peoples. The Committee has attached special importance to Obama's vision of and work for a world without nuclear weapons," http://www.nobelprize.org/nobel_prizes/peace/laureates/2009/press.html (accessed 1-28-2015).

9. Transcript: Obama's Speech Against the Iraq War," http://www.npr.org/templates/story/story.php?storyId=99591469 (accessed 1-30-2014).

10. George W. Bush, "Prepared Text of Bush's Knesset Speech," http://www.wsj.com/articles/SB121083798995894943 (accessed 12-30-2014).

11. *Washington Times*, "McCain Decries 'Obama's Socialism,'" http://www.washingtontimes.com/news/2008/oct/19/mccain-decries-obamas-socialism/#ixzz3MO7dPmNL (accessed 12-20-2014).

12. Paul Roderick Gregory, "Is President Obama Truly a Socialist?," http://www.forbes.com/sites/paulroderickgregory/2012/01/22/is-president-obama-truly-a-socialist/ (accessed 12-19-2014).

13. Merrill Matthews, "Comparing Obama's Policies with French Socialist Hollande," http://www.forbes.com/sites/merrillmatthews/2012/05/10/comparing-obamas-policies-with-french-socialist-hollande-2/ (accessed 12-19-2014).

14. Josh Feldman, "Bill O'Reilly: 'Socialist-Communist Vision' Fueling Liberal Fight for Obamacare," http://www.mediaite.com/tv/bill-oreilly-socialist-communist-vision-fueling-liberal-fight-for-obamacare/ (accessed 12-19-2014).

15. The White House, Office of the Press Secretary, "News Conference by President Obama," http://www.whitehouse.gov/the-press-office/news-conference-president-obama-4042009 (accessed 1-2-2015).

16. Sarah Palin, *America by Heart: Reflections on Family, Faith, and Flag* (New York: HarperCollins, 2010), 69.

17. Rush Limbaugh, "President Obama's Cairo

Speech: Outrageous, Absurd, Embarrassing," http://www.rushlimbaugh.com/daily/2009/06/04/president_obama_s_cairo_speech_outrageous_absurd_embarrassing (12-17-2014).

18. C-SPAN, "Wisconsin Faith and Freedom Coalition," http://www.c-span.org/video/?305242-1/wisconsin-faith-freedom-coalition (accessed 12-21-2014).

19. Wall Street Journal, "Text of Mitt Romney's Speech on Foreign Policy at The Citadel," http://blogs.wsj.com/washwire/2011/10/07/text-of-mitt-romneys-speech-on-foreign-policy-at-the-citadel/ (accessed 12-21-2014).

20. Mallie Jane Kim, "Osama bin Laden Is Dead—Does Obama or Bush Deserve Credit?," http://www.usnews.com/opinion/articles/2011/05/05/osama-bin-laden-is-dead-does-obama-or-bush-deserve-the-credit (accessed 1-2-2015).

21. Bridget Kendall, "UN's Del Ponte Says Evidence Syria Rebels 'Used Sarin,'" http://www.bbc.com/news/world-middle-east-22424188 (accessed 1-3-2015).

22. New York Times, "A Plea for Caution from Russia: What Putin Has to Say to America About Syria," http://www.nytimes.com/2013/09/12/opinion/putin-plea-for-caution-from-russia-on-syria.html?pagewanted=all&_r=0 (accessed 1-2-15).

23. Matthew Rothschild, "Obama Bows to American Exceptionalism at West Point," http://www.progressive.org/news/2014/05/187714/obama-bows-american-exceptionalism-west-point (accessed 12-21-2014).

24. New York Times editorialist William Safire wrote, "Jacques Chirac's scheme to win French companies fat contracts in reconstructing Iraq has run into realpolitik: anti–U.S. actions have consequences," in "Chirac's Latest Ploy." http://www.nytimes.com/2003/04/24/opinion/chirac-s-latest-ploy.html (accessed 1-28-2015).

25. Alex Lefebvre, "French concessions on Iraq Met by U.S. threats," http://www.wsws.org/en/articles/2003/05/fran-m01.html (accessed 1-28-2015).

26. Nile Gardiner, "Nicolas Sarkozy Mocks Barack Obama as 'Not a Leader but a Follower'; He's Spot On," http://blogs.telegraph.co.uk/news/nilegardiner/100234571/nicolas-sarkozy-mocks-barack-obama-as-not-a-leader-but-a-follower-hes-spot-on/ (accessed 12-31-2014).

27. Hillary Clinton, interview with Jeffrey Goldberg, Atlantic, http://www.theatlantic.com/international/archive/2014/08/hillary-clinton-failure-to-help-syrian-rebels-led-to-the-rise-of-isis/375832/?single_page=true (accessed 12-20-2014).

28. Stuart Jeffries, "Does Nicolas Sarkozy have short-man syndrome?," http://www.theguardian.com/lifeandstyle/2009/sep/09/mens-fashion-nicolas-sarkozy (accessed 3-30-2015).

29. Quoted in Gardner, "Nicolas Sarkozy mocks Barack Obama," http://blogs.telegraph.co.uk/news/nilegardiner/100234571/nicolas-sarkozy-mocks-barack-obama-as-not-a-leader-but-a-follower-hes-spot-on/ (accessed 12-31-2014).

30. Jules Ferry, "Les fondements de la politique coloniale," discours prononcé à la Chambre des députés: le 28 juillet 1885.

Chapter 2

1. Leon Bocquet and Ernst Hosten, Un fragment de l'épopée sénégalaise, quoted in Bakari Kamian, Des Tranchées de Verdun à l'Eglise Saint-Bernard-80.000 combattants maliens au secours de la France (1914–18 et 1935–45) (Paris: Editions Karthala, 2001), 57.

2. Ibid.

3. Quoted in Christian Koller, "Representing Otherness: African, Indian and European Soldiers' Letters and Memoirs," in Race, Empire and First World War Writing, ed. Santanu Das, 127–142 (Cambridge: Cambridge University Press, 2011), 129.

4. Ibid., 130.

5. Ibid., 132.

6. Raphaël Granvaud, "De l'armée coloniale à l'armée néocoloniale (1830–1909)," (Paris: Collections Dossiers Noirs, No 23, 2009), 8.

7. Joe Harris Lunn, "Kande Kamara Speaks: An Oral History of the West African Experience in France, 1914–18," in Africa and the First World War, ed. Melvin E. Page (New York: St. Martin's, 1987), 36.

8. Quoted in Lunn, 38.

9. Richard S. Fogarty, Race and War in France: Colonial Subjects in the French Army, 1914–1918 (Baltimore: Johns Hopkins University Press, 2008), 174–81.

10. Marc Michel, "Les troupes noires—la grande guerre et l'Afrique noire française après 1918," http://www.troupesdemarine.org/traditions/histoire/fiches/pg000028.htm (accessed 1-9-2015).

11. Ibid.

12. Christian Koller, "The recruitment of colonial troops in Africa and Asia and their deployment in Europe during the First World War," University of Zurich Open Repository and Archive, 2008.

13. Christian Koller, "Representing Otherness: African, Indian and European Soldiers' Let-

ters and Memoirs," in *Race, Empire and First World War Writing*, ed. Santanu Das, 127–142 (Cambridge: Cambridge University Press, 2011), 132.

14. For a full account of the invention and exploitation of blacks' images in the interwar period, see Dana S. Hale's resourceful *Races on Display: French Representations of Colonial peoples, 1886–1940* (Bloomington: Indiana University Press, 2008).

15. For further detailed statistics, see Albert Sarraut, *La Mise en valeur des colonies françaises* (Paris: Payot, 1923).

16. Ibid., 51.

17. Ibid.

18. Ibid., 58.

19. Ibid., 63.

20. Fabrice Grenard, "Manifestations de travailleurs à Paris pour protester contre la montée du chômage en 1933," http://fresques.ina.fr/jalons/fiche-media/InaEdu02019/manifestations-de-travailleurs-a-paris-pour-protester-contre-la-montee-du-chomage-en-1933.html (accessed 1-15-2015).

21. Corinne Dalle and Jean-Michel Viallet, "L'Exposition coloniale internationle de 1931," Archives départementales du Puy-de-Dôme, http://www.archivesdepartementales.puydedome.fr/n/l-exposition-coloniale-internationale-de-1931/n:30 (accessed 1-7-2015).

22. Marc Michel, *op. cit.*

23. Sarraut, 59–60.

24. Ibid., 73.

25. Richard S. Fogarty, *Race and War in France: Colonial Subjects in the French Army, 1914–1918* (Baltimore: Johns Hopkins University Press, 2008), 56.

26. Dana S. Hale, *Races on Display: French Representations of Colonial Peoples, 1886–1940* (Bloomington: Indiana University Press, 2008), 94.

27. Christian Koller, "Representing Otherness," 128.

28. Lunn, 29.

29. Bakari Diallo, *Force-bonté* (Paris: Rieder, 1926), 123.

30. Marc Michel, *op. cit.*

31. Fogarty, *Race and War in France*, 231.

32. See Martin Evans, *Algeria: France's Undeclared War* (New York: Oxford University Press, 2012), 49.

33. Granvaud, 7.

34. Marc Michel, *op. cit.*

35. Hale, 178.

36. Darién J. Davis and Judith Michelle Williams, "Pan-Africanism, Negritude, and the Currency of Blackness: Cuba, the Francophone Caribbean, and Brazil in Comparative Perspec-

tive, 1930–1950s," in *Beyond Slavery: The Multilayered Legacy of Africans in Latin America and the Caribbean*, ed. Darién J. Davis, (Rowman & Littlefield, 2007), 151.

37. Raphael Granvaud, "De l'armée coloniale à l'armée néocoloniale (1830–1990)," (Paris) *Collections Dossiers Noirs*, no. 23, 2009), 22.

38. Ibid.

39. Walter Hines Page and Arthur Page, "The Life and Letters of Walter H. Page," in *The World's Works*, vol. 43 (New York: Doubleday, Page, 1922), 156.

40. Dossiers Thématiques, "Appel du 18 juin 1940 du général de Gaulle : texte et circonstances," http://www.charles-de-gaulle.org/pages/l-homme/dossiers-thematiques/1940–1944-la-seconde-guerre-mondiale/l-appel-du-18-juin/documents/l-appel-du-22-juin-1940.php (accessed 1-11-2015).

41. For detailed statistics, see David Killingray, *Fighting for Britain: African Soldiers in the Second World War* (Woodbridge: James Currey, 2010).

42. Thierry Amougou, "Deuxième guerre mondiale: du rôle oublié de l'Afrique dans le débarquement," http://www.dakaractu.com/Deuxieme-Guerre-mondiale-du-role-oublie-de-l-Afrique-dans-le-debarquement_a68077.html (accessed 1-16-2015).

43. Dossiers Thématiques, "Les troubles de Madagascar et leurs répercussions sur la politique intérieure française—A Dakar, M. Vincent Auriol exalte l'union des populations métropolitaines et africaine," *Nouvelliste Valaisan*, no. 93 (April 22, 1947), 2.

44. "The Battle of Berlin, 1945," Eye Witness to History, http://www.eyewitnesstohistory.com/berlin.htm (accessed 1-12-2015).

45. Drew Middleton, "U.S. and Red Armies Join, Split Germany," *New York Times*, April 28, 1945.

46. Albert Axell, interview with Olga Dimitrieva, http://www.telegraph.co.uk/sponsored/rbth/6281732/Russia-Now-Remembering-Russias-sacrifice-in-World-War-Two.html (accessed 1-12-2015).

47. Peter Sheremushkin, "Remember the Russian People's Role in World War II, Defeating Nazi Germany," http://www.telegraph.co.uk/sponsored/rbth/opinion/7737591/russian-role-defeating-nazi-germany.html (accessed 1-12-2015).

48. Ibid.

49. Ali A. Mazrui, "Africa and the Legacy of the Second World War: Political, Economic and Cultural Aspects," 13–26, in *Africa and the Second World War: Report and Papers of the Symposium*

Organized by UNESCO at Benghazi, Libya, Arab Jamahiriya, from 10–13 November 1980; The General History of Africa; Studies and Documents 10 (Paris: United Nations, 1985), 14.

50. Ibid., 15.

51. François Maspéro, "Préface," in Yves Benot, *la IVe République et la mise au pas des colonies françaises* (Paris: Découverte, 2001), III.

Chapter 3

1. See Martin Evans' *Algeria: France's Undeclared War* (New York: Oxford University Press, 2012).

2. Ibid., 19.

3. Ibid., 11.

4. Youssef Girard, "Le passé génocidaire de la France en Algérie," http://www.ism-france.org/analyses/Le-passe-genocidaire-de-la-France-en-Algerie-article-16433 (accessed 1-17-2015).

5. Evans, 14–17.

6. Alistair Horne, *A Savage War of Peace: Algeria, 1954–1962*, (New York: Viking, 1978), 37.

7. Ibid., 16–17.

8. Quoted in Girard.

9. Ibid.

10. Evans, 83.

11. For more detailed information on Messali Hadj as a political figure, see Evans, 57.

12. Horne, 38.

13. Ibid.

14. For more on Ben Badis and the Association of Algerian Ulema, see Evans, 52.

15. Quoted in Horne, 37.

16. Ibid., 36.

17. Ibid., 37.

18. Ibid., 40.

19. Yves Benot, *Massacres coloniaux, 1944–1950: la IVe République et la mise au pas des colonies françaises* (Paris: La Découverte, 2001), 10–11.

20. Evans, 88–89.

21. Rebellyon.info, "8 mai 1945: massacre de Sétif!" http://rebellyon.info/8-Mai-1945-Massacre-de-Sétif.html (accessed 1-16-2015).

22. Evans, 87.

23. Bernard Droz, "1er novembre 1954 : la Toussaint rouge," http://www.histoire.presse.fr/collections/l-espagne/1er-novembre-1954-la-toussaint-rouge-07-04-2002-9978 (accessed 1-19-2015).

24. Evans, 91.

25. Benjamin Stora, *Algeria, 1830–2000*, trans. Jane Marie Todd (Ithaca: Cornell University Press, 2001), 19.

26. "Alger, Algérie: documents algériens: Série économique agriculture: Place et rôle du paysanat dans l'économie algérienne," http://alger-roi.fr/Alger/documents_algeriens/economique/pages/61_paysanat.htm, no 61, May 20, 1949, (accessed 1-19-2015).

27. Most of these statistics are drawn from Roger Lequy's excellent thesis, "L'Agriculture algérienne de 1954 à 1962," http://www.persee.fr/web/revues/home/prescript/article/remmm_0035-1474_1970_num_8_1_1081 (accessed 1-19-2015).

28. Ibid., 58.

29. "Alger, Algérie: documents algériens: Série économique agriculture: Place et rôle du paysanat dans l'économie algérienne," http://alger-roi.fr/Alger/documents_algeriens/economique/pages/61_paysanat.htm, no 61, May 20, 1949, (accessed 1-19-2015).

30. Evans, 24.

31. Ibid.

32. Benot, 47.

33. Frantz Fanon, *The Wretched of the Earth*, preface by Jean-Paul Sartre (New York: Grove Press, 1963), 39.

34. Ibid.

35. Algeria Watch, "Proclamation du F.L.N. Appel de l'A.L.N 1er novembre 1954," http://www.algeria-watch.org/farticle/1954–62/proclamation1nov.htm (accessed 2-4-2015).

36. Quoted in Horne, 97.

37. Ibid., 98.

38. Ibid.

39. Evans, 127.

40. Lequy, 58.

41. Ibid., 60.

42. Ibid., 61.

43. Granvaud, 27.

44. Raphaëlle Branche, "Torture and Other Violations of the Law by the French Army During the Algerian War," in *Genocide, War Crimes and the West: History and Complicity*, ed. Adam Jones, trans. Jo Jones, 135–45 (London: Zed Book, 2004), 135.

45. Ibid., 139.

46. Ibid., 141.

47. Nadia Agsous, "Indépendance: nous femmes d'Algérie," http://www.huffingtonpost.fr/nadia-agsous/independance-algerie-role-des-femmes-_b_2358381.html (accessed 1-20-2015).

48. Branche, 143.

49. Granvaud, 10.

50. Stora, 50.

51. Ibid.

52. Daniel Yergin, *The Prize: The Epic Quest for Oil, Money and Power* (New York: Free Press, 2008), 508.

Chapter 4

1. Quoted in François-Xavier Verschave, *Complicité de génocide?: La politique de la France au Rwanda* (Paris: Éditions la Découverte, 1994), 37.

2. See K. Martial Frindéthié, *Francophone African Cinema: History, Culture, Politics and Theory* (Jefferson, NC: McFarland, 2009).

3. Fausto Biloslavo, "Un secret de Sarkozy bien gardé: l'exécution de Kadhafi," http://www.agoravox.fr/actualites/politique/article/un-secret-de-sarkozy-bien-garde-l-154064 (accessed 5-10-2015).

4. McCain has called Obama "the most naïve president in history," http://politicalticker.blogs.cnn.com/2014/02/21/mccain-calls-obama-most-naive-president-in-history/comment-page-1/ (accessed 1-27-2015). As for Mathew Rothschild, Obama's war in Libya is "unconstitutional, naïve, hypocritical," http://www.progressive.org/news/2011/03/158978/obama%E2%80%99s-libya-war-unconstitutional-na%C3%AFve-hypocritical (accessed 1-27-2015).

5. "Obama and Sarkozy Killed Gaddafi to Silence Him: Le Canard Enchaîné," http://www.lbcgroup.tv/news/8432/obama-and-sarkozy-killed-gaddafi-to-silence-him-le (accessed 12-29-2014).

6. Peter Allen, "Gaddafi Was Killed by French Secret Serviceman on Orders of Nicolas Sarkozy, Sources Claim," http://www.dailymail.co.uk/news/article-2210759/Gaddafi-killed-French-secret-serviceman-orders-Nicolas-Sarkozy-sources-claim.html (accessed 12-29-2014).

7. Lise Labott, "U.S. to Restore Relations with Libya," http://www.cnn.com/2006/U.S./05/15/libya/index.html?section=cnn_world (accessed 12-26-2014).

8. *BBC News*, "Blair hails new Libyan relations," http://news.bbc.co.uk/2/hi/uk_news/politics/3566545.stm (accessed 1-1-2015).

9. Richard Spencer, Heidi Blake, and Jon Swaine, "Tony Blair 'Visited Libya to Lobby for JP Morgan,'" http://www.telegraph.co.uk/news/politics/tony-blair/8772418/Tony-Blair-visited-Libya-to-lobby-for-JP-Morgan.html (accessed 1-1-2015).

10. In December 2014, Dassault Aviation entered negotiations with Indian authorities for a prospective sale of Rafale jets to be finalized in January 2015. On February 16, 2015, Egypt ordered 24 Rafale jets. On October 4, 2015, Indian Prime Minister Narandra Modi announced on a visit to France that his country would purchase 36 Rafales; and on April 30, 2015, Qatar ordered

24 Rafales. Finally, the war on Gaddafi has proven lucrative for Dassault. The Rafales tested well and were being sold outside of France.

11. On February 25, 2011, at a joint news conference with Turkish President Abdullah Gul in Ankara, Sarkozy demanded that Gaddafi step down. Two days later, Obama reportedly made an untelevised, lukewarm appeal for the resignation of Gaddafi. See Alex Spillius, "Libya: Barack Obama Calls on Col. Gaddafi to Step Down," http://www.telegraph.co.uk/news/worldnews/africaandindianocean/libya/8350246/Libya-Barack-Obama-calls-on-Col-Gaddafi-to-step-down.html (accessed 3-25-2015).

12. "Security Council Approves 'No-Fly Zone' Over Libya, Authorizing 'All Necessary Measures' to Protect Civilians, by Vote of 10 in Favour with 5 Abstentions," http://www.un.org/press/en/2011/sc10200.doc.htm (accessed 12-30-2014).

13. Saïf Al-Islam Gaddafi, Interview with AFP, http://fr.euronews.com/2013/03/01/xyz-affaire-gueant-sarkozy-kadhafi-les-accusations-de-saif-al-islam/ (accessed 12-15-2015).

14. Boris Thiolay, "Sarkozy et l'argent libyen: les pistes du soupçon," http://www.lexpress.fr/actualite/societe/justice/sarkozy-et-l-argent-libyen-les-pistes-du-soupcon_1543003.html (accessed 12-28-2014).

15. Is it not France that orchestrated the Rwandan genocide? Is it not France that orchestrated the Congolese and the Cameroonian massacres? Is it not the French army that shot 64 unarmed Ivorian youths in 2004?

16. Paul Vale, "Russia's Sergei Lavrov Says Obama's State of the Union Address Proves America Wants 'World Domination,'" http://www.huffingtonpost.co.uk/2015/01/21/russias-sergei-lavrov-says-obamas-state-of-the-union-address-proves-america-is-bent-on-world-domination_n_6515970.html (accessed 1-21-2015).

17. See Martial Frindéthié, *Globalization and the Seduction of Africa's Ruling Class: An Argument for a New Philosophy of Development* (Jefferson, NC: McFarland, 2010).

18. LEXPRESS.fr, "Kadhafi, 'roi des rois d'Afrique,'" http://www.lexpress.fr/actualite/monde/afrique/kadhafi-roi-des-rois-d-afrique_738116.html (accessed 12-31-2014).

19. Jean-Paul Pougala, "Les vraies raisons de la guerre en Libye," http://www.alterinfo.net/Les-vraies-raisons-de-la-guerre-en-Libye_a57616.html (accessed 4-14-2015).

20. John Watkins, "Libya's Thirst for 'Fossil Water,'" http://news.bbc.co.uk/2/hi/science/nature/4814988.stm (accessed 12-27-2014).

21. Ibid.

22. Celestin Bedzigui, "Hypocrisie: Kadhafi, 'la communauté économique et nous,'" http://guerre.libreinfo.org/manipulations/mensonges-de-guerre/99-guerre-libye/548-kadhafi-hypocrisie.html (accessed 12-26-2014).

23. James Petras and Robin E. Abaya, "The Euro-U.S. War on Libya: Official Lies and Misconceptions of Critics," http://www.globalre search.ca/the-euro-us-war-on-libya-official-lies-and-misconceptions-of-critics/24033 (accessed 12-26-2014).

24. Mathaba, "Libya's "Water Wars" and Gaddafi's Great Man-Made River Project," Center for Research on Globalization, http://www.globalresearch.ca/libyas-water-wars-and-gad dafis-great-man-made-river-project/5334868 (accessed 1-21-2015).

25. Damien McElroy, "Gaddafi's Death: Libya's New Rulers 'Stained' by Manner of His Death, Says Philip Hammond," http://www.telegraph.co.uk/news/worldnews/africaand indianocean/libya/8844744/Gaddafis-death-Libyas-new-rulers-stained-by-manner-of-his-death-says-Philip-Hammond.html (accessed 12-27-2014).

26. Vittorio de Filippis, "Pétrole: l'accord secret entre le CNT et la France," http://www.liberation.fr/monde/2011/09/01/petrole-l-accord-secret-entre-le-cnt-et-la-france_758320 (accessed 2-14-2015).

27. See Jean-Charles Tiémélé, "Libye: Kadhafi est mort, vive Total!," http://regardscroises.ivoire-blog.com/archive/2015/02/13/libye-kadhafi-est-mort-vive-total.html (accessed 2-14-2015).

28. Ibid.

29. See Pierre Laniray, François-Xavier Verschave: l'homme qui voulait soulever les montagnes (Paris: Éditions les Arènes, 2006), 119.

30. Judge Eva Joly details her investigation of Elf in her book Justice Under Siege: One Woman's Battle Against a European Oil Company, trans. Emma Kemp (London: Citizen Press, 2006).

31. Ibrahima Aidara, "Pourquoi Areva refuse-t-elle de payer un juste taux d'imposition au Niger?," http://www.nextafrique.com/finance/fiscalite-legacy/3124-pourquoi-areva-refuse-t-elle-de-payer-un-juste-taux-d-imposition-au-niger (accessed 2-15-2015).

32. Thomas Hofnung and Yann Philippin, "Affaire Uramin: Perquisition chez Anne Lauvergeon," http://www.liberation.fr/economie/2014/06/03/affaire-uramin-perquisition-chez-areva-et-lauvergeon_1032757 (accessed 24-4-2015).

33. See Aidara, op. cit.

34. Léopold Nséké, "Les Multinationales françaises en Afrique," http://www.afrique expansion.com/france-afrique-du-sud/12340-les-multinationales-francaises-en-afrique.html (accessed 2-14-2015).

35. See Gary K. Busch, "Consensual Rape in the Françafrique Currency Markets," http://www.academia.edu/5096732/Consensual_Rape_in_the_Francafrique_Currency_Markets (accessed 2-21-2015).

Chapter 5

1. J-S Lia, "Hommage à Bohoun-Bouabré: Le père du budget sécurisé a tiré sa révérence," http://news.abidjan.net/h/422495.html (accessed 2-17-2015).

2. Ibid.

3. Koureyssi Bâ, Interview with Abdou Salam Diop, in L'Harmattan, no. 854–9056 (January 2, 2005).

4. Ibid.

5. Ibid.

6. Michel Camdessus, quoted by Jean-Pierre Béjot, La Dépêche diplomatique, July 14, 2003.

7. Marcel Amondji, "Forfaiture et impunité L'affaire Ouattara (1990–1993) et la crise de l'houphouéto-foccartisme 3e partie," http://cerclevictorbiakaboda.blogspot.com/2012/07/laffaire-ouattara-1990-1993-et-la-crise.html (accessed 3-12-2015).

8. Ibid.

9. Ibid.

10. See Assié-Lumumba and Lumumba Kasongo.

11. Jeune Afrique, issue 1231 (August 8, 1984), 21.

12. Christophe Champlin, "Portrait d'Alassane Ouattara," http://www.rfi.fr/afrique/20101126-portrait-alassane-ouattara/ (accessed 2-2-2015).

13. "Ivory Coast: Election Critique, 10/17/'95," http://www.africa.upenn.edu/Urgent_Action/Apic_1017.html (accessed 2-24-2015).

14. Quoted in Amondji.

15. Philippe David, La Côte d'Ivoire (Paris: Editions Karthala, 2009), 51.

16. See Yacouba Konaté, "Le Destin d'Alassane Dramane Ouattara," in Côte d'Ivoire: l'année terrible, 1999–2000, ed. Marc le Pape and Claudine Vidal, 253–310 (Paris: Editions Karthala, 2002), 272.

17. Quoted in Epiphane Zoro-Bi, Juge, désarmer la violence en Côte d'Ivoire (Paris: Karthala, 2004), 54.

18. Judith Rueff, "Côte-d'Ivoire: mandat

d'arrêt contre Ouattara. L'opposant est inculpé de 'faux et usage de faux' concernant ses cartes d'identité," http://www.liberation.fr/monde/ 1999/12/09/cote-d-ivoire-mandat-d-arret-contre-ouattara-l-opposant-est-inculpe-de-faux-et-usage-de-faux-concern_291422 (accessed 2-26-2015).

19. Interview with RFI, http://discours.viepublique.fr/notices/003000264.html (accessed 2-26-2015).

20. Interview with Julia Ficatier, *La Croix*, January 10, 2000.

21. Quoted in Leslie Varenne, *Abobo la guerre* (Paris: Editions Mille et une nuits, 2012), chapter 4.

22. Claudine Vidal, "Du conflit politique aux menaces entre voisins," in *La Côte d'Ivoire-l'année terrible, 1999–2000*, ed. Marc Le Pape and Claudine Vidal, 215–52 (Paris: Editions Kathala, 2002), 222.

23. Djedjro Francisco Meledje, "The Making, Unmaking and Remaking of the Constitution of Côte d'Ivoire: An Example of Chronic Instability," in *Fostering Constitutionalism in Africa*, ed. Charles Fombad and Christina Murray (Pretoria University Press, 2010), 119.

24. Edwige Hardmong, "Côte d'Ivoire: Les auteurs du putsch de 1999 lavent Ouattara de toute responsabilité," http://www.jeuneafrique. com/Article/ARTJAWEB20110920101238/ (accessed 3-1-2015).

25. Most of this section is inspired by the works of Bertin Kadet, https://fr-fr.facebook. com/lamajoritepresidentielle/posts/ 295256017260060 (accessed 2-19-2015), and Robert Krassault, "Côte d'Ivoire: Le parcours d'un homme atypique: Laurent Gbagbo, le resistant," http://www.afrik53.com/Cote-d-Ivoire-Le-parcours-d-un-homme-atypique-Laurent-Gbagbo-le-resistant_a13700.html (accessed 2-19-2015).

26. Macaire Etty, "Faut-il regretter le parti unique?" http://le-filament.blogspot.com/2012/ 04/faut-il-regretter-le-parti-unique.html (accessed 3-5-2015).

27. Francis Akindès, "Des Origines des crises politiques récentes au sein de l'histoire en Côte d'Ivoire," in *La Métaphore du politique au Nord et au Sud,* ed. Karthala (Paris: Karthala, 2004), 139.

28. Edward P. Lipton, *Religious Freedom in Africa* (Hauppauge: Nova Science, 2002), 44.

29. For more development of the concept of Ivoirité, see Frindéthié, *Francophone African Cinema* (McFarland, 2009).

30. See "Ivoiriens et leur Ivoirité," *Fraternité Matin*, February 23, 1998.

31. See Chrysantus Ayangafac, "The Politics of Post-Conflict Elections in Côte d'Ivoire," in *From Civil Strife to Peace Building: Examining Private Sector Involvement in West Africa Reconstruction,* ed. Hany Besada, 33–52 (Wilfrid Laurier University Press, 2009).

32. See Akindès, 141.

33. "Ouverture du procès de l'ex-chef de la junte militaire, voici ceux qui avaient intérêt à tuer Robert Guéi," http://www.lecridabidjan. net/voici_ceux_qui_avaient_interet_a_tuer_ robert_guei.html (accessed 3-16-2015).

34. Mamadou Koulibaly, *La guerre de la France contre la Côte d'Ivoire* (Abidjan: La Refondation, 2003).

35. Interview with Elio Comarin, "Côte d'Ivoire: Gbagbo dénonce la 'complicité' du Burkina," http://www1.rfi.fr/actufr/articles/ 034/article_17719.asp (accessed 3-17-2016).

36. Pierre Sané, "Côte d'Ivoire: The Logic of the Absurd," http://www.pambazuka.net/ en/category/features/71588 (accessed 3-18-2015).

37. As recounted by Manwane Ben Yahmed in "Accord de Linas-Marcoussis: la vraie histoire du 'oui' de Gbagbo à Chirac," http://www. jeuneafrique.com/Article/LIN02033lavra carihc0/ (accessed 3-21-2015).

38. Jean Du Bois De Gaudusson, "L'accord de Marcoussis, entre droit et politique," in *Afrique Contemporaine* 2, no. 206 (2003), 14.

39. Dakouri Gadou, "Conflit et mobilisations patriotiques en Côte d'Ivoire: les protagonistes entre imaginaire national et positionnement politico-économique," in *Côte d'Ivoire: La réinvention de soi dans la violence,* ed. Francis Augustin Akindès, 82–132 (Dakar: CODESRIA, 2011).

40. Ibid.

Chapter 6

1. Thabo Mbeki, "What the World Got Wrong in Côte d'Ivoire," http://www.foreign policy.com/articles/2011/04/29/what_the_ world_got_wrong_in_cote_d_ivoire?page=full (accessed 4-9-2015).

2. See "Mémo sur le déroulement du scrutin du 28 novembre 2010 dans les régions du nord de la Côte d'Ivoire (zone CNO)," http://regard-scroises.ivoire-blog.com/tag/fraudes+au+ second+tour+de+l'%C3%A9lection+ pr%C3%A9sidentielle (accessed 5-5-2015).

3. CEDEAO-ECOWAS Press Release, "ECOWAS Calls on All Stakeholders to Seek Consensual Solutions," http://news.ecowas.int/

presseshow.php?nb=186&lang=en&annee=2010 (accessed 5-5-2015).

4. Susan Rice on *Morning Joe*, March 9, 2012, http://atlanticsentinel.com/2012/03/rice-rules-out-syrian-intervention-then-doesnt/ (accessed 3-9-2015).

5. Interview with Tanguy Berthemet, "Laurent Gbagbo: 'Il y a un complot contre moi,'" http://www.lefigaro.fr/international/2010/12/26/01003-20101226ARTFIG00129-laurent-gbagbo-il-y-a-un-complot-contre-moi.php (accessed 3-9-2015).

6. "Paris Rejects Nationalisation of two French Banks by Gbagbo," http://www.panapress.com/Paris-rejects-nationalisation-of-two-French-banks-by-Gbagbo—12-759710-lang2-4-index.html (accessed 3-14-2015).

7. Unicef, "Fighting malaria is an investment in future!," http://www.unicef.org/cotedivoire/health_nutrition_2167.html (accessed 3-11-2015).

8. Patrick Slavin, "En Côte d'Ivoire, en pleine crise, une mise en garde contre une pénurie des médicaments de première nécessité," http://www.unicef.org/french/infobycountry/cotedivoire_57599.html (accessed 3-11-2015).

9. Médecins sans frontières, "La population ivoirienne prise dans l'étau du conflit," http://www.msf.fr/presse/communiques/population-ivoirienne-prise-etau-conflit (accessed 3-13-2015).

10. Daily Express Reporter, "Britain to send £3m aid to Libya," http://www.express.co.uk/news/uk/267823/Britain-to-send-3m-aid-to-Libya (accessed 3-13-2015).

11. European Commission Press Release, "The Commission establishes humanitarian presence in Tripoli and boosts funding for emergency operations in Libya's capital," http://europa.eu/rapid/press-release_IP-11-993_en.htm?locale=en (accessed 3-13-2015).

12. *Le Parisien*, "Côte d'Ivoire: l'UE ne reconnaît pas les ambassadeurs de Gbagbo," http://www.leparisien.fr/international/cote-d-ivoire-l-ue-ne-reconnait-pas-les-ambassadeurs-de-gbagbo-29-12-2010-1206364.php (accessed 3-15-2015).

13. Tanguy Berthemet, "Côte d'Ivoire: Ouattara appelle à la grève générale," http://www.lefigaro.fr/international/2010/12/27/01003-20101227ARTFIG00423-cote-d-ivoire-ouattara-appelle-a-la-greve-generale.php (accessed 4-6-2015).

14. UN Security Council Press Release, "Security Council Demands End to Violence in Cote d'Ivoire, Imposing Sanctions Against Former

President and Urging Him to 'Step Aside,' in Resolution 1975," http://www.un.org/press/en/2011/sc10215.doc.htm (accessed 3-15-2015).

15. Pascal Airault, "Côte d'Ivoire: secrets de guerre," http://www.jeuneafrique.com/Article/JA2672p040.xml0/ (accessed 4-5-2015).

16. Alain Bouikalo, "Amadou Soumahoro Planifie un Génocide," http://ivoire.telediaspora.net/fr/texte.asp?idinfo=69881 (accessed 3-10-2015).

17. Rapport, MIDH, FIDH, LIDHO, "Côte d'Ivoire: Choisir entre la justice et l'impunité: Les autorités ivoiriennes face à leurs engagements," December 11, 2014, 19.

18. Emphasis added.

19. S-2014-729, Security Council Report, "Letter dated 10 October 2014 from the Chair of the Security Council Committee established pursuant to resolution 1572 (2004) concerning Côte d'Ivoire addressed to the President of the Security Council," 19.

20. Human Rights Watch World Report 2014 on Côte d'Ivoire. http://www.hrw.org/world-report/2014/country-chapters/cote-d-ivoire?page=2 (accessed 3-13-2015).

21. Laurent Gbagbo, interview with Tanguy Berthemet, *op. cit.*

22. UN Daily Press Briefing, http://www.unmultimedia.org/tv/webcast/2011/01/daily-press-briefing-40.html (accessed 3-10-2015).

23. "Congressional Record 112th Congress (2011–2012)," http://thomas.loc.gov/cgi-bin/query/z?r112:S07AP1-0024: (accessed 3-9-2015).

24. Sarah Stockman and Milton Valencia, "U.S. officials thought a BU post might ease Gbagbo out," http://www.boston.com/news/education/higher/articles/2011/04/13/us_officials_thought_a_bu_post_might_ease_gbagbo_out/ (accessed 3-9-2015).

25. François Soudan, "Côte d'Ivoire: Simone Gbagbo, une femme puissante," http://www.jeuneafrique.com/Article/JA2708p024-032.xml1/ (accessed 3-7-2015).

26. Thomas Hofnung, "La Dame d'Ivoire," http://www.liberation.fr/portrait/2007/05/22/la-dame-d-ivoire_93719 (accessed 3-7-2015).

27. Ibid.

28. Boga Sivori, Transcripts of Simone Gbagbo's Trial, "Simone Gbagbo devant la cour d'assises: 'Ouattara n'a pas gagné les élections,'" http://www.notrevoie.com/develop.asp?id=61673 (accessed 3-6-2015).

29. Robert Krassault, "Côte d'Ivoire: Le parcours d'un homme atypique: Laurent Gbagbo, le résistant," http://www.afrik53.com/Cote-d-Ivoire-Le-parcours-d-un-homme-atypique-

Laurent-Gbagbo-le-resistant_a13700.html (accessed 2-18-2015).

30. "Procès Gbagbo devant la CPI: la défense se plaint de manquer de moyen," http://www.rfi.fr/afrique/20111215-proces-gbagbo-devant-cpi-defense-plaint-manquer-moyens/ (accessed 3-5-2015).

31. André Sylver Konan, "Côte d'Ivoire: Plus de 700 millions FCFA sur un compte de Laurent Gbagbo," http://www.jeuneafrique.com/Article/ARTJAWEB20120515135424/ (accessed 3-4-2015).

32. Nathalie Schuck and Frédéric Gerschel, *Ça reste entre nous, hein?: Deux ans de confidence de Nicolas Sarkozy* (Paris: Flammarion, 2014), 39.

33. Achille Mbembe and Célestin Monga, "Côte d'Ivoire: la démocratie au bazooka?" http://blogs.mediapart.fr/edition/les-invites-de-mediapart/article/260111/cote-divoire-la-democratie-au-bazooka (accessed 4-8-2015).

34. Ibid.

35. "Kidnappings in Nigeria: A Clueless Government," http://www.economist.com/news/middle-east-and-africa/21601839-incompetence-nigerias-president-and-government-hurting-countrys (accessed 3-24-2015).

36. Dan Merica, "Hilary Clinton Faults Nigerian Government's Handling of Search for Kidnapped Girls," http://politicalticker.blogs.cnn.com/2014/05/07/hillary-clinton-faults-nigerian-governments-handling-of-search-for-kidnapped-girls/ (accessed 3-24-2015).

37. Aliou Tall, "Abdoulaye Wade insulte tous les Africains en confortant les théories racistes sur le Nègre," http://congo-liberty.com/?p=11337 (accessed 3-24-2015).

38. Ferdinand de Jong and Vincent Foucher, "La tragédie du roi Abdoulaye?: Néomodernisme et Renaissance africaine dans le Sénégal contemporain," in *Conjecture* (Paris: Karthala, 2010).

39. http://nonalamonarchieausenegal.unblog.fr/bougeons-nous/democratie-ou-monarchie/ (accessed 3-25-2015).

40. Quoted in Marwane Ben Yahmed, "Jusqu'où Ira Macky Sall?" http://www.jeuneafrique.com/Article/LIN20018jusquedawmi0/?art_cle=LIN20018jusquedawmi0 (accessed 3-25-2015).

41. Francis Kpatindé, "BCEAO: Les Dessous d'un hold-up," http://www.jeuneafrique.com/Article/LIN23113bceaopudloh0/ (accessed 3-26-2015).

42. U.S. Department of State Daily Briefing, http://www.state.gov/r/pa/prs/dpb/2012/01/182675.htm#SENEGAL (accessed 3-22-2015).

Chapter 7

1. See Video at https://www.facebook.com/photo.php?v=128446120645986&set=vb.100004417961800&type=2&theater.

2. "Côte d'Ivoire: 'It Looks like Nothing Ever Happened Here': Still No Justice One Year After Nahibly Camp Attack," London: Amnesty International Publications, 2013, p. 5.

3. See "Remarks by National Security Advisor Susan E. Rice: 'Human Rights: Advancing American Interests and Values,'" http://www.whitehouse.gov/the-press-office/2013/12/04/remarks-national-security-advisor-susan-e-rice-human-rights-advancing-am (accessed 3-8-2015).

4. Colum Lynch, "Obama's new national security advisor has sharp elbows, a tart tongue, and a taste for the shadows," http://foreignpolicy.com/2013/07/01/susan-rice-finally-has-her-perfect-job-head-knocker-in-chief/ (accessed 3-8-2016).

5. Cyril Bensimon, "IB, une personnalité bien encombrante de la scène ivoirienne," http://www.rfi.fr/afrique/20110429-ib-une-personnalite-bien-encombrante-scene-ivoirienne/ (accessed 4-15-2016).

6. François Mattei, interview with Laurent Correau, http://www.rfi.fr/afrique/20140627-verite-justice-crise-cote-ivoire-livre-gbagbo-francois-mattei/ (accessed 2-16-2015).

7. Ferloo, "Guillaume Soro: 'Mon meilleur souvenir au Sénégal, c'est quand Me Wade m'a acheté ma première veste,'" http://www.seneweb.com/news/People/guillaum-soro-laquo-mon-meilleur-souveni_n_152511.html (accessed 4-15-2015).

8. Thomas Hofnung, "D'ex-chefs de guerre à l'école française," http://www.liberation.fr/monde/2012/05/29/d-ex-chefs-de-guerre-a-l-ecole-francaise_822255 (accessed 4-16-2015).

9. Philippe Duval, "Le Bombardement de Bouaké, dernier secret de la Françafrique," http://mondafrique.com/lire/international/2014/11/07/neuf-soldats-tues-a-bouake-une-bavure-francaise (accessed 4-18-2015).

10. Pascal Airault, "Côte d'Ivoire: mourir pour Bouaké," http://www.jeuneafrique.com/Article/JA2744p046.xml0/ (accessed 4-18-2015).

11. Philippe Duval, "Le Bombardement de Bouaké, dernier secret de la Françafrique," http://mondafrique.com/lire/international/2014/11/07/neuf-soldats-tues-a-bouake-une-bavure-francaise (4-18-2015).

12. Airault, *op. cit.*

13. Duval, *op. cit.*

14. Abel Florentin, "Côte d'Ivoire: Bombardement de Bouaké: les généraux français au rapport," http://www.jeuneafrique.com/Article/JA2755p042.xml2/ (accessed 4-19-2015).

15. Joseph Warungu, "Letter from Africa: Kenya Passes Electoral Test—but What Next?" http://www.bbc.com/news/world-africa-21745501 (accessed 4-10-2015).

16. Aimé Césaire, *Discourse on Colonialism,* trans. Joan Pinkham (New York: Monthly Review Press, 1972), 23, originally published as *Discours sur le colonialisme* by Editions Presence Africaine, 1955.

17. President Barack Obama, "Remarks by the President at National Prayer Breakfast," February 5, 2015, http://www.whitehouse.gov/the-press-office/2015/02/05/remarks-president-national-prayer-breakfast (accessed 2-6-2015).

18. "Krauthammer 'Stunned' By Obama's 'Banal & Offensive' Prayer Breakfast Remarks," http://insider.foxnews.com/2015/02/05/krauthammer-i-was-stunned-obamas-banal-offensive-prayer-breakfast-remarks (accessed 2-7-2015).

19. "Krauthammer on Obama Prayer Speech: 'Everything He Does Is to Minimize What's Happening, to Hold Us Back,'" http://www.realclearpolitics.com/video/2015/02/05/krauthammer_on_obama_prayer_speech_everything_he_does_is_to_minimize_whats_happening_to_hold_us_back.html (accessed 2-7-2015).

20. Lawrence O'Donnell, "Obama Went Back 800 Years for Comparison, Seems to Be Saying He Knows What Real Islam Is," http://www.realclearpolitics.com/video/2015/02/05/lawrence_odonnell_obama_went_back_800_years_ago_to_make_comparison_seems_to_be_saying_that_he_knows_what_real_islam_is.html (accessed 2-7-2015).

21. Mark Levin, Obama "A Nihilist, a Narcissist and an Extremist; Warns 'We Are Going To Get Hit Again,'" http://www.realclearpolitics.com/video/2015/02/05/mark_levin_obama_a_nihilist_a_narcissist_and_an_extremist_warns_we_are_going_to_get_hit_again.html (accessed 2-7-2015).

22. "Scarborough on Obama Prayer Speech: 'Where Did He Go to Church? Where Would He Get Such Ideas From?," http://www.realclearpolitics.com/video/2015/02/06/scarborough_on_obamas_prayer_speech_where_did_he_go_to_church_where_would_he_get_such_ideas_from.html (accessed 2-7-2015).

23. A.O. Scott, "A Sniper Does His Deeds, but the Battle Never Ends: 'American Sniper' Review, a Clint Eastwood Film with Bradley Cooper," http://www.nytimes.com/2014/12/25/movies/american-sniper-a-clint-eastwood-film-starring-bradley-cooper.html?_r=0 (accessed 2-8-2015).

24. Brooks Barnes, "'Sniper' Rules Weekend Box Office," http://www.nytimes.com/2015/01/19/movies/sniper-rules-weekend-box-office.html (accessed 2-8-2015).

25. Sarah Gray, "Noam Chomsky discusses terrifying 'American Sniper' mentality: Chomsky compares the mentality of Chris Kyle to America's drone operation," http://www.alternet.org/watch-chomsky-blasts-american-sniper-and-media-glorifies-it (accessed 2-8-2015).

26. "Harry Belafonte Disappointed with Obama," http://marquee.blogs.cnn.com/2011/07/30/harry-belafonte-disappointed-with-obama/ (accessed 2-9-2015).

27. Peroshni Govender, "Obama protesters rally near hospital treating Mandela," A http://www.reuters.com/article/2013/06/28/mandela-idUSL5N0F414P20130628 (accessed 2-9-2015).

28. "Transcript of Clinton's Confirmation Hearing," http://www.npr.org/templates/story/story.php?storyId=99290981 (accessed 4-13-2015).

29. Abdul Karim Bangura, ed., "The Crisis in Côte d'Ivoire," in *Assessing Barack Obama's Africa Policy: Suggestions for Him and African Leaders* (Lanham: University Press of America, 2015), 128.

30. Adekeye Adebajo, "Obama failing to live up to his pledges on Africa," http://www.bdlive.co.za/opinion/columnists/2015/02/23/obama-failing-to-live-up-to-his-pledges-on-africa (accessed 3-8-2015).

31. Takunda Maodza, "President Raps Obama's Naivety," http://www.herald.co.zw/president-raps-obamas-naivety/ (accessed 3-8-2015).

32. Richard Miniter, "6 Signs That the White House's Susan Rice Is Clueless About Africa," http://www.forbes.com/sites/richardminiter/2014/02/28/6-signs-that-the-white-houses-susan-rice-is-clueless-about-africa/ (accessed 3-8-2015).

33. Ibid.

34. Interview with Thomas Frank, Cornel West: "He posed as a progressive and turned out to be counterfeit: We ended up with a Wall Street presidency, a drone presidency," http://www.salon.com/2014/08/24/cornel_west_he_posed_as_a_progressive_and_turned_out_to_be_counterfeit_we_ended_up_with_a_wall_street_presidency_a_drone_presidency/ (accessed 2-9-2015).

Chapter 8

1. See "American voters take on the crisis in Syria," http://www.foxnews.com/transcript/2013/09/16/american-voters-take-crisis-syria/ (accessed 4-23-2015).

2. This is what the Germans allegedly responded when confronted with evidence of their massacres in Africa: "This is ancient history."

3. As notes David Fieldhouse, all happened as if "the ability to decide a country's destiny, its collective mind, had been cut out surgically and transplanted into another mind" in a Western country. See *The West and the Third World: Trade, Colonialism, Dependence and Development* (Malden: Blackwell, 1999), 72.

4. See George Martelli, *Leopold to Lumumba: A History of the Belgian Congo, 1877–1960* (London: Chapman and Hall, 1962), 109.

5. See E.D. Morel, *The Black Man's Burden: The White Man in Africa from the Fifteenth Century to World War I* (New York: Modern Reader, 1969), 116.

6. Martelli, 138.

7. Quoted in Martelli, 124.

8. Morel, 116.

9. Ibid.

10. See John Hope Franklin, *George Washington Williams: A Biography* (Chicago: University of Chicago Press, 1985), 243–44.

11. Quoted in Martelli, 167.

12. Roger Casement, "The Casement Report," House of Commons, Accounts and Papers, vol. 62, 1904, p. 23.

13. Ibid.

14. Ibid., 26.

15. Ibid.

16. Morel, 162.

17. Martelli, 168.

18. See George Watson Macalpine, *Report of the Commission of Enquiry into the Administration of the Congo Free State*, published for the Baptiste Missionary Society by Jaas. Clarke (Southampton Row: The Kingsgate Press), 20.

19. Ibid., 19.

20. Ibid., 22.

21. Martelli, 176–79.

22. Morel, 162.

23. See Georges Nzongola-Ntalaja, *The Congo from Leopold to Kabila: A People's History* (London: Zed Books, 2002), 24.

24. Martelli, 185.

25. Ibid., 186.

26. For an elaborate discussion of the Belgian commercial exploitation of the Congo, see Nzongola-Ntalaja, 27–33.

Chapter 9

1. Much of the information in this chapter has been developed at greater length in a previous study. See Martial Frindéthié, *Francophone African Cinema: History, Culture, Politics and Theory* (Jefferson, NC: McFarland, 2009), 171–223.

2. See George Martelli, *Leopold to Lumumba: A History of the Belgian Congo, 1877–1960* (London: Chapman and Hall, 1962), 226.

3. See Thomas Kanza, *Conflict in the Congo: The Rise and Fall of Lumumba* (London: Penguin, 1972), 73.

4. Ibid., 123.

5. See Frantz Fanon, *The Wretched of the Earth* (New York: Grove Press, 1963), 43.

6. See Georges Nzongola-Ntalaja, *The Congo from Leopold to Kabila: A People's History* (London: Zed, 2002), 88.

7. Ibid., 285.

8. Ibid.

9. Martelli, 224.

10. Kanza 119.

11. Adamoekula, "L'histoire est têtue, c'est mon oncle Ambroise Boimbo qui a arraché l'épée du roi Baudouin 'reportage à Monkoto,'" http://emiradamo.com/2014/10/04/video-exclu-lhistoire-est-tetuecest-mon-oncle-ambroise-boimbo-qui-a-arrache-lepee-du-roi-baudouin-reportage-a-monkoto-3/ (accessed 5-7-2015).

12. Kanza, 119.

13. Ibid., 181.

14. Ibid., 201.

15. Ibid., 244.

16. Ludo de Witte, *The Assassination of Lumumba*, trans. Ann Wright and Renée Fenby (London: Verso, 2001), 13.

17. Ibid., 12.

18. Ibid., 13.

19. Kanza, 271.

20. Ibid, 287.

21. Nzongola-Ntalaja, 109.

22. Kanza, 305.

23. De Witte, 17.

24. Chevalier Jacques Brassine, "Enquête sur la mort de Lumumba," PhD dissertation, Université Libre de Bruxelles, 1991, p. 9.

Chapter 10

1. Raphaël Granvaud, *De l'armée coloniale à l'armée néocoloniale (1830–1909)* (Paris: Collections Dossiers Noirs, no. 23, 2009), 22.

2. Ibid., 55.

3. James Petras and Henry Veltmeyer, "World Development: Globalization or Imperialism?," in Globalization and Antiglobalization: Dynamics of Change in the New World Order, ed. Henry Veltmeyer (Burlington: Ashgate, 2004), 12–29.

4. Quoted in Granvaud, 10.

5. Ibid., 11.

6. Ibid.

7. "Barack Obama Is Not a Christian in Any Meaningful Way," http://www.redstate.com/2015/02/06/barack-obama-is-not-a-christian-in-any-meaningful-way/ (accessed 2-7-2015).

8. In Wittgenstein's terms, grammatical propositions are those propositions that "shape what counts as an intelligible description of reality," that lay down the rules of the language game; whereas empirical propositions are those propositions that are merely descriptive without having rule-defining power in the language game. Nevertheless, "empirical propositions can harden into grammar and therefore be removed from the traffic of doubt. It isn't that grammatical propositions can't be proven; it is that they no longer need to be proven." They need not be proven because they have been imposed by a whole machinery of power as truth. See Peg O'Connor, Oppression and Responsibility: A Wittgensteinian Approach to Social Practices and Moral Theory (University Park: Pennsylvania State University Press, 2002), 34.

9. See Steven C. Ward, Modernizing the Mind: Psychological Knowledge and the Remaking of Society (Westport: Praeger, 2002), 10–19.

10. For further discussion of how the Third World has failed to be competitive in the industry of truth fabrication and dissemination, see Martial Frindéthié, Globalization and the Seduction of Africa's Ruling Class: An Argument for a New Philosophy of Development (Jefferson, NC: McFarland, 2010), chapter 3.

11. Edward Paice, Tip and Run: The Untold Tragedy of the Great War in Africa (London: Weidenfeld & Nicolson, 2007), 352.

12. Ibid., 354.

13. Ibid.

14. Quoted in William Gallois, A History of Violence in the Early Algerian Colony (New York: Palgrave MacMillan, 2013), 145.

15. See Martin Evans, Algeria: France's Undeclared War (New York: Oxford University Press, 2012), 86.

16. Josh Israel, "Republican Presidential Hopeful Says There's No Such Thing as a War Crime," http://thinkprogress.org/security/2015/02/16/3623391/ben-carson-no-war-crimes-rules/ (accessed 2-18-2015).

17. Eugene Robinson, "President Obama's Immoral Drone War," http://www.washingtonpost.com/opinions/eugene-robinson-president-obamas-immoral-drone-war/2013/12/02/f25cc0aa-5b82-11e3-a49b-90a0e156254b_story.html (accessed 4-13-2015).

18. See Yves Benot, Massacres coloniaux, 1944–1950: la IVe République et la mise au pas des colonies françaises (Paris: La Découverte, 2001), 36–37.

19. From Bare Hands Victory, by Sidiki Bakaba, director (Abidjan: Kepri Creations, 2005).

20. Benot, 44.

21. Fanon, 35–36.

Conclusion

1. Bashkar Chakravori, "China's New Development Bank Is a Wake-Up Call for Washington," https://hbr.org/2015/04/chinas-new-development-bank-is-a-wake-up-call-for-washington (accessed 5-23-2015).

Bibliography

Adamoekula. "L'histoire est têtue, c'est mon oncle Ambroise Boimbo qui a arraché l'épée du roi Baudouin 'reportage à Monkoto.'" 4–10–14. http://emiradamo.com/2014/10/04/video-exclu-lhistoire-est-tetuecest-mon-oncle-ambroise-boimbo-qui-a-arrache-lepee-du-roi-baudouin-reportage-a-monkoto-3/ (accessed 5–7–2015).

Adebajo, Adekeye. "Obama failing to live up to his pledges on Africa." 2–23-2015. http://www.bdlive.co.za/opinion/columnists/2015/02/23/obama-failing-to-live-up-to-his-pledges-on-africa (accessed 3–8–2015).

Agsous, Nadia. "Indépendance: nous femmes d'Algérie." 12–24-2012. http://www.huffingtonpost.fr/nadia-agsous/independance-algerie-role-des-femmes_b_2358381.html (accessed 1–20-2015).

Aidara, Ibrahima. "Pourquoi Areva refuse-t-elle de payer un juste taux d'imposition au Niger?" 3–1-2014. http://www.nextafrique.com/finance/fiscalite-legacy/3124-pourquoi-areva-refuse-t-elle-de-payer-un-juste-taux-d-imposition-auniger (accessed 2–15-2015).

Airault, Pascal. "Côte d'Ivoire: mourir pour Bouake." http://www.jeuneafrique.com/Article/JA2744p046.xml0/. 8–23-2013 (accessed 4–18–2015).

_____. "Côte d'Ivoire: secrets de guerre." 3–4-2012. http://www.jeuneafrique.com/Article/JA2672p040.xml0/ (Accessed 4–5–2015).

Akindès, Francis. "Des Origines des crises politiques récentes au sein de l'histoire en Côte d'Ivoire." In *La Métaphore du politique au Nord et au Sud*. Edited by Karthala, Paris: Karthala, 2004.

Allen, Peter. "Gaddafi Was Killed by French Secret Serviceman on Orders of Nicolas Sarkozy, Sources Claim." 9–30-2012. http://www.dailymail.co.uk/news/article-2210759/Gaddafi-killed-French-secret-serviceman-orders-Nicolas-Sarkozy-sources-claim.html (accessed 12–29-2014).

Amondji, Marcel. "Forfaiture et impunité L'affaire Ouattara (1990–1993) et la crise de l'houphouéto-foccartisme 3e partie." 7–29–12. http://cerclevictorbiakaboda.blogspot.com/2012/07/laffaire-ouattara-1990–1993-et-la-crise.html (accessed 3–12-2015).

Axell, Albert. "Remembering Russian Sacrifice in World War II." Interview with Olga Dimitrieva, 10–9–2009. http://www.telegraph.co.uk/sponsored/rbth/6281732/Russia-Now-Remembering-Russias-sacrifice-in-World-War-Two.html (accessed 1–12-2015).

Ayangafac, Chrysantus. "The Politics of Post-Conflict Elections in Côte d'Ivoire." In *From Civil Strife to Peace Building: Examining Private Sector Involvement in West Africa Reconstruction*. Edited by Hany Besada. Waterloo: Wilfrid Laurier University Press, 2009.

Bâ, Koureyssi. Interview with Abdou Salam Diop, in *L'Harmattan*, no. 854–9056 (January 2, 2005).

Bakaba, Sidiki. *Bare Hands Victory*. Abidjan: Kepri Creations, 2005.

Bangura, Abdul Karim, ed. "The Crisis in Côte d'Ivoire." In *Assessing Barack Obama's Africa Policy: Suggestions for Him and African Leaders*. Lanham, MD: University Press of America, 2015.

Barnes, Brooks. "'Sniper' Rules Weekend Box Office." 1–19-2015. http://www.nytimes.com/2015/01/19/movies/sniper-rules-weekend-box-office.html (accessed 2–8–2015).

Bedzigui, Celestin. "Hypocrisie: Kadhafi, 'la communauté économique et nous.'" http://guerre.libreinfo.org/manipulations/mensonges-de-guerre/99-guerre-libye/548-kadhafi-hypocrisie.html (accessed 12–26-2014).

Benot, Yves. *Massacres coloniaux, 1944–1950: la IVe République et la mise au pas des colonies françaises*. Paris: La Découverte, 2001.

Bensimon, Cyril. "IB, une personnalité bien encombrante de la scène ivoirienne." 4–29-2011 http://
     www.rfi.fr/afrique/20110429-ib-une-personnalite-bien-encombrante-scene-ivoirienne/
     (accessed 4-15-2016).
Berthemet, Tanguy. "Côte d'Ivoire: Ouattara appelle à la grève générale." 12–28-2010. http://www.
     lefigaro.fr/international/2010/12/27/01003-20101227ARTFIG00423-cote-d-ivoire-ouattara-
     appelle-a-la-greve-generale.php (accessed 4–6-2015).
Biloslavo, Fausto. "Un secret de Sarkozy bien gardé: l'exécution de Kadhafi." 7–4-2014. http://
     www.agoravox.fr/actualites/politique/article/un-secret-de-sarkozy-bien-garde-l-154064
     (accessed 5–10-2015).
Bocquet, Leon, and Ernst Hosten. "Un fragment de l'épopée sénégalaise." In Bakari Kamian, Des
     Tranchées de Verdun à l'Eglise Saint-Bernard: 80.000 combattants maliens au secours de la France
     (1914–18 et 1935–45). Paris: Editions Karthala, 2001.
Bouikalo, Alain. "Amadou Soumahoro Planifie un Génocide." 6–19-2012. http://ivoire.telediaspora.
     net/fr/texte.asp?idinfo=69881 (accessed 3–10-2015).
Branche, Raphaëlle. "Torture and Other Violations of the Law by the French Army During the
     Algerian War.," In Genocide, War Crimes and the West: History and Complicity. Edited by Adam
     Jones. Translated by Jo Jones. London: Zed Book, 2004.
Brassine, Chevalier Jacques. "Enquête sur la mort de Lumumba." PhD dissertation, Université Libre
     de Bruxelles, 1991.
Busch, Gary K. "Consensual Rape in the Françafrique Currency Markets." http://www.academia.
     edu/5096732/Consensual_Rape_in_the_Francafrique_Currency_Markets (accessed 2–21-
     2015).
Bush, George W. "Prepared Text of Bush's Knesset Speech." 5–15–208. http://www.wsj.com/
     articles/SB121083798995894943 (accessed 12–30-2014).
Casement, Roger. "The Casement Report," House of Commons. Accounts and Papers, vol. 62.
     1904.
Césaire, Aimé. Discourse on Colonialism. Translated by Joan Pinkham. New York: Monthly Review
     Press, 1972. Originally published as Discours sur le colonialisme by Editions Présence Africaine,
     1955.
Chakravorti, Bashkar. "China's New Development Bank Is a Wake-Up Call for Washington." 4–20-
     2015. https://hbr.org/2015/04/chinas-new-development-bank-is-a-wake-up-call-for-washing-
     ton (accessed 5–23-2015).
Champlin, Christophe. "Portrait d'Alassane Ouattara." 11–26-2010. http://www.rfi.fr/afrique/
     20101126-portrait-alassane-ouattara/ (accessed 2–2-2015).
Chapman, Steve. "Every President Is a War President." 5–6-2012. http://articles.chicagotribune.
     com/2012–05–06/news/ct-oped-0506-chapman-20120506_1_anti-war-candidate-air-war-
     barack-obama (accessed 1–2-2015).
Clinton, Hillary. Interview with Jeffrey Goldberg. Atlantic, 8–1-2014. http://www.theatlantic.com/
     international/archive/2014/08/hillary-clinton-failure-to-help-syrian-rebels-led-to-the-rise-of-
     isis/375832/?single_page=true (accessed 12–20-2014).
_____. "Transcript of Clinton's Confirmation Hearing." 1–13-2009. http://www.npr.org/
     templates/story/story.php?storyId=99290981 (accessed 4–13-2015).
C-SPAN. "Wisconsin Faith and Freedom Coalition." 3–31-2012. http://www.c-span.org/video/
     ?305242–1/wisconsin-faith-freedom-coalition (accessed 12–21-2014).
Dalle, Corinne, and Jean-Michel Viallet. "L'Exposition colonial international de 1931." Archives
     départementales du Puy-de-Dôme. http://www.archivesdepartementales.puydedome.fr/n/l-
     exposition-coloniale-internationale-de-1931/n:30 (accessed 1–7-2015).
David, Philippe. La Côte d'Ivoire. Paris: Editions Karthala, 2009.
Davis, Darién J., and Judith Michelle Williams. "Pan-Africanism, Negritude, and the Currency of
     Blackness: Cuba, the Francophone Caribbean, and Brazil in Comparative Perspective, 1930–
     1950s." In Beyond Slavery: The Multilayered Legacy of Africans in Latin America and the Caribbean.
     Edited by Draién J. Davis. Rowman & Littlefield, 2007.
Diallo, Bakari. Force-bonté. Paris: Rieder, 1926.
Droz, Bernard. "1er novembre 1954: la Toussaint rouge." April 2002. http://www.histoire.presse.
     fr/collections/l-espagne/1er-novembre-1954-la-toussaint-rouge-07–04-2002–9978 (accessed
     1–19-2015).
Duval, Philippe. "Le Bombardement de Bouaké, dernier secret de la Françafrique." 11–7–2009.

http://mondafrique.com/lire/international/2014/11/07/neuf-soldats-tues-a-bouake-une-bavure-francaise (accessed 4-18-2015).

Erickson, Erick. "Barack Obama Is Not a Christian in Any Meaningful Way." 2-6-2015. http://www.redstate.com/2015/02/06/barack-obama-is-not-a-christian-in-any-meaningful-way/ (accessed 2-7-2015).

Etty, Macaire. "Faut-il regretter le parti unique?" 4-1-2012. http://le-filament.blogspot.com/2012/04/faut-il-regretter-le-parti-unique.html (accessed 3-5-2015).

Evans, Martin. *Algeria: France's Undeclared War.* Oxford: Oxford University Press, 2012.

Fanon, Frantz. *The Wretched of the Earth.* Preface by Jean-Paul Sartre. New York: Grove Press, 1963.

Feldman, Josh. "Bill O'Reilly: 'Socialist-Communist Vision' Fueling Liberal Fight for Obamacare." http://www.mediaite.com/tv/bill-oreilly-socialist-communist-vision-fueling-liberal-fight-for-obamacare/ (accessed 12-19-2014).

Ferloo. "Guillaume Soro: 'Mon meilleur souvenir au Sénégal, c'est quand Me Wade m'a acheté ma première veste.'" 4-13-2015. http://www.seneweb.com/news/People/guillaum-soro-laquo-mon-meilleur-souveni_n_152511.html (accessed 4-15-2015).

Ferry, Jules. "Les fondements de la politique coloniale." Discours prononcé à la Chambre des députés: le 28 juillet 1885.

Fieldhouse, David Kenneth. *The West and the Third World: Trade, Colonialism, Dependence and Development.* Malden: Blackwell, 1999.

Filippis, Vittorio de. "Pétrole: l'accord secret entre le CNT et la France." 9-1-2011. http://www.liberation.fr/monde/2011/09/01/petrole-l-accord-secret-entre-le-cnt-et-la-france_758320 (accessed 2-14-2015).

Flint, John E. *Cecil Rhodes.* Boston: Little, Brown, 1974.

Florentin, Abel. "Côte d'Ivoire: Bombardement de Bouaké: les généraux français au rapport." 11-12-2013. http://www.jeuneafrique.com/Article/JA2755p042.xml2/ (accessed 4-19-2015).

Fogarty, Richard. *Race and War in France: Colonial Subjects in the French Army, 1914-1918.* Baltimore: Johns Hopkins University Press, 2008.

Franklin, John Hope. *George Washington Williams: A Biography.* Chicago: University of Chicago Press, 1985.

Frindéthié, Martial. *Francophone African Cinema: History, Culture, Politics and Theory.* Jefferson, NC: McFarland, 2009.

_____. *Globalization and the Seduction of Africa's Ruling Class: An Argument for a New Philosophy of Development.* Jefferson, NC: McFarland, 2010.

Gaddafi, Saïf Al-Islam. Interview with AFP. 3-1-2013. http://fr.euronews.com/2013/03/01/xyz-affaire-gueant-sarkozy-kadhafi-les-accusations-de-saif-al-islam/ (accessed 12-15-2015).

Gadou, Dakouri. "Conflit et mobilisations patriotiques en Côte d'Ivoire: les protagonistes entre imaginaire national et positionnement politico-économique." In *Côte d'Ivoire: La réinvention de soi dans la violence.* Edited by Francis Augustin Akindès. Dakar: CODESRIA, 2011. 82-132.

Gallois, William. *A History of Violence in the Early Algerian Colony.* New York: Palgrave MacMillan, 2013.

Gardiner, Nile. "Nicolas Sarkozy Mocks Barack Obama as 'Not a Leader but a Follower': He's Spot On." 9-6-2013. http://blogs.telegraph.co.uk/news/nilegardiner/100234571/nicolas-sarkozy-mocks-barack-obama-as-not-a-leader-but-a-follower-hes-spot-on/ (accessed 12-31-2014).

Gaudusson, Jean Du Bois de. "L'accord de Marcoussis, entre droit et politique." In *Afrique Contemporaine,* no. 206 (2003/2).

Gbagbo, Laurent. Interview with Elio Comarin, "Côte d'Ivoire: Gbagbo dénonce la 'complicité' du Burkina." http://www1.rfi.fr/actufr/articles/034/article_17719.asp. 10-25-2002 (accessed 3-17-2016).

_____. Interview with Tanguy Berthemet. "Laurent Gbagbo: 'Il y a un complot contre moi.'" 12-26-2010. http://www.lefigaro.fr/international/2010/12/26/01003-20101226ARTFIG00129-laurent-gbagbo-il-y-a-un-complot-contre-moi.php (accessed 3-9-2015).

Girard, Youssef. "Le passé génocidaire de la France en Algérie." 12-26-2011. http://www.ism-france.org/analyses/Le-passe-genocidaire-de-la-France-en-Algerie-article-16433 (accessed 1-17-2015).

Gordon, David T. "The Roots of de Tocqueville's American Exceptionalism." 4-1 -2011. http://www.visionandvalues.org/2011/04/the-roots-of-tocqueville-s-american-exceptionalism/ (accessed 1-25-2015).

Govender, Peroshni. "Obama protesters rally near hospital treating Mandela." 6–28–2013. http:// www.reuters.com/article/2013/06/28/mandela-idUSL5N0F414P20130628 (accessed 2–9– 2015).

Granvaud, Raphaël. *De l'armée coloniale à l'armée néocoloniale (1830–19909)*. Paris: Collections Dossiers Noirs, no. 23 (2009).

Gray, Sarah. "Noam Chomsky discusses terrifying 'American Sniper' mentality: Chomsky compares the mentality of Chris Kyle to America's drone operation." 1–26–2015. http://www.alternet. org/watch-chomsky-blasts-american-sniper-and-media-glorifies-it (accessed 2–8–2015).

Gregory, Paul Roderick. "Is President Obama Truly a Socialist?" 1–22–2012. http://www.forbes. com/sites/paulroderickgregory/2012/01/22/is-president-obama-truly-a-socialist/ (accessed 12–19–2014).

Grenard, Fabrice. "Manifestations de travailleurs à Paris pour protester contre la montée du chômage en 1933." http://fresques.ina.fr/jalons/fiche-media/InaEdu02019/manifestations-de-travail leurs-a-paris-pour-protester-contre-la-montee-du-chomage-en-1933.html (accessed 1–15–2015).

Hale, Dana S. *Races on Display: French Representations of Colonial Peoples, 1886–1940*. Bloomington: Indiana University Press, 2008.

Hardmong, Edwige. "Côte d'Ivoire: Les auteurs du putsch de 1999 lavent Ouattara de toute respon- sabilité." 9–20–2011. http://www.jeuneafrique.com/Article/ARTJAWEB20110920101238/ (Accessed 3–1–2015).

Heggoy, Alf Andrew. *Insurgency and Counterinsurgency in Algeria*. Bloomington: Indiana University Press, 1972.

Hochschild, Adam. *King Leopold's Ghost: A Story of Greed, Terror, and Heroism in Colonial Africa*. Boston: Houghton Mifflin, 1998.

Hofnung, Thomas. "D'ex-chefs de guerre à l'école française." 5–29–2012. http://www.liberation. fr/monde/2012/05/29/d-ex-chefs-de-guerre-a-l-ecole-francaise_822255 (accessed 4–16– 2015).

Hofnung, Thomas, and Yann Philippin, "Affaire Uramin: Perquisition chez Anne Lauvergeon." 6– 3–2014. http://www.liberation.fr/economie/2014/06/03/affaire-uramin-perquisition-chez- areva-et-lauvergeon_1032757 (accessed 24–4–2015).

Horne, Allistair. *A Savage War of Peace: Algeria, 1954–1962*. New York: Viking, 1978.

Human Rights Watch. *Criminal Politics: Violence, "Godfathers" and Corruption in Nigeria* 19, no. 16 (October 2007).

_____. *The Niger Delta: No Democratic Dividend* 14, no. 7(A) (October 2002).

Israel, Josh. "Republican Presidential Hopeful Says There's No Such Thing as a War Crime." 2–16– 2015. http://thinkprogress.org/security/2015/02/16/3623391/ben-carson-no-war-crimes- rules/ (accessed 2–18–2015).

Jeffries, Stuart. "Does Nicolas Sarkozy have short-man syndrome?" 9–9–2009. http://www. theguardian.com/lifeandstyle/2009/sep/09/mens-fashion-nicolas-sarkozy (accessed 3–30– 2015).

Joly, Eva. *Justice Under Siege: One Woman's Battle Against a European Oil Company*. Translated by Emma Kemp. London: Citizen Press, 2006.

Jong, Ferdinand de, and Vincent Foucher. "La tragédie du roi Abdoulaye?: Néomodernisme et Ren- aissance africaine dans le Sénégal contemporain." In *Conjecture*. Paris: Karthala, 2010.

Kadet, Bertin. "Président Laurent Gbagbo, un modèle de combattant pour les libertés démocra- tiques/Un destin forgé par ses parents/Les faits marquants de sa vie retracés par Bertin Kadet." https://fr.facebook.com/lamajoritepresidentielle/posts/295256017260060. 12–3–2012 (accessed 2–19–2015).

Kanza, Thomas. *Conflict in the Congo: The Rise and Fall of Lumumba*. London: Penguin, 1972.

Kendall, Bridget. "UN's Del Ponte Says Evidence Syria Rebels 'Used Sarin.'" 5–6–2013. http:// www.bbc.com/news/world-middle-east-22424188 (accessed 1–3–2015).

Killingray, David. *Fighting for Britain: African Soldiers in the Second World War*. Woodbridge: James Currey, 2010.

Kim, Mallie Jane. "Osama bin Laden Is Dead—Does Obama or Bush Deserve Credit?" 5–5–2011. http://www.usnews.com/opinion/articles/2011/05/05/osama-bin-laden-is-dead-does-obama- or-bush-deserve-the-credit (accessed 1–2–2015).

Koller, Christian. "The recruitment of colonial troops in Africa and Asia and their deployment in Europe during the First World War." University of Zurich Open Repository and Archive, 2008.

_____. "Representing Otherness: African, Indian and European Soldiers' Letters and Memoirs." In *Race, Empire and the First World War Writing*. Edited by Santanu Das. Cambridge: Cambridge University Press, 2011.

Konan, André Sylver. "Côte d'Ivoire: Plus de 700 millions FCFA sur un compte de Laurent Gbagbo." http://www.jeuneafrique.com/Article/ARTJAWEB20120515135424/ (accessed 3–4–2015).

Konan, Venance. "Ivoiriens et leur Ivoirité." *Fraternité Matin*, February 23, 1998.

Konaté, Yacouba. "Le Destin d'Alassane Dramane Ouattara." In *Côte d'Ivoire: l'année terrible: 1999– 2000*. Edited by Marc le Pape and Claudine Vidal. Paris: Editions Karthala, 2002.

Koulibaly, Mamadou. *La guerre de la France contre la Côte d'Ivoire*. Abidjan: La Refondation, 2003.

Kpatindé, Francis. "BCEAO: Les Dessous d'un hold-up." 11–20-2003. http://www.jeuneafrique.com/Article/LIN23113bceaopudloh0/ (accessed 3–26–2015).

Krassault, Robert. "Côte d'Ivoire: Le parcours d'un homme atypique: Laurent Gbagbo, le résistant." 3–22-2013. http://www.afrik53.com/Cote-d-Ivoire-Le-parcours-d-un-homme-atypique-Laurent-Gbagbo-le-resistant_a13700.html (accessed 2–19-2015).

Labott, Lise. "U.S. to Restore Relations with Libya." 5–15-006. http://www.cnn.com/2006/U.S./05/15/libya/index.html?section=cnn_world (accessed 12–26-2014).

Laniray, Pierre. *François-Xavier Verschave: l'homme qui voulait soulever les montagnes*. Paris: Éditions les Arènes, 2006.

Las Casas, Bartolomé de. *Brevisima Relacion de la Destruccion de las Indias*. London: Printed by J.C. for Nath. Brook, at the Angel in Cornhill, 1656.

Lefebvre, Alex. "French concessions on Iraq Met by U.S. threats." 5–1-2003. http://www.wsws.org/en/articles/2003/05/fran-m01.html (accessed 1–28-2015).

Lequy, Roger. "L'Agriculture algérienne de 1954 à 1962." Master's thesis. http://www.persee.fr/web/revues/home/prescript/article/remmm_0035-1474_1970_num_8_1_1081 (accessed 1–19-2015).

Levin, Marc. "Obama 'a Nihilist, a Narcissist and an Extremist'; Warns 'We Are Going To Get Hit Again.'" 2–5-2015. http://www.realclearpolitics.com/video/2015/02/05/mark_levin_obama_a_nihilist_a_narcissist_and_an_extremist_warns_we_are_going_to_get_hit_again.html (accessed 2–7-2015).

Lia, J-S. "Hommage à Bohoun-Bouabré: Le père du budget sécurisé a tiré sa révérence." (1–12-2012. http://news.abidjan.net/h/422495.html (accessed 2–17-2015).

Limbaugh, Rush. "President Obama's Cairo Speech: Outrageous, Absurd, Embarrassing." 6–4-2009. http://www.rushlimbaugh.com/daily/2009/06/04/president_obama_s_cairo_speech_outrageous_absurd_embarrassing (accessed 12–17-2014).

Lipton, Edward P. *Religious Freedom in Africa*. Hauppauge: Nova Science, 2002.

Lunn, Joe Harris. "France's Legacy to Demba Mboup?: A Senegalese Griot and his Descendants Remember His Military Service During the First World War." In *Race, Empire and the First World War Writing*. Edited by Santanu Das. Cambridge: Cambridge University Press, 2011.

_____. "Kande Kamara Speaks: An Oral History of the West African Experience in France, 1914–18." In *Africa and the First World War*. Edited by Melvin E. Page. New York: St. Martin's, 1987.

Lynch, Colum. "Obama's new national security advisor has sharp elbows, a tart tongue, and a taste for the shadows." 7–1-2013. http://foreignpolicy.com/2013/07/01/susan-rice-finally-has-her-perfect-job-head-knocker-in-chief/ (accessed 3–8-2016).

Macalpine, George Watson. *Report of the Commission of Enquiry into the Administration of the Congo Free State*. Published for the Baptiste Missionary Society by Jaas. Clarke. Southampton Row: Kingsgate, n.d.

Maodza, Takunda. "President Raps Obama's Naivety." 12–5-2014. http://www.herald.co.zw/president-raps-obamas-naivety/ (accessed 3–8-2015).

Martelli, George. *Leopold to Lumumba: A History of the Belgian Congo, 1877–1960*. London: Chapman and Hall, 1962.

Maspéro, François. "Préface." In *La IVe République et la mise au pas des colonies françaises*. Vol. 3. Paris: Découverte, 2001.

Mathaba. "Libya's 'Water Wars' and Gaddafi's Great Man-Made River Project." Center for Research on Globalization. 5–13-13. http://www.globalresearch.ca/libyas-water-wars-and-gaddafis-great-man-made-river-project/5334868 (accessed 1–21-2015).

Mattei, François. Interview with Laurent Correau, 6–27-2014. http://www.rfi.fr/afrique/20140627-verite-justice-crise-cote-ivoire-livre-gbagbo-francois-mattei/ (accessed 2–16-2015).

Matthews, K.J. "Harry Belafonte Disappointed with Obama." 7-30-2011. http://marquee.blogs.cnn.com/2011/07/30/harry-belafonte-disappointed-with-obama/ (accessed 2-9-2015).

Matthews, Merrill. "Comparing Obama's Policies with French Socialist Hollande." 5-10-2012. http://www.forbes.com/sites/merrillmatthews/2012/05/10/comparing-obamas-policies-with-french-socialist-hollande/2/ (accessed 12-19-2014).

Mazrui, Ali A. "Africa and the Legacy of the Second World War: Political, Economic and Cultural Aspects." In *Africa and the Second World War: Report and Papers of the Symposium Organized by UNESCO at Benghazi, Libya, Arab Jamahiriya, from 10–13 November 1980; The General History of Africa; Studies and Documents 10.* Paris: United Nations, 1985.

Mbeki, Thabo. "What the World Got Wrong in Côte d'Ivoire." 4-29-2011. http://www.foreignpolicy.com/articles/2011/04/29/what_the_world_got_wrong_in_cote_d_ivoire?page=full (accessed 4-9-2015).

Mbembe, Achille, and Célestin Monga. "Côte d'Ivoire: la démocratie au bazooka?" 1-26-2011. http://blogs.mediapart.fr/edition/les-invites-de-mediapart/article/260111/cote-divoire-la-democratie-au-bazooka (accessed 4-8-2015).

McElroy, Damien. "Gaddafi's death: Libya's new rulers 'stained' by manner of his death, says Philip Hammond." 10-23-2011. http://www.telegraph.co.uk/news/worldnews/africaandindianocean/libya/8844744/Gaddafis-death-Libyas-new-rulers-stained-by-manner-of-his-death-says-Philip-Hammond.html (accessed 12-27-2014).

Médecins sans frontières. "La population ivoirienne prise dans l'étau du conflit." 3-15-2011. http://www.msf.fr/presse/communiques/population-ivoirienne-prise-etau-conflit (accessed 3-13-2015).

Meledje, Djedjro Francisco. "The Making, Unmaking and Remaking of the Constitution of Côte d'Ivoire: An Example of Chronic Instability." In *Fostering Constitutionalism in Africa.* Edited by Charles Fombad and Christina Murray. Pretoria University Press, 2010.

Merica, Dan. "Hilary Clinton Faults Nigerian Government's Handling of Search for Kidnapped Girls." 5-7-2014. http://politicalticker.blogs.cnn.com/2014/05/07/hillary-clinton-faults-nigerian-governments-handling-of-search-for-kidnapped-girls/ (accessed 3-24-2015).

Middleton, Drew. "U.S. and Red Armies Join, Split Germany." *New York Times*, April 28, 1945.

Miniter, Richard. "6 Signs That the White House's Susan Rice Is Clueless About Africa." 2-28-2014. http://www.forbes.com/sites/richardminiter/2014/02/28/6-signs-that-the-white-houses-susan-rice-is-clueless-about-africa/ (accessed 3-8-2015).

Morel, E.D. *The Black Man's Burden: The White Man in Africa from the Fifteenth Century to World War I.* New York: Modern Reader, 1969.

Nséké, Léopold. "Les Multinationales françaises en Afrique." 10-24-2013. http://www.afriqueexpansion.com/france-afrique-du-sud/12340-les-multinationales-francaises-en-afrique.html (accessed 2-14-2015).

Nzongola-Ntalaja, George. *The Congo from Leopold to Kabila: A People's History.* London: Zed Books, 2002.

Obama, Barack H. "News Conference by President Obama." 4-4-2009. http://www.whitehouse.gov/the-press-office/news-conference-president-obama-4042009 (accessed 1-2-2015).

_____. "Remarks by the President at National Prayer Breakfast." 2-5-2015. http://www.whitehouse.gov/the-press-office/2015/02/05/remarks-president-national-prayer-breakfast (accessed 2-6-2015).

_____. "Transcript: Obama's Speech Against the Iraq War." 1-20-2009. http://www.npr.org/templates/story/story.php?storyId=99591469 (accessed 1-30-2014).

O'Connor, Peg. *Oppression and Responsibility: A Wittgensteinian Approach to Social Practices and Moral Theory.* University Park: Pennsylvania State University, 2002.

O'Donnell, Lawrence. "Obama Went Back 800 Years for Comparison, Seems to Be Saying He Knows What Real Islam Is." 2-5-2015. http://www.realclearpolitics.com/video/2015/02/05/lawrence_odonnell_obama_went_back_800_years_ago_to_make_comparison_seems_to_be_saying_that_he_knows_what_real_islam_is.html (accessed 2-7-2015).

Page, Walter Hines, and Arthur Page. "The Life and Letters of Walter H. Page." In *The World's Work.* Vol. 43. New York: Doubleday, Page, 1922.

Paice, Edward. *Tip and Run: The Untold Tragedy of the Great War in Africa.* London: Weidenfeld and Nicolson, 2007.

Palin, Sarah. *America by Heart: Reflections on Family, Faith, and Flag.* New York: HarperCollins, 2010.

Petras, James, and Henry Veltmeyer. "World Development: Globalization or Imperialism?" In *Globalization and Antiglobalization: Dynamics of Change in the New World Order.* Edited by Henry Veltmeyer. Burlington: Ashgate, 2004.

Petras, James, and Robin E. Abaya, "The Euro-U.S. War on Libya: Official Lies and Misconceptions of Critics." 3–30-2011. http://www.globalresearch.ca/the-euro-us-war-on-libya-official-lies-and-misconceptions-of-critics/24033 (accessed 12–26-2014).

Pfaff, William. "Every President Needs a War of His Own." 9–15-2009. http://www.williampfaff.com/modules/news/print.php?storyid=431&PHPSESSID=4bce6c3dd0877862ce81c30ae 19f90a8 (accessed 1–2-2015).

Piettey, Betsey. "Wachovia Admits Slave Trade Profits." http://www.workers.org/2005/us/wachovia-0616/ (accessed on 1–11/2015).

Pougala, Jean-Paul. "Les vraies raisons de la guerre en Libye." 4–16-2011. http://www.alterinfo.net/Les-vraies-raisons-de-la-guerre-en-Libye_a57616.html (accessed 4–14-2015).

Putin, Vladimir. "A Plea for Caution from Russia: What Putin Has to Say to America About Syria." 9–12-2013. http://www.nytimes.com/2013/09/12/opinion/putin-plea-for-caution-from-russia-on-syria.html?pagewanted=all&_r=0 (accessed 1–2-15).

Rice, Susan E. "Human Rights: Advancing American Interests and Values." 12–4-2013. http://www.whitehouse.gov/the-press-office/2013/12/04/remarks-national-security-advisor-susan-e-rice-human-rights-advancing-am (accessed 3–8-2015).

Robinson, Eugene. "President Obama's Immoral Drone War." 12–2-2013. http://www.washingtonpost.com/opinions/eugene-robinson-president-obamas-immoral-drone-war/2013/12/02/f25cc0aa-5b82-11e3-a49b-90a0e156254b_story.html (accessed 4–13-2015).

Romney, Mitt. "Text of Mitt Romney's Speech on Foreign Policy at The Citadel." 10–7-2011. http://blogs.wsj.com/washwire/2011/10/07/text-of-mitt-romneys-speech-on-foreign-policy-at-the-citadel/ (accessed 12–21-2014).

Rothschild, Matthew. "Obama Bows to American Exceptionalism at West Point." http://www.progressive.org/news/2014/05/187714/obama-bows-american-exceptionalism-west-point (accessed 12–21-2014).

Rueff, Judith. "Côte-d'Ivoire: mandat d'arrêt contre Ouattara; L'opposant est inculpé de 'faux et usage de faux' concernant ses cartes d'identité." 12–9-1999. http://www.liberation.fr/monde/1999/12/09/cote-d-ivoire-mandat-d-arret-contre-ouattara-l-opposant-est-inculpe-de-faux-et-usage-de-faux-concern_291422 (accessed 2–26-2015).

Safire, William. "Chirac's Latest Ploy." 4–24-2003. http://www.nytimes.com/2003/04/24/opinion/chirac-s-latest-ploy.html (accessed 1–28-2015).

Sané, Pierre. "Côte d'Ivoire: The Logic of the Absurd." 3–1-2011. http://www.pambazuka.net/en/category/features/71588 (accessed 3–18-2015).

Sarraut, Albert. *La Mise en valeur des colonies françaises.* Paris: Payot, 1923.

Scarborough, Joe. "Where Did [Obama] Go To Church? Where Would He Get Such Ideas From?" 2–6-2015. http://www.realclearpolitics.com/video/2015/02/06/scarborough_on_obamas_prayer_speech_where_did_he_go_to_church_where_would_he_get_such_ideas_from.html (accessed 2–7-2015).

Schuck, Nathalie, and Frédéric Gerschel. *Ça reste entre nous, hein?: Deux ans de confidence de Nicolas Sarkozy.* Paris: Flammarion, 2014.

Scott, A.O. "A Sniper Does His Deeds, but the Battle Never Ends, 'American Sniper' Review, a Clint Eastwood Film with Bradley Cooper." 12–25-2014. http://www.nytimes.com/2014/12/25/movies/american-sniper-a-clint-eastwood-film-starring-bradley-cooper.html?_r=0 (accessed 2–8-2015).

Sheremushkin, Peter. "Remember the Russian people's role in World War II, defeating Nazi Germany." 5–18-2010. http://www.telegraph.co.uk/sponsored/rbth/opinion/7737591/russian-role-defeating-nazi-germany.html (accessed 1–12-2015).

Sivori, Boga. Transcripts of Simone Gbagbo's Trial. "Simone Gbagbo devant la cour d'assises: 'Ouattara n'a pas gagné les élections.'" 5–5-2015. http://www.notrevoie.com/develop.asp?id=61673 (accessed 3–6-2015).

Slavin, Patrick. "En Côte d'Ivoire, en pleine crise, une mise en garde contre une pénurie des médicaments de première nécessité." http://www.unicef.org/french/infobycountry/cotedivoire_57599.html (accessed 3–11-2015).

Soudan, François. "Côte d'Ivoire: Simone Gbagbo, une femme puissante." 2–23-2015. http://www.jeuneafrique.com/Article/JA2708p024–032.xmll/ (accessed 3–7-2015).

Spencer, Richard, Heidi Blake and Jon Swaine. "Tony Blair 'visited Libya to lobby for JP Morgan.'" 9–18-2011. http://www.telegraph.co.uk/news/politics/tony-blair/8772418/Tony-Blair-visited-Libya-to-lobby-for-JP-Morgan.html (accessed 1–1-2015).

Spillius, Alex. "Libya: Barack Obama Calls on Col. Gaddafi to Step Down." 2–27-2011. http://www.telegraph.co.uk/news/worldnews/africaandindianocean/libya/8350246/Libya-Barack-Obama-calls-on-Col-Gaddafi-to-step-down.html (accessed 3–25-2015).

Stockman, Sarah, and Milton Valencia. "U.S. officials thought a BU post might ease Gbagbo out." 4–13-2011. http://www.boston.com/news/education/higher/articles/2011/04/13/us_officials_thought_a_bu_post_might_ease_gbagbo_out/ (accessed 3–9-2015).

Stora, Benjamin. *Algeria, 1830–2000: A Short History.* Ithaca: Cornell University Press, 2001.

Tall, Aliou. "Abdoulaye Wade insulte tous les Africains en confortant les théories racistes sur le Nègre." 3–4-2015. http://congo-liberty.com/?p=11337 (accessed 3–24-2015).

Thiolay, Boris. "Sarkozy et l'argent libyen: les pistes du soupçon." 5–15-2014. http://www.lexpress.fr/actualite/societe/justice/sarkozy-et-l-argent-libyen-les-pistes-du-soupcon_1543003.html (accessed 12–28-2014).

Tiémélé, Jean-Charles. "Libye: Kadhafi est mort, vive Total!" 2–13-2015. http://regardscroises.ivoire-blog.com/archive/2015/02/13/libye-kadhafi-est-mort-vive-total.html (accessed 2–14-2015).

Unicef. "Fighting malaria is an investment in future!" http://www.unicef.org/cotedivoire/health_nutrition_2167.html (accessed 3–11-2015).

Vale, Paul. "Russia's Sergei Lavrov Says Obama's State of the Union Address Proves America Wants 'World Domination.'" 1–21-2015. http://www.huffingtonpost.co.uk/2015/01/21/russias-sergei-lavrov-says-obamas-state-of-the-union-address-proves-america-is-bent-on-world-domination_n_6515970.html (accessed 1–21-2015).

Varenne, Leslie. *Abobo la guerre.* Paris: Editions Mille et une nuits, 2012.

Verschave, François-Xavier. *Complicité de génocide?: La politique de la France au Rwanda.* Paris: Éditions la Découverte, 1994.

Vidal, Claudine. "Du conflit politique aux menaces entre voisins." In *La Côte d'Ivoire-l'année terrible, 1999–2000.* Edited by Marc Le Pape and Claudine Vidal. Paris: Editions Kathala, 2002.

Warungu, Joseph. "Letter from Africa: Kenya passes electoral test—but what next?" 3–12-2013. http://www.bbc.com/news/world-africa-21745501 (accessed 4–10-2015).

Ward, Steven C. *Modernizing the Mind: Psychological Knowledge and the Remaking of Society.* Westport: Praeger, 2002.

Watkins, John. "Libya's Thirst for 'Fossil Water.'" 3–18-2006. http://news.bbc.co.uk/2/hi/science/nature/4814988.stm (accessed 12–27-2014).

West, Cornel. Interview with Thomas Frank. "He posed as a progressive and turned out to be counterfeit; We ended up with a Wall Street presidency, a drone presidency." 8–24-2014. http://www.salon.com/2014/08/24/cornel_west_he_posed_as_a_progressive_and_turned_out_to_be_counterfeit_we_ended_up_with_a_wall_street_presidency_a_drone_presidency/ (accessed 2–9-2015).

Witte, Ludo de. *The Assassination of Lumumba.* Translated by Ann Wright and Renée Fenby. London: Verso, 2001.

Yahmed, Manwane Ben. "Accord de Linas-Marcoussis: la vraie histoire du 'oui' de Gbagbo à Chirac." 3–4-2003. http://www.jeuneafrique.com/Article/LIN02033lavracarihc0/ (accessed 3–21-2015).

_____. "Jusqu'où Ira Macky Sall?" 1–21-2008. http://www.jeuneafrique.com/Article/LIN20018jusquedawmi0/?art_cle=LIN20018jusquedawmi0 (accessed 3–25-2015).

Yergin, Daniel. *The Prize: The Epic Quest for Oil, Money and Power.* New York: Free Press, 2008.

Zoro-Bi, Epiphane. *Désarmer la violence en Côte d'Ivoire.* Paris: Karthala, 2004.

Index

Abako 214, 217–220
Abbas, Ferhat 52–53
Abdallah, Ahmed 82
Abidjan 9, 35, 68, 85–86, 97–98, 101, 105,
    113–115, 118–120, 124, 126, 128, 135–137,
    139–143, 149–151, 154, 158, 168, 170, 174,
    178–180, 182–184, 198, 240–241, 248,
    256n1, 257n33, 257n34, 262n19, 263, 267
L'Abidjanaise 119
Abobo 140–141, 149, 151, 170–174, 257n21,
    270
Accra 117, 124, 193, 215, 217–218
Achiary, André 53
Adamoekula 262n11
Addis-Ababa 142
Adebajo, Adekeye 194, 260n30, 263
Adjamé 140
Adouala, Cyrille 216
Afghanistan 16, 18, 21, 142, 239
African Union (AU) 2, 42, 120, 128–130,
    142, 156, 192, 195
Afrika Korps 42
Agence Nationalie pour l'Organisation de la
    Conférence Islamique (ANOCI) 163–164
Agsous, Nadia 254n47, 263
Ahoussou, Jeannot 168
AIC see Association Internationale du
    Congo
Aidara, Ibrahima 256n31, 256n33, 263
Airault, Pascal 258n15, 259n10, 259n12, 263
Akan 111
Akindès, Francis 257n27, 257n32, 257n39
Akodjénou, Arnauld 144
Akoto, Paul Yao 118
al-Assad, Bashar 18–19, 70, 80, 197
Albert I (King) 211
Algeria 4, 6–7, 10–11, 23, 25, 29, 32, 38, 42,
    47–66, 81, 215–218, 227, 236, 238, 243,
    253n32, 254n1, 254n6, 254n14, 254n25,
    254n35, 254n44, 262n14, 264, 270
Allen, Peter 255n6, 263
L'Alliance pour la République (APR) 165

Allied Forces 5, 42–44, 104
Alliot-Marie, Michèle 182
al-Mamoudi, Ali Baghdadi 72
ALN see Armée de Libération Nationale
al-Qaida 18, 178
Alsace 6, 25, 41, 58
Altit, Emmanuel 171
Amara, Essy 120
Amnesty International 96, 169, 178–179, 210,
    239, 259n2
Amondji, Marcel 90–91, 256n7, 256n14, 263
Amougou, Thierry 253n42
Anaky, Innocent Kobena 118
Angola 98, 142, 156, 243–244
Ankara 255n11
Annan, Kofi 119
Anoblé, Félix 174
ANOCI see Agence Nationalie pour l'Or-
    ganisation de la Conférence Islamique
Aokas 6, 54, 62
APR see L'Alliance pour la République
Arab League 72
Arab Spring 7, 67–69, 80, 246
Aragon, Louis 39
Areva 82–83, 256n31, 256n32, 263, 266
Armajaro 116
Armée de Libération Nationale (ALN) 6, 59,
    61, 65
Arnaud, Gerard 131, 147
Assié-Lumumba 256n10
Association Internationale du Congo (AIC)
    199
Association of Algerian Ulema 51, 254n14
Attécoubé 140
AU see African Union
Auriol, Vincent 43, 253n43
Auschwitz 44
Australia 188, 212, 237
Austria 26
Austria-Hungary 26
Axelrod, David 192
Ayangafac, Chrysantus 257n31, 263

Bâ, Koureyssi 89, 256n3, 263
Bacongo 214
Baga 160
Bakayoko, Soumaïla 126
Bakayoko, Youssouf 130–134
Bakwanga 231
Balan, Jean 181–182
Baluba 214, 216, 220
Bamako 117, 135
Bamba, Kassoum 177
Bamba, Mamadou 124
Bambara 35
Bamiléké 82
Banco (natural park) 172–173
Banco 2 (quarter) 140
Bangala 202–203, 214, 220
Bangolo 145
Bangura, Abdul Karim 194, 260n29, 263
Bank of America 12
Banny, Charles Konan 166
La Banque Centrale des Etats de l'Afrique de
　l'Ouest (BCEAO) 84, 94, 97, 11, 135,
　259n41, 267
Baoulé 107
Barnes, Brooks 190, 260n24, 263
Baudouin I 9, 199, 218, 223–227, 261n11,
　263
BCEAO see La Banque Centrale des Etats
　de l'Afrique de l'Ouest
Bédié, Aimé Henry Konan 8, 86, 88–89, 91–
　104, 108–115, 118–120, 126, 128, 153–154,
　177, 234
Bedouin 236
Bedzigui, Celestin 76, 256n22, 263
Beernaert, August 200
Behanzin, King of Dahomey 176
Bejaia 55
Belafonte, Harry 191, 260n26, 268
Belgium 29, 40, 42, 199–200, 204, 208–212,
　216–220, 222–228
Belkacem, Karim 55
Ben Ali, Zine El Abidine 7, 67–68
Ben Badis, Sheikh Abd al-Hamid 51, 254n14
Ben Bella, Ahmed 55
Ben Kettani 228, 230
Ben Yahmed, Béchir 94
Ben Yahmed, Manwane 259n40
Benghazi 17, 74, 80, 253n49, 268
Beni-Menasser 236
Benin 38, 42, 84, 178
Benot, Yves 58, 254n51, 254n19, 254n32,
　262n18, 262n20, 263
Bensimon, Cyril 259n5, 264
Berdennikova, Maria 171
Berlin (Battle of) 253n44
Berlin Conference (1885) 3, 25, 34, 49, 199–
　200, 202–204, 237, 247

Berthemet, Tanguy 258n5, 258n13, 258n21,
　264, 265
Bété 111
Biden, Joe 80
Biloslavo, Fausto 255n3, 264
bin Laden, Osama 18, 178, 245, 252n20, 266
Bismarck, Otto Von 25–26, 237
black force 31, 38
Black Shame 29–31
Blair, Tony 70, 255n8, 270
Blake, Heidi 255n9, 270
Blunck, Hans Friedrich 28
Bobos 34
Bocquet, Leon 252n1, 264
Boehner, John Andrew 17
Boka, Ernest 107
Bokassa, Jean-Bedel 68, 81
Boko Haram 81, 160–161
Bolikango, Jean 220
Bollardière, Jacques Paris de 65
Bolloré 82, 85, 88
Bolobo 206
Boma 207
Bomboko, Justin 225, 229–230
Bondoukou 179
Bongo, Ali 156
Bongo, Omar 81, 119, 154–156
Bordeaux 41
Bordj 54
Borno 54
Bosch, Jean van den 225
Boston 149, 258, 270
Botswana 42
Bouabré, Paul-Antoine Bohoun 87–88, 124,
　256n1, 267
Bouaké 105, 114–115, 117, 123, 129–130, 142,
　165–166, 177, 180–184, 241, 259n9,
　259n10, 259n11, 260n14, 263, 264, 265
Boudiaf, Mohamed 55
Bouikalo, Alain 258n16, 264
Boundiali 130
Bouygues 82, 85–86
Bouzizi, Tarek 67
BP (British Petroleum) 70
Brassine, Chevalier Jacques 261n24, 264
Brazil 75, 78, 165, 248, 253n36, 264
Brazzaville Conference (1944) 233
Brega 78
Breton, André 39
Bretton Woods 75, 83, 87, 248
BRICS states 248
British Petroleum (BP) 70
Brokaw, Tom 45
Brown, Gordon 24
Brussels 138, 198–199, 207, 219, 220–221,
　225–226, 239
Bugeaud, Thomas (Marshal) 29, 48, 50

Burkina Faso 9, 42, 82, 83, 93–94, 101, 110–111, 113–114, 116, 125, 135, 145–146, 158, 165–167, 240, 257n35, 265
Busch, Gary K. 83–84, 256n35, 264
Bush, George W. 9, 14, 15, 16, 18, 21, 97, 185, 194, 251n10, 252n20, 264, 266
Bush vs. Gore 9

Caen 23
Cairo 15–16, 188, 251n17, 267
Calvar, Patrick 73
Cambon, Jules 50
Camdessus, Michel 90, 256n6
Cameroon 42, 76, 82–83, 161, 255n16
Caprivi, Leo von 237
Carson, Ben 238, 262n16, 266
Carson, Jonnie 185
Carter, Jimmy 13
Carter, Philip, III 9, 131–134
Casement, Roger 204–208, 210, 261n12, 264
Castro, Fidel 15
Cavell, John 55
CEMAC see Communauté Économique et Monétaire de l'Afrique Centrale
Central African Economic and Monetary Community (CEMAC) see Communauté Économique et Monétaire de l'Afrique Centrale
Central Bank of West African States see La Banque Centrale des Etats de l'Afrique de l'Ouest
Central Intelligence Agency (CIA) 230–231, 17
Césaire, Aimé 39, 186, 260n16, 264
CFA franc 76, 81, 83, 88, 95–96, 135, 137, 153, 165, 172
Chad 42, 83, 157, 234
Chakravorti, Bahskar 249, 264
Chamois, Jacqueline 105
Champlin, Christophe 256n12, 264
Chapman, Steve 13, 251n7, 264
Char, René 39
Charles X 48
Charlie Hebdo 160
Chechnya 81
Cheremushkin, Peter 45
Chibok 160
Chirac, Jacques 8, 21, 23, 68, 85, 95, 106, 114, 118–120, 123, 154, 170, 175, 180–181, 183, 241, 252n24, 257n37, 269
Choi, Young-Jin 131, 134–135, 137, 147
Chomsky, Noam 191, 260n25, 266
Christianity 17, 38, 48, 105, 120, 188–191, 236, 252n3, 262n7, 265
Churkin, Vitaly 19
CIA 230–231, 17
Cissé, Hadja Nabintou 102

The Citadel 17, 252n19, 269
Claparède, René 210
Clémenceau, Georges 25–26, 30, 34, 37
Clinton, Bill 20–21, 193, 196
Clinton, Hillary 21–22, 148, 150–151, 161, 193, 252n27, 259n36, 260n28, 264
CNSP see Comité National du Salut Public
Cocody 105, 183, 185
Cold War 45
Colleville-sur-Mer 24
Comarin, Elio 257n35, 265
Comité National du Salut Public (CNSP) 99
Commando invisible 141, 171–174, 178
Communauté Économique et Monétaire de l'Afrique Centrale (CEMAC) 83
Communism 225
Compaoré, Blaise 9, 113, 116, 125, 135, 145–146, 158–159, 161, 166–167
Compaoré, Jean-Baptiste 135
Compiègne 40
Conakat 214, 216, 220
Constantine 51
Cooper, Anderson 246
Copé, Jean-François 186
Cordier, Andrew 229–230
Coulibaly, Adama 177
Coulibaly, Aly 140
Coulibaly, Ibrahima 114, 173–174, 177, 179
Coulibaly, Lanzeni 91
Coulibaly, Ousmane (aka bin Laden) 91
Crusades 188–189

Dabakala 130
Dabou 94, 178
Dacoury-Tabley, Louis 124
Dacoury-Tabley, Philippe Henry 135
Dahomey 176
Dakar 38, 43, 117, 162–164, 166, 253n42, 253n43, 253n39, 265
Dalle, Corinne 253n21, 264
Dansokho, Amath 165–166
Darguina 6, 54, 62
Das, Santanu 252n3, 252n13, 267
David, Philippe 96, 256n15, 264
Davis, Darién J. 253n36, 264
Dayal, Rajeshwar 229
DeBeers 163
Deby, Idriss Itno 157
de Gaulle, Charles 23, 41, 43–44, 62, 73, 77, 81, 141, 215, 233, 241, 253n40
Déli, Gaspard 119
Del Ponte, Carla 19, 252n21, 262
Delvaux, Albert 229
Denard, Bob 82
Dernburg, Bernard 237
Derrière Rails 171–172
Deval, Pierre 48

De Witte, Ludo 261n16, 261n23, 270
Diabaté, Daouda 140
Diabaté, Henriette Dagri 120, 124
Diabaté, Lamine 109, 112
Diagne, Blaise 37–38, 40
Diallo, Bakari 36, 253n29, 264
Diarra, Seydou 119–120, 122–124
Diarrasouba, Oumar (aka Zaga Zaga) 101
Dien Bien Phu 23, 242
Dimbokro 94, 97
Diomi, Gaston 215
Diop, Abdou Salam 256n3, 263
Dioulo, Nicolas 102
Djédjé, Alcide 140
Djédjé, Madi 139
Djéni, Georges Kobenan 92–93
Doctors Without Borders see Médecins Sans
    Frontières
Doe, Samuel 115
Doh, Félix 119
Doherty, Glen 17
Doron Baga 160
Dos Santos, José Eduardo 142, 156
Doué, Mathias 181, 183
Doukouré 171
Doumergue, Gaston 38
Dozo 168–169
Droz, Bernard 254n23, 264
Dubai 164
DuBois, W. E.B. 210
Duékoué 145, 169
Dulles, Allen 230
Duncan, Kablan 120

Eastman-Abaya, Robin 78, 256n23, 269
Eastwood, Clint 190, 260n23, 269
Ebola 238
Economic Community of West African States
    (ECOWAS) 117–119, 125, 129, 158, 257n3
ECOWAS see Economic Community of
    West African States
Egypt 1, 4, 8, 13, 26, 42, 70, 79, 189, 192–
    193, 224, 246, 255n10
Eisenhower, Dwight 43, 225
El Obeidi, Rami 70
El-Kader, Abd 48
Elbe 44
Elf 68, 256
Elisabethville 224, 229, 231
Eluard, Paul 39
Elysée 71, 78, 114, 143, 154, 158, 181, 186
Entebbe 142
Equatorial Guinea 83
Erickson, Erick 236, 265
Eritrea 42
Estaing, Valéry Giscard d' 68, 73
Ethiopia 42, 142, 226–227

Etty, Macaire 106, 257n26, 265
European Union (EU) 2, 7, 12, 77, 88, 96,
    136, 138–139, 186, 194, 239, 249
Evans, Martin 48, 238, 253n32, 254n1,
    254n5, 254n10, 254n11, 254n14, 254n20,
    254n22, 254n24, 254n30, 254n39, 262n15,
    265
Exposition coloniale internationale 5, 34, 39,
    253n21, 264

FANCI see Forces Armées Nationales de
    Côte d'Ivoire
Fanon, Frantz 58, 215, 221–222, 243–244,
    254n33, 261n5, 262n21, 265
Faye, Mbackiyou 162
Fédération Estudiantine de Côte d'Ivoire
    (FESCI) 176
Feldman, Josh 251n14, 265
Felzenberg, Alvin 18
Ferkessédougou 130
Ferloo 259n7, 265
Ferry, Jules 25–26, 32, 252n30, 265
FESCI see Fédération Estudiantine de Côte
    d'Ivoire
Ficatier, Julia 257n20
Fieldhouse, David 261n3, 265
Filippis, Vittorio de 256n26, 265
Fillon, François 186
Firestone 42
Flint, John E. 265
FLN see Front de Libération Nationale
Florentin, Abel 260n14, 265
FN (Forces Nouvelles) 125–126, 177
Foccart, Jacques 81, 90, 107, 256n7, 263
Foch, Ferdinand 34
Fofana, Losseni 145
Fogarty, Richard 29, 252n9, 253n25, 253n31,
    265
Folloroux, Loïc 116
Force Licorne 141, 185
La Force noire 37
Forces Armées Nationales de Côte d'Ivoire
    (FANCI) 115, 126
Forces Nouvelle (FN) 125–126, 177
Forces Républicaines de Côte d'Ivoire
    (FRCI) 144–146, 168–69, 179, 185
Fote, Memel 107
Foucher, Vincent 259n38, 266
Fozié, Tuo 179
Françafrique 89–91, 241–242, 256n35,
    259n9, 259n11, 264
François-Ferdinand 26
Frank, Thomas 260n34, 270
Franklin, John Hope 261n10, 265
FRCI see Forces Républicaines de Côte
    d'Ivoire
Fréjus 105

Frilet, Alain 91
Front de Libération Nationale (FLN) 6, 23, 55–56, 59, 61–62, 65
Fuentes, Jean-Jacques 181

Gaddafi, Muammar 2, 7–8, 18, 69–80, 138, 156, 170, 187, 246–248, 255n5, 255n6, 255n10, 255n11, 255n13, 256n24, 256n25, 263
Gaddafi, Saif el-Islam 70, 72–73, 255n13, 265
Gado, Lélé Marguerite 105
Gadou, Dakouri 257n39, 265
Gagnoa 104–105
Gallois, William 262n14, 265
Gambia 42
Gardiner, Nile 21, 24, 252n26, 252n29, 265
Gaudusson, Jean Du Bois de 121, 257n38, 265
Gazeau-Secret, Anne 97
Gbagbo, Simone Ehivet 106, 149–151, 178, 258n25, 258n28, 269, 270
Gbagbo, Zèpè Koudou Paul 104–105
Georgieva, Kristalina 138
Germany 4–5, 15, 23, 25–26, 29–31, 35, 39–41, 49–50, 72, 76, 212, 237, 239, 253n45, 253n47, 268, 269
Gerschel, Frédéric 157, 259n32, 269
Ghana 42, 124, 142, 215, 217, 224, 226–227, 240
Girard, Youssef 48, 254n4, 254n8, 265
Giuliani, Rudy 192
Gizenga, Antoine 227, 231
Gléléban 94
GMMRP ("Great Man-Made River Project") 76–77, 256n24, 267
Gnagbé, Kragbé 107
Gnanduillet, Ange 180
Gnassingbé, Eyadema 82, 117
Gobelet 140
Gold Coast 42
Goldberg, Jeffrey 252n27, 264
Golf Hotel 116, 130–131, 134, 172
Gordon, David T. 251n5, 265
Gore, Albert 9, 185
Gorée 38, 162
Gotlieb, Sydney 231
Goudé, Charles Blé 123, 241
Govender, Peroshni 260n27, 266
Graham, Lindsay 187
Grant, Mark Lyall 72
Granvaud, Raphaël 39, 233–234, 251n1, 252n6, 253n7, 253n37, 254n43, 254n49, 261n10, 262n4, 266
Gray, Sarah 260n25, 266
Great Britain 26, 30, 35, 42, 44–45, 79, 138, 163, 204–205, 207, 212, 237
"Great Man-Made River Project" (GMMRP) 76–77, 256n24, 267

Gregory, Paul 15, 251n12, 266
Grenard, Fabrice 253n20, 266
Guadeloupe 36
Guéant, Claude 73, 255n13, 265
Guébié 107
Gueï, Robert 8, 90, 92, 95–99, 101–104, 112–115, 120, 126, 177, 183, 234, 257n33
Guelma 6, 51, 53–54, 62, 238
Gueu, Michel 123–124
Guggenheim 212
Guillaud, Édouard 143
Guillaumat, Pierre 81
Guinea (Conakry) 29, 42, 145–146, 215, 224, 226–227, 240
Gul, Abdullah 255n11
Gulf of Guinea 234
Guyana 32

Habbé 34
The Hague 2, 9, 70, 79, 84, 147, 152, 171, 174–175, 180–198
Haiti 142, 176
Hale, Dana S. 253n14, 253n26, 253n35, 266
Hammarskjöld, Dag 225–229
Hammond, Philip 79, 256n25, 268
Hannity, Sean 189, 197
Hardmong, Edwige 257n24, 266
Hawaii 44
Heggoy, Alf Andrew 266
Hemelrijck, Maurice van 215, 217, 219
Hereros 237
Hiroshima 239
Hitler, Adolf 14, 41, 144–145
Hochschild, Adam 251n4, 266
Hocine, Ahmed 55
Hoenberg, Sophie de 26
Hofnung, Thomas 256n32, 258n26, 259n8, 266
Hollande, François 15, 157, 186, 251n13, 268
Horne, Alistair 52, 254n6, 254n12, 254n15, 254n32, 266
Hortefeux, Brice 73
Hosten, Ernst 252n1, 264
Hôtel Ivoire 141, 183–184
Houphouët, Boigny Felix 90–95, 98, 104–109, 112, 120, 123, 135, 141, 149, 151, 171, 241, 256n7, 263
House Edward M. 40
HRW *see* Human Rights Watch
Hrykiwin, Zenko 246
Huch, Florie 170
Human Rights Watch (HRW) 146, 178, 210, 258n20, 266
Huntziger, Charles 40
Hutus 68

IHAA *see* Institut d'Histoire d'Art et
   d'Archéologie Africain
Ileo, Joseph 216
India 8, 28, 71, 75, 78, 226, 229, 248, 251n3,
   252n3, 252n13, 255n10, 267
Indochina 4–6, 32, 43, 62–63, 81, 242
Indonesia 226
Inhofe, James Mountain 141, 148
Inquisition 188–189
Institut d'Histoire d'Art et d'Archéologie
   Africain (IHAA) 105
International Criminal Court 2, 152–153,
   174–175, 185, 249
International Crisis Group 178
Iran 13, 81, 193
Iraq 14, 16, 18, 21, 23, 78–79, 81, 138–139,
   190–191, 239, 251n9, 252n24, 252n25, 267,
   268
Ireland 226
ISIS 188–189
Israel, Josh 262n16, 266
Israel 14, 16–17
Italy 26, 30, 42, 49, 114
Ivanovic, Natacha 171
Ivoirité 96, 98–99, 110–112, 153–154,
   257n29, 257n30, 267
Ivorian Defense Force 96, 115, 122–123, 173,
   183

Jacobs, Dov 171, 174
Janssens, Emile 224
Japan 44, 76, 87
Jim Crow 188
John Paul II 114
Joly, Eva 82, 256n30, 266
Jonathan, Goodluck 9, 158–161
Jonathan, Patience 160
Jong, Ferdinand de 259n38, 266
Jospin, Lionel 95
Josselin, Charles 98
JP Morgan 12, 255n9, 270
Juppé, Alain 72, 143, 167

Kabakouma 114
Kabila, Joseph 246, 261n23, 261n6, 268
Kadet, Bertin 257n25, 266
Kagamé, Paul 156
Kalonji, Albert 216, 224, 229, 231
Kandé, Salifou Kamara 29, 252n7, 267
Kanza, Antoine 220
Kanza, Daniel 219
Kanza, Thomas 227, 229–230, 261n3,
   261n10, 261n12, 261n19, 261n22, 266
Kasai 213–214, 216, 228–231
Kasavubu, Joseph 213–214, 217–220, 223–
   224, 228–231
Kasengulu 229

Kasongo, Joseph 222, 256n10
Kassaraté, Edouard Tiapé 185
Katanga 201, 211, 214, 216, 224–226, 228–
   231
Katiola 115, 130
Kazakhstan 82
Kédio-Babré 104
Keitel Wilhelm 41
Kendall, Bridget 252n21, 266
Kennedy, John F. 231–232
Kenya 13, 42, 173, 185–186, 248, 260n15,
   270
Kenyatta, Jomo 13
Kenyatta, Uhuru 185–186, 248
Kerry, John 19, 148
Kheris, Sabine 181, 184
Kherrata 6, 51, 54, 62, 238
Ki-Moon, Ban 9, 131, 139, 142, 170
Kieffer, Guy André 116
Killingray, David 266
Kim, Mallie Jane 252n20, 266
Kipré, Pierre 140, 151
Kléber 118–120, 122–124, 177
Kodja, Hussein 48
Koffi, Charles Yao 140
Koffi, Paul Koffi 144
Koffigoh, Joseph Kokou 129
Koller, Christian 36, 252n3, 252n12, 252n13,
   253n27, 266
Konan, André Sylver 259n31, 267
Konan, Venance 111, 267
Konaté, Yacouba 256n16, 267
Koné, Abdoulaye 97
Koné, Messemba 179
Koné, Nadia 145
Kongo Kingdom 214
Korea *see* North Korea; South Korea
Korhogo 114–115, 129–130, 142, 165–166,
   177
Koudouss, Idriss 140
Kouibly 145
Koulibaly, Mamadou 257n34, 267
Koumassi 140
Krassault, Robert 257n25, 258n29, 267
Krauthammer, Charles 1, 189, 260n18,
   260n19
Kuznetzov, Vasily 225
Kyle, Chris 191, 260n26, 266

Labot, Lise 255n7, 267
Lamoricière, Christophe Léon Louis Juchault
   de 48
Laniray, Pierre 256n29, 267
Lapsley, Samuel 210
Las Casas, Bartolomé de 251n3, 267
Lauvergeon, Anne 83, 256n32, 266
Lavrov, Sergey 19, 73, 255n16, 270

Layas, Mohammed 8, 70, 77
Le Lidec, Gildas 85, 103, 106, 147, 180, 241–242
Lee, Matthew Russell 147
Lefebvre, Alex 252*n*25, 267
Lenin, Vladimir 15
Leningrad 44
Leopold II 9, 199–211, 216, 218, 223–227, 251*n*4, 261*n*4, 261*n*23, 261*n*2, 261*n*6, 266, 267
Leopoldville 223, 227, 231
Lequy, Roger 59, 254*n*27, 254*n*40, 267
Leriche, Ulysse 37
Lesotho 42
Levin, Mark 189, 260*n*21, 267
Levy, Henry Bernard 69
Lia, J-S 256*n*1, 267
Liberia 42, 115, 144, 178–179, 226, 240
Libreville 95
Libya 1–4, 7–8, 13, 17, 30, 42, 69–73, 75–81, 138–139, 156, 187–188, 192–193, 239, 246–248, 267
Limbaugh, Rush 17, 251*n*17, 267
Linas-Marcoussis 118–123, 127, 171, 177, 179–180, 257*n*37, 257*n*38, 265, 270
Lincoln, Abraham 189, 196
Lipton, P. Edward 257*n*28, 267
Lissouba, Pascal 68, 175
Lockerbie 70
Loi Cadre 215
Lomé 98, 117
Longuet, Gerard 143
Lord Lansdowne 204, 207
Lorraine 6, 25, 41, 58
Louverture, Toussaint 176
Luce, Edward 16
Lumumba, Kasongo 256*n*11
Lundula, Victor 229
Lunn, Joe Harris 252*n*7, 252*n*8, 253*n*28, 267
Luntz, Franck 197
Lycée Classique d'Abidjan 105, 151
Lycée Descartes 180
Lynch, Column 259*n*4, 267
Lynden, Harold d'Aspremont 226

Mabri, Toikeusse 139
Macalpin, George Watson 261*n*18, 267
Madagascar 26, 32, 36, 253*n*43
Maghreb 7, 11, 32, 43
Mahmoud, Jibril 70, 80
Makola, Khomotso 192
Malaria 48, 137, 238, 258*n*7, 270
Malawi 42
Mali 34–35, 42, 81, 83, 93, 109–111, 135, 144–146, 157–158, 171, 176, 226, 234, 239, 252*n*1
Mamie Faitai 171

Man 115, 123, 143
Mandela, Nelson 192, 245, 260*n*27, 266
Mandingos 34
Mangin, Charles 37–38, 52
Mangou, Philippe 126, 185
Mao Zedong 15
Maodza, Takunda 260*n*31, 267
Marcory 97
Marseille 48
Martinique 32
Maspéro, François 254*n*51, 267
Massu, Jacques 65
Mathaba 256*n*24, 267
Mattei, François 174, 259*n*6, 267
Matthews, K.J. 268
Matthews, Merrill 15, 251*n*13, 268
Mazeaud, Pierre 119
Mazrui, Ali 46, 253*n*49, 268
Mbaye, Keba 119
Mbeki, Thabo 127–128, 142, 257*n*1, 268
Mbembe, Achille 159, 259*n*33, 268
Mbuj-Mayi 229
McCain, John 14, 20, 187, 251*n*11, 255*n*4
McDonald, Eric 170
McElroy, Damien 256*n*25, 268
McGovern, Mike 156–159, 161
Médecins Sans Frontières 137, 258*n*9, 268
Mel Eg, Theodore 118
Meledje, Djedjro Francisco 257*n*23, 268
Mendès-France, Pierre 61
Merica, Dan 259*n*36
Merivale, Herman 237
Messali Hadj 51, 254*n*11
MFA *see* Mouvement des Forces de l'Avenir
Michel, Marc 252*n*10, 253*n*22, 253*n*30, 253*n*34
Middleton, Drew 253*n*45, 268
Miniter, Richard 195, 260*n*32, 268
Missouri, Moftah 72
Misurata 79
Mitchell, Andrew 79
Mitterrand, François 61, 68, 78, 175
MJP *see* Mouvement pour la Justice et la Paix
MNC *see* Mouvement National Congolais
Mobutu, Sese Seko 81, 229–232
Mockey, Jean-Baptiste 107
Modi, Narandra 255*n*10
Monga, Célestin 159, 259*n*33, 268
Montagnac, Lucien de 50, 236
Morel, E.D. 203–204, 207, 210, 261*n*5, 261*n*8, 261*n*16, 261*n*22, 268
Morocco 32, 139, 226–227, 248
Morrison, William 210
Moscow 19, 26, 224, 228
Mossis 35
Mount Peko 145

Mouvement des Forces de l'Avenir (MFA) 118, 124
Mouvement National Congolais (MNC) 213–218, 220
Mouvement Patriotique de Côte d'Ivoire (MPCI) 117, 119–120, 124, 177
Mouvement Populaire Ivoirien du Grand Ouest (MPIGO) 119, 124, 177
Mouvement pour la Justice et la Paix (MJP) 118, 124, 177
Mozambique 98
MPCI see Mouvement Patriotique de Côte d'Ivoire
MPIGO see Mouvement Populaire Ivoirien du Grand Ouest
Mpolo, Maurice 231
MSF see Médecins Sans Frontières
Mubarak, Hosni 80, 246
Munongo, Godefroid 231

Nagasaki 239
Nahibly 144, 168–169, 259n2
Naouri, Jennifer 171
Napoleon III 25, 51
NATO 7, 15, 69–70, 72–73, 78–79
Nazi 14, 44–45, 50, 53, 105, 253n47, 269
NDB see New Development Bank
N'Diaye, Sada 165
N'diaye, Souleymane N'déné 163
N'dré, Yao 121
New Development Bank (NDB) 248, 262n1, 264
New York 19, 190, 225, 227, 251, 252n22, 268
Ngalula, Joseph 215, 217
N'Gbo, Gilbert Marie Aké 131
N'Goran, Kouassi Pierre 129
Nguesso, Sassou 68, 82
Niger 82–83, 85, 256n31, 263
Nigeria 9, 42, 76, 81, 158–161, 205, 234, 259n35, 259n36, 266, 268
Nisco, Baron 207
Nkrumah, Kwame 215
Noiret, Philippe 37, 167
Normandy 24
North Atlantic Treaty Organization (NATO) 7, 15, 69–70, 72–73, 78–79
North Korea 152–163, 193
Northern Charter 108–110, 112, 120
Nséké, Léopold 256n34, 268
Nuland, Victoria 167
Nzeza, Simon 219
Nzongola-Ntalaja, Georges 210, 261n23, 261n26, 262n6, 261n21, 268

O'Connor, Peg 262n8, 268
Odiénné 94, 109, 115, 178

O'Donnell, Lawrence 189, 260n20, 268
Okito, Joseph 231
Oklahoma 141, 148
Olympio, Sylvanus 82
Opération Dignité 181, 241
O'Reilly, Bill 15, 251n14
Ouagadougou 113–114, 116, 125–126, 128
Oueï, Patrice 180
Ouffas 236
Ouodraogo, Rémi (Amadé Ourémi) 145–146
Ouolof/ Wolof 34, 164
Ouragahio 104–105
Ousmane, Chérif 101, 125–126, 177
Ovambos 237

Paganini, Agostino 137
Page, Arthur 253n39, 268
Page, E. Melvin 252n7, 267
Page, Walter H. 40, 253n39, 268
Paice, Edward 251n4, 262n11, 268
Pakistan 226, 239
Palin, Sarah 16, 251n16
Pan-Africanism 86, 215, 222, 253n36, 264
Pan Am Flight 103 70
Papua New Guinea 186
Park, E. 210
Parti de l'Indépendance et du Travail (PIT) 165
Parti Démocratique Sénégalais (PDS) 164–165
Parti Ivoirien des Travailleurs (PIT) 96, 102, 118
Party Démocratique de Côte d'Ivoire (PDCI) 91–93, 106, 109, 111–113, 118, 124
PDCI see Party Démocratique de Côte d'Ivoire
PDS see Parti Démocratique Sénégalais
Pearl Harbor 44
Pentagon 69
Pétain, Philippe 29, 41, 44
Petersburg 44
Petras, James 78, 256n23, 262n3, 269
Pfaff, William 13, 251n6, 269
Pheasant 80
Philadelphia 248
Philippin, Yann 76, 256n32, 266
Philippines 76
Piettey, Betsey 251n2, 269
PIT (Parti de l'Indépendance et du Travail) 165
PIT (Parti Ivoirien des Travailleurs) 96, 102, 118
Pleven, René 83
Pokou, Abla 107
Poland 14
Poncet, Henri 181–182, 184
Pongo, Gilbert 231

Pope Francis 188
Port-Bouët 98, 178, 183
Portugal 30, 98, 237
Pougala, Jean-Paul 75–76, 255n19, 269
Powell, Collin 21
Pretoria 192
Prussia 40, 49, 237
Puga, Benoît 143
Putin, Vladimir 11, 19–20, 187, 252n22, 269

Qatar 8, 20, 255n10

RASCOM (Regional African Satellite Communication Organization) 76
Rassemblement des Houphouëtistes pour la Démocratie et la Paix (RHDP) 146, 171
Rassemblement des Républicains (RDR) 84, 93–96, 98–100, 102, 109, 111, 113–114, 118, 121, 124, 129, 168–169
rattrapage ethnique 144, 178
Rawlings, Jerry 142
RDR *see* Rassemblement des Républicains
Red Army 44–45
Red Cross 138, 179
Refondation (politics of) 8, 86–89, 170, 198–199, 257n34, 267
Regional African Satellite Communication Organization (RASCOM) 76
Reims 5, 23, 43
Remblais 140
Reunion 32, 38
RHDP *see* Rassemblement des Houphouëtistes pour la Démocratie et la Paix
Rhineland 29–30, 36–37
Rhodes, Cecil 11, 265
Rice, Condoleezza 70
Rice, Susan 9, 72, 131–132, 147, 150, 168–170, 193, 258n4, 259n3, 259n4, 260n32, 266, 267, 268, 269
Ricoux, René 49
Robinson, Eugene 239, 262n17, 269
Rockefeller 212
Rommel, Erwin 42
Romney, Mitt 17, 252n19, 269
Rose, Charlie 21
Rothschild, Matthew 20, 252n23, 255n4, 269
Rueff, Judith 256n18, 269
Rufisque 38
Rumsfeld, Donald 18
Ruto, William 248
Rwanda 68, 78, 156, 175, 198, 255n1, 255n15, 270

Saab 71
Saal, Bouzid 53

Saddam, Hussein 14, 21, 80, 138
Safire, William 252n24, 269
Saint Cyr 114
Saint Dominique Savio 105
Saint-Louis 38
Sall, Macky 161–162, 164–165, 259n40, 270
San Pédro 88, 137, 141, 145, 178
Sané, Pierre 257n36, 269
Sankara, Thomas 82
Sankuru River 231
Sanwi 107
Sarajevo 26
Sarkozy, Nicolas 4, 7–9, 22–24, 66–77, 79, 81, 83–84, 139, 142–143, 147–149, 157–159, 161, 166, 169–170, 174–175, 184, 186–187, 199, 252n26, 252n28, 252n29, 255n3, 255n5, 255n6, 255n11, 255n13, 255n14, 259n32, 263, 264, 265, 266, 269, 270
Sarraut, Albert 31–33, 35, 253n15, 253n23, 269
Sartre, Jean-Paul 254n33, 255
Scarborough, Joe 1, 131, 189–190, 260n22, 269
Scheyven, Raymond 219
Schlenner, Kurt 28
Schollaert, Frans 210
Schrijver, Auguste 219
Schuck, Nathalie 157, 259n32, 269
Schumacher, Edmond de 207
Scotland 70
Scott, A.O. 260n23, 269
Séché, Alphonse 31, 52
Séguéla 105, 130
Selassie, Haile 233, 243
Sendwe, Jason 213–214, 216
Senegal 5, 9, 28, 30, 36–38, 42, 83, 89, 119, 139, 158, 161–167, 177, 234, 252, 259, 264–267
Senghor, Léopold Sédar 38, 40
Senufo 34
Serbia 26
Sereres 34
Setif 6, 47, 51–54, 62, 238, 254n21
Sevez, François 44
Shammam, Mahmoud 80
Shanghai 248
Sheppard, William Henry 210
Siaka Koné Market 171
Sidiki, Bakaba 262n19, 263
Sierra Leone 42, 115, 205
Simon, Jean-Marc 9, 131, 134, 139
Sirte 69, 76, 80, 156
Sivori, Boga 123, 258n28, 269
Slavin, Patrick 258n8, 269
Smahine, Barys 180
Smith Walter 43

Société Internationale Forestière et Minière
    du Congo 209
Soilih, Ali 82
Somaliland 205
Soro, Kigbafori Guillaume 115, 119–120, 123,
    125, 130, 139, 165, 174, 176–178, 259n7,
    265
Soudan, François 258n25, 270
Souk El- Tenine 54
South Africa 42, 87–88, 127–128, 192, 216,
    237, 243–245, 248
South Korea 76, 137
Soviet Union 43–45, 51, 225, 228
Spain 15, 49, 48, 58, 74, 248
Spencer, Richard 255n9, 270
Spillius, Alex 255n11, 270
Stanley Pool 204, 206
Stanley, Henri Morton 199, 204, 206, 213,
    218, 231
Stanleyville (Kisangani) 213, 218, 231
Stasi, Bernard 95
Stevens Christopher 17
Stockman, Sarah 258n24, 270
Stora, Benjamin 254n25, 254n50, 270
Strasbourg 15–16
Stuart, Jeffries 252n28, 266
Sudan 35, 81, 164, 226
Sufi 41, 51
Sukhos, Yuri 180
Sunni 48
Susloparov, Ivan 43
Swaine, Jon 255n9, 270
Swaziland 42
Sweden 226
Switzerland 91–92, 210
Syria 18–19, 22, 70, 79, 81, 252n21, 252n22,
    258n4, 261n1, 264, 266, 269

Tagro, Désiré 125
Tall, Aliou 162, 259n37
Tanzania 42
Taylor, Charles 178
Texaco 163
Thesier, Wilfred 202
Thiolay, Boris 255n14, 270
Thompson, Emeka 161
Thorez, Maurice 39
Thysville 231
Tiémélé, Jean-Charles 80, 256n27, 270
Tiffany and Co. 12
Timberlake, Clare 228
Tocqueville, Alexis de 4, 12, 24, 251n5, 265
Total 68, 80–82, 256n27, 270
Toure, Samory 176
Touré, Sékou 215, 222
Traoré, Dramane 145
Tripoli 71, 73–74, 77, 80, 138, 258n11

Trotha, Lothar von 237
Tshombe, Moïse 213–214, 216, 221, 224–
    226, 229–231
Tunisia 2, 7, 32, 44, 66–69, 72, 226–227
Turkey 76
Tutsis 68
Twain, Mark 210

UDCY see Union Démocratique et
    Citoyenne
UDPCI see Union pour la Démocratie et
    pour la Paix en Côte d'Ivoire
Uganda 42, 142
UNHCR (United Nations High Commis-
    sioner for Refugees) 146
UNICEF (United Nations Children's Fund)
    137, 258n7, 258n8, 269, 270
Union Démocratique et Citoyenne (UDCY)
    118, 124
Union des Intérêts Sociaux Congolais
    (UNISCO) 214
Union Minière du Haut Katanga 209, 211
Union pour la Démocratie et pour la Paix en
    Côte d'Ivoire (UDPCI) 118, 124
UNISCO see Union des Intérêts Sociaux
    Congolais
United Kingdom 72, 76
United Nations High Commissioner for
    Refugees (UNHCR) 146
United Nations Children's Fund (UNICEF)
    137, 258n7, 258n8, 269, 270
United Nations in Côte d'Ivoire (UNOCI)
    141, 144, 147, 168–169
UNOCI see United Nations in Côte d'Ivoire
Upper Volta 34, 94, 102

Vale, Paul 255n16, 270
Valencia, Milton 258n24, 270
Valero, Bernard 135, 139
Van Bilsen, Joseph 217
van der Meersch, Ganshof 220
Vandervelde, Emile 204, 210
Varenne, Leslie 142, 257n21, 270
Varga, Kristztina 170
Veltmeyer, Henry 262n3, 269
Verschave, François-Xavier 255n1, 256n29,
    267, 270
Viallet, Jean-Michel 253n21, 264
Vichy 41–42, 44
Vidal, Claudine 256n16, 257n22, 267, 270
Villepin, Dominique de 118, 120, 123, 177, 182
Violette, Maurice 52–53
von Horn, Carl 228

Wachovia Bank 12, 251n2, 269
Wade, Abdoulaye 9, 13, 158–159, 161–167,
    177, 259n37, 259n7, 265, 270

WAEMU *see* West African Economic and Monetary Union
Wahis, Baron 204
Ward, Anthony 116
Ward, Steven C. 236, 262n9, 270
Warungu, Joseph 260n15, 270
Washington, Booker T. 210
Washington, D.C. 2, 46, 77, 140, 152, 167, 169, 193, 198, 222, 226, 230
Watkins, John 255n20, 270
West, Cornel 196, 260n34, 270
West African Economic and Monetary Union (WAEMU) 83
West Indians 32
West Point 20, 252n23, 269
White, Molly 188
White House 1, 24, 147, 195, 225, 251n15, 260n32, 268
WHO *see* World Health Organization
Wigny, Pierre 224
Wilhelm II 237
William, George Washington 203–204, 208
William, Judith Michelle 253n36, 264
Wilson, Woodrow 13
Winfrey, Oprah 192

Wisconsin 17
Witting, Peter 72
Wodié, Francis 96, 102, 118
Woods, Tyrone 17
World Health Organization (WHO) 139
Wurzelbacher, Samuel Joseph (Joe the Plumber) 14

Yacé, Philippe Grégoire 91
Yacine, Kateb 54
Yamoussoukro 91–92, 115, 124, 182–183
Yaosséhi 140
Yaoundé 76
Yeke 214, 216
Yergin, Daniel 254n52, 270
Yopougon 95, 113, 140, 171, 178
Yugoslavia 19

Zadi, Zahourou 151
Zambia 42, 94
Zimbabwe 42, 142, 156, 193, 195, 244
Zoro-Bi, Epiphane 256n17, 270
Zulu, Justine B. 94
Zuma, Jacob 142

www.ingramcontent.com/pod-product-compliance
Lightning Source LLC
Chambersburg PA
CBHW031413270326
41929CB00010BA/1443